Cognitive Development
of Children and Youth
A LONGITUDINAL STUDY

EDUCATIONAL PSYCHOLOGY

Allen J. Edwards, Series Editor
Department of Psychology
Southwest Missouri State University
Springfield, Missouri

Cognitive Development of Children and Youth

A LONGITUDINAL STUDY

Herbert J. Klausmeier

Department of Educational Psychology
The University of Wisconsin—Madison
Madison, Wisconsin

Patricia S. Allen

The Wisconsin Research and Development Center
for Cognitive Learning
The University of Wisconsin—Madison
Madison, Wisconsin

ACADEMIC PRESS   New York San Francisco London 1978
A Subsidiary of Harcourt Brace Jovanovich Publishers

ACADEMIC PRESS, INC.
111 Fifth Avenue, New York, New York 10003

United Kingdom Edition published by
ACADEMIC PRESS, INC. (LONDON) LTD.
24/28 Oval Road, London NW1

Library of Congress Cataloging in Publication Data

Klausmeier, Herbert John, Date
 Cognitive development of children and youth:
 A longitudinal study

 (Educational psychology series)
 Bibliography: p.
 1. Cognition in children. 2. Cognition in children––Research. I. Allen, Patricia S., joint author. II. Title.
BF723.C5K57   155.4'13   78–13306
ISBN 0–12–411355–9

PRINTED IN THE UNITED STATES OF AMERICA

Contents

Preface

This book is designed for persons who are interested in the cognitive development of children and youth, including upper-division and graduate students in psychology, educational psychology, and education—and more broadly, for those in the behavioral sciences and helping professions. A theory of cognitive development is presented, including descriptive information and conclusions based on a longitudinal study. The topics covered and the treatment of research methods suggest that the book is suitable as a basic text in a course that emphasizes cognitive learning and development and as a supplementary text in courses that emphasize other areas of learning or development.

Several features of the book will be of interest to many persons. First, four highly significant products of learning are dealt with—namely, concepts, principles, structures of knowledge, and problem-solving skills. These are the products that make it possible for human beings to interpret the physical and social world and also to acquire knowledge on their own. Second, the findings and conclusions of a comprehensive longitudinal study are presented for the first time. This is believed to be the only available empirically based description of cognitive development of American children and youth, Grade 1 through Grade 12. Third, knowledge concerning cognitive learning and development is combined with the results of experiments carried out in school settings in a design of instruction that is intended to nurture more effectively the cognitive development of children and youth. Applications of the design to developing instructional materials and to carrying out instruction in the classroom are explained in sufficient detail to guide the interested reader in carrying out these activities.

Acknowledgments

Continuous funding was received by the senior author, initially from the United States Office of Education and later from the National Institute of Education, to support the three major areas of study that are reported: the longitudinal study of cognitive development of children and youth which was planned in 1972; controlled experimentation in laboratories and school settings to clarify the internal and external conditions of concept learning, begun in 1968; and intervention studies to change conditions of instruction and schooling so that they become more conducive to the educational development of children and youth, started in 1965. The studies of the following graduate advisees of the first author were supported with this funding: Ronald W. Ady, Carma Jo Averhart, Michael Bernard, J. Kent Davis, Marcus C. S. Fang, Dorothy A. Frayer, Wayne C. Fredrick, John Gaa, Richard Gargiulo, Patricia Kalish, Selena Katz, Barbara Kennedy, Peter A. Lamal, Daniel Lynch, Richard Marliave, Barbara Marten, Dean L. Meinke, Gregory Mize, Gerry W. Miller, Barbara A. Nelson, Gordon K. Nelson, Winston E. Rampaul, James Ramsey, Joan Schilling, Joseph A. Scott, Nancy Smuckler, Terrence J. Snowden, James Swanson, Roger C. Sweet, Glenn E. Tagatz, Katherine Vorwerk, and Suzanne P. Wiviott.

Assistance of the former graduate students and other persons who served on the research teams of the first author from 1968 to 1978 is deeply appreciated. During the years 1972–1978, Thomas Sipple, project associate, made the arrangements with the participating schools to carry out the longitudinal study and to administer the data-gathering instruments. He also coordinated the computer processing of the information and the preparation of the tables and figures appearing in this book. Keith White, project assistant, did most of the test administration in the participating schools. Trudy Dunham and Samuel R. Mathews II, graduate students in Educational Psychology, assisted in the preparation and review of part of Chapter 4.

The participation of the children and youth of several school districts, their parents, their teachers, and the school administrators is acknowledged with the deepest gratitude. No persons are identified in order to protect the privacy of all the participants.

Special recognition is due Elizabeth Schwenn Ghatala and Dorothy Frayer, co-authors with the first author of *Conceptual Learning and Development: A Cognitive View* (Academic Press, 1974). The basic elements of the theory of conceptual learning and development in that book are continued in the present volume and served as the framework for conducting the longitudinal study. The large amount of new information from the longitudinal study and from other recently completed experiments made it possible to include only short segments from the earlier work in their original form.

Helpful suggestions from several persons were received concerning the design of the studies, data analysis, and other matters. The suggestions of Chester Harris and Margaret Harris were followed in carrying out the factorial analyses. Lawrence Hubert and Michael Subkoviak provided many constructive suggestions in connection with test construction and data processing. Benton Underwood consulted on the design of several experiments on concept learning.

Chapters or the complete manuscript were carefully reviewed by Chester Harris, Elizabeth Ghatala, Frank Hooper, and Sue Markle. These reviewers contributed significantly to improvement of the manuscript.

The second author, Patricia S. Allen, who is a specialist in developmental psychology, served as a research associate starting in 1973. She coordinated the preparation of the annual cross-sectional reports and the early longitudinal reports that were brought out as technical reports of the Wisconsin Research and Development Center for Cognitive Learning. Most important, she wrote the first drafts of Chapters 2, 6, 7, and 8, the chapters that report the design and results of the longitudinal study. She also made many useful suggestions on the final drafts of all the chapters.

The first author's dedicated administrative secretary over many years, Arlene Knudsen, was responsible for coordinating the preparation of the manuscript.

Cognitive Development
of Children and Youth
A LONGITUDINAL STUDY

1

Introduction

The study of cognitive development deals with the many changes that occur from birth to maturity in the cognitive structure, the cognitive operations, and the related observable and inferrable behaviors of the individual. These changes are often observed to be orderly and progressive. The cognitive structure of the individual at any point in time includes everything the individual has learned. The products, or outcomes, of learning may be categorized as perceptual information, verbal information and skills, concepts, principles, structures of knowledge including taxonomies, and problem-solving skills, including strategies of learning. These products are learned initially, represented internally, organized, and stored in the form of images, symbols, meanings, and relations among images, symbols, and meanings. The cognitive structure changes from birth onward as a result of learning and maturation and simultaneously has both molecular and molar features. The simplest perceptions are included, such as an image of the sun sinking beyond the horizon, as well as the most abstract ideas, such as those involved in theorizing about the origin of the sun.

Persons without specialization in human learning and development probably accept growth of the cognitive structure from infancy into adulthood as the most significant attribute of human beings but do not study it further. They also may observe differences among their acquaintances in the substance or content of the cognitive structure, the rate at which it develops, and the final level of development and functioning.

Attempts to understand and describe these phenomena have proven very difficult for psychological scientists, philosophers, and others. The infinite

1

variations in the experiences of human beings, the great changes that occur in the physical and social world of each succeeding generation, and the unbelievably rapid rate at which persons from infancy onward develop cognitively make description and explanation exceedingly tentative. The repertoire of psychological methods and tools and the financial resources to carry out the experimentation are very limited in relation to the magnitude of the task. It is hoped that this attempt to describe conceptual development during the school years may further advance our substantive knowledge and also our methodology.

An earlier theoretical framework of conceptual learning and development (Klausmeier, 1971; Klausmeier, Ghatala, & Frayer, 1974) was based mainly on an analysis and synthesis of experiments on concept learning conducted in laboratories and in school settings and on the content analyses and behavioral analyses of the tasks used in the experimentation. The propositions set forth in 1974 provided the theoretical framework for conducting the comprehensive longitudinal–cross-sectional studies of cognitive development during the school years reported in this book and also for the less comprehensive studies of instruction designed to facilitate cognitive growth.

In this chapter, the four products of learning of primary concern—concepts, principles, problem solving, and structures of knowledge—are discussed first. These products when learned and incorporated into the cognitive structure enable a person to interpret the physical and social world with independence and also to continue to learn without explicit guidance or instruction from others.

The accuracy of the description of cognitive development in this book rests primarily on the identification of the mental operations required to attain concepts at four successively higher levels and on the conceptualization of the four levels. The tests of conceptual development used in the longitudinal study were constructed explicitly and as directly as possible to measure the operations at each of the four levels. In this chapter the mental operations presumed to be sufficient for attaining concepts at four successively higher levels are specified.

Concepts are essential for understanding principles of which the concepts are a part. Moreover, to understand exclusive–inclusive relations embodied in taxonomies, such as the plant and animal kingdom, the concepts embodied in the taxonomy must be understood. Solving problems also requires the use of concepts. An overview of these uses of concepts, which were also investigated in the longitudinal–cross-sectional study, is given in the chapter.

Extensive study of the relationship among words, word meanings, and concepts is of very recent origin, despite the general observation that we communicate our intentions, experiences, and meanings primarily in words. An introduction to this area is given in this chapter, preceding an indication of the plan of the book.

Before proceeding further it may be helpful to differentiate among the terms *maturation, learning,* and *development.* As we use the terms, *maturation* refers to growth under normal environmental conditions that results from the individual's biological inheritance. Differences among individuals in the onset of prehensile grasping, taking first steps, and puberty are judged to be more closely related to differences in biological inheritance than to learning. *Learning* refers to permanent changes in inferrable and observable behaviors resulting from practice or experience. For example, a child learns to discriminate the letters of the alphabet, to write, to count. Unless learning occurs, none of these performances will be achieved. *Development* is a product of both maturation and learning, and developmental changes occur across longer time periods and by many means, as Flavell (1977) describes. This view of development is different from Piaget's (1964). According to Piaget, development results in the formation of general structures of knowledge that are common to all members of the species; the general structures permit learning, which is always specific, to take place. There are other differences between our views regarding learning and development and those in Piagetian theory. No attempt is made in this book to interpret Piaget. However, three groups of students of our longitudinal study in Grades 1 through 9 received both Piagetian tasks and the concept attainment tests. The relationship between students' performances on the two sets of measures are reported elsewhere (Klausmeier & Associates, in preparation).

CONCEPTS AND THE COGNITIVE STRUCTURE

Concepts, principles, taxonomic and other hierarchical relations, and problem solving are powerful outcomes of learning in the cognitive domain. Progressive acquisition of these outcomes is accompanied by increasing independence in learning. It is reasonable, therefore, that much formal education is directed toward these outcomes in various subject fields. This is not to minimize outcomes in the affective domain, such as values and interests, or outcomes in the psychomotor domain, such as motor skills. Rather, these domains also deserve full book treatments.

Concepts

Each sentence that appears in this book and other books can be subdivided into units of meaning. Some units are single words; others are groups of words. The meanings of the units are lexical concepts. The author has one set of meanings; if the reader has the same meanings the communication is effective. If the reader has different meanings, the communication is ineffective. When one considers the great variety of words and word groupings that represent concepts, it becomes understandable that persons may approach their study of concept learning or concept development (or indeed of any area) with different purposes and from different psychological or philosophical backgrounds. In general, however, psychologists and others attempt to analyze global constructs into more discrete and manageable parts and also to synthesize and organize a large amount of information into a high level of abstract general propositions or conclusions.

MENTAL CONSTRUCT—SOCIETALLY ACCEPTED MEANING

A concept is both a mental construct of the individual and the societally accepted meaning of one or more words that represent the particular concept. Concepts as mental contructs change greatly from early childhood into late adolescence, whereas the societally accepted meanings are more stable. However, they too change as new knowledge is generated about the social and physical world. Examples of concepts that are changing noticeably in recent years are *intelligence, cancer,* and *space.*

Concepts as mental constructs are the critical component of a maturing individual's continuously changing, enlarging cognitive structure. When considered from a learning point of view over short time periods, a person's concepts provide the basis for interpreting and organizing incoming information and also for forming principles and other complex relations among concepts. Maturing individuals attain concepts according to their unique informal and formal learning experiences and their maturational patterns. The role of concepts in thinking is well stated by Kagan (1966):

> Concepts are the fundamental agents of intellectual work. The theoretical significance of cognitive concepts (or, if you wish, symbolic mediators) in psychological theory parallels the seminal role of valence in chemistry, gene in biology, or energy in physics. Concepts are viewed as the distillate of sensory experience and the vital link between external inputs and overt behaviors. The S–O–R model of a generation ago regarded O as the black box switch that connected behavior with a stimulus source. The O is viewed today as a set of concepts or mediators [p. 97].

The word *concept* not only designates mental constructs of individuals but also the meanings of words and other symbols accepted by social groups who speak the same language. Attempts to verbalize these meanings are found in dictionaries, encyclopedias, and other books. Thus the meanings of the words comprise the societally accepted, or public, concepts of groups of persons who speak the same language. An unabridged dictionary is probably the best single source of societally accepted word meanings. For many words, however, the dictionary definition is not a complete societally accepted concept or word meaning (Markle, 1975).

Carroll (1964a) related concepts, words, and word meanings this way: Words in a language can be thought of as a series of spoken or written entities. There are meanings for words that can be considered a standard of communicative behavior that is shared by those who speak a language. Finally, there are concepts, that is, the classes of experiences formed in individuals either independently of language processes or in close dependence on language processes. Putting the three together, Carroll stated:

> A "meaning" of a word is, therefore, a societally-standardized concept, and when we say that a word stands for or names a concept it is understood that we are speaking of concepts that are shared among the members of a speech community [p. 187].

CATEGORIES OF CONCEPTS

There are a number of different ways to classify concepts. One is in accordance with the six form classes of words: nominals, adjectivals, verbals, adverbials, prepositionals, and conjunctivals (Carroll, 1964b). Words and groups of words that can be categorized as belonging in each of these form classes represent concepts as shown in Table 1.1. We may consider the nominals and verbals in more detail.

Nominals include nouns, pronouns, and noun phrases. Examples of these are as follows: nouns—*chair, Americans, thought,* and *symmetry;* pronouns—*she, who, themselves;* noun phrases—*the broken chair,* the *ugly Americans, a brilliant thought.* The meaning that you have for each example given is your concept of the class of things it represents. The meaning you have of *noun, pronoun,* and *noun phrase* is your concept of each of them as a subclass of nominals. It is recognized that the meaning ascribed to words, and particularly to pronouns, is related to the context in which they are experienced.

Verbals include verbs and verb phrases that refer to events, relationships, or states whose location or distribution in a time dimension can be specified. Examples of verbs are *hit, love, throw, is,* and *was* and of verb phrases, *has been hit, will be hit.* We might examine adjectivals, adverbials, prepositionals, and conjunctivals, but assume that the reader can do so independently. It is noted in passing that the concepts represented by prepositionals (e.g., *between, in*), conjunctivals (e.g., *but, because*), adjectivals (e.g., *red, smooth*) differ in many respects, one of which is the number and kind of attributes that define each form class.

CONCRETE–ABSTRACT CONCEPTS

Another means for classifying concepts is in terms of whether the defining attributes can be perceived. Mussen, Conger, and Kagan (1974) indicate that concepts having perceptible attributes (e.g., *animal, swim, color*) are concrete, whereas concepts whose attributes cannot be directly perceived (e.g., *nominals, imagine, however*) are abstract. Gagné (1974) uses the term *concrete concept* in much the same way as Mussen *et al.,* but he uses the term *defined concepts* to refer to concepts whose attributes cannot be "pointed to." Markle (1977) makes a useful distinction between "generic" and "specific" concepts to take into account inclusiveness. The concept *animal* is more inclusive than *cow,* but the examples of *animal* are as concrete as those of *cow*—both can be pointed to.

TABLE 1.1 Major Form–Class Concepts[a]

Class	Linguistic manifestation[b]	Approximate conceptual meaning— the class of experiences that includes:
Nominals	Nouns, pronouns, noun phrases	Objects, persons, ideas, and relations whose location or distribution in space, actually or metaphorically, can be specified
Adjectivals	Adjectives, adjective phrases	Qualities or attributes perceived as applying to nominals, either on an all-or-none basis (presence–absence) or in terms of degree
Verbals	Verbs, verb phrases	Events, relationships, or states whose location or distribution in a time dimension can be specified
Adverbials	Adverbs, adverb phrases	Qualities or attributes perceived as applying to adjectivals and verbals, either on an all-or-none basis or in terms of degree
Prepositionals	Prepositions, prepositional phrases	Relations of spatial, temporal, or logical position relative to nominals
Conjunctives	Conjunctions	Logical relations occurring whenever any two or more members of any class (or construction) are considered together

[a] From John B. Carroll, *Language and Thought*, © 1964, pg. 92. Reprinted by permission of Prentice-Hall, Inc., Englewood Cliffs, New Jersey.

[b] In each case it is to be understood that derivations from other form classes are to be included.

A CONCEPT OF *CONCEPT*

While it may serve a useful purpose to think of all concepts as being either concrete or abstract or concrete and defined, the approach taken in this book calls for a somewhat more analytical treatment. Thus, the class of learning outcomes called concepts may be considered as mental constructs of individuals and also as societally accepted meanings of words and word phrases shared by persons of similar environmental backgrounds who speak the same language. Further, the term *concept* itself can be defined in terms of attributes. The eight attributes of *concept* are learnability, usability, validity, generality, power, structure, instance abstractness, and instance numerousness. These attributes are presumed to be applicable to any public concept, that is, to the societally accepted meaning of any word that stands for a concept and also to concepts as mental constructs of individuals.

Learnability. Any concept must be learned; it does not emerge solely as a product of maturation. The learnability varies among concepts in the sense that some are learned more readily than others by individuals who share similar cultural experiences and language. For example, concepts that have many concrete examples, such as *dog* and *tree*, are learned more readily than are concepts without concrete examples, such as *noun* and *eternity*. The relative ease of learning different concepts requires sophisticated research.

While public concepts vary in learnability, the level to which a particular concept as a mental construct is attained by a given individual also varies, increasing with further learning. For example, with more learning, an individual's concept of *plant* comes closer to the concept held by the botanist.

The level of mastery of any public concept also varies among individuals of roughly equivalent maturational and experiential levels. For example, high school seniors vary widely in their mastery of the concept of *valence*. This variability among persons of roughly the same age and experience pertains to the other seven attributes as well; therfore, we shall not refer to it further.

Usability. As will be discussed later in this chapter, having mature concepts aids us (a) to generalize to new examples and to discriminate nonexamples of the concept; (b) to understand exclusive–inclusive, hierarchical, and part–whole relationships; (c) to understand cause and effect, correlational, probability, and axiomatic relationships among concepts; and (d) to solve problems involving the concept. These uses of concepts in turn reduce the necessity for constant learning and relearning of concepts and also make possible the highest levels of human intellectual functioning.

Concepts vary in their usability in the sense that some can be employed more than others in understanding and forming principles and in solving problems. The mathematical concepts of *number* and *set* are probably used more frequently in understanding mathematical principles and in solving a variety of problems than are the concepts of *proportion* and *ratio*. Concepts as mental constructs of the individual become more usable as they are attained at successively higher levels.

Validity. One means of determining validity is by reference to persons who are most knowledgeable about a subject. In this sense a concept is valid to the extent that experts agree on its meaning. Concepts comprising well-defined taxonomic systems within zoology, botany, and chemistry have greater validity than do many concepts in the behavioral sciences, for example, *intelligence, democracy, liberal,* and *group dynamics.* Experts are in greater agreement concerning the meanings of the first group of concepts than they are about the second group. The validity of the concepts of maturing individuals increases as their concepts come to agree with those of the experts or, more generally, of the larger social community.

Generality. Concepts have been organized into taxonomic systems, into other hierarchies, and into other structures of knowledge related to various disciplines. Within the same taxonomy the higher the concept, the more general it is in terms of the number of subclasses or subordinate concepts it includes. *Living things* is highly general; *vertebrate, mammal,* and *man* are successively less general. In the terminology of Markle (1977), the latter three concepts are increasingly specific.

As noted earlier, individuals organize and relate their own store of concepts in the cognitive structure. If their organization of concepts is the same as that of any of the socially accepted taxonomies and other structures, then their concepts also vary in generality in an analogous manner.

Power. The attribute of power refers to the extent to which a particular concept facilitates or is essential to the attainment of other concepts. Bruner (1960), for example, stated that there are certain big ideas, or fundamental concepts, in each of the various disciplines. He recommended that these should be taught first so that other less powerful concepts and factual information could be related to them. Ausubel (1963, 1966, 1968) dealt with the power of concepts indirectly through the construct of advance organizers. He stated that an advance organizer—that is, introductory material to a lesson—should include concepts at a higher level of generality than those in the lesson so that the concepts presented in the new material could be related to those in the advance organizer. When learned, these more general and inclusive concepts in the advance organizer would enable the individual to relate new information to them.

Structure. Any concept defined in terms of attributes has a structure, a relatedness of the defining attributes. Bourne (1970) described an internally consistent structure of concept attributes, which he called conceptual rules. The rules were derived from the calculus of propositions that generates a total of 16 possibilities for partitioning a stimulus population, using two stimulus dimensions at most. According to Bourne, 10 of the possibilities are unique and nontrivial as related to concept structure and can be reduced to five pairs, each pair consisting of a primary and a complementary stimulus partition, or conceptual rule. The basis of the five pairs is that any instance which is positive under one rule is negative under its complement. The conceptual rules are given in Table 1.2. The primary rules appear in the left columns and are labeled the affirmative, the conjunctive, the inclusive disjunctive, the conditional, and the biconditional conceptual rules.

Bourne (1973) has done much experimentation on rule identification with universes of concepts expressly developed for the rule–identification experi-

TABLE 1.2 Conceptual Rules Describing Binary Partitions of a Stimulus Population[a]

	Primary rule			Complementary rule	
Name	Symbolic description[b]	Verbal description	Name	Symbolic description	Verbal description
Affirmative	R	All red patterns are examples of the concept	Negation	$\bar{R}$	All patterns that are not red are examples
Conjunctive	R ∩ S	All patterns that are red and square are examples	Alternative denial	R ∣ S [$\bar{R}$ ∪ $\bar{S}$]	All patterns that are either not red or not square are examples
Inclusive disjunctive	R ∪ S	All patterns that are red or square or both are examples	Joint denial	R ↓ S [$\bar{R}$ ∩ $\bar{S}$]	All patterns that are neither red nor square are examples
Conditional	R → S [$\bar{R}$ ∪ S]	If a pattern is red, then it must be square to be an example	Exclusion	R ∩ $\bar{S}$	All patterns that are red and not square are examples
Biconditional	R ↔ S [(R ∩ S) ∪ ($\bar{R}$ ∩ $\bar{S}$)]	Red patterns are examples if and only if they are square	Exclusive disjunctive	R $\bar{\cup}$ S [(R ∩ $\bar{S}$) ∪ ($\bar{R}$ ∩ S)]	All patterns that are red or square but not both are examples

[a] From L. E. Bourne, Jr. Knowing and using concepts. *Psychological Review*, 1970, 77, 547. Copyright 1970 by the American Psychological Association. Reprinted by permission.

[b] R and S stand for red and square (relevant attributes), respectively. Symbolic descriptions using only three basic operations, ∩, ∪, and negation, are given in brackets.

ments. These universes consist of displays such as of geometric figures, each figure having two or more dimensions, each dimension having two values (e.g., form—triangle or square; color—red or blue; size—large or small; orientation on display—horizontal or vertical; and edge of figure—broken line or solid line). Concepts can be created from this display involving any of the 10 rules given in Table 1.2 (e.g., affirmative—all the red figures; conjunctive—figures that are large and horizontal; inclusive disjunctive—figures that are either red or have solid edges, etc.).

Most concepts taught in school may be defined in terms of attributes joined by rules; but they have many different patterns and kinds of attributes, and the values across concepts cannot be attended to and discriminated as readily as they are with the universes of concepts used in rule-identification experiments. This is true, for example, of the different classes of animals in the animal kingdom and the form classes of words. The rules joining the attributes defining these multi-attribute concepts are primarily affirmative or conjunctive. The conclusions regarding the learning of binary rules for joining attributes based on experiments with the created universes of concepts have limited generalizability to learning these multi-attribute concepts (Neimark & Santa, 1975).

Abstractness of examples. Concepts vary with respect to the extent to which examples of the concepts can be sensed. For example, *plant* has many examples which can be manipulated, seen, and smelled, whereas *eternity* has no perceptible examples. Between these poles are concepts whose examples can be represented by drawings and other means. For example, we can generate drawings of concepts such as *point* and *line segment* but cannot provide observable examples of either one as defined technically in geometry.

With increasing age, individuals are able to identify the less obvious attributes of concept examples. Also, the various sensory modalities can be used in combination. The maturing child is successively able to interact with and represent the environment enactively, iconically, and symbolically, and then to combine these modes of interaction and representation, according to Bruner (1964, 1973). It is the symbolic mode that frees us from the concrete, the here and now, and enables us in the sweep of a few seconds to analyze a present situation in terms of what we have experienced before and intend to accomplish in the future.

Numerousness of examples. Most concepts have examples or commonly used verbal or pictorial representations. The number of examples ranges from one to an infinite number: one example, *the earth's moon*; a small number, *the continents*; a large number, *living persons*; or an infinite number, *integers*. Certain concepts may have imaginary rather than actual examples, for example, *pilotless passenger airplanes*.

Most individuals continue to encounter new examples, or pictorial or verbal representations of examples of the same concepts, with increasing age. But there is great variability among individuals with respect to the number and nature of examples of the same concepts encountered. Many younger children living in desert regions do not encounter swamplands; those who live in the lowlands along rivers, lakes, and oceans do not encounter desert lands; some children living in our inner cities encounter no kind of land except the asphalt of the city streets.

The particular examples of some of the same concepts that different individuals encounter vary markedly. For example, we all encounter examples of *mother, father, fear, love,* and *death,* but the examples encountered are clearly unique for each of us. Concepts that evoke strong affective responses are more nearly noncommunicable mental constructs of the particular individual than are concepts of *plant, numeral,* and the like that have many highly similar instances that are experienced without much emotion.

We may now attempt a formal definition of concept in terms of defining attributes. Concepts are mental constructs, that is, part of the organized cognitive structure of the individual, a category of learning outcomes. They are learned, and as learned to higher levels may be used increasingly to generalize to new examples and to discriminate nonexamples of the concept; to understand exclusive–inclusive, hierarchical, and part–whole relationships; to understand cause and effect, correlational, probability, and axiomatic relationships among concepts; and to solve problems involving the concept. The validity of an individual's concepts increases as they come closer to agreeing with the societally accepted concepts of the larger social community; the power of the concept also increases as learning to higher levels proceeds. Concepts are also societally accepted meanings of words used by persons of similar environmental experiences who speak the same language. Concepts as societally accepted meanings vary in learnability, usability, validity, generality, power, structure, abstractness of examples, and numerousness of examples.

DEFINING ATTRIBUTES OF CONCEPTS

We should clarify what is meant by the terms *attribute* and *defining attribute of a concept.* Bruner, Goodnow, and Austin (1956) defined an attribute narrowly as "any discriminable feature of an event that is susceptible of some discriminable variation from event to event [p. 26]." Some attributes are merely "discriminable features" of events, but others are not. An attribute may be a directly observable or inferrable intrinsic property of an object, event, or process, an observable or inferrable use thereof, or an observable or inferrable function thereof, or it may be an observable or inferrable relation between objects, events, or processes. Things that are members of taxonomies—for example, most members of the plant and animal kingdom—have observable or readily inferrable intrinsic attributes. The same things that have intrinsic attributes may also have uses—for example, the classes of plants and animals that are used for food by persons of particular cultural–ethnic groups. Also, there are observable or inferrable relations between and among members of classes—for example, between dogs and human beings generally or between a particular dog and a child who has it for a pet.

Many valid and powerful concepts do not have directly observable attributes in the same sense as plants and animals—for example, the concepts comprising the form classes of the English language discussed earlier. Here some of the attributes of the classes can be expressed in terms of the functions of each class when used in a sentence, and this implies a relationship with the functions of other form classes of words in the same sentence. The attributes of events and processes in hierarchically organized systems and models also may be expressed in terms of relationships. One attribute of the concept *learning hierarchy* as formulated by Gagné (1970) is that attainment of each successively higher intellectual skill has attainment of the lower skills as its prerequisite. As another example, the attributes of signed numbers can probably best be expressed as relations between positive and negative numbers.

Observable and inferrable attributes of things may be continuous or discrete. Color, height, and weight are examples of continuous attributes and are often referred to as dimensions rather than attributes. Other attributes are discrete. For example, there are no gradations along the pregnancy dimension—a woman is either pregnant or she is not; a man is either a bachelor or he is not. Other attributes that are discrete may have more than two values, such as the number of sides different polygons have.

Three other key terms related to attributes require clarification: *defining, critical,* and *variable. Defining attributes* of a concept include all the attributes that are necessary to determine whether any instance experienced is or is not an example of a concept. The defining attributes of *equilateral triangle* are plane, simple, closed, three equal angles, and three sides of equal length.

Critical attributes of a concept are those necessary to distinguish members of one coordinate class from members of other coordinate classes. The critical attributes of *equilateral triangle* are three equal angles and three sides of equal length. These attributes are necessary and sufficient for discriminating between equilateral triangles and triangles of coordinate classes, including right triangles.

Variable attributes are those which are necessary for discriminating among members within a given class (e.g., black, green, and blue spruce trees). The same variable attribute, such as size or color, may be found across coordinate classes and also across supraordinate and subordinate classes. For example, equilateral triangles vary in size from very small to very large; right triangles (coordinate class) do also. Scalene triangles, of which equilateral triangles and right triangles are two subordinate classes, also vary in size. In the animal kingdom certain attributes are critical in discriminating mammals from other coordinate classes of vertebrates, including birds and reptiles. Certain variable attributes, such as of color and size, are needed to discriminate among members within each class: mammal, bird, reptiles. The defining attributes of each mammal, bird, and reptile include not only the critical attributes of each class but also the attributes of vertebrate (to distinguish from invertebrate) and of animal (to distinguish from plant). A more complete discussion of defining, critical, and variable attributes may be found in Markle (1977) and Tiemann, Kroeker, and Markle (1977). The attempt has been made throughout this book to use the three terms consistently and to avoid continuing the misconceptions associated with less precise terms used earlier, such as *relevant* and *irrelevant* *attributes*.

Principles

A principle is defined formally as a relationship between two or more concepts. To understand any principle, the concepts embedded in it must also be understood. Like a concept, a principle serves both as a mental construct of the individual and as the societally accepted meaning of the words, symbols, or statements that represent the principle. Most principles are expressed in verbal statements. However, the task in learning a principle is not to learn to state a verbal definition; rather, to understand a principle is to be able to use it to predict consequences from known conditions and also to explain phenomena that are encountered. In this way principles, like concepts, are the powerful tools we need for interpreting many phenomena and for solving problems.

Four basic types of relationships expressed in principles are *cause-and-effect*, *correlation*, *probability*, and *axiomatic*. An example of each of the first three follows:

> Tuberculosis is caused by the organism *Myobacterium tuberculosis*. (Cause-and-effect)
>
> Sample correlations between two sets of scores on standardized reading achievement tests of the same children taken at yearly intervals during the successive elementary school years range from .70 to .90. (Correlation)
>
> The probability of giving birth to a boy during any one pregnancy is .52. (Probability)

Axioms are universally accepted truths or conditions. They represent the largest class of principles. The class of axiomatic relationships may be divided into five subclasses: fundamentals, laws, rules, theorems, and axioms. What each class of axioms is called and how they function vary among disciplines such as mathematics, physics, and psychology.

The structure of knowledge in a discipline refers to the organization of the concepts and principles of the discipline. The structure of knowledge in algebra involves the solution of equations of the unknown, and the ability to solve equations rests upon understanding the principles of commutation, distribution, and association. The structure of spoken language may be thought of as the ways that individual phonemes are organized into morphemes, morphemes into phrases, phrases into the proper sequence to form sentences, and a string of sentences into an utterance.

Problem Solving

Problem-solving ability is the most important of all outcomes of learning inasmuch as a person, when capable of solving problems, can learn independently. Problem-solving techniques are learned and become part of the individual's cognitive structure. Both concepts and principles are used in solving many kinds of problems.

Individuals are confronted with a problem when they encounter a situation where they must respond but do not have immediately available the specific information, concepts, principles, or methods to arrive at a solution. Some simple problems, such as finding a shorter route to get from one building to another, may be solved very quickly using information immediately available through the sensory organs. Other problems involve using already learned information and methods and also learning some new information, methods, or both.

Much current knowledge concerning problem solving has been organized around sequences of mental operations involved in problem solving (Klausmeier, 1977a). Three similar formulations of the operations are given in Table 1.3. We may note the parallel terminology. In the first part of the sequence we have these parallel operations, reading the top part from left to right: "Need or difficulty observed," "Experiencing a difficulty," and "Preparation." Other operations that are parallel are shown, though the number of operations is not identical in the three sets. The five-step sequence consisting of preparation, analysis, production, verification, and reapplication described by Merrifield, Guilford, Christensen, and Frick (1960) was found useful in studying the differential behaviors of boys and girls of low, average, and high IQ during their problem-solving activities (Klausmeier & Loughlin, 1961).

Taxonomies and Hierarchies

Throughout the recorded history of humanity, persons have been adding to their individual and collective knowledge, organizing it, and putting it into communicable forms, primarily symbolic. Two organizational focuses for both an individual's cognitive structure and the communicable knowledge of a group who share the same language and cultural experiences are taxonomies and other hierarchies. Concepts comprise the key building block of these focuses of organized knowledge.

Though a taxonomy may be considered as a hierarchy, a useful distinction may be made between a taxonomy and other hierarchies. A taxonomy involves

TABLE 1.3   **Phases in Problem Solving and Creative Production**[a]

Rossman (1931)	Dewey (1933)	Merrifield et al. (1960)
Need or difficulty observed	Experiencing a difficulty	Preparation
Problem formulated	Locating and defining the problem	Analysis
Information gathered		
Solutions formulated	Suggesting possible hypotheses	Production
	Mental elaboration	
Solutions tested	Testing hypotheses	Verification
New ideas formulated		Reapplication
New ideas tested and accepted		

[a] From H. J. Klausmeier & W. Goodwin. *Learning and Human Abilities: Educational Psychology* (4th ed.). New York: Harper & Row, 1975.

inclusive–exclusive relationships among classes of things, whereas a hierarchy implies relationships among things ordered by some principle other than inclusiveness–exclusiveness, such as of importance, priority, or dependency. The main relationships among classes of things in a taxonomy such as of the plant kingdom and the animal kingdom are supraordinate, subordinate, and coordinate. Each class of things successively lower in a taxonomy has all the attributes of the supraordinate generic class and also the critical attributes that are needed to discriminate members of the particular subordinate class from the members of coordinate classes.

One important kind of relationship in a hierarchy is dependency. Gagné's (1968, 1974) concept of a learning hierarchy is illustrative. A learning hierarchy is a set of sequentially related skills of the kind where each preceding skill must be learned before the succeeding one can be. For example, a normally developing child speaks a word before reading it and reads it before spelling it correctly.

Despite the importance of principles, structures of knowledge, and problem solving in human cognitive functioning, psychologists during the early 1970s gave relatively little attention to these products of learning. In their review of

266 publications dealing with thinking and concept attainment Neimark and Santa (1975) did not report any research dealing with the learning of principles or of structures of knowledge. They reported a declining interest in problem solving. One exception to this trend was the comprehensive information theory of problem solving formulated by Newell and Simon (1972). More recently, Scandura (1977) provided a detailed analysis of problem solving while Bernard (1975b) and Tiemann, Kroeker, and Markle (1977) reported pioneering experiments on teaching coordinate concepts.

MENTAL OPERATIONS IN CONCEPT LEARNING

One way of explaining the internal conditions of learning across short time intervals is to identify the mental operations that are involved in bringing about changes in observable behavior, or inferrable behavior. Scientific methods of accomplishing this include the behavioral analysis of learning tasks, directed observation as the learning tasks are performed, controlled experimentation, and factor analysis of measured performances and mental operations. One way of explaining development across long time spans is to observe and measure the changes that occur at specified time intervals and to infer the determinants of the observed changes. Two problems encountered in these methodological approaches are the identification of learning tasks appropriate for maturing individuals of greatly different ages and the development and validation of the measuring instruments and procedures. These problems can be resolved if an adequate theoretical framework is established to guide the inquiry methods. The basic elements of the framework to be described here involve identifying the levels at which the same concept is learned from its earliest manifestation through its most mature understanding and also identifying and describing the mental operations involved at each level.

As shown in Figure 1.1, four successive levels of attaining the same concept are designated *concrete, identity, classificatory,* and *formal.* The ability to learn a concept at each of the four successive levels may be explained in terms of the individual's becoming capable of certain mental operations. The initial manifestation of a particular mental operation is presumed to be a product of both maturation and learning or, more broadly, of development. Maturing individuals progress invariantly from one level to the next in the attainment of the same concept as they become capable of the new mental operations required to learn a particular level and as they have attained the concept at the prior level.

The proposition that the same concept is attained at these four successively higher levels applies to concepts that (a) have more than one example, (b) have observable examples or representations, and (c) are defined in terms of perceptible and function attributes. Not all concepts are of this kind. Some concepts have only one example (e.g., *the earth's moon*). Some do not have observable examples (e.g., *atom, eternity, soul*). Still others are defined in terms of a

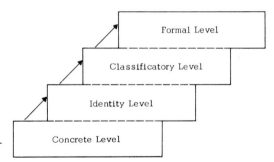

Figure 1.1. Levels of concept attainment.

dimension (e.g., *rough, thin*) or in terms of a variety of relations, including spatial (e.g., *south, between, above*), temporal (e.g., *before, after*), and deictic (e.g, *they, whom*). Not all four levels are applicable to each of these kinds of concepts. However, the attainment of any concept that has only one observable example or that has many observable examples of identical form or quality may be explained in terms of the concrete, identity, and formal levels. The classificatory level does not apply. Concepts defined by an observable single dimension and in terms of observable relationships may be explained primarily in terms of the classificatory level. The formal level is applicable to the many concepts that have neither observable, classifiable examples nor nonsymbolic representations. With this introduction to the four levels and kinds of concepts under consideration, the mental operations pertaining to each level will be discussed.

Concrete Level

A young child attends to a clock on the wall, discriminates it from other objects in the environment, represents the image of the clock internally, maintains the image (remembers), and then, after a period of time, attends to the clock and again recognizes it as the same thing attended to earlier. This child has attained a concept of this particular clock at the concrete level, not necessarily as a clock, but as an object with permanence. The operations involved in attaining this level, as shown in Figure 1.2, are attending to an object, discriminating it from other objects, representing it internally as an image, and maintaining the representation (remembering).

Identity Level

Attainment of a concept at the identity level is inferred by the individual's recognition of an object, quality, event, or relation as the same one previously encountered when the thing is observed from a different spatiotemporal perspective or sensed in a different modality, such as hearing or seeing. For example, the child who recognizes the clock as the same one when it is

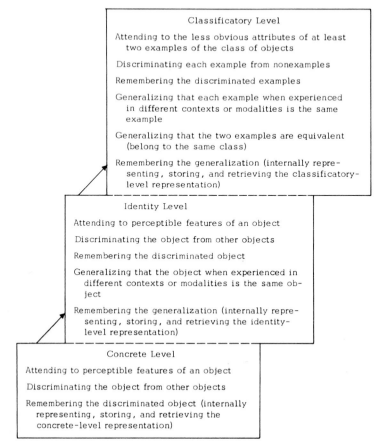

Classificatory Level

Attending to the less obvious attributes of at least
two examples of the class of objects

Discriminating each example from nonexamples

Remembering the discriminated examples

Generalizing that each example when experienced
in different contexts or modalities is the same
example

Generalizing that the two examples are equivalent
(belong to the same class)

Remembering the generalization (internally representing, storing, and retrieving the classificatory-
level representation)

Identity Level

Attending to perceptible features of an object

Discriminating the object from other objects

Remembering the discriminated object

Generalizing that the object when experienced in
different contexts or modalities is the same object

Remembering the generalization (internally representing, storing, and retrieving the identity-
level representation)

Concrete Level

Attending to perceptible features of an object

Discriminating the object from other objects

Remembering the discriminated object (internally
representing, storing, and retrieving the
concrete-level representation)

Figure 1.2.   Mental operations in concept attainment at the concrete, identity, and classificatory
levels.

removed from the wall of one room and placed in another room has attained
the concept of the particular clock at the identity level. Similarly, the child who
recognizes the family poodle whether seen from straight ahead, from the side,
or from various angles has attained the concept of the particular poodle at the
identity level. As shown in Figure 1.2, the operations of attending, discriminating, and remembering are involved in attainment at the identity level as well as
at the concrete level. However, concept attainment at the concrete level
involves only the discrimination of an object from other objects, whereas
attainment at the identity level involves not only discriminating various forms
of the same object from other objects, but also generalizing the forms of the
particular object as equivalent, or generalizing across different contexts in
which the same object is experienced. Generalizing is the new operation
postulated to emerge as a result of learning and maturation that makes attainment at the identity level possible.

Most psychologists (e.g., Gagné, 1970) until recently have treated concepts at the concrete and identity levels as discriminations, not as concepts. Piaget (1970) does not differentiate the concrete and identity levels but refers to object concepts. Nelson (1974) questions Piaget's ideas concerning object concepts and theorizes that infants as young as 12 months of age attain concepts. She explains how this initial learning of concepts precedes learning the words that represent the concepts.

Our interest here is less in concept learning during infancy and more in attainment of the concrete and identity levels by kindergarten and primary school children. We should recognize, too, that as we meet many new and different persons for very short time periods throughout our adult lives, we are continuously attaining concepts of individual persons at the identity level. However, we already have the concept *person* at both the classificatory and formal levels, so our task is much easier than that of the young child.

Classificatory Level

As shown in Figure 1.2, the new mental operation that makes possible attainment of concepts at the classificatory level is generalizing that two or more things are equivalent. The lowest level of attainment of a concept at a classificatory level is inferred when the individual responds to at least two different examples of the same class of objects, events, or actions as equivalent. For example, the child who treats the clock on the wall and the one on the desk as equivalent in some way (e.g., both have the same shape, have moving parts, and are used to tell time), has attained a concept of *clock* at a beginning classificatory level. At this beginning level children seem to base their classifications on some of the perceptible and function attributes of the concept examples they have experienced, but they cannot state the basis of their classifications.

Individuals are still at the classificatory level when they can correctly identify a large number of things as examples and others as nonexamples but cannot use the societally accepted defining attributes of the concept in evaluating examples and nonexamples. At this higher phase in attaining concepts at the classificatory level, children discriminate some of the less obvious attributes of the concepts and generalize correctly to a great variety of examples, some of which are very much like the nonexamples. Also, they are able to make the basis of their classification more explicit, though it is still incomplete.

Formal Level

Persons demonstrate a concept of *tree* at the formal level if, when shown some examples of trees, shrubs, and herbs, they properly identify the trees and call them "trees," discriminate and name the defining attributes of *tree*, give a societally accepted definition of *tree*, and evaluate how examples of trees differ from examples of shrubs and herbs in terms of the defining attributes of *tree*.

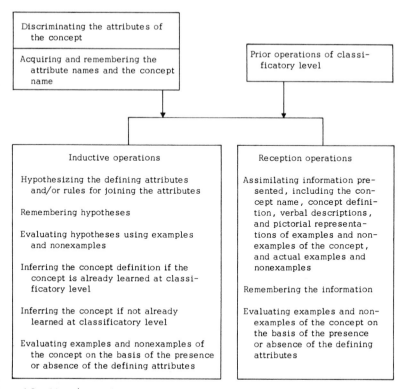

Figure 1.3. Mental operations in concept attainment at the formal level.

When individuals can do these things, it is inferred that they have learned the concept at the formal level through performing the operations as shown in Figure 1.3.

The inductive pattern involves formulating, remembering, and evaluating hypotheses regarding the attributes of the concept and then inferring the concept definition, if the concept has already been attained at the classificatory level, or inferring the concept itself if it has not been learned at the classificatory level. (A high school student encountering the concept *trigonometry* or *valence* for the first time illustrates the latter.) The operations involved in the inductive hypothesis-testing strategy characterize individuals who secure information potentially available to them from both examples and nonexamples of the concept. These individuals apparently reason like this: "Thing 1 is land totally surrounded by water. It is a member of the class. Thing 2 is land that is only partially surrounded by water. It is not a member of the class. Therefore, lands totally surrounded by water belong to the class, but lands only partially surrounded by water do not." The individual has hypothesized a defining attribute, remembered it, and evaluated the hypothesis, and is making progress toward inferring a definition of *island* in terms of its defining attributes.

A reception strategy, rather than an inductive one, is often employed in school settings, to enable students to move from merely being able to classify examples of concepts to being able to understand the concepts at a mature level. In expository instruction using a reception strategy students are given the name of the concept and its defining attributes. Explanations and illustrations must be provided by the teacher; information may also be made available in books and visuals. As will be explained more fully in Chapter 3, the students' main task is to attend to, receive, and process the information that is provided and then to retrieve it when needed.

In school settings much effective concept learning at the formal level involves some combining of the inductive and reception operations. It is very time-consuming for students to infer the defining attributes independently through an hypothesis-testing approach. However, to be told everything and not to do any hypothesizing or evaluating may result in lack of understanding. It may be well to re-emphasize that learning a definition is not learning a concept at the formal level. Further, much verbal instruction in school settings that has not utilized examples and nonexamples of the concepts has led to rote memory of information; it has not resulted in being able to classify or to understand concepts fully.

CONCEPT UTILIZATION

Concepts are the building blocks of cognitive development, not only because they enable one to interpret many discrete phenomena, but also because they provide the basis for vertical and horizontal transfer. As noted earlier, there is vertical transfer from one level to the next as individuals attain the successively higher levels of the same concept. There are four directions of horizontal transfer, corresponding to the four categories of uses that may be made of attained concepts.

The individual who has formed a concept at any of the four levels may use it as shown in Figure 1.4. A concept attained only to the concrete or identity level may be used in solving simple perceptual problems that do not require thinking with the use of symbols. Concepts learned at the classificatory and formal levels can be used in generalizing to examples and discriminating nonexamples when encountered, in understanding taxonomic and other hierarchical relationships involving the concept, in understanding principles, and in solving problems.

Generalizing to Examples and Discriminating Nonexamples

The attainment of a concept at the classificatory and formal levels reduces the need for relearning the concept primarily because the individual is able to generalize to new examples as they may be encountered and to discriminate

LEVELS OF CONCEPT ATTAINMENT   CONCEPT EXTENSION AND USE

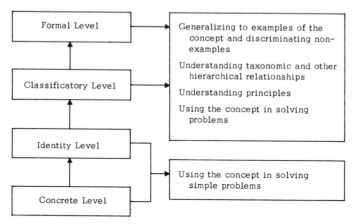

Figure 1.4. Levels of concept attainment and use.

nonexamples. Having a concept also provides us with expectations that help us deal effectively with new examples of it. Once we identify a plant as poison ivy, we treat it gingerly.

Not only does having a concept enable a person to identify examples and nonexamples and act appropriately toward them, but direct and verbal experiences with the new examples increase the validity and power of the concept for the individual. For example, the Canadian visiting in the Southern Hemisphere during January, when it is summer there, may attain more valid and powerful concepts of *flower* and *plant*. Similarly, by learning that human beings are mammals, we come to realize that human beings have many of the same attributes as monkeys and other mammals. Hence, our concept of *human being* has greater validity.

Cognizing Taxonomic and Other Hierarchical Relationships

Individuals can use their concepts attained at the formal level, and to a lesser extent at the classificatory level, in understanding exclusive–inclusive relationships of the kind embodied in taxonomies and also dependency and other systematic relationships that are the bases for hierarchies. Further, understanding one or more of the concepts representing a class in a taxonomy facilitates learning the other concepts of the taxonomy.

The relationship among examples or members of these classes is inclusive–exclusive. The lowest level of understanding these relationships is inferred when the individual puts examples of concepts in their proper groups. For example, an individual upon request puts all the red and blue equilateral triangles in a grouping of equilateral triangles, all the equilateral triangles and right triangles in a grouping of triangles, and all the triangles and rectangles in a grouping of polygons. At a higher level of attainment, the individual explains each group formed on the basis of its attributes, indicating that equilateral triangles include all the triangles that have three equal sides and three equal angles, triangles include all the polygons that have three sides, and polygons include all the simple closed, planar figures that have three or more sides.

Many inclusive–exclusive relationships are embodied in the preceding taxonomy. For example, the sum of the members of the supraordinate class equals the sum of the members of the subordinate classes; or conversely, the sum of the members of the subordinate classes equals the sum of the members of the supraordinate class. Another: No member of one coordinate class is a member of another coordinate class. Another: Each member of a subordinate class is also a member of the supraordinate class.

Hierarchical relations among members of classes are stated in terms of the particular kind of relationship. For example, the relationship between attaining the four levels of the same concept is hierarchical in the sense that attaining each lower level is prerequisite to attaining the next higher level.

Understanding of hierarchical and coordinate–supraordinate–subordinate relationships among sets of concepts increases the validity and usability of the involved concepts. For example, knowing the attributes of acid and also that vinegar is an acid leads to the inference that vinegar has the attributes of all acids, as well as the attributes peculiar to vinegar. Thus, all of the things known about acids—for example, how they react with bases—are true for vinegar also. In this way, learning that *acid* is a concept supraordinate to *vinegar* increases the validity and usability of the concept of *vinegar* for the individual.

Understanding Principles

Consider the following principle: Observing objects and events is prerequisite to drawing inferences regarding them. To understand this principle the concepts incorporated in it must be understood. The person who does not have any one of the concepts—*observing, objects, events, prerequisite, drawing inferences*—will not understand the principle fully.

Understanding principles permits us to understand lawful relationships among the classes of things represented by the concepts rather than among individual things. In the principle given, *prerequisite* is the key term, the comprehension of which enables us to understand the relationship between incidences of *drawing inferences* and *observing objects and events*. Or, consider this relationship: When two substances at different temperatures come into contact, the temperatures of the substances tend to equalize. This relationship permits us to infer what will happen in such diverse situations as putting ice cubes in warm soda pop or being lost in a snowstorm.

In all cases, being able to understand and use a lawful relationship depends on knowing the concepts that are related. Only then can the principle or axiom be applied to the appropriate phenomena.

Using Concepts in Problem Solving

We can clarify the role of concepts in problem solving with an example. Assume that a person has attained a concept of *equilateral triangle* at the formal level and therefore knows that all equilateral triangles have three sides of equal length and three angles of 60 degrees each. How will this concept aid the person in solving this problem?

Given that sides a, b, and c are equal in length and that line d bisects angle A, how many degrees are there in angles D and C combined?

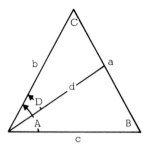

To solve the problem, the individual must

Retrieve and use the information that since the sides of the triangle are equal, the triangle is an equilateral triangle.

Retrieve and use the information that each angle has 60 degrees.

Retrieve or learn the new concept *bisect*.

Divide 60 degrees by 2 and get 30 degrees.

Add 60 degrees and 30 degrees.

It should be clear that without having a concept of *equilateral triangle*, or by some other means knowing that the three angles are equal, a person cannot solve the problem without actually measuring the angles.

In addition to having and applying knowledge, the individual also engages in a sequence of problem-solving operations as outlined earlier in this chapter.

WORDS FOR CONCEPTS AND THEIR DEFINING ATTRIBUTES

Until human infants can represent their experiences with natural language they are imprisoned in their own separate cognitive worlds (Flavell, 1977).

With the development of language they can not only represent more of the things and events they experience but also communicate verbally and start to become socialized by other human beings. Eventually good command of language permits sophisticated communication with others and also very rapid thought regarding past, present, and future events. Having words to represent concepts rather than merely images or other nonverbal representations of specific examples of the concepts facilitates this kind of communication and thinking.

The words representing a concept and some of its attributes may become associated with an example of the concept at any of the first three levels—concrete, identity, or classificatory—as indicated by the broken lines in Figure 1.5. However, having the concept name and the name of the attributes is prerequisite to attaining the formal level as portrayed by the solid line. The latter proposition follows logically from an analysis of the kinds of operations specified for attaining concepts at the formal level both by an inductive process and by meaningful reception.

Our purpose in this book is not to deal with language development but to indicate some relationships between words, word meanings, and the levels of concept development. The semantic aspect of language, rather than the syntactical, is of interest. As indicated by Dale (1976), this field of study is very promising; and Miller and Johnson-Laird (1976) have developed a theory of meaning around which to organize empirical findings, as is explained in Chapter 5.

Deaf individuals and others who lack normal speech development may attain concepts at the formal level. By our definition, the individual must know the defining attributes of the concept and must be able to communicate this knowledge. Verbalizing is normally used in this kind of communication. Other types of symbolic communication—for example, sign language—may also be

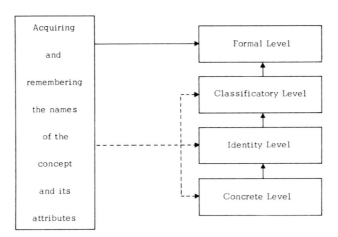

Figure 1.5.   Levels of concept attainment and acquisition of words.

employed. Speech per se is not necessary for the attainment of concepts, but some means for symbolizing and communicating the concept in the absence of examples is necessary at the formal level.

PLAN OF THIS BOOK

An overview of a theory of conceptual learning and development (CLD) has been presented in this chapter. In Chapter 2 the methods used in a combined longitudinal–cross-sectional study are described. Chapters 3, 4, and 5 are devoted respectively to an elaboration of the operations involved in attaining concepts at successively higher levels, memory and cognitive development, and the relationship between language development and cognitive development. In these chapters, some findings from the longitudinal–cross-sectional study are presented but the main purpose in the chapters is to elaborate CLD theory.

In Chapters 6, 7, and 8 the results of the longitudinal–cross-sectional study are presented. In Chapter 6 descriptive information is provided to support the proposition that concepts are attained at four successively higher levels in an invariant sequence. In Chapter 7 developmental curves are presented that depict the course of cognitive growth across the school years. In addition, descriptive information is presented regarding two other propositions central to CLD theory: Concepts are attained at successively higher levels at different rates, and concepts learned at successively higher levels are used more effectively in understanding principles and taxonomic relationships, and in solving problems. In Chapter 8, interindividual and intraindividual differences in rates and patterns of cognitive growth are described and hypotheses are offered concerning conditions contributing to the greatly different rates of cognitive development that were identified.

We have tried to summarize and synthesize information from the longitudinal–cross-sectional study in these chapters while still presenting concrete illustrative cases to capture some of the individuality of the 292 boys and girls who participated in the study and to whom we are deeply indebted. The surprisingly large interindividual differences found bear testimony to the richness of human individuality and the regularities observed to the qualities common to the human species.

Even before the present longitudinal–cross-sectional study started, the senior author, along with graduate advisees and other project personnel, was conducting controlled experiments in school settings to identify the instructional variables that facilitate concept learning. Results of these studies are included in Chapter 9, where a design of instruction is presented. The design includes a set of guidelines for carrying out instruction related to the different levels of concept attainment and for preparing instructional materials to teach concepts at the classificatory and formal levels.

The senior author and some of his colleagues at the Wisconsin Research and Development Center for Cognitive Learning have been involved in the reform and renewal of education since 1965 and have developed a kind of schooling called Individually Guided Education that is intended to make it possible to adapt instruction, particularly in the cognitive domain, to the characteristics of the individual student (Klausmeier, 1977b; Klausmeier, Rossmiller, & Saily, 1977). Individually Guided Education is described in Chapter 10, and the results of one large-scale study are included that indicate the means by which cognitive growth can be accelerated markedly in this kind of school setting.

The point of view reflected in Chapters 9 and 10 is that practitioners need more than knowledge about cognitive learning and development in order to facilitate cognitive development across the school years. They need high-quality materials and strategies for teaching based on sound instructional design. They need much continuing assistance in creating facilitative learning environments in the school, environments in which the individual child becomes the focus of instruction, rather than the familiar age-graded classroom group of 20 to 40 students. Chapter 11 is given to a review, elaboration, and extension of CLD theory, based on the results of the longitudinal study and also on the review and synthesis of other research and theory.

Knowledge in the field of cognitive learning and development continues to grow at an accelerating rate, making it impossible to treat any set of topics either in breadth or depth in a single volume. To provide greater coverage, we have annotated a group of recent books and articles at the end of most chapters. Two kinds of suggested readings are included. The first is a general treatment of the sort found in textbooks designed for upper-division and beginning graduate students. This kind of book or article presents an overview of a field and usually includes differing viewpoints or approaches to the field. The second is a more intensive treatment that summarizes and synthesizes research and theory for the more advanced student. Here, a more concentrated and detailed analysis of material presented in the chapter, a somewhat different perspective on a particular topic, or both may be found.

FOR FURTHER STUDY

Brainerd, C. J. *Piaget's theory of intelligence*. Englewood Cliffs, New Jersey: Prentice-Hall, Inc., 1978.

Piagetian theory is presented as a system of hypotheses that should be submitted to scientific test. Research that supports or refutes the hypotheses is included. Separate chapters are given to each of the four stages. Key metatheoretical concepts including stage, structure, and schema are treated in objective and neutral language. Education based on Piagetian theory is discussed.

Bruner, J. S. *Beyond the information given*. New York: W. W. Norton and Company, 1973. Pp. 313–351.

Chapters 18 and 19 of this book are reprints of Bruner's key papers dealing with the course of cognitive growth. The enactive, iconic, and symbolic modes of representation are explained.

Erickson, J. R., & Jones, M. R. Thinking. In M. R. Rosenzweig & L. W. Porter (Eds.), *Annual review of psychology* (Vol. 29). Palo Alto, Calif.: Annual Reviews Inc., 1978. Pp. 61–90.

Erickson and Jones review the recent experimental literature related to problem solving, concept learning, and reasoning. They relate concept learning to semantic memory, problem solving to perception and learning, and reasoning to inferential processes. Their review provides a context for relating the experimental psychology of learning to the theory and research presented in this introductory chapter and Chapters 3–8 of this book.

Farnham-Diggory, S. Development of logical operations and reasoning. In V. Hamilton & M. D. Vernon (Eds.), *The development of cognitive processes*. London: Academic Press, 1976. Pp. 359–412.

Farnham-Diggory reviews four general approaches to the study of the development of human logical skill: general intelligence testing, Piagetian theory, psycholinguistics, and information processing. The attempt is made to show how principles of growth are being formulated and analyzed by current workers in the field.

Flavell, J. H. *Cognitive development*. Englewood Cliffs, New Jersey: Prentice-Hall, Inc., 1977. Pp. 1–148.

Flavell, a major American interpreter and friendly critic of Piaget, describes cognitive development from infancy through adolescence in Chapters 1–4 of this highly readable textbook. Not only are Piaget's ideas explained clearly but American research is included that questions some of Piaget's theoretical formulations.

Gelman, R. Cognitive development. In M. R. Rosenzweig & L. W. Porter (Eds.), *Annual review of psychology* (Vol. 29). Palo Alto, Calif.: Annual Reviews Inc., 1978. Pp. 297–332.

Gelman reviews the recent research on cognitive development, with an emphasis on the study of younger children. The growing evidence that the cognitive capacities of young children have been underestimated is summarized. Gelman's review provides a context for relating the developmental aspects of the theory and research presented in this chapter and Chapters 3–8 of this book.

Klausmeier, H. J., & Harris, C. W. (Eds.). *Analyses of concept learning*. New York: Academic Press, 1966.

Sixteen scholars—psychologists, philosophers, subject-matter and curriculum specialists—deal with four main topics: schemes for classifying and relating concepts, the learning of concepts, learning–teaching processes, and concepts in various subject fields. Chapter 10, Meaningful Reception Learning and the Acquisition of Concepts by David Ausubel is an especially readable overview of meaningful reception learning. The other 15 chapters also are pertinent to the overview of cognitive learning and development presented in this introductory chapter and in later chapters of this book.

2

Methods of Studying
Cognitive Development

In American psychology, the dramatic increase in attention to cognitive development since the 1950s can be attributed in part to a revival of interest in Piaget's work, in part to a renewed commitment toward improving American education, and in part to increasingly sophisticated methodologies for studying developmental questions. Carrying out the longitudinal study reported in this book and refining the theory of conceptual learning and development on which it is based reflect interest in the improvement of education, as well as in extending knowledge of cognitive development. Students of school age, Grade 1 through Grade 12, were selected to participate in the study in order that patterns of growth related to concepts, principles, structures of knowledge, and problem-solving skills might be clarified during these important years. They are particularly critical years since most students must attend school where they receive much instruction that is directed toward development in the cognitive domain.

As a background for considering the design of the present longitudinal–cross-sectional study, several different methods used in studying human development are discussed briefly. Then the design and methods of the present research are explained, including a description of the students who were studied longitudinally and those who served as the control groups for repeated testing and year of birth. Some significant effects related to repeated testing and to year of birth were found. These effects are summarized and their implications for interpreting the main findings of the study are discussed in the last part of this chapter. Inasmuch as very few studies have included repeated testing or cohort control groups, considerable attention is given to this important aspect of longitudinal methodology.

METHODS OF STUDYING COGNITIVE LEARNING AND DEVELOPMENT

Over the past two decades a great deal of research on cognition and cognitive growth has accumulated, encompassing a full range of research methodologies: from normative, descriptive, and correlational studies to rigorously controlled laboratory experiments. An exhaustive and detailed survey of the many research strategies that have been used to study cognitive development is beyond the scope of this chapter. For a more comprehensive discussion of these research methods, the interested reader is referred to Kessen (1960), Nesselroade and Reese (1973), and Wohlwill (1973).

Experimental Study of Cognitive Learning and Development

Many investigators have obtained information about cognition and cognitive processes by using the experimental method. Essential characteristics of this scientifically rigorous method are control, which is usually exerted most efficiently in the laboratory, and objective measurement of changes in both independent variables (those factors independently manipulated by the experimenter) and dependent variables (usually the behavioral phenomena of interest). This method has supplied us with a great deal of precise and reliable knowledge about learning, memory, attention, reasoning, problem solving, and other cognitive processes.

Although experimental research has greatly increased our understanding of cognitive processes, it has seldom been directly addressed to cognitive *development* per se. The experimental approach usually poses questions about how independently manipulated experimental variables influence learning either alone or in interaction, rather than about how performance is influenced by an age factor. That is, the experimental manipulative method is not typically used to demonstrate a relation between behavior and developmental level. An age factor may be included to increase the precision of the research but does not necessarily reflect a developmental interest, as Spiker (1966) has observed. Reese and Lipsitt (1970) have noted, however, that a study in which age level is not varied may still have indirect relevance for developmental theory or suggest a developmental hypothesis. The Kendlers' (1959) work on reversal and non-reversal shifts in concept learning and the mediation hypothesis is an example.

In a recent theoretical paper, McCall (1977) discusses a number of challenges facing contemporary developmental psychology and suggests that many of the important questions that should be examined in developmental psychology are not addressed effectively by experimental, laboratory research methods. In order to achieve full understanding of cognitive growth, we must use methodologies that are directly amenable to the study of development and sensitive to developmental change. The two traditional developmental assessment methodologies are the cross-sectional method and the longitudinal method.

Cross-sectional Study of Cognitive Development

Development implies change. Developmental research is commonly defined as the study of behavioral changes that are associated with age changes. Historically, this formulation has generated a great deal of normative information about the typical age at which a given behavior occurs.

First of all, let us consider the factor of age. The age variable has a unique status in developmental research. Aging cannot be directly, experimentally manipulated; it must occur naturally. Moreover, age is regarded by contemporary developmentalists as a powerful index variable, but not as a causal variable. Some time ago Kessen (1960) and Bijou and Baer (1963), among others, warned that the age variable as used in developmental paradigms must be interpreted with caution. If it is found that age bears a systematic relation to some behavioral change, then we can only determine that the change was produced by some variable or variables also correlated with age. Vocabulary acquisition in very early childhood, for example, may be highly correlated with age, but age per se cannot be regarded as producing the change in the number of words in the child's repertoire. Explaining language development requires analysis in terms of other, psychologically significant variables. The study of cognitive development, then, involves not only the discovery of regularities in the relation between behavior and age, but also analysis of that relationship in order to provide psychological explanations that go beyond simple age-functional generalizations.

Although a broad statement of the developmental method implies the observation of behavior over time, there is a widely used shortcut for studying the progress of chronological aging that is known as the cross-sectional method. The cross-sectional method is used in order to compare measurements on some variable for different age groups who are tested once at approximately the same time; this method enables the investigator to study differences in behavior at one age versus another.

Nunnally (1973) has suggested that there are two major reasons for using the cross-sectional method. The first is to survey behavioral differences in individuals of different ages at a particular point in time. For example, the purpose of a cross-sectional study might be to compare political attitudes in various age groups in 1977 because that information is of current social relevance. The second reason for using cross-sectional methodology is to approximate the developmental function for a particular behavior. This is the usual purpose of the cross-sectional design in studying human development. In fact, Wohlwill (1973) has estimated that more than 90% of developmental research has relied on cross-sectional age-group comparisons. For example, using a cross-sectional design, Meinke, George, and Wilkinson (1975) investigated the ability of abstract and concrete thinkers in three age groups (fourth-, sixth-, and eighth-grade children) to categorize examples of complex concepts, such as freedom and justice. Statistical analyses showed that abstract thinkers did better than concrete thinkers at every grade and categorizing ability improved significantly with increasing age. The improvement in performance with increasing age was attributed to the increase in cognitive ability to deal with abstract concepts. That is, behavioral differences across Grades 4, 6, and 8 were taken to approximate a cognitive developmental progression.

Nunnally (1973) has also pointed out several potential problems which must be considered if the cross-sectional method is used to study behavioral differences at one point in time. The age groups studied must be comparable. An attempt can be made to ensure comparability of the age groups in several ways, depending upon the purposes of the study. For example, consider a cross-sectional study designed to determine whether differences exist in attitudes toward school as expressed by fifth-, eighth-, and eleventh-grade students in one particular city. A sample of individuals from each of these three grades might be drawn at random, in order that each is as representative as possible of the larger population of students in the city at that age–grade level. Or, the age groups in a cross-sectional study might be selected and matched on variables that could influence the outcome of the research. In a cross-sectional developmental study of problem-solving ability in 5-, 8-, and 12-year-olds, for example, the age groups might be matched on important variables that are not age related (IQ, motivation, or socioeconomic level) in order to ensure that any differences obtained between age groups are due to differences in developmental level and not to differences in extraneous variables. Most researchers using the cross-sectional method are aware of the importance of ensuring comparability of the age groups studied.

A second problem encountered when using the cross-sectional method involves making certain that the measures used are equivalent, or mean the same thing at the different ages studied. That is, the researcher must ensure that the tests or measures being used are appropriate for different age groups and are measuring the same behaviors at the different ages. Comparability of measures across different age groups may be a problem, especially when a wide age span is studied, but clearly is contingent on the type of measure that is used. Again, most researchers using the cross-sectional method attempt to ensure comparability of measures across the age groups studied.

The cross-sectional method involves another potential problem. In a cross-sectional study, each of the various age groups represents a different cohort (population of individuals born in the same year). Widely different age groups, say 5-, 10-, 15-, and 18-year-olds studied cross-sectionally, not only differ in age but also come from cohorts that encompass a 13-year span in year of birth. There is a possibility that these cohorts have experienced different environmental and sociocultural conditions that might be related to the dependent measure.

Consider a hypothetical example cited by Kessen (1960). If the fears of 5-, 10-, 15-, and 18-year-olds had been studied cross-sectionally in London during the late 1950s, the older children might have been found to exhibit many more fears than the younger children. It would be erroneous to interpret this finding as a developmental phenomenon, that is, that fears show a significant rise in mid- to late adolescence. The older children in Great Britain had lived through the traumatic events of World War II; the profound differences in the sociocultural conditions experienced by the age groups in this example cannot be discounted in interpreting the findings.

Cohort differences may be apparent in a replication of a study done much earlier. In fact, replications are sometimes conducted to determine the impact of sociocultural change. Barnes (1971) replicated a study by Parten (1932) on play behaviors in preschoolers. Barnes found a much lower frequency for cooperative and associative behaviors than had Parten. These findings were attributed to large sociocultural changes that had occurred between the 1930s and 1970s: exposure of children to mass media, smaller families, different types of toys, and so on.

Undoubtedly, cross-sectional differences among age groups on some dependent measures may reflect differences in cultural or environmental experiences. Interests, values, and attitudes would seem to be particularly susceptible to changing sociocultural conditions.

In summary, what can be said about the usefulness of the cross-sectional method as a way of studying human development? We have briefly discussed some of the problems that may be encountered when this method is used. The cross-sectional method is, however, very efficient and economical of research time and, as we have already seen, has been used quite extensively in studying development. If cross-sectional studies have been carefully and adequately designed in order to investigate behaviors at different ages that do not appear to be highly susceptible to changing sociocultural conditions, then they may not only provide reasonable approximations of a growth function but also constitute valuable sources of information about human development.

One final comment is in order. As many developmental methodologists (e.g., Nunnally, 1973; Schaie, 1965; Wohlwill, 1973) have noted, cross-sectional studies do not permit investigating developmental change directly. The change must be *inferred* from differences found among the age groups. For this reason, the cross-sectional method should be regarded as a method of studying age *differences*.

Longitudinal Study of Cognitive Development

In contrast to the cross-sectional approach, the conventional longitudinal method typically involves repeated (or dependent) observations taken on a single group of same-age individuals over some extended period of time. The longitudinal method enables us to study developmental change in individuals and groups of individuals and individual differences in growth patterns. In exchange for the increased sensitivity of longitudinal data to developmental change, however, the researcher loses the economy and efficiency of the cross-sectional method.

Longitudinal research is not new. Among the earliest longitudinal reports are the so-called "baby biographies" (e.g., Preyer, 1882), which attempted to record and describe as completely as possible the early development of an individual child. Among the best-known longitudinal investigations of cognitive development are the classic growth studies initiated in the 1920s and early 1930s: The Stanford Studies of Gifted Children (Terman, 1925), the Berkeley Growth Study (Bayley, 1954, 1968), and the Fels Study (Sontag, Baker, & Nelson, 1958) are examples. Some of these longitudinal studies are still ongoing and well into their fifth decade of data collection. Among the longitudinal studies that have had the most theoretical importance for cognitive development are Piaget's (1951, 1954, 1963) early descriptions of his own children.

Just as was true for cross-sectional methodology, however, a number of potential difficulties have been identified in the conventional longitudinal method. Baltes (1968) discussed five problems that may affect the validity of longitudinal research: selective sampling, selective survival, selective dropout, testing effects, and generation or cohort effects. Some of these problems may also affect the cross-sectional method and were discussed earlier. We will consider each of these possible problems in turn.

Most researchers know that the samples of individuals studied must be representative of the larger population from which the samples are drawn in order for the findings to be generalizable to the population. How can sampling problems uniquely affect longitudinal research? Selective or nonrepresentative sampling is a potential problem in longitudinal research that requires a commitment from adult subjects to participate in the study over a long period—10 to 20 years or longer. Individuals who agree to participate in this sort of long-term longitudinal research tend to be of higher intelligence and higher socioeconomic status (Baltes, 1968). Nonrepresentative sampling seems unlikely to affect short-term longitudinal research studying children over a period of a few years. Methods of ensuring comparability of different age groups studied cross-sectionally were previously discussed.

Selective survival implies that a given cohort (individuals with a common year of birth) will become less representative of the original population as chronological age increases. For example, the physically and psychologically less healthy members of the cohort will probably not live as long. Selective survival thus tends to be a positive biasing effect, in that it results in improved performance with age, and may present a problem for both longitudinal and cross-sectional methods. Developmental research covering the entire life span is likely to have to contend with this bias. Cross-sectional or longitudinal research covering a short age span is less vulnerable to this problem; selective survival would not appear to be a significant factor across the span of the school years.

Selective dropout is a problem whenever individuals in a longitudinal study—who are measured, for example, once each year over a period of several years or longer—are lost on some systematic or nonrandom basis so that a relation exists between whatever is being measured and some characteristic of the individuals who have dropped out of the study. Selective dropout is not a problem that can affect cross-sectional research because individuals are measured only once. Longitudinal research can directly determine whether or not dropout was selective by statistically comparing the last available performances of individuals who were lost with those of individuals who remained.

It is possible for repeated testing of the same individuals to influence the findings in longitudinal research. Whenever individuals are repeatedly measured, the practice they gain may positively bias the dependent measures: Performance may progressively improve as a result of practice and experience. Or, on the other hand, satiation, fatigue, and general disinterest over repeated measurements may negatively bias the measurements: Performance may deteriorate as a result of boredom. Again, longitudinal research can be designed to determine whether repeated testing has influenced the results by including appropriate control groups.

Generation or cohort effects, as we have seen, may be a problem in the internal validity of cross-sectional studies because the researcher cannot assume that the age samples selected differ in age only. We have already discussed the fact that year of birth differences are confounded with age differences in cross-sectional research and may present a problem, particularly with dependent measures that are highly sensitive to cultural shifts. A longitudinal sample shares a common year of birth, so generation effects within the sample do not exist. However, findings from a conventional longitudinal study are cohort-specific and may have questionable external validity for generalizations to other generations or cohorts, depending upon the susceptibility of the dependent measure to sociocultural changes. Longitudinal research can also employ designs to determine whether significant year-of-birth differences exist. If cohorts do differ, then the researcher must judge whether and to what degree the developmental function is altered by year-of-birth differences.

It should be clear at this point that neither cross-sectional nor longitudinal methods, as conventionally used, are without potential problems. The cross-sectional method will no doubt continue to dominate the developmental literature simply because it is so much more economical. It is a useful research strategy to describe how individuals differ in behavior at one age versus another, or to approximate the developmental function. If, however, a researcher is primarily interested in examining intraindividual change and interindividual differences in change, the longitudinal method must be used.

In summary, a great deal of attention has been devoted in the past decade to identifying and analyzing the methodological deficiencies of conventional cross-sectional and longitudinal designs. Developmental methodologists have devised alternative and far more complex designs (e.g., cross-sectional sequential, longitudinal sequential, and convergence designs) in order to circumvent the shortcomings of the conventional designs (see, for example, those reviewed by Wohlwill, 1973).

The methods of any scientific discipline benefit from periodic and constructive reevaluation. However, McCall (1977) points out that recent criticisms of developmental methodology, and particularly of longitudinal research, should not be overgeneralized. Some of the alternative designs to the conventional developmental methods that have been suggested with the intention of taking into account all extraneous variables (e.g., cohort, year of measurement) are so demanding that they have the ultimate effect of rendering "correct" developmental methodology beyond the realm of what is reasonable in terms of time and financial commitments. As McCall (1977) has observed,

> age, secular year of measurement, and birth year are *inevitably* confounded and can *never* be teased apart without making *some* assumptions. The issue for developmental psychology is which assumptions shall we make. The milestone longitudinal studies (e.g., Fels and Berkeley) tacitly assumed that their massive programs of repeated assessments did not change their subject's behavior relative to children not experiencing such intensive testing and that any age changes observed in the data were caused by generalizable developmental processes and were not produced by unusual historical events that children born in other decades do not experience at the same age, if ever (e.g., a world war, permissive attitudes in child rearing, etc.). That is, they assumed no effects for repeated testing or secular change (i.e., cohort differences). The tenability of such assumptions should be debated, but it is not always clear that the assumptions required by some of the suggested alternative research designs are more palatable [p. 340].

As McCall implies, the design of each specific developmental study must be understood within the context of the particular situation and the purposes of the study. For example, existing cohort differences need not totally alter the shape of the developmental function, even though the growth curve of a later-born cohort may begin and end at a higher level than that of an earlier-born group of children. Moreover, some aspects of cognitive development would reasonably appear to be immune to cohort effects. As McCall remarks, who would argue that the ontogenetic course of Piaget's sensimotor stages differs depending on whether children were studied in 1960 or in 1970? On the other hand, any researcher interested in investigating developmental change in values or attitudes (e.g., toward sex roles, divorce, abortion) must be immediately sensitive to the profound impact of rapid changes in our sociocultural milieu.

In conclusion, both cross-sectional and longitudinal methodologies have virtues and potential limitations. Cross-sectional research is economical and enables the researcher to compare differences in behavior at one age versus another, and to approximate the developmental function. Longitudinal research is more time-consuming, but enables the researcher to study changes over time in individuals and groups of individuals. Refinements in developmental methodology enable the investigator to assess several of the potential biases that were discussed earlier. For example, control groups for repeated testing and cohort differences can be incorporated in the design of developmental studies; special attention can be given to sampling biases and to the possible changing nature of a longitudinal sample over time.

Combined Longitudinal–Cross-sectional Methodology

A study that combines the best features of the cross-sectional *and* the longitudinal method enables the researcher to study cognitive development over a relatively broad age span in a fashion that is both economical and methodologically and conceptually sound, if attention is given to potential biases and if assumptions regarding the operation and interpretation of extraneous variables are made explicit.

In discussing mixed designs, Nunnally (1973) has noted:

> it would be very useful to employ designs that combine some of the economy of the cross-sectional design with the conceptual advantages of the longitudinal design. . . . such mixed designs potentially can supply some useful forms of information that cannot be supplied either by cross-sectional or longitudinal designs separately. One purpose of such research strategies would be to estimate truly longitudinal curves from partly cross-sectional data [p. 93].

The present design was cross-sectional in that four different age groups (students in first, fourth, seventh, and tenth grades) were initially selected for study. The design was longitudinal in that each of these age groups was tested once a year over a 3-year period. The strategy of combining cross-sectional and longitudinal measurement permitted the study of cognitive development over the entire span of the school years, Grades 1–12, as well as the study of individual differences in growth patterns.

The longitudinal and cross-sectional methods were combined in order to take advantage of the best features of each. But how can the possible difficulties associated with each method be resolved? A brief summary of these potential problems follows, along with the rationale for discounting some of them and the strategies used to deal with others.

In terms of the cross-sectional aspect of the study, the remaining sections of this chapter will describe the procedures followed to ensure that the four age groups studied, though differing in age–grade, were comparable and representative of the larger population of American students of school age. The dependent measures used in the study, based on extensive pilot work, were determined to measure comparable (i.e., the same kind of) cognitive abilities at each age; when certain measures, through earlier testing, were found to be inappropriate (too easy or too difficult) for some age groups, they were not administered in the final study. The confound between cohort differences and age differences that affects the internal validity of a cross-sectional design was taken into account by using control groups for year of birth. However, cohort differences were not expected to be a significant factor for two reasons: (1) Cognitive abilities should be less susceptible to year-of-birth differences than other kinds of behavioral phenomena, and (2) the four age groups studied did not represent widely differing cohorts.

In terms of the longitudinal aspect of the study, selective sampling and selective survival appeared to be insignificant factors in short-term longitudinal research with age groups spanning the school years. The possibility of selectivity in drop-out was examined. Effects of repeated testing were taken into account by using control groups that were tested on a single occasion. Finally, in the present study four groups of children, each representing a different cohort, were followed longitudinally.

In the remainder of this chapter, we shall describe in detail the design of the present combined longitudinal–cross-sectional study of cognitive development. But first of all, we will delineate the objectives and purposes of the study, which will in turn aid in explication of the methodology.

OBJECTIVES OF THE PRESENT STUDY AND DEVELOPMENT OF CONCEPT ASSESSMENT BATTERIES

Objectives of the Present Study

The objective of the present study was to chart the course of cognitive development across the school years, Grades 1–12. Concepts, principles, structures of knowledge, and problem-solving skills were selected for study. The theory of conceptual learning and development described in Chapter 1 provided the substantive framework for designing and carrying out the study.

The CLD theory encompasses four propositions. These propositions are stated in abbreviated form as predictions to be verified and explained by analysis of the data collected.

1. *Individuals will attain four successively higher levels of the same concept in an invariant sequence: concrete, identity, classificatory, and formal.* This prediction is based on three premises. The first is that mental operations emerge with learning and maturation. The second is that the ability to attend to larger amounts of complex material and to process increasing amounts of information also emerges with learning and maturation. A third premise is that language emerges with learning and maturation. The three conditions combined—new and higher-level mental operations, the ability to attend to and process more

complex material, and the ability to use language—make it possible to attain concepts at the four successively higher levels. As noted in Chapter 1, language is not prerequisite for attainment of the first three levels but it is for the formal level.

2. *Individuals will vary in the rate of attaining the same concepts and also in uses of concepts.* This proposition implies that because of differences among children in the emergence of mental operations, in the ability to attend to and process information, and in language development, there will also be differences in rate of attaining concepts and using the concepts.

3. *The same level of various concepts will be attained by the same individual at different ages.* Concepts vary widely in the number of examples and also in how the examples are experienced. Some have many concrete examples that are widely distributed in the environment, for example, *cutting tool* and *tree*. Others have examples that are usually observed as drawings (e.g., *equilateral triangle*). Still others are expressed only by words or other symbols which stand for classes of things, *noun*, for example. It is predicted that the successively higher levels of concepts that have concrete or pictorial examples will be acquired earlier than will the levels of concepts that have only verbal examples.

4. *Concepts learned at successively higher levels will be used more effectively in understanding taxonomic relationships, in understanding principles, and in solving problems.* This prediction holds that facility in using a concept is related to and dependent upon the level of concept attainment.

Criteria for Selecting Concepts

The CLD theory attempts to account for concept attainment from the earliest discrimination of an object, event, quality, or relation as one of permanence different from other things through a high level of attainment. A high school or college student who can classify examples and nonexamples and also indicate the defining attributes of the concept has attained the concept to a high level. Measurement to chart change of this magnitude across the years requires careful selection of the concepts, guided by explicitly formulated criteria.

First, the concept should be of the kind that potentially can be attained at each of the four levels and used in the three ways specified by CLD theory; further, it should be of high validity so that attainment of the four levels and three uses can be measured reliably. This criterion calls for concepts representing things that have actual examples or representations of examples that are experienced by individuals, starting during the early years of life. The examples should be entities of permanence such that they can be presented to the individual, removed, and then presented again. This is necessary for determining attainment of the concrete, identity, and classificatory levels. The concept should also have a societally accepted definition stated in terms of its defining attributes. The attributes may be stated as properties intrinsic to the examples of the concept, as functional properties—that is, as indicators of what can be done with the examples of the concept or what they can do—or as dependency relations between the given examples and other examples in a hierarchy. Having a societally accepted definition is essential for measuring attainment at the formal level.

Although many concepts satisfy this set of criteria, others do not meet at least one or more of them. For example, such important concepts as *love, fear, time, space,* and *death* have societally accepted definitions, but examples and nonexamples of them cannot be depicted readily at the concrete and identity levels so that young children's attainment of those levels can be measured reliably. Disagreement among experts concerning other powerful concepts such as *intelligence, democracy, justice,* and *morality* does not permit the development of reliable measures of their attainment at the formal level (or any other level).

The second set of criteria of concept selection deals with possible commonalities of the operations, the levels, and the uses across families of concepts, such as found in taxonomies and other hierarchical structures of knowledge. Harris and Harris (1973), in factor analytic studies involving children completing the fourth grade, identified a separate factor associated with the achievement of concepts in each subject field: language arts, mathematics, science, and, to a lesser degree, social studies. They also found that tests measuring achievement of many different concepts within each subject field loaded on the one subject-field factor. Rampaul (1976) obtained similar results with fourth- and seventh-grade students.

To assure generalizability and the possibility of comparison across subject fields, *equilateral triangle* was selected from mathematics, *noun* from English, and *tree* from science. The fourth concept, *cutting tool,* may be more closely related to science than to the other subject areas; however, it was selected because it is not typically taught at any time during the school years. Growth of this kind of concept can be related to the other concepts that are typically included in school curricula.

The third criterion deals with possible generalizability involving a concrete–abstract dimension of concepts. Most persons experience many examples of cutting tools and trees in their immediate environments. Examples of equilateral triangles are experienced typically as drawings, edges of surfaces, or boundaries of surface areas. Nouns are represented by single words, phrases, or clauses that in turn represent observable things and have clearly defined functions in a sentence, as is implied in the following definition:

> A word that is the name of a subject of discourse (as a person, animal, plant, place, thing, substance, quality, idea, action, or state)

and that in the English language is singular or plural, possessive or not possessive, and is used in a sentence as a subject or object of a verb, as an object of a preposition, as an appositive, or as a predicated element after a copula (intransitive verb).

The concepts used in the present study have three categories of examples: those that can be experienced by seeing and touching, those that have pictorial representations that can be seen, and those that can be experienced only in oral or written form. In the present study, the examples and nonexamples of *cutting tool, tree,* and *equilateral triangle* used at the concrete, identity, and classificatory levels were represented in drawings and those for *noun* in words. The test items of *noun* at the concrete and identity levels require attending to and discriminating words, rather than drawings of things.

Concepts from music, such as of *harmony* and *rhythm,* might have been used. These and other concepts involving the auditory modality were considered. They were not selected because of the difficulties and costs involved in constructing reliable measuring instruments.

Criteria for Test Construction

In addition to the usual criteria of reliability and usability, tests for each of the four concepts were constructed in accord with criteria of validity related to CLD theory.

First, the test items in each concept assessment battery should measure the operations specified for each of the four levels, i.e., attending, discriminating, generalizing, etc. Here the attempt was made to measure the final operation required at the level rather than the operations thought to be prerequisite to the final one. At the concrete level discriminating the target example from the nonexamples was measured rather than attending to the target example. At the identity level, generalizing across the different orientations or other situational contexts in which the same target example was presented was measured. At the classificatory level, generalizing across two or more different examples was measured. At the formal level the two prerequisites of being able to discriminate the defining attributes and having the concept name and the names of the attributes were measured separately. Recognition of the definition of the concept and evaluation of examples and nonexamples in terms of the presence or absence of the defining attributes were also measured separately. These four measures were combined to assess attainment of the formal level rather than attempting to construct tests to measure the formulating of hypotheses, testing the hypotheses, and inferring the concept. Though many concept-identification experiments have been done, based on the assumption that hypothesizing and inferring are the key operations in inductive concept learning (Bourne, Ekstrand, & Dominowski, 1971; Klausmeier, Ghatala, & Frayer, 1974), reliable measurement of these operations has proved to be elusive (Marliave, 1976).

The second criterion for test construction was that the tests for the four levels should measure the CLD operations on more material and on increasingly complex material of the kind exprienced by many human beings from infancy through adulthood. The amount of material within each level of each test was controlled by varying the number of nonexamples included in the items of the test. Complexity was controlled by varying the number of defining attributes and variable attributes shared by the examples and nonexamples. As more nonexamples were used and as they become more like the target example in both the defining and the variable attributes, greater demands were placed on the individual in terms of attending, discriminating, remembering and generalizing.

A third criterion was that tests should measure the three uses of concepts specified by CLD theory. This called for a test to be constructed for each of the three uses of each concept: understanding principles, understanding taxonomic relationships, and solving problems. Taxonomic relations involving supraordinate–subordinate–coordinate relations were specified, rather than other hierarchical relations, because of the large amount of research already completed in this field and also because of the importance of taxonomies as organizing frameworks of many areas of human knowledge. At the time of constructing the tests, we had no evidence as to which of the uses would be mastered earlier or later, and no order of mastery is assumed by CLD theory.

Test Construction and Validation

The construction of the four batteries of tests used in the present study occurred during a 3-year period. The selection of concepts and early test construction proceeded concurrently rather than independently during the first year. That is, from a larger number of possible concepts that were considered initially and analyzed according to concept analysis procedures outlined in Chapter 9, only certain ones were used—those that met the preceding criteria.

The first pilot study involving *equilateral triangle* and *cutting tool* was carried out with 50 children—10 each of nursery-school, kindergarten, third-, sixth-, and eighth-grade age (Frayer, Klausmeier, & Nelson, 1973). For *equilateral triangle*, 36 three-dimensional blocks of three shapes, three colors, two sizes (surface area), and two thicknesses were used. For *cutting tool,* 36 drawings on 3-inch × 5-inch cards were used; the drawings depicted five kinds of cutting tools and four kinds of noncutting tools. The test administrations were individual and oral. Problems were identified with some of the questions and materials used in the first tryout and the attempt was made to correct them.

The next pilot test for *equilateral triangle* (Klausmeier, Sipple, & Frayer, 1973) involved 280 students, 40 each of seven grade groups: preschool, kindergarten, second, fourth, sixth, eighth, and tenth. (Pilot studies of this magnitude were conducted for every battery.) The administration was also individual, and three-dimensional blocks were used.

The technical characteristics of the tests of the four levels and three uses were such that it appeared feasible to undertake the present longitudinal–cross-sectional study. However, three major problems remained. The three-dimensional blocks worked reasonably well at the concrete, identity, and classificatory levels with younger children but not at the formal level with older students. The older students know that *equilateral triangles* are plane, simple, closed figures and three-dimensional blocks are not plane, simple, or closed. Also, some questions called for the student to use terms such as *equilateral triangel, equal angles,* and *plane.* The examiner, despite repeated questioning to elicit acceptable verbal responses, frequently had difficulty in deciding whether to score answers as correct or incorrect. The individual administrations were also very time-consuming. To eliminate these three problems and to maintain consistency across all four batteries, the decision was made to use a

TABLE 2.1.   Number of Items and Criteria for Mastery of Each of the Twenty-Eight CLD Tests

Battery, test, and abbreviation	Number of items	Criteria for mastery
Cutting tool, concrete (CTCO)	8	7
Cutting tool, identity (CTID)	8	7
Cutting tool, classificatory (CTCL)	8	7
Cutting tool, formal (CTFO)	18	15
Cutting tool, principle (CTPR)	5 pairs	4 pairs
Cutting tool, taxonomic relations (CTTAX)	4 pairs	3 pairs
Cutting tool, problem solving (CTPS)	5	4
Tree, concrete (TRCO)	8	7
Tree, identity (TRID)	8	7
Tree, classificatory (TRCL)	8	7
Tree, formal (TRFO)	35	28
Tree, principle (TRPR)	10 pairs	8 pairs
Tree, taxonomic relations (TRTAX)	4 pairs	3 pairs
Tree, problem solving (TRPS)	10	8
Equilateral triangle, concrete (ETCO)	8	7
Equilateral triangle, identity (ETID)	8	7
Equilateral triangle, classificatory (ETCL)	3	3
Equilateral triangle, formal (ETFO)	18	15
Equilateral triangle, principle (ETPR)	5 pairs	4 pairs
Equilateral triangle, taxonomic relations (ETTAX)	4 pairs	3 pairs
Equilateral triangle, problem solving (ETPS)	6	5
Noun, concrete (NNCO)	8	7
Noun, identity (NNID)	8	7
Noun, classificatory (NNCL)	8	7
Noun, formal (NNFO)	25	20
Noun, principle (NNPR)	5 pairs	4 pairs
Noun, taxonomic relations (NNTAX)	4 pairs	3 pairs
Noun, problem solving (NNPS)	5	4

paper–pencil format in which the correct responses had to be recognized rather than supplied, to use line drawings instead of three-dimensional figures, and to administer the tests to groups, except in the case of young children who might need clarification of the instructions on an individual basis. The instructions were read to all students who participated in the study. Test items were also read to the younger children if they were judged not to have some of the words of the test items in their reading vocabularies.

Further tryouts of the *cutting tool* and *equilateral triangle* batteries and tryouts for *tree* and *noun* consisted of administering them in paper–pencil format in schools of another district under conditions identical to those of the district in which the longitudinal–cross-sectional data were gathered. As noted earlier, only the *equilateral triangle* battery was ready for administration to the longitudinal samples of kindergarten, third-, sixth-, and ninth-grade students in the spring semester of 1973.

Four final scaled batteries were constructed for each of four concepts: *equilateral triangle* (Klausmeier, Ingison, Sipple, & Katzenmeyer, 1973a), *noun* (Klausmeier, Ingison, Sipple, & Katzenmeyer, 1973b), *tree* (Klausmeier, Marliave, Katzenmeyer, & Sipple, 1974), and *cutting tool* (Klausmeier, Bernard, Katzenmeyer, & Sipple, 1973). A technical manual was also developed for each battery (DiLuzio, Katzenmeyer, & Klausmeier, 1975a, 1975b, 1975c, 1975d). The manuals give the technical characteristics of the tests, based on the responses of the total number of students who were tested during the first year of the cross-sectional–longitudinal study. The test titles, abbreviations, number of items per tests, and the criteria for mastery of each test are given in Table 2.1.

DESIGN AND METHODS OF THE PRESENT
COMBINED LONGITUDINAL–CROSS-SECTIONAL STUDY

Design

Four longitudinal samples (Table 2.2) participated in the study; in 1973 each consisted of 50 boys and 50 girls. The four longitudinal samples, each corresponding to a different grade, were designated Blocks A, B, C, and D. These 400 students were administered one battery of seven scaled tests designed to measure the attainment of the four levels and three uses of the concept *equilateral triangle*. By 1974, the three other batteries had been constructed and validated. In 1974, 1975, and 1976, the four batteries were administered to the students in each grade block. (Results of the 1973 assessment are reported as a cross-sectional study [Klausmeier, Sipple, & Allen, 1974a] and are referred to infrequently in this book.)

Of the 400 children in the study in the spring of 1973, 292 remained in the final year of assessment, 1976. These 292 children were distributed fairly evenly across the four grade blocks and by sex: Block A: 32 boys, 30 girls;

TABLE 2.2   Design of Combined Longitudinal–Cross-sectional Study

Grade in school each year of measurement				N in 1976[b]	Control group designation
1973[a]	1974	1975	1976		
Kg →	1 →	2 →	3	62	*Longitudinal Block A*
		1 →	2	23–26	Cohort Control 1
			1	33	Cohort Control 2
		2		34–40	Retest Control 1
			3	32–40	Retest Control 2
3 →	4 →	5 →	6	77	*Longitudinal Block B*
		4 →	5	36–37	Cohort Control 1
			4	34–36	Cohort Control 2
		5		34–40	Retest Control 1
			6	37–40	Retest Control 2
6 →	7 →	8 →	9	80	*Longitudinal Block C*
		7 →	8	32	Cohort Control 1
			7	35	Cohort Control 2
		8		33–40	Retest Control 1
			9	37–40	Retest Control 2
9 →	10 →	11 →	12	73	*Longitudinal Block D*
		10 →	11	32–33	Cohort Control 1
			10	38	Cohort Control 2
		11		33–40	Retest Control 1
			12	34–40	Retest Control 2

[a] One battery, *equilateral triangle,* was administered in 1973; the complete set of four batteries was administered in 1974, 1975, and 1976 to the four longitudinal blocks of students. The cohort and retest control groups that received all four batteries starting in 1975 are shown above; the 1974 cohort and retest control groups for *equilateral triangle* are not shown.

[b] Unequal Ns for the four longitudinal groups and the various control groups and ranges in Ns within some of the control groups resulted mainly from differing incidences of attrition among the various groups and from absenteeism for one or more tests within the same control group.

Block B: 40 boys, 37 girls; Block C: 39 boys, 41 girls; and Block D: 36 boys, 37 girls. Of the 108 children who did not complete the longitudinal study, 65 moved out of the city, 22 entered parochial schools, and 21 left for other reasons. Statistical analyses of the students' test scores showed no significant differences between students who left the study after the first and second years and those who remained.

Control groups were incorporated into the design to permit evaluations of possible cohort differences (i.e., differences among children born in different years) and possible effects of repeated testing (also referred to as retesting) of the longitudinal groups.

For each of the four longitudinal blocks there were two cohort control groups. The first set of cohort groups consisted of individuals of the same age–grade as each of the longitudinal blocks but who were born 1 year later.

This set of four cohort groups was administered all batteries in 1975 and again in 1976. The second set of cohort groups consisted of individuals of the same age–grade as each of the longitudinal blocks but who were born 2 years later. The second set of four cohort groups was tested only in 1976.

For each longitudinal block there were also two retest control groups. Each retest control group, of the same age–grade as the longitudinal block, was tested only once. The first set of retest control groups was administered all batteries in 1975 in order to compare their performances with those of the longitudinal blocks that had been tested twice. The second set of retest control groups was administered all batteries in 1976 in order to compare their performances with those of the longitudinal blocks that had been tested three times.

The children in the cohort and retest control groups were drawn at random from the same schools and classrooms from which the children in Longitudinal Blocks A-D had been drawn in 1973. Each control group initially contained 20 boys and 20 girls. Conditions accounting for the loss of some of the longitudinal-block students also accounted for the loss of some control-group students. The greatest loss occurred with Longitudinal Block A and the cohort control groups for this block. Many of these original children entered parochial schools upon completing kindergarten.

Locale

To permit generalizability of the results across school districts, a small industrial Midwestern city was selected in which the public school population reflects the racial mix, distribution of socioeconomic levels, and achievement level of the student population of the United States. This manufacturing– industrial city had a 1972 population of approximately 36,000, of which 7% were black. The economic level was slightly above the average for Midwest industrial communities. The public school system, which enrolled about 10,000 students at the time this study was begun in 1973, had 14 elementary schools, 3 junior high schools, and 1 senior high school. The four longitudinal samples of 50 boys and 50 girls were drawn at random from 4 elementary schools, 1 junior high school, and the senior high school, all of which were representative of the socioeconomic, ethnic, and general demographic classifications found in the city.

Data Collection and Treatment

The four test batteries were administered to groups of 20–30 children each year with the exception that first-grade children were tested in small groups of 5–8 children in order to reduce distractibility and, in general, to enable the test administrators to supervise the test-taking situation more closely. Occasionally control-group children of elementary school age were tested in small groups of 6–8.

Not all tests were administered to every grade group of children. Tests responded to on a chance basis in a lower grade because of their difficulty were not administered and tests that all students at one grade level got correct were not administered to the next higher grade. These decisions were based on results of administering the tests to similar samples of students in a different school district. Table A.1 of the Appendix indicates the grades at which tests were and were not administered.

During the first year of data collection two test administrators were responsible for testing. Thereafter, the same person administered all tests. The same two administrators also scored the tests and coded the test information for subsequent data analyses.

Data were quantified to compute the frequencies and proportions of students who fully attained, or mastered, each concept level and each use during each year of the study. Criterion for full attainment was set at 80–85% of the items correct, to the nearest whole item. Means and standard deviations were also computed using the raw scores on all tests administered at each grade level for each year of the study. Each of the predictions derived from the theory of conceptual learning and development was evaluated by analysis of the frequencies and proportions or the mean scores.

All data presented and discussed in the remaining chapters were combined for boys and girls. Following each yearly administration of the tests, the data were examined cross-sectionally (e.g., Grades 1, 4, 7, 10; Grades 2, 5, 8, 11) for sex differences in performance (Klausmeier, Sipple, & Allen, 1974b; Klausmeier, Allen, Sipple, & White, 1976a; Klausmeier, Allen, Sipple, & White, 1976b). Since no statistical evidence for strong or systematic sex differences was found, it was concluded that boys and girls did not differ in their performances on these tests.

Reliability of the Tests

The reliability of the tests for each of the 3 years they were administered to the longitudinal samples was assessed by means of Hoyt reliability coefficients based on the tests administered each year. The number of items per test in each battery, the Hoyt reliability coefficients, and the numbers of students on which each coefficient is based are given in Table 2.3. Tests were not administered at the grade level following the grade where the students had answered all the items correctly during the tryout. Other tests were not administered at a grade where this earlier research indicated that students performed at a chance level.

In order to eliminate spurious ceiling or floor effects on the statistical reliabilities of the various tests, a procedure was established for determining which grades to include in deriving each coefficient. It was required that the

TABLE 2.3 Hoyt Reliability Coefficients and Standard Errors of Measurement for Separate Tests and Combined Tests Used in Longitudinal–Cross-sectional Study[a]

	Year								
	1, 1974			2, 1975			3, 1976		
	Grades 1, 4, 7, 10			Grades 2, 5, 8, 11			Grades 3, 6, 9, 12		
Test and battery	N	Hoyt	SE_M	N	Hoyt	SE_M	N	Hoyt	SE_M
Concrete									
Cutting tool (8 items)	*			*			*		
Tree (8 items)	*			*			*		
Equilateral triangle (8 items)	*			*			*		
Noun (8 items)	62	.39	.79	*			*		
Identity									
Cutting tool (8 items)	*			*			*		
Tree (8 items)	*			*			*		
Equilateral triangle (8 items)	*			*			*		
Noun (8 items)	62	.67	1.01	62	.70	.59	62	.67	.49
Classificatory									
Cutting tool (8 items)	219	.72	.50	142	.63	.46	*		
Tree (8 items)	219	.82	.68	139	.66	.57	62	.90	.39
Equilateral triangle (3 items)	219	.46	.34	139	.48	.24	*		
Noun (8 items)	230	.76	.90	292	.76	.89	219	.77	.80
Formal									
Cutting tool (18 items)	292	.77	1.38	292	.74	1.34	292	.81	1.08
Tree (35 items)	292	.91	2.09	292	.86	2.08	292	.92	2.07
Equilateral triangle (18 items)	292	.84	1.62	292	.82	1.60	292	.83	1.34
Noun (25 items)	230	.85	2.07	292	.92	1.91	292	.87	2.06
Combined levels									
Cutting tool (42 items)	139	.73	1.70	139	.66	1.61	62	.49	1.61
Tree (59 items)	139	.86	2.54	139	.82	2.52	139	.88	2.56
Equilateral triangle (37 items)	139	.70	2.02	139	.71	1.92	139	.76	1.64
Noun (49 items)	157	.82	2.44	139	.90	2.25	139	.79	2.47
Principle									
Cutting tool (10 items)	292	.72	1.26	292	.76	1.26	292	.75	1.10
Tree (20 items)	230	.85	1.79	292	.92	1.68	292	.91	1.72
Equilateral triangle (11 items)	230	.78	1.36	230	.73	1.34	292	.76	1.25
Noun (10 items)	230	.70	1.30	230	.69	1.29	292	.77	1.29
Taxonomic relations									
Cutting tool (8 items)	292	.58	.89	292	.58	.90	292	.70	.75
Tree (8 items)	292	.72	1.01	292	.65	1.03	292	.76	.95
Equilateral triangle (8 items)	292	.67	1.10	292	.69	1.07	292	.79	.95
Noun (8 items)	230	.62	1.08	230	.61	1.05	292	.64	1.13
Problem solving									
Cutting tool (5 items)	292	.59	.80	292	.55	.81	292	.43	.69
Tree (10 items)	292	.68	1.24	292	.67	1.28	292	.75	1.21

(continued)

TABLE 2.3   (*Continued*)

	Year								
	1, 1974			2, 1975			3, 1974		
	Grades 1, 4, 7, 10			Grades 2, 5, 8, 11			Grades 3, 6, 9, 12		
Test and battery	N	Hoyt	SE_M	N	Hoyt	SE_M	N	Hoyt	SE_M
Equilateral triangle (6 items)	230	.66	.91	230	.65	.89	292	.66	.82
Noun (5 items)	230	.52	.84	230	.41	.87	292	.60	.86
Combined uses									
Cutting tool (23 items)	292	.81	1.86	292	.83	1.87	292	.81	1.63
Tree (38 items)	230	.89	2.51	292	.93	2.47	292	.93	2.42
Equilateral triangle (25 items)	230	.85	2.09	230	.84	2.04	292	.86	1.92
Noun (23 items)	230	.83	1.99	230	.81	1.97	292	.86	2.02

[a] An asterisk indicates that mean items correct for each block equalled or exceeded 95% of subtest items.

mean items correct on a subtest be within the range of 5–95% of the subtest items. These cutoff points were set in order that grade groups would not be included in which there was very little variance because the test was either very easy or very hard for all the students. All grade groups that met the 5–95% criterion for any year of the study were then combined for deriving the reliability coefficient for a particular test, the combined levels tests, and the combined uses tests. Carrying out these procedures resulted in the unequal Ns given in Table 2.3 and also in the lack of coefficients for 22 tests at the concrete, identity, and classificatory levels.

Tests from the *cutting tool* battery follow as examples of applying the procedure. All four grade blocks (i.e., A 1–3, B 4–6, C 7–9, D 10–12) in all years were administered the classificatory level test, but the mean score of each of the four grades administered the test in 1976 (i.e., Grades 3, 6, 9, and 12) exceeded 7.6 (i.e., 95% of the eight classificatory items). These four grade groups were eliminated because of the ceiling effect, and consequently a Hoyt reliability coefficient was not calculated for the classificatory test of *cutting tool* in 1976. All grade groups in each year, N = 292, were also administered the formal test; the mean score of each grade was within the range of 5–95%; therefore, all grades were included in computing this coefficient. Related to the coefficients for the four combined levels of *cutting tool,* 139 first- and fourth-grade students in 1974 and the same 139 students in 1975 as second- and fifth-graders took all four tests; their mean scores fell within the 5–95% range, and they were included in computing the coefficient. Students of Grades 7–12 were not administered the concrete and identity level tests, so they were not included.

Shortcomings of this procedure are apparent. Since there are no reliability

TABLE 2.4   Hoyt Reliability Coefficients for the Levels Tests of *Equilateral Triangle*[a]

	Combined group (N = 160)	Normal (N = 80)	EMR (N = 80)
Concrete level	.82	.80	.83
Identity level	.72	.79	.67
Classificatory level	.65	.55	.76
Formal level	.26	.27	.25

[a] Based on Gargiulo, 1974.

coefficients for 22 tests, their reliabilities may be inferred only when included as part of a combined test. Second, many Ns were reduced markedly, which tended to lower the coefficient. Third, when some of the mean scores were close to the cutoff point, the variance generally was small and the derived reliability coefficient was also quite low. Examples of low coefficients related to easy tests and/or small Ns are as follows: *Noun*, concrete level in 1974, $N = 62$, Hoyt = .39; *cutting tool*, combined levels test in 1976, $N = 62$, Hoyt = .49.

The effects on reliability of a range of scores on a test are indicated in Table 2.4, drawn from an experiment carried out by Gargiulo (1974) in which the *equilateral triangle* battery was used. The four levels tests were administered to 80 educable mentally retarded children whose MAs ranged from 5.0 to 10.0 and 80 normally developing younger children of comparable mental age. The Hoyt *rs* obtained were higher for the concrete and identity levels, which were of appropriate difficulty for these children, than for the classificatory and formal levels, which were more difficult.

Hoyt reliability coefficients were also obtained in 1974 when the tests were first administered to the longitudinal blocks of students (DiLuzio, Katzenmeyer, & Klausmeier, 1975a, 1975b, 1975c, 1975d). They are reported for the combined grades in Appendix Table A.8. These coefficients were based on larger numbers of students (including those who dropped out later) and did not take into account the ceiling and floor effects with the 95 and 5% criterion. For these reasons the coefficients in Appendix Table A.8 are either somewhat higher or lower than those reported in Table 2.3.

One may infer from the coefficients derived from the longitudinal samples and the Gargiulo experiment that the tests are reasonably reliable and generally acceptable for comparing the mean performances of groups. However, any individual's pattern of growth related to any area measured by these tests must be interpreted with caution, particularly when the percentage correct is quite high or quite low.

RESULTS PERTAINING TO COMPARISONS BETWEEN CONTROL GROUPS AND LONGITUDINAL BLOCKS

Earlier in this chapter we saw that control groups were included in the design of the study. One kind of control group, cohort, was included to ascertain the effects of being born 1 or 2 years later than the students of each longitudinal block. Another kind of control group, repeated testing, was included to determine what effects receiving the same four batteries of tests at 12-month intervals had on the performances of the students of the longitudinal blocks. The hypothesis was that neither of these effects would be significant for any comparison involving a control group and a longitudinal group. The hypothesis was rejected. Some significant differences were found when comparing pairs of cohort and longitudinal groups and also when comparing pairs of repeated-testing and longitudinal groups. The statistically significant differences that were found and their relevance for testing the predictions stated earlier in this chapter are now considered.

Cohort Effects

To identify mean differences significant at the .01 level, t tests were run between each of 91 pairs of mean scores of the longitudinal blocks and their first cohort control groups in 1975; t tests were run also for each pair of 91 mean scores of the longitudinal blocks and both their first- and second-year cohort controls in 1976. These significance tests were run for the pairs of mean scores for each level and each use of each of the four concepts. The results are shown in Table 2.5. In 1975 18 tests were significant at the .01 level; 14 of the 18 comparisons indicated that significantly higher mean scores were obtained by the students of the longitudinal blocks. The remaining four favored the cohorts who were born 1 year later. In 1976, 20 differences significant at the .01 level were found, 11 favoring the longitudinal blocks and 9 favoring the cohorts. Since the 1976 cohorts had taken the four batteries twice, retesting effects may have been present for this group. The significant effects varied somewhat across the four concepts, as examination of Table 2.5 reveals.

Some significant differences were found between the mean scores of the second set of cohort groups and the longitudinal blocks; 25 favored the cohorts who were born 2 years later than the longitudinal groups, and 10 favored the longitudinal groups. The number of differences favoring the cohorts or the longitudinal blocks also varied for the four concepts, as shown in Table 2.5. It is noteworthy that in 1976, the last year of the study, about 71% of the significant effects favored children and youth of the cohort groups who were born 2 years later than those of the longitudinal groups.

The data-processing procedures, conditions of test administrations, and possible changes in the school situation of the children and youth were examined very carefully to try to identify sources of the inconsistent pattern of significant differences. None of these factors accounted for the finding that in the first year the majority of effects favored the longitudinal blocks and in the second year the cohort controls, and that in 1976, 25 differences favored the later-born cohort groups and 10 the longitudinal groups. Similarly, sources of the differences in the effects according to the four concepts could not be identified.

TABLE 2.5 Grade Blocks in Which There Were Significant Differences between the Mean Scores of the Longitudinal Groups and the Retesting and Cohort Control Groups[a]

	Cutting tool		Tree		Equilateral triangle		Noun	
	1975	1976	1975	1976	1975	1976	1975	1976
Concrete								
Retest	—	—	—	—	—	—	—	—
1st Cohort	—	—	A,B	<u>A</u>	—	—	—	—
2nd Cohort		—		—		—		—
Identity								
Retest	—	—	—	—	—	—	—	—
1st Cohort	—	—	—	—	—	—	—	—
2nd Cohort		—		<u>B</u>		—		<u>A</u>
Classificatory								
Retest	—	—	—	—	B	A	—	D
1st Cohort	—	—	—	—	B	—	A	C
2nd Cohort		<u>D</u>		—		—		A,<u>B</u>,C
Formal								
Retest	—	—	D	—	D	B,D	D	D
1st Cohort	A	—	<u>A</u>,D	B,C,D	D	—	<u>B</u>	A
2nd Cohort		A,<u>C,D</u>		<u>A</u>,B,D		<u>A,B</u>		<u>B</u>
Principle								
Retest	—	—	—	—	—	—	D	—
1st Cohort	A	<u>B</u>	—	A,B,C	D	<u>B</u>	<u>B</u>	—
2nd Cohort		<u>B,C,D</u>		C,D		<u>B,C</u>		D
Problem solving								
Retest	—	<u>C</u>	—	—	<u>C</u>	—	—	—
1st Cohort	A	—	—	<u>A,C,D</u>	—	<u>B</u>	—	<u>D</u>
2nd Cohort		A,<u>D</u>		<u>A,B,C</u>		<u>B,C</u>		<u>D</u>
Taxonomic relations								
Retest	—	—	—	—	D	<u>A</u>	D	D
1st Cohort	A,B	A	—	A	A,D	<u>B</u>	<u>B</u>	C
2nd Cohort		A		—		<u>B,C,D</u>		—

[a] (1) Results for each subtest based on *t* tests ($p < .01$) for significant differences between mean scores of longitudinal blocks and control groups.

(2) Underlining indicates control group obtained significantly higher mean than longitudinal block.

(3) A dash (—) indicates differences not significant at .01.

(4) Children in first cohort control group were tested in 1975 and retested in 1976. Children in second cohort control group were tested only in 1976.

Repeated Testing Effects

To ascertain the effects of testing the longitudinal groups in 1974, 1975, and 1976 with the same test batteries, t tests were run between the mean scores of the four longitudinal blocks and their retest control groups. The tests of significance were run between the pairs of mean scores of each test administered to the longitudinal and control groups; a total of 187 pairs of scores were tested. (See Appendix Table A.1 to see the grades where the tests were too easy or too difficult and were therefore not administered.) Eight differences significant at the .01 level were found for the statistical comparisons in 1975 and 8 in 1976; 13 favored the longitudinal blocks and 3 the retest controls, as shown in Table 2.5. The differences favoring the longitudinal blocks or the retest controls varied somewhat for each concept. Careful analyses of the test data and the conditions of testing provided no clues as to why 3 of the 16 significant differences favored the control groups who were tested only once. Since 187 pairs of mean scores were compared, 2 significant differences at the .01 level could be expected on the basis of chance.

Differences between Longitudinal Blocks

As noted earlier, cohort and retesting effects were not anticipated (and the large majority of tested differences were not significant). Had there been none, the mean scores of the students of the longitudinal blocks when in Grades 4, 7, and 10 in 1974 should have been as high or higher than the mean scores of the students in the preceding block in 1976 when in Grades 3, 6, and 9. This assumes that some increase should have accrued on each test across each grade until near perfect performance was achieved and that the mean score, once near perfect, should not have fallen. Some significant retesting and cohort effects were found; also there were other substantial differences that did not reach statistical significance at the .01 level. Retesting effects favoring the students of the longitudinal groups and cohort effects favoring students born later than the longitudinal groups would result in higher mean scores for the students in 1976 when in Grades 3, 6, and 9 than for the students in 1974 when in Grades 4, 7, and 10. To determine whether this had occurred, the mean test scores were compared between Grades 3 and 4, 6 and 7, and 9 and 10. Thirty-seven of these comparisons were significant, as shown in Table 2.6. Of the 37 significant differences, 29 favored students in 1976 when in Grades 3, 6, and 9; 8 favored students in 1974 when in Grades 4, 7, and 10.

The 29 differences favoring Grades 3, 6, and 9 were fairly evenly distributed across the four concepts. However, only 6 were found at the concrete, identity, and classificatory levels of concept attainment, whereas there were 10 for the formal level, 7 for the use of principles, 8 for problem solving, and 6 for taxonomic relations. Seven of the 8 significant differences favoring Grades 4, 7, and 10 involved the formal level and principles. Further, 5 of the 8 involved the concept tree.

TABLE 2.6 Significantly Different Mean Scores between Grade Blocks A–B, B–C, and C–D[a]

	Cutting tool			Tree			Equilateral triangle			Noun		
Blocks	A–B	B–C	C–D	A–B	B–C	C–D	A–B	B–C	C–D	A–B	B–C	C–D
Grades	3–4	6–7	9–10	3–4	6–7	9–10	3–4	6–7	9–10	3–4	6–7	9–10
Concrete	—	—	—	—	—	—	—	—	—	—	—	—
Identity	—	—	—	—	—	—	Y	—	—	—	—	—
Classificatory	—	Y	Y	—	Y	Y	—	—	—	Y	—	—
Formal	Y	Y	Y	0	0	0	0	Y	—	Y	Y	—
Principle	—	Y	Y	0	0	—	Y	Y	—	—	—	0
Problem solving	—	Y	—	Y	Y	Y	Y	Y	—	Y	—	Y
Taxonomic relations	0	Y	—	—	Y	Y	—	Y	—	—	Y	—

[a] A Y indicates a significant difference between adjacent blocks as determined by t tests ($p <$ .01) favoring the younger retested students when in Grades 3, 6, and 9; and 0 favoring the older students who had been tested only once when in Grades 4, 7, and 10.

A comparison of these significant differences with the significant differences involving the retest and cohort control groups presented in Table 2.5 shows considerable agreement. For example, 11 of the 13 significant cohort effects involving the formal level and principles related to *tree* favored the longitudinal blocks rather than the later-born cohorts. On the other hand, all 12 of the significant cohort effects for *equilateral triangle* in 1976 favored the later-born cohorts.

Significant Effects and Testing the Predictions

Earlier in this chapter, we indicated that the four longitudinal groups of students were drawn from the population of students of one school district (the control groups were drawn from the same population). This was done with the expectation that the differences in the performances of students in successive grades and adjacent blocks (i.e., Grades 3–4, 6–7, and 9–10) would be of about the same magnitude as the differences across two testings within the same blocks (e.g., Grades 2–3, 5–6, 8–9), except that there might be some deceleration as the students neared full attainment of a concept level or use. Another expectation was that the mean scores for Grades 4, 7, and 10 would be as high or higher than the mean scores for Grades 3, 6, and 9, because students in Grades 4, 6, and 10 were a year older.

Contrary to expectations, the mean differences between the blocks generally favored the younger students of Grades 3, 6, and 9, apparently because of retesting effects, cohort effects, or a combination of the two. The retesting effects generally resulted in somewhat higher scores across the years of testing within each block. The cohort effects were associated with the relatively lower performances of the older Grade 4, 7, and 10 students and the higher performances of the younger (and later-born) students. As noted earlier, there were some exceptions to this general pattern of retesting and cohort effects. Since the exceptions are in accordance with the expectations, they will not be dealt with in detail. We will now consider the implications of the significant differences between the longitudinal blocks for verifying the main predictions of the longitudinal–cross-sectional study and also for charting the course of cognitive growth, Grade 1–Grade 12.

That the mean scores of the students in their third year of the study were generally higher than expected as a result of retesting was judged not to have affected the test of the first prediction (i.e., that the four levels of each of the four concepts would be attained in an invariant sequence). As will be described in Chapter 6, evidence for this prediction was derived from the order in which each individual *within each block* achieved full attainment of the four levels. Though students might have fully attained the levels earlier as a result of the retesting, except in the case of the formal level for *tree* and *equilateral triangle*, the earlier attainment should not have influenced full attainment of one level more than another. Further, of the total 37 significant effects, only 6 were found at the three lower levels of attainment as reported in Table 2.6.

The increase in the third-year mean scores within each block that resulted from repeated testing was also judged not to have influenced the identification of the differences among students in the rate at which the various levels and uses of the concept were attained (prediction number 2). As will be shown in Chapter 8, differences in the rate of acquisition were identified by analyzing the data *within the longitudinal blocks,* not across the blocks. We assume that the retest effects were of about the same magnitude for all the students within each block. (As noted earlier, 13 of the 16 retest differences favored the longitudinal blocks.) Two conditions may have had some effect on the range. For the levels and uses where there was rapid growth within a block, the rapid developers may have increased more as a result of retesting than the slow developers, thus increasing the range. For those levels and uses where the rapid developers within a block were already at or near full attainment prior to their third year, the slow developers may have gained more as a result of retesting, thereby reducing the variability among the students somewhat.

The higher mean scores for the third-year students were also judged not to influence the testing of the remaining predictions: (3) The same level of various concepts will be mastered at different ages; (4) Concepts learned at successively higher levels will be used more effectively in understanding taxonomic relationships, in understanding principles, and in solving problems. As with the other predictions, the effect of retesting that favored the longitudinal blocks was to accelerate the rate of development within each block somewhat until full attainment was reached. This acceleration, when experienced by all students, however, would not materially influence the differences in age at which the individuals would attain any level of the different concepts or their ability to use the concepts when attained at the successively higher levels.

Empirical Curve Fitting

One purpose of the study was to chart the course of cognitive growth throughout the school years. The means of portraying normative growth was to construct curves that show the form and rate of growth, Grades 1–12. These results are presented in Chapter 7.

The combined effects of retesting and cohort differences which resulted in generally higher mean scores for grades 3, 6, and 9 than for Grades 4, 7, and 10 for certain levels and uses of concepts distorted these mean scores. Empirical curve fitting, rather than drawing curves that connect the obtained mean scores, was employed to eliminate these distortions. Other possible distortions taken into account by the empirical curve-fitting process are related to the unexplainable second-year cohort effects that favored the longitudinal groups, the three unexplainable retest effects favoring the control groups that had been tested only once, and error of measurement.

The empirical curve-fitting process employed in the study followed a two-step sequence. First, the obtained mean score on each test administered in Grades 1–12 was graphed. The mean scores for each test were connected, as shown in Figure 2.1 for three tests. The resulting curves for each test, one for each of the four longitudinal blocks of students, were analyzed and compared. For the many tests where the mean scores of the students in Grades 1 or 2 were below 40% correct and where the mean score at Grade 6 or later approached 95%, the curves across blocks, when connected, were in the form of a quadratic. For the tests where the mean scores were near or below 40% correct in Grades 1 or 2 and where the mean score in Grade 12 was near 85% or less, the curves across blocks, when connected, were in the form of a natural log curve. For the tests where the mean score in Grade 1 was near 70% or higher but a level of 95% or higher was not reached until Grade 6 or thereafter, the curves across blocks, when connected, were in the form of a straight line. Also, a straight line best fits the mean scores that showed about the same amount of increase across each grade within each longitudinal block.

The subsequent empirical curve fitting was based on these analyses of the observed means in the following manner. The obtained mean scores from each test, changed to percentages, were used in deriving a smoothed curve. A computer program involving regression analysis was employed that empirically determined whether the curve based on the obtained mean scores (one for each grade except where a test was not administered) was in the form of a straight line, a quadratic curve, or natural log curve.[1]

[1] The REGAN 3 computer program was used; it is part of the STATJOB package, 1977, Madison Academic Computing Center, University of Wisconsin, Madison, Wisconsin.

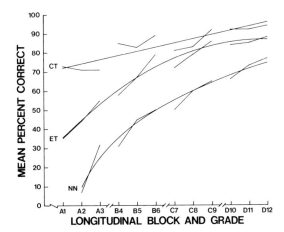

Figure 2.1. Observed means and smoothed curves for *cutting tool,* taxonomic relations (straight line); *equilateral triangle,* formal (quadratic curve); *noun,* formal (natural log curve).

The best-fitting curve of the three was identified by determining the least difference between the sum of the squares of the deviations of the predicted values from the observed values. In turn, the predicted values were plotted and the smoothed curves were drawn by connecting the predicted values.

Figure 2.1 shows the curves that connect only the three observed means of each longitudinal block and the smoothed curves that connect all grades. In this figure and in all figures in which smoothed curves are presented in this book, the obtained mean scores, having been changed to percentages, permit all "y" axes to be of identical length. All "X" axes showing the 12 grades are also of identical length. This procedure was followed to facilitate direct comparison of various sets of curves.

Earlier in this section, possible sources of distortion of the true developmental curves were discussed. In Figure 2.1 distortions due primarily to the effects of repeated testing, being born later, or both, are reflected in the *observed* means for *equilateral triangle* and *noun* between Grades 3 and 4, 6 and 7, and 9 and 10. Distortions primarily due to error of measurement are illustrated in the observed mean scores for *cutting tool* between Grades 1, 2, and 3 and between Grades 4 and 5. The effects of repeated testing, being born later, or both, as well as error of measurement are reflected in the higher mean score for *cutting tool* in Grade 6 than in Grade 7.

The three smoothed curves shown in Figure 2.1 and those that will be presented in later chapters are assumed to reflect quite reliably developmental trends for children and youth currently enrolled in American schools, Grades 1–12, where the dropout rate does not exceed 15–20%, where mean school achievements are near the median of national norms, and where the population of the school reflects that of the nation in terms of racial mix and socioeconomic status. The reader may wish to plot the obtained mean scores, changed to percentages, as given in Appendix Table A.2, to compare the obtained scores within the longitudinal blocks and the smoothed curves.

FOR FURTHER STUDY

Baltes, P. B., Cornelius, S. W., & Nesselroade, J. R. Cohort effects in behavioral development: Theoretical and methodological perspectives. In W. A. Collins (Ed.), *Minnesota Symposia on Child Psychology* (Vol. 11). Hillsdale, New Jersey: Lawrence Erlbaum Associates, 1978.

The authors examine in depth cohort effects in behavioral development, including their theoretical and methodological importance.

Datan, N., & Reese, H. W. (Eds.), *Life-span developmental psychology: Dialectical perspectives on experimental research.* New York: Academic Press, 1977.

The contributors to this book apply dialectical methods and interpretations to the general issue of the relation between theory and method and to more specific issues in experimental research such as learning and memory and cognitive development.

Feldman, C. F., & Toulmin, S. Logic and the theory of mind. In W. J. Arnold (Ed.), *Nebraska symposium on motivation 1975: Conceptual foundations of psychology.* Lincoln: University of Nebraska Press, 1975. Pp. 409–476.

For the advanced student, this paper provides an excellent and sophisticated examination of the epistemological problems that must be faced by theories of cognitive development which emphasize formal or logical mental structures and stages (e.g., Piaget). Parallels between the problems encountered by these theories of psychological development and theories in physics, biology, and chemistry are discussed, as well as possible new lines of theory development in psychology designed to deal with the confusions that exist in present structuralist theories of cognitive development.

McCall, R. B. Challenges to a science of developmental psychology. *Child Development,* 1977, *48,* 333–344.

In discussing some of the conceptual and methodological issues in contemporary developmental psychology, McCall concludes that insufficient data exist that are truly developmental. He suggests several reasons for the under-use of longitudinal methodology and urges that developmentalists must exploit methods that are sensitive to developmental change.

Nunnally, J. C. Research strategies and measurement methods for investigating human development. In J. R. Nesselroade and H. W. Reese (Eds.), *Life-span developmental psychology: Methodological issues.* New York: Academic Press, 1973. Pp. 87–109.

The author reviews the research strategies and methods used in the study of development and explains the kind of information regarding the age function that each provides. Nunnally also describes mixed designs that combine cross-sectional and longitudinal methods and explains the unique advantages that this strategy provides.

Postman, L. Methodology of human learning. In W. K. Estes (Ed.), *Handbook of learning and cognitive processes: Approaches to human learning and motivation* (Vol. 3). New York: John Wiley, 1976. Pp. 11–70.

Postman explains the methodology for studying human learning. Comparison of this methodology with that of longitudinal methodology reveals both likenesses and differences.

Wohlwill, J. *The study of behavioral development.* New York: Academic Press, 1973.

Wohlwill treats systematically many important questions of methodology and research strategy in the study of development. In dealing with the major paradigms in developmental research, Wohlwill focuses on problems of design and data analysis as they relate specifically to the study of development.

3

Mental Operations and
Levels of Concept Attainment

Two lines of investigation continue to be of much interest to theorists and practitioners. One deals with what is learned initially, stored, retrieved from memory, and used. A second deals with the processes that may be involved in initially acquiring information, organizing, and representing it in memory, and then retrieving and using it. Both of these areas of inquiry involve inferring the contents and processes of thought.

As we shall see in Chapter 4, Miller and Johnson-Laird (1976) explain the acquisition–retention–use of information in terms of four basic operations: perceiving, intending, remembering, and feeling—which in turn make knowing possible. In deriving their theory, these authors have used information from various sources, including computer simulations and laboratory experiments involving sensation, perception, learning, and memory.

Guilford (1967) took a somewhat different approach in formulating and validating a structure of intellect. Results from laboratory experiments were used to arrive at the initial formulation of 120 separate abilities, each one defined as one of five operations on one of six products in one of four content areas. The five operations are cognition, memory, productive thinking convergent, productive thinking divergent, and evaluation. The six products are units, classes, relations, systems, transformations, and implications. The areas of content are figural, symbolic, semantic, and behavioral. To identify the abilities, Guilford and his staff constructed tests to measure each hypothesized ability, administered the tests, and submitted the results to factor analysis.

The present effort is more delimited than either of the preceding in that only the content domain of concepts is dealt with. However, it is more complex in that the attempt is made to describe the changes that may occur developmentally during the school years, whereas both Guilford and Miller and Johnson-Laird present explanations typical of adult functioning only.

In the initial identification of the mental operations involved in attaining concepts at successively higher levels as shown earlier in Figures 1.2 and 1.3, results of experiments in the area of concept learning were examined (Klausmeier, Ghatala, & Frayer, 1974). Also, analyses were made of the tasks employed in the experiments. As was noted in Chapter 2, the tests used in the longitudinal study were constructed specifically to measure the operations at each level. In this chapter research and theory regarding the operations are presented. Also results from the longitudinal–cross-sectional study are given to provide descriptive information concerning the operations and the levels.

ATTENDING AND DISCRIMINATING

Attending to and discriminating things (objects—both animate and inanimate—events, relations, and processes) are fundamental to attaining concepts at the concrete, identity, and classificatory levels. Attending to and discriminating the defining attributes of the class of objects, events, or processes are prerequisite for attaining a concept at the formal level. Although discrimination of the societally accepted defining attributes is prerequisite for attaining the formal level, these attributes may be discriminated successively as individuals progress from the concrete to the formal level in their attainment of a concept. More attributes and less perceptibly obvious attributes are attended to, discriminated, and represented internally at each successively higher level.

Attending and Discriminating at the Concrete Level

Attending, in the sense of orienting one's sensory organs so that external stimulation may be received, is fundamental to concept learning and, indeed, to any type of learning. Woodruff (1961) stressed the importance of receiving external stimulation in concept learning:

> All learning begins with some form of personal contact with actual objects, events, or circumstances in life. The contacts occur through our sensory organs. The process by which the senses transmit meaning to the brain is known as perception. From these constantly occurring acts of perception we formulate our concepts [p. 66].

The operation of attending in this sense must logically precede all other operations in concept learning. The role of attention in concept learning, however, is not limited to this initial orienting response. Rather, attending is basic to discrimination, and acquiring a concept at the concrete level involves discriminating between one thing and other things or representations of the things (e.g., drawings or symbols).

We designate the internal representation of a discriminated object as attainment of the concept at the concrete level. To illustrate, a child at about age 2 acquires a concept of a particular picture book at the concrete level when seeing it, forming an internal representation of it, and recognizing it as the same object when seeing it later in the identical place. To do this, the child attends to features of the book that serve to differentiate it from other objects.

The first attainment of a few concepts at the concrete level probably involves discrimination of the particular object (a picture book) from other objects (a cereal box, a music box, a large plastic block, for example) that have none of the critical attributes of the class of things (book) and no more than one variable attribute (for example, form, size, color, texture, or function). When children are able to discriminate two objects that are alike in one or two critical attributes and one or two variable attributes, they can also probably attain the concept at the classificatory level.

Concepts at the concrete level are also formed for things that are coded representations of the environment, that is, symbols of various kinds. For example, the child attains a concept of each letter of the alphabet and each digit. The letters and digits are discriminated from one another on the basis of their distinctive orthographic and acoustic features and are represented internally for later recognition.

The perceptual learning theory of Gibson (1969) indicates what is attended to and discriminated at the concrete level:

> Complex objects in real life can seldom be differentiated on the basis of single properties which render them unique. They are apt to be uniquely identifiable only by virtue of a bundle of properties. They are differentiated (and thereby identified) by their distinctive features. These features are not constructed by the mind but are discovered by the perceiver. When he is exposed to a new set of objects, what he learns are the distinctive features of each object and of the set. Distinctive features are relational, having contrasts or different values within a set. There may be many such features, some shared by certain members of a set, some by others, so that each member must be distinguishable from the others by its bundle of features. This bundle of distinctive features constitutes a potential higher order structure [p. 82].

According to Gibson, discrimination is achieved by discovering those features that are present in two or more different things and on which they actually differ. A distinctive feature of an object is any property (e.g., color, form, texture, angularity) on which it may differ from other objects. The features of an object that are discriminated obviously depend upon the other object or objects from which it is discriminated.

Gibson (1969) also hypothesized that differentiation of pictured objects is learned at the same time that the distinctive features of real objects are learned. That is, the features of an object are recognized, even by young children, when they are presented in photographs or outline drawings. It would seem, therefore, that the same operations of attending to and discriminating distinctive features are involved when stimuli are two-dimensional representations as when stimuli are actual objects.

As indicated in Chapter 1 in the overview of CLD theory, not only instrinsic features but also functional and other relationships of an object with other things, including persons, may be used in attaining concepts at any level. These relationships, like any instrinsic features, must be discriminated for a concept to be attained at the concrete level.

Attending and Discriminating at the Identity and Classificatory Levels

Attainment of a concept at the identity level requires that the individual be able to recognize a thing as being the same thing previously experienced despite changes in its appearance, the context in which it is experienced, or the modality in which it is experienced. For example, an infant who recognizes a particular toy as being the same toy despite changes in its orientation or of the modality in which it is sensed (visual, tactile) has a concept of the particular toy at the identity level. This level of concept attainment involves discriminating and internally representing those properties of the thing that may be relevant to its identity. Thus, discrimination of some perceptible attributes, not merely global features, is necessary at the identity level. At the classificatory level of concept attainment, the individual can discriminate at least two different instances of the concept, but treats them as equivalent on the basis of the intrinsic, functional, or other attributes that they have in common. At the classificatory level, these attributes may be perceptible properties of instances, or they may be nonperceptible. Bruner, Olver, and Greenfield (1966) suggest that young children tend to form classifications on the basis of perceptible attributes (e.g., color, size, shape). Older children are able to classify more on the basis of nonperceptible attributes, such as functional attributes (what things are used for or what they do) and nominal classifications (societally designated defining attributes). Moreover, with increasing age, children become increasingly able to discriminate and name the defining attributes (of whatever type) of concepts (Wiviott, 1970).

Rydberg and Arnberg (1976) studied attention in 6-year-old children and adults in a series of concept identification experiments. The concepts to be identified were defined by combinations of one of three values of one of four dimensions. Without pretraining or instruction, adults could attend to the four dimensions during a single trial and identify the concept the experimenter had in mind. Some 6-year-old children could attend to one dimension and identify the concept; those who attended to more than one dimension during a single trial failed to identify the concept. Subsequently, the 6-year-olds were given instruction prior to starting the experiment that included (1) familiarization with the four stimulus objects, (2) discrimination of the four dimensions of each object and the three values of each dimension, (3) naming of each dimension and giving a number 1, 2, 3 to the three values of each dimension, (4) broadening of the child's attention so as to attend to the four dimensions, and (5) memorizing of the dimensions and values.

Thirteen of 18 children succeeded and 5 failed to identify the concepts after this instruction. Those who succeeded were slightly more effective (used less time in identifying a series of concepts) than adults who had not received instruction; and they were far more effective than 6-year-olds who did not receive instruction. To assure that attention was being observed and measured reliably, active-touch overt attending was employed; that is, the experimental subjects could touch the objects with the index finger but could not sense the object visually or in any other way, except during the familiarization and discriminating instruction, where overt touch and vision were employed.

In this series of experiments, the 6-year-olds who were instructed and were successful learned to attend to more dimensions and values during preexperimental instruction and then, after attending to the four dimensions, selectively attended to a particular dimension and value in each successive trial. In fact, 13 of the 18 learned to discriminate and also to classify about as well as adults. Rydberg and Arnberg hypothesized that young children who are unable to classify may experience memory overload when the attentional demands related to the dimensions and values are heavy.

Attending and Discriminating at the Formal Level

Attending to and discriminating the defining attributes of the class of things is essential for attaining a concept at the formal level, whether an inductive or a meaningful reception approach is used. Logically, being able to discriminate all the defining attributes of the concept is prerequisite to hypothesizing the attributes and testing them. It is also prerequisite to understanding a definition of the concept that is stated in terms of the defining attributes. Earlier cognitive theories of learning (e.g., Krechevsky, 1932; Lashley, 1938) and more recent hypothesis-testing theories of concept learning (e.g., Bower & Trabasso, 1964; Levine, 1966; Restle, 1955) take as their starting point the discrimination of the attributes by which examples and nonexamples may be classified.

Perceptual Theory and Attending and Discriminating

Gibson and Levin (1975) applied perceptual learning theory to reading. They treat perception in a manner similar to the present treatment of attending and discriminating. They define perception as the process of extracting information from stimulation emanating from objects, places, and events. Three kinds of information are abstracted: the distinctive features of all kinds of things, including people, objects, and symbols; invariants of events; and invariant relations between distinctive features or between the invariants of events. The relations may be of a whole formed by the subordinate features or of the parts in relation to the whole.

According to Gibson and Levin, it is the perception of distinctive features, invariants of events, and invariants of relations that enables the individual first to recognize specific objects, events, or relations as the same ones experienced earlier. This corresponds to attaining concepts of things, events, and relations at the concrete and identity levels. Perception of the same three kinds of information also is involved in learning concepts at the classificatory and formal levels, as these levels were discussed earlier in this section.

In addition to reporting experiments dealing with the perception of different kinds of information, Gibson and Levin also outlined trends in perceptual development, giving particular attention to the perceptual processes involved in learning to read, including the discrimination and recognition of single letters. One trend in perceptual development is in the improvement, or optimization, of attention. With increasing age, the distinctive features of things and the invariants of events, corresponding to the defining attributes of concepts, are increasingly attended to and discriminated. Nondefining variable attributes of concepts and irrelevant contextual information are increasingly ignored.

This trend was observed by Nodine and Evans (1969) and Nodine and Lang (1971), who studied the visual attending behaviors of kindergarten and third-grade children. In these studies the children were instructed to compare two sets of letters to decide whether they were the same or different. The children's eye movements were photographed as they made the judgment. The children were shown paired sets of four-letter nonsense syllables. Half of the pairs were the same and half were different. A same pair might be EROI–EROI; a corresponding different pair might be EROI–EORI. The difference between two syllables always consisted of a juxtaposition of the two medial letters; this was an appropriate target spot for concentrating fixations. Half of the pairs contained middle letters that were easily confusable (e.g., OEFU), whereas the other half had middle letters of low confusability (e.g., OFWS). The researchers reasoned that if the high-confusability syllables were fixated longer in the target area, the child was attending to the distinctive features of the letters.

The kindergarten children scanned much less efficiently, requiring an average of four more fixations and 1.25 seconds longer for each matching test than the third-grade children. The third-grade children exhibited significantly more systematic scans from one syllable to the other, comparing the corresponding letters in the pair of syllables. Though both groups spent more fixations on target-letter positions than on non-target-letter positions, the older group spent relatively more time on target letters than the younger. The kindergarten children scanned more within syllables than between. In summary, the visual scanning of the older children was greater in specificity and economy. They attended selectively to informative details and tended to ignore irrelevant and redundant information.

A second developmental trend is that there is increasing specificity of what is attended to and discriminated (Gibson & Levin, 1975). As children mature and have more encounters with things and events in their environment, their perceptions become progressively more differentiated and incorporate specific information. In an experiment clarifying this phenomenon, Gibson, Gibson, Pick, and Osser (1962) studied the development of discrimination of letterlike forms in children from 4 through 8 years of age. In their study a set of graphic forms was constructed that were comparable to the Roman capital letters. The forms were constructed so as to embody as nearly as possible the distinctive features that characterize these letters, and special attention was given to kinds of transformation of symbols that have been thought to give children either much or only a little trouble. The transformations included straight to curved, rotation and reversal, perspective or orientation (such as occurs when a book is tilted back or to one side away from the line of sight), and open form to closed form or vice versa. There were three degrees of change for the straight-curved transformation so that the effect of amount of change in this important contrast could be measured. Examples of these transformations are shown in Figure 3.1.

The forms were drawn on small cards. The child's task was to compare a standard form with each of its transformations and copies of itself, and then to select and hand to the experimenter only the exact copies of the standard. Thus the children matched for 12 different standards, each with all 12 transformations.

The number of errors declined markedly from age 4 to age 8. A single straight–curved transformation elicited many errors at 4 years, but scarcely any were made involving three transformations. The older children rarely made an error on this item. The children progressively increased the specificity of their discrimination in accordance with changes in the material provided.

A final trend in perceptual development is the increasing economy with which information is processed (Gibson & Levin, 1975). Maturing children progressively process information more efficiently by detecting order and structure present in the available stimulus information. One contributor to economical processing is to use one key distinctive feature for making a perceptual decision regarding membership in a set. Yonas (1969) conducted a discrimination reaction time experiment in which the subjects had to decide whether a letter projected on a small screen belonged to a positive set that had been previously defined by the experimenter. There were three treatments in the experiment and all the subjects participated in all three, in counterbalanced

Standard Form	One Transformation	Two Transformations	Three Transformations

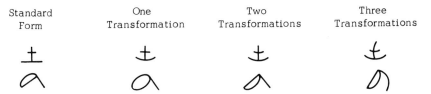

Figure 3.1. Transformations in straight–curved features of a letterlike form. (Reprinted from *The Psychology of Reading* by E. J. Gibson & H. Levin by permission of The M.I.T. Press, Cambridge, Massachusetts. © 1975 by the M.I.T. Press.)

order. The reaction times for each treatment were averaged for blocks of 30 trials, yielding five blocks with increasing practice. In Treatment 1, only one letter belonged to the positive set. It was interspersed with eight others, all of which were projected one at a time in random order. In Treatment 2, three of the nine letters chosen at random were positive. In Treatment 3, there were also three of nine letters in the positive set, but the positive and other set were so arranged experimentally that the presence or absence of diagonality of lines served to differentiate all the positive from all the other letters. Attending to and using this single feature were sufficient for a correct decision.

Treatment 1 had the fastest reaction time. Treatments 1 and 2 had equal and lower reaction times in the first block of trials; however, reaction time dropped more rapidly across blocks of trials in Treatment 3 than in Treatment 2 and eventually was close to that in Treatment 1. Second-grade children showed this trend toward economical processing, although their mean reaction time was slower than that for sixth-grade children or adults. The older children and adults were able to perceive the relationship of the diagonality feature, process the obtained information, and use it in decision making more effectively than the younger children.

We may summarize this descriptive account of perceptual development. Individuals with experience and practice are able, with greater economy and flexibility, to discriminate more specific features of things, invariants of events, and invariants of relationships. As children become increasingly capable of these discriminations, they are also increasingly able to discriminate among things and events that are more similar and also among the qualities and relations thereof. Gibson and Levin (1975) explain this kind of perceptual development in terms of the individual's learning (1) to orient the sense organs selectively to certain features and invariants while ignoring others, (2) to abstract the features or invariants, and (3) to filter the incoming sensations so as to retain relevant features or invariants but not the irrelevant. Flavell (1977) in addition to recognizing the preceding trends, presumes that individuals become increasingly able to monitor and guide their own attentional-discrimination behavior. That individuals are able to attain concepts at the successively higher levels appears to be interpretable in part by these explanations of developmental trends in attending and discriminating. The trends which we identified in attending and discriminating at the concrete level and in discriminating the defining attributes of concepts follow immediately.

Developmental Trends in Attending–Discriminating and in Attribute Discrimination

Attending and discriminating are essential operations at all four levels of concept attainment. The information which follows from the longitudinal study indicates trends in attending and discriminating similar to those found in the preceding studies of perceptual development.

ATTENDING–DISCRIMINATING

Developmental trends in attending and discriminating were inferred from the results of the concrete-level tests administered to the young children of Block A. The children had to attend to and discriminate among drawings for the *cutting tool, tree,* and *equilateral triangle* test items and among typewritten words for the *noun* items.

To measure the ability to attend to and discriminate increasingly complex material, test items for the concrete level in all four batteries were constructed to require attending to an increasing amount of information and making finer discriminations. The amount of information to attend to was increased by increasing the number of nonexamples in the items. The discrimination requirement was increased by making the nonexamples more like the example in terms of common variable attributes and defining attributes, including the critical attributes.

To illustrate, the eight *equilateral triangle* test items were constructed in four pairs as follows: Item 1 consisted of three nonexamples, each of which differed from the target example in two of the five defining attributes, the two critical attributes that are italicized (*three sides of equal length, three angles of equal degrees,* plane, simple, closed), and in both of the two variable attributes (color and size). Item 2 had six nonexamples, each of which also differed in two of the defining attributes and both of the two variable attributes. Item 1, along with the instructions, follows (the letters under the forms indicate their colors):

Instructions: Look at the drawing.

Y

(Target was removed from sight for five seconds)

Instructions: Mark the drawing that looks the same as the one you just saw.

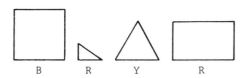

B   R   Y   R

Items 3 and 4 also had three and six nonexamples, respectively, but each nonexample differed from the target example in zero to two critical attributes and one to two variable attributes. Items 5 and 6 also had three and six nonexamples; each nonexample differed from the target example in zero to two critical attributes and one variable attribute. The equilateral triangles used as nonexamples differed from the target example only in either color or size.

Items 7 and 8 had nine nonexamples that varied from the target example in the same manner as in Items 5 and 6. The target example and nonexamples for Item 8 follow:

```
Instructions:  Look at the drawing.
```

```
(Target was removed from sight for five seconds)
```

```
Instructions:  Mark the drawing that looks the same as the one you
               just saw.
```

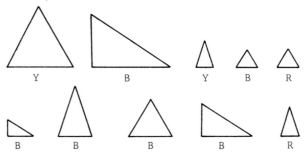

Table 3.1 gives the percentage of each item answered correctly by the same 62 children when in kindergarten and Grades 1 and 3 for *cutting tool, tree, equilateral triangle,* and *noun.* (Only the equilateral triangle battery was administered to kindergarten children, as noted in Chapter 2.)

Since 92% or more of the first-grade children answered all the items for *cutting tool* and *tree,* trends across items and grades cannot be inferred readily for these concepts. However, more errors were made on the last two pairs of items for *equilateral triangle* and *noun* than on preceding items by the kindergarten and Grade 1 children. Also, the Grade 3 children performed better than the younger ones on these items. Increasing the amount of information to attend to and discriminate and increasing the similarity of the nonexamples and the target example in both the number of defining attributes and the variable attributes increased the difficulty of attending and discriminating. With increasing age the children attended and discriminated a larger amount of more similar material.

ATTRIBUTE DISCRIMINATION

One test at the formal level was constructed to measure the extent to which the defining attributes of the concepts were discriminated. The number of items

TABLE 3.1 Development Related to Attending and Discriminating

					Battery				
	Cutting tool		Tree			Equilateral triangle		Noun	
Item	Grade 1	Grade 3	Grade 1	Grade 3	Kg	Grade 1	Grade 3	Grade 1	Grade 3
1	100	100	100	100	97	100	100	94	100
2	100	100	100	100	97	100	100	98	100
3	100	100	98	100	97	100	100	95	97
4	98	100	98	100	89	100	100	98	97
5	98	100	98	98	87	100	100	89	97
6	100	100	95	98	90	100	100	90	98
7	97	100	92	100	82	94	100	53	97
8	98	100	97	100	85	92	100	76	92

used for the various concepts was as follows: *cutting tool,* 6; *tree,* 10; *equilateral triangle,* 5; and *noun,* 7. The item for the three-equal-angles attribute of *equilateral triangle* follows:

Instructions: Below are four drawings. Put an X on the one that has three equal angles.

Figure 3.2 gives the smoothed curves showing the developmental trends in discriminating the attributes of the four concepts. For both *noun* and *equilateral triangle,* which had relatively low mean percentages correct in Grade 2 and Grade 1 respectively, there is a rapid increase for Longitudinal Block A (Grades 1–3) and Block B (Grades 4–6). The rate of increase decelerates for Block C (Grades 7–9) and D (Grades 10–12). Already in Grade 1 the students discriminated a high percentage of the defining attributes of *cutting tool* (mean percentage correct 76) and *tree* (mean percentage correct 86) and the rate of increase thereafter was slow but uniform across the school years.

It is clear that the defining attributes of concepts that have actual examples widely distributed in the environment, i.e., *cutting tool* and *tree*, are attended to and discriminated much more readily than are the attributes of more abstract concepts. Also, even though children when in Grade 3 are able to discriminate many defining attributes of concepts, the ability to discriminate is still increasing for some students from Grades 11 to 12.

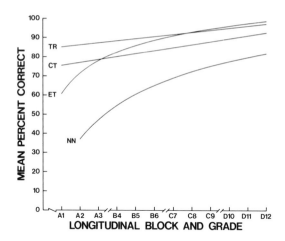

Figure 3.2. Development related to discriminating the defining attributes of concepts.

GENERALIZING

Generalizing that an object, quality, or event is the same one when experienced in different contexts or by means of different sensory modalities is considered necessary for attaining a concept at the identity level. In addition, generalizing that two or more examples are equivalent is necessary for attainment at the classificatory level. Attainment of a concept at the formal level presumes that the concept has already been attained at the classificatory level or that the person is capable of attainment at that level. It is possible, however, that from the earliest attainment of the formal level to a final mature level a person may learn to generalize to increasingly unique or remote examples of the concept—for example, to generalize that an amoeba is an animal.

Generalizing at the Identity Level

The distinction between the identity and classificatory levels of attaining the same concept corresponds to the distinction between "identity" and "equivalence" categorizing made by Bruner et al. (1956). These authors pointed out that identity categorization may be defined as responding to a variety of stimuli as *forms of the same thing.* Equivalence categorization refers to responding to a set of discriminably different things as the *same kind of thing* or as *amounting to the same thing.* According to these analyses, attainment of a concept at the identity level is logically prerequisite to the attainment of the same concept at the classificatory level, since the identity of two or more particular things must be conserved across changes in orientation, apparent size, and other transformations before these same two things can reliably be put into an equivalence class. It is noted that the identity → classificatory sequence applies to objects or events that are examples of the same concept. It is possible, however, to classify certain objects—for example, a basketball and a volleyball as balls or things to play with—before being able to recognize other objects as forms of the same thing—for example, the paperback being read by Mother is the same one that earlier lay on the table.

Attaining the identity level requires the individual to generalize across orientation, distance, background, and other spatiotemporal dimensions and also across modalities. The object, quality, or relation remains identical or essentially identical; however, it may be perceived as not identical because of the differences in the spatiotemporal dimensions.

Being able to generalize an object, quality, or relationship as the same one regardless of a change in its orientation or the context in which it is experienced occurs early in life before children start to school. However, there is variability among concepts in the age at which they are attained at the identity level, as may be inferred from the following percentages of 62 first- and third-grade children who had attained the identity level of the four concepts: 100% and 100%, *cutting tool*; 97% and 97%, *tree*; 95% and 100%, *equilateral triangle*; and 23% and 94%, *noun*.

Generalizing at the Classificatory and Formal Levels

When children or adults treat at least two discriminably different things as equivalent but are unable to indicate the basis for their classifying in terms of attributes, we say they have attained a concept at the classificatory level. The basic operation at the classificatory level in addition to attending, discriminating, and remembering is generalizing among instances on the basis of their common attributes. Generalizing presumes that a representation of a class of things is held in memory; this internal representation serves as a basis for testing newly encountered examples and nonexamples. As more classes become represented in memory, there is increased reliability of identification of class members and a concomitant decrease in the need for representations of each specific member of each class.

Vernon (1970) points out that as the child encounters more and more objects, the accumulation of internal representations of single things would become prohibitively large. In the identification of any new thing, it would be necessary to review the memorial representations of all similar things previously experienced. If, however, a representation can be attached to a *class* of things, then any new thing that is encountered may be identified by relating it to this class.

We may infer that the ability to generalize across changes in the orientation of objects and drawings of objects (i.e., *cutting tool, tree,* and *equilateral triangle*) is already well developed by children when in Grade 1. Generalizing across changes in the orientation and the upper and lower case of words that represent nouns develops later and is probably associated directly with the ability to read.

We presume that the generalization process at the classificatory level follows much the same pattern as at the identity level but with two important additions or refinements. First, some of the defining attributes of two things rather than of only one thing, must be discriminated, and the two things must be generalized as equivalent. This assumes that a prior concept of each thing must have been developed at the identity level, as explained in the preceding discussion. Second, more of the defining attributes are discriminated at the classificatory level than at the identity level.

Persons can form concepts at the classificatory level without having the names for either the concepts or the defining attributes. LeFurgy, Woloshin, and Sandler (1969) demonstrated that subjects can learn to identify examples and nonexamples of a complex concept without being able to indicate the defining attributes of the concept. In their experiment, the children (14 years old) had only minimal opportunity for explicit hypothesis testing during the learning trials. Yet 42 out of 48 subjects attained a level of nonrandom responding on test and generalization stimuli. Of these 42 subjects, only 16 could articulate a rule for discriminating examples from nonexamples.

Developmental Trends in Generalizing

The items in the four batteries that measured attainment of the concepts at the classificatory level necessarily varied according to the nature of the examples and nonexamples, but all the items were constructed to measure the students' ability to generalize from a given target example to one or more examples presented with three or more nonexamples. The successive items in all four batteries were constructed to require generalizing to a greater variety of examples while discriminating from nonexamples increasingly like the target example.

Figure 3.3 depicts development related to generalizing as measured by the classificatory-level tests of the four batteries. The smoothed curve for *cutting*

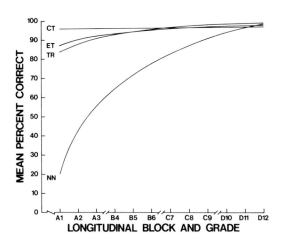

Figure 3.3. Development related to generalizing.

tool is essentially flat; the children of Block A when in Grade 1 readily generalized across different examples of cutting tools. The curves for *tree* and *equilateral triangle* start quite high in Grade 1 and rise gradually until Grade 6, when over 95% correct is achieved. The curve for *noun* rises very sharply from Grade 1 to Grade 2 and continues to rise thereafter through Grade 12 at a decelerating rate of increase. Based on these data, a consistent increase across the school years in the ability to generalize across examples of concepts may be inferred. Also, children when in Grade 1 readily generalize across concrete concept examples that are distributed widely in the environment.

We saw earlier that generalizing at the identity level came much later for *noun* than for the other concepts. Here we observe that generalizing across different examples starts much later for *noun* than for any other concept and somewhat earlier for *cutting tool* than for the other concepts. This order for *noun* and *cutting tool* with *tree* and *equilateral triangle* between but close to *cutting tool* is interpretable on the basis of the concrete–abstract dimension of concept examples that was discussed earlier in Chapter 1.

INDUCTIVE OPERATIONS AT THE FORMAL LEVEL

Attainment of a concept at the formal level is assessed by determining whether the individual can define the concept in terms of its defining attributes, can evaluate actual or verbally described examples and nonexamples of the particular concept in terms of the presence or absence of the defining attributes, and can give the name of the concept and its attributes. When individuals can do these things, we infer that they are also capable of performing both the inductive and the deductive operations at the formal level, as shown earlier in Chapter 1.

Inferring the Concept or the Concept Definition by Testing Hypotheses

Many concept-identification experiments have been conducted to elucidate an inductive, hypothesis-testing approach to concept attainment. An hypothesis in a concept-identification experiment is operationalized as the subject's prediction of the defining attributes of the concept (Levine, 1959, 1963). In concept-identification experiments in which the universe of concepts used by the experimenter differs on a number of attributes and each particular concept is defined by one attribute or some combination of attributes, the subject's task is viewed as one of hypothesizing the attributes that in turn provide the basis for correct classification of the examples of the concept. The subject does this by adopting an hypothesis concerning the defining attribute(s) and responding on the basis of that hypothesis until informed by the experimenter that an error has been made. At that time, the subject abandons the hypothesis and selects a new one. When an hypothesis is made that leads to no errors, the subject has inferred the concept. When the concept is inferred, the subject also has identified the defining attributes of the concept and, in the experimental situation, may be called on to state the definition of the concept, not merely to classify correctly.

Starting from this very general statement of hypothesis-testing experimentation, we shall examine various aspects of formulating hypotheses, remembering hypotheses, and evaluating hypotheses.

HYPOTHESIZING RELEVANT ATTRIBUTES

Levine (1966) developed a procedure for directly ascertaining the nature of subjects' hypotheses in concept-identification tasks. In Levine's procedure, subjects had to choose one of two letters on each of eight cards that comprised the experimental concept population. As shown in Figure 3.4, the letters differed in color (*black* or *white*), form (*X* or *T*), position (*right* or *left*), and size (*small* or *large*). Before beginning the task, the subjects were instructed as to the structure of the universe of concepts and the nature of possible solutions (i.e., a single attribute value was the correct basis for solution). Thus, the subject could choose among eight different hypotheses—all black letters, all white letters, all *X*s, all *T*s, etc. The subject was shown a stimulus card and told which of the two choices was correct (e.g., the black letter, the *X*). The subject was then required to respond to four cards selected by the experimenter as being members of the concept without receiving any feedback from the experimenter. The cards were constructed in such a way that the experimenter could infer from the pattern of the subject's four responses (yes, it is; no, it is not) which, if any, of the possible hypotheses the subject used. The assumption was that the subjects would respond on the basis of the same hypothesis on all four trials because they received no feedback on any of them. A further assumption was that on the fifth trial, the experimenter could predict the subject's response on the basis of the hypothesis inferred from the four no-feedback trials. On the fifth trial, the experimenter told the subjects "right" or "wrong" according to a prearranged scheme. Then the subjects received another four no-feedback trials from which their new hypotheses could be inferred. Finally, another trial with feedback was given, followed by a third set of trials with no feedback.

One conclusion of the study was that the subjects formulated hypotheses—approximately 92% of the response patterns agreed with one of the eight possible hypotheses. Also, the subjects' hypotheses, which the experimenter inferred from the block of four no-feedback trials, could be used to predict their

Figure 3.4. Stimuli used in concept-identification task. (From M. Levine, Hypothesis behavior by humans during discrimination learning. *Journal of Experimental Psychology*, 1966, *71*, 331. Copyright 1966 by the American Psychological Association. Reprinted by permission.)

responses on the fifth trial in about 98% of the cases. Many other experiments have confirmed these findings concerning hypothesis formulation and testing (Erickson, 1968; Levine, Leitenberg, & Richter, 1964; Rourke & Trabasso, 1968).

As might be expected, Levine (1966) found that maintaining or changing hypotheses is directly related to the feedback received. If the experimenter says "right" following a subject's response, there is a high probability that the hypothesis will be retained (about 95% of the time); however, if the response leads to the pronouncement of "wrong," the hypothesis is usually rejected and a new one adopted (only 2% of the time was a hypothesis retained following a "wrong").

During the course of learning a concept, the successive hypotheses formulated are dependent upon the information gained by the subject through comparing previous hypotheses with the attributes of subsequent concept examples and nonexamples encountered. Some hypothesis-testing theories of concept learning (e.g., Restle, 1962) postulate that the subject retains a hypothesis if it results in a correct choice, but resamples with replacement if it results in an incorrect choice. If resampling is done the subject still has an equally large number of hypotheses remaining to be tested. There is evidence to support the notion that resampling of hypotheses does occur after an incorrect choice (e.g., Erickson, 1968; Levine, 1966; Rourke & Trabasso, 1968). However, other evidence has indicated that such resampling is *without* replacement—that is, the incorrect hypothesis is not returned to the pool, thereby reducing the pool of hypotheses remaining to be tested (e.g., Erickson, 1968; Erickson, Zajkowski, & Ehrman, 1966; Levine, 1966). Moreover, Levine's (1966) data indicate that subjects do not merely exclude a single hypothesis after an incorrect choice, but they utilize information from an error trial to exclude logically other hypotheses that they may not have been testing directly.

Dodd and Bourne (1969), Levine (1966), and Nahinsky and Slaymaker (1969) suggest that modification of the hypothesis pool may occur on correct trials as well as on error trials. Subjects can use information gained on correct trials to eliminate hypotheses logically in the same way as on error trials. Of course, what subjects have learned on correct trials will not be evident until they make an error; a new hypothesis following the error will be compatible with information gained from previous correct trials. Thus, whereas subjects tend to change hypotheses only after an error, they process information on both error and correct trials.

REMEMBERING HYPOTHESES

Memory for hypotheses serves two functions. First, subjects maintain the current hypothesis in storage and respond on the basis of that hypothesis until it leads to an incorrect classification. Second, their memory of prior hypotheses guides the selection of a new hypothesis to test when the current hypothesis is disconfirmed. Subjects systematically exclude from further testing those hypotheses that have been found to be incorrect. Also, memory of prior information about the concept population is utilized when a current hypothesis is rejected and a new one is formulated. Subjects may retrieve the information they have stored about the concept population and formulate a new hypothesis that is logically consistent with this information. Once a new hypothesis is formulated in this manner, it is evaluated against new information.

One kind of experimentation that has been used to investigate memory for hypotheses provides subjects misinformative feedback. Subjects are given some trials with random reinforcement, and after that, without the subjects' knowing it, the experimenter begins to reinforce a particular solution consistently. If subjects sample hypotheses at random and with replacement, the random reinforcement trials should not delay solution once the real problem is begun. However, if subjects remember which hypotheses they have tested and rejected, then random reinforcement should retard solution. In fact, even small amounts of misinformative feedback have been found to retard concept learning (Levine, 1962).

In an interesting variation of the misinformative feedback experiment, Stein and Erickson (1967) were able to determine not only that subjects remembered hypotheses but also that memory of the successive hypotheses was greatest for the most recent of those tested and least for the earliest ones. The authors interpreted their results as favorable to the notion of short-term storage of previously tried hypotheses.

Experiments using latency measures during concept learning provide another approach to investigating memory for hypotheses. Erickson et al., (1966) argued that response latencies should be related to the size of the pool of hypotheses from which a subject is sampling. The more hypotheses to be considered, the more time the sampling process should take. If subjects sample with replacement, then the latencies should be constant on trials before the last error. In an experimental test of this assumption it was found that latencies after errors decreased considerably on trials before the last error. This implies that subjects were able to exclude hypotheses, and this in turn suggests that subjects have some memory for past hypotheses.

If memory is overloaded by presenting several problems simultaneously, memory for hypotheses may diminish. For example, in a later experiment by Erickson and Zajkowski (1967) in which subjects were given three concurrent concept learning tasks, the latencies after errors before the last error trial did not decrease but remained constant, indicating no memory for hypotheses. Other studies employing the multiple task technique (e.g., Restle & Emmerich, 1966) have indicated that under these conditions, subjects' performance is retarded. In fact, performance approaches that predicted by the sampling-with-replacement assumption.

EVALUATING HYPOTHESES

Hypothesis evaluation can be viewed in a global fashion as follows. First, subjects may test to see whether the current hypothesis agrees with the information they have in memory. If the answer is no, then they select a new hypothesis (not one already rejected) and apply the same test until an hypothesis is found that is consistent with past data. Following this first test, subjects may attempt to determine whether the current hypothesis agrees with *present* data. If it does, they maintain the hypothesis and either accept it as the correct solution or seek further information. If the current hypothesis does not agree with present information, then it is rejected and another hypothesis is selected. Thus, the process of formulating hypotheses, testing, reformulating, and retesting of hypotheses proceeds in an iterative cycle very much like the Test–Operate–Test–Exit (TOTE) units described by Miller, Galanter, and Pribram (1960).

Inferring the Concept by Cognizing Attributes Common to Examples

The preceding hypothesis testing strategy involves using information from examples and nonexamples. There may be another approach to inferring concepts that entails less demand upon logical reasoning. Tagatz (1967) and Tagatz, Walsh, and Layman (1969) identified a commonality strategy in concept learning. Subjects who employ this approach arrive at the concept by identifying those attributes that the examples have in common, instead of actively hypothesizing and testing attributes by utilizing information from examples and nonexamples.

Tagatz (1967) instructed fifth- and sixth-grade students in one of two strategies. Instructions for a commonality strategy directed the children to give their entire attention to examples and explained that attributes common to all examples were relevant to the concept. Conservative focusing instructions directed the child to attend to both examples and nonexamples and explained that if only one attribute differed between an example and a nonexample, that dimension was critical.

The children were presented with a series of four exercises. For each exercise two examples and two nonexamples were given. Time to criterion was significantly less for subjects receiving the commonality instructions than for those receiving the conservative focusing instructions. At the completion of all four exercises, the subjects were asked which cards they had used, in order to determine which strategy they had actually employed. From this questioning, it was learned that many children instructed in a conservative focusing strategy actually changed to a commonality strategy. This result indicates that the focusing strategy that requires explicit testing of attributes with the use of examples and nonexamples is difficult for children of this age.

It is possible that the commonality strategy is used primarily with less complex concepts of the kind used in the Tagatz studies by persons who, for lack of inductive reasoning ability, have difficulty in securing information from nonexamples, and by persons who, for affective reasons, do not process the available information from nonexamples. Some persons, when told that their choice of a nonexample is not a member of the concept, apparently interpret this feedback as a kind of punishment just as they do when told that a word is misspelled or an arithmetic answer is wrong. Further research regarding the use of a commonality strategy is necessary to clarify the variables, including instruction, that may lead to its use.

OPERATIONS INVOLVING MEANINGFUL RECEPTION LEARNING AT THE FORMAL LEVEL[1]

Much concept learning at the formal level by upper elementary, high school, and college students follows from expository instruction. In expository instruction students are given the name of the concept, a verbal definition, and verbal or pictorial examples and nonexamples; the student relates this new information to information already in the cognitive structure. The concept thus learned can be used later in evaluating examples and nonexamples in terms of the presence or absence of the defining attributes. Learning a concept at the formal level in this manner entails meaningful reception learning as described by Ausubel (1968).

To relate the assimilation process in meaningful reception learning to concept attainment at the formal level, let us assume that students have learned the concept *tree* (T) at the classificatory level. Assume further that the students' individual mental constructs of T are such that (1) they can discriminate most trees from shrubs and herbs; (2) they have the name *tree* in their vocabulary and the name represents the concept, not merely specific examples of trees; (3) they have in their vocabulary most of the words that are used in the defining attributes of *tree*; (4) they can discriminate most or all the defining attributes of *tree*; and (5) they have learned some but not all the defining attributes of *tree*. Assume further that they have mental constructs pertaining to *shrubs* (S) and *herbs* (H). The existing cognitive structure may now be symbolized as T, S, H. Through lecture, printed material, audiovisual means, or combinations thereof, the students receive (1) the definition of tree, which is stated in terms of the defining attributes (d); (2) explanations and possibly illustrations of each defining attribute (a); (3) some examples of trees in the form of drawings or pictures (e); and (4) some nonexamples of trees in the form of pictures or drawings of both shrubs and herbs (ne). The new information may be symbolized as d, a, e, ne.

In the assimilation process, the new information received (d, a, e, ne) is related by the individual to the existing cognitive structure (T, S, H); the new product constructed by the individual from this interaction is (d', a', e', ne', T', S', H'). If the relating of the new information to the existing cognitive structure has proceeded as intended by the instruction, this new product is the concept of *tree* at the formal level, and also a more advanced concept of *shrub* and *herb* at the classificatory level.

---

[1] In an earlier book (Klausmeier, Ghatala, & Frayer, 1974), the operations at the formal level involving meaningful reception learning were subsumed under "cognizing the common attributes."

The individual's concept of *tree* at the formal level will now include the definition of the word *tree*, the names of the defining attributes and the ability to discriminate them, the semantic representation of *tree*, and also, possibly some visual representation of trees experienced earlier. This mental construct, if fully developed, will enable the person to identify examples and nonexamples of *tree* with high reliability, to generalize that certain things are trees and discriminate others as not trees, and to explain the basis of the generalizations and discriminations in terms of the presence or absence of the defining attributes.

We can see that the assimilative process in meaningful reception learning is an active process but not inductive, as is the hypothesis-testing approach. Though it is useful to identify the salient features and processes in both approaches, it is possible that most concept learning at the formal level involves some of both, rather than one or the other exclusively.

Developmental Trends in Evaluating Examples and Nonexamples

Three prerequisites for attaining a concept at the formal level are (1) having attained the concept at the classificatory level, (2) having discriminated the defining attributes of the concept, and (3) having acquired the names of the concept and its defining attributes. Being able to evaluate examples and nonexamples of the concept in terms of the presence or absence of the defining attributes is the primary test of full attainment of the formal level. Earlier, in Figure 3.2, developmental trends related to attribute discrimination were given. In Chapter 5, similar information about acquiring the names of concepts and concept attributes will be given. In this section, developmental trends are indicated regarding the evaluation of examples and nonexamples.

Separate tests were constructed as part of the formal-level tests to measure evaluation of examples and nonexamples of *cutting tool, tree, equilateral triangle,* and *noun*. A sample item for each concept follows. The choice with the asterisk indicates the defining attribute that is not present in the nonexamples given in one item.

Thing X is different from the other things in a certain way. How is it different?

Thing X

a. X is used for holding or turning.

*b. X is used to cut.

c. X is used to strike other objects.

d. X is made from metal.

e. I don't know.

The things in Group X are different from the things in Group Y in a certain way. How are they different?

Group X   Group Y

   a. The things in Group X need either air or light.

   b. The things in Group X need either food or water.

*c. The things in Group X have either broad leaves or needles.

   d. The things in Group X have either teeth or legs.

   e. I don't know.

Drawing X is different from <u>all</u> the other drawings in a certain way. How is it different?

     X

   a. X is a solid figure.

   b. X is an accurate figure.

   c. X is a complex figure.

*d. X is a closed figure.

   e. I don't know.

The things in group X are different from the things in group Y in a certain way. How are they different?

Rome city	Zuk has
group X	group Y

*a. The things in group X name either a particular thing or class of things.

b. The things in group X are either words or not words.

c. The things in group X may be used as the verb or adverb of a sentence.

d. The things in group X name either an action or a condition.

e. I don't know.

The smoothed curves indicating development related to evaluating examples and nonexamples are presented in Figure 3.5. The curves are based on the percentage correct.

The ability to evaluate examples and nonexamples of *cutting tool* was relatively high for Grade 1 students and it increased at a uniform rate through Grade 12. The mean percentage correct for *equilateral triangle* and *tree* in Grade 1 is what would be expected on a chance basis; the same is true for *noun* in Grades 2 and 3. Stated differently, when in Grades 1 and 2, children of Longitudinal Block A were essentially unable to evaluate the given examples and nonexamples in terms of the absence of the defining attributes in the nonexamples.

The curves for evaluating examples and nonexamples of *equilateral triangle*,

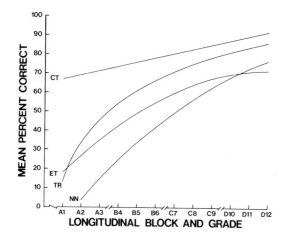

Figure 3.5. Development related to evaluating examples and non-examples of concepts.

tree, and *noun* are characterized by a rapid rate of increase between the first 2 years and a decelerating rate of increase thereafter. The rate of increase until Grade 9 is quite rapid. It is possible that had younger children been tested for *cutting tool*, a curve of the same form would have been obtained.

The following conclusions may be drawn to summarize the discussion of the developmental curves. The ability to evaluate examples and nonexamples of some concrete concepts is present in children of primary school age. There is regular progression of this ability throughout the school years; however, the mean performances of students increase markedly between Grades 10 and 12 and even in Grade 12 are considerably below 100%. There are large differences among concepts in terms of when evaluating examples and nonexamples can first be performed effectively and also in the final level of performance attained. These differences among concepts appear to be related to the concrete–abstract dimension of concept examples discussed earlier and the nature of the informal experiences and formal education of the students.

FOR FURTHER STUDY

Flavell, J. H. *Cognitive development*. Englewood Cliffs, New Jersey: Prentice-Hall, Inc., 1977. Pp. 149–182.

In the first part of Chapter 5 Flavell summarizes and synthesizes American studies dealing with the development of visual and auditory perception. Flavell relates the development of perception to age spans, infancy through adolescence, rather than to stages or levels of development.

Mackworth, J. F. Development of attention. In V. Hamilton & M. D. Vernon (Eds.), *The development of cognitive processes*. London: Academic Press, 1976. Pp. 111–152.

Mackworth indicates that attention is the crucial requirement of learning and problem solving of all kinds. Selective attention is active in all phases of the information processing of an event, from the initial study of the environmental stimuli through final synthesis in long-term memory. The development of attention is related to early infancy, infancy to about age 4 or 5, and childhood. Mackworth gives attention about the same role in learning and development as attention and discrimination are given in CLD theory and perception in Gibson's theory.

Vurpillot, E. Development of identification of objects. In V. Hamilton & M. D. Vernon (Eds.), *The development of cognitive processes*. London: Academic Press, 1976. Pp. 191–236.

In this chapter three means of object identification are dealt with: individual identification which refers to the identification of individual objects, identification by referring to a figurative model of the object, and identity or nonidentity of two objects simultaneously present. Much of the chapter deals with object identification during the preschool years.

4

Memory and Levels of
Concept Attainment

Memory is involved at each level of concept attainment—concrete, identity, classificatory, and formal. At any point in time, the type of information that is stored in memory and the form in which it is stored are related to the level which the individual has attained, to the individual's unique mode of storing information, and also to the external conditions of learning the individual has experienced related to the particular concept. Our main purpose in this chapter is to deal with memory at each level of concept attainment. We first consider an information-processing account of memory (Miller & Johnson-Laird, 1976) as a context for the more detailed treatment of memory at each level. Other sources that may be used to supplement this analysis include Brown (1975) and Kail and Hagen (1976).

THE MEMORY SYSTEM

Persons who find an information-processing theory helpful in understanding human memory are concerned with four main phenomena. First, they are interested in the storage of information, from the first reception of external stimulating conditions to the long-term retention of experiences. Terms such as *buffer memory, primary memory*, and *secondary memory* are used in connection with the time dimension of memory. Second, the form of the internal representation of experiences and their organization into related fields at any level of development and also across the developmental years is of much interest. We recognize that there are great differences in the form and organization of memory for a 2-year-old attaining a concept of *tree* at the concrete level and for a high school senior attaining it at the formal level. Third, the relation of memory to initially securing information and subsequently to carrying out actions requires explanation. Finally, information-processing theorists try to identify the strategies and processes that human beings use in searching secondary memory for information. Although the memory requirements and other features of the memory system change according to the level of concept attainment, the description in this section, drawn mainly from Miller and Johnson-Laird (1976), is, according to them, typical of adult functioning only.

Memory Stores

Miller and Johnson-Laird (1976) delineate a three-phase memory system consisting of a buffer memory, a primary memory, and a secondary memory. Other theorists who explain human learning as information processing employ other terms for the three phases, including *sensory register, short-term memory* or *working memory*, and *long-term memory*. Wickelgren (1973) critically evaluated the evidence regarding the time dimension and concluded that a distinction between short-term and long-term memory could be made but that further division of long-term memory into two or more time durations was not warranted.

The essential elements of the human information processing system are shown in Figure 4.1. The information processor itself includes primary memory, where incoming information is presumably related to information that may be retrieved from secondary memory, and also the various translating mechanisms and processes between primary memory and other aspects of the memory system. For example, inputs to the sensory register by means of the various sense organs are filtered and patterned in the sensory register. The patterned information is then translated into the neural form in which it is received in primary memory. Similarly, visual or kinesthetic information held in primary memory may be translated, or encoded, into symbolic form when transferred to secondary memory.

Some kind of internal controlling capability, called *executive control*, is presumed that, within the limits imposed by the characteristics of the human species, determines all aspects of the input, processing, and storing of information as well as the actions that follow after processing. Conscious control over all aspects of the system varies in many ways. For example, we may consciously develop and carry out a plan for committing a passage to memory, but we are not always able to exclude hearing a sound, feeling heat, or seeing something. Similarly, once we understand the spoken language well, we are not always consciously able to control receiving, processing, and storing the substance of what we hear.

We may follow the flow of information from input to overt actions in the Miller and Johnson-Laird (1976) model as depicted in Figure 4.1 and simultaneously deal with the three memory stores.

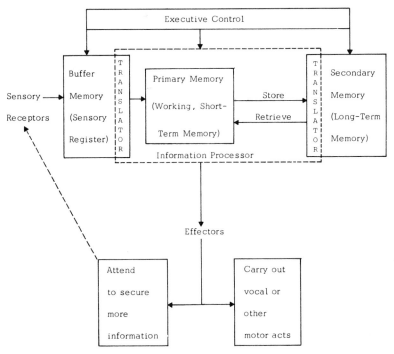

Figure 4.1. A model of human information processing. (Based on Miller & Johnson-Laird, 1976.)

BUFFER MEMORY

The individual attends to environmental conditions. This attention to the environment may originate in three ways. First, the greater intensity of some feature of the perceptual field may control the attention of the observer. In other words, if any particular feature of the perceptual field is sufficiently intense to exceed an individual's threshold for determining a "just noticeable difference," that individual's attention will be directed to the attribute or feature that is perceived as being different. Second, an individual's attention may be directed by some intentional search of the perceptual field in response to a request by another person for information or action. For example, one person may invite another to locate a particular reference work in the library. Attention may also be directed by an internal process—for example, when additional information is required from the perceptual field for the solution of an internally generated problem. Thus, properties of the perceptual field, requests for information by another individual, or internally generated demands for information may direct attention in the perceptual field.

Stimulation from the perceptual field activates the receptors and the information received is transformed to neural information in the buffer memory. Here the stimulus-induced, transformed information persists in its entirety for a very short period of time. This storage, lasting only hundredths of a second, is described by Sperling (1960) for visual information, and by Crowder and Morton (1969) for acoustic information. The duration of time that information is retained in its entirety in buffer memory is exceedingly brief. The duration of time for that portion which is patterned in accordance with selective attention is also very brief, up to one-tenth of a second; and it is this patterned information that is presumed to be translated and transferred to primary memory.

PRIMARY MEMORY

In primary memory, or working memory, patterned information from the sensory register is stored briefly and processed further. It may be rehearsed or elaborated and then translated and stored in secondary memory, or it may be translated into commands to the effectors. Incoming information is held in primary memory for about one second and may remain if undisturbed for as much as 10 seconds. Rehearsal of the information—for example, repeating the lines of a poem or the digits of a telephone number—and also deeper processing of information—for example, relating the content of a sentence just heard to information retrieved from secondary memory—extends the amount of time it can be held in working memory, up to about 30 seconds. Both the information from the immediate sensory experiences and the information retrieved from secondary memory are processed in working memory. (The word *information* is used in this discussion to include all forms of internal and external inputs and their translations, or transformations.)

SECONDARY MEMORY

In order for information to be stored in secondary memory, it must be translated into an appropriate form. This is presumed to occur within the information processor. The translation process is referred to also as encoding (Melton & Martin, 1972; Paivio, 1974). The two main forms of encoding are percepts and lexical concepts, or word meanings, according to Miller and Johnson-Laird (1976) and images and language according to Paivio (1974).

Secondary memory in adults is characterized by virtually unlimited capacity and high stability over long periods of time. Although there is not always conscious control by the individual as to whether information goes into secondary memory, it is clearly possible for individuals consciously to attempt to process and store information so that it will be remembered.

Theorists generally assume that thinking about anything occurs in limited processing space, that is, in primary memory. Percepts, concepts, and information of other kinds are stored in a more capacious space for long periods of time, that is, in secondary memory. There is continuous information flow from secondary memory to primary memory and from primary to secondary as we engage in a continuous mental activity, such as reading or concentrating on solving a problem.

ACTION

Information processing in primary memory may be followed by commands leading to overt actions. Stated differently, the output resulting from the processing of incoming information with that retrieved from secondary memory may be translated and transmitted to appropriate effectors. In some cases, vocalization may result, such as responding to a question or command orally. In other cases, other motor activity may be carried out—for example, putting one's thoughts into written form by handwriting or typing. In still other cases, further information may be sought through attending to the environment.

This approach of Miller and Johnson-Laird to human learning as *consciously controlled* information gathering, information storage, information processing, and action bears little resemblance to the reflex arc model of human learning that served as the foundation of early stimulus–response theory. Rather, it is based upon an analogy with information processing by computers. One possible limitation of the analogy with computer information processing is that information processing by computer is sequential and the information is alphanumeric. We know, however, that human beings have various sensory receptors and that they often simultaneously secure information by means of three or four different sensory organs. We presume that the several forms of incoming information are processed simultaneously. Thus, an explanation of human information processing based upon the analysis of computer simulations of human information processing may be overly simplified. Miller and Johnson-Laird have drawn from psychological research, as well as from epistemology, in formulating their theory. The present authors draw on several cognitive theories, including those of Ausubel (1968) and Bruner (1973), to supplement information-processing theory.

Memory Fields and Organization of Memory

Ausubel (1968) defined the cognitive structure of the individual as all the information that the individual has about any particular area of experience. He further hypothesized that the cognitive structure is organized in a hierarchical fashion, with the most generalized principles or concepts at the core around which are organized the successively more specific concepts and units of information. This interpretation of the organization of knowledge stored in the secondary memory appears to be generally accepted for semantic content. The memory field, or location, for semantic content is called *semantic memory*.

Tulving (1972) made a sharp distinction between semantic memory and episodic memory. According to Tulving, *episodic memory* is a temporally organized record of a person's experiences. For example, one ate particular things for breakfast, drove a car by a particular route to work, and attended a party at a certain time. Semantic memory, on the other hand, includes all the organized knowledge a person has gained through understanding the meaning of words and other symbols and their relationships, as well as ways and means of doing things. According to this view, events that one has experienced are located in episodic memory, whereas the knowledge gained about the physical and social world is located in semantic memory.

Miller and Johnson-Laird (1976) indicate that the distinction between episodic and semantic memory is useful in considering how information may be stored and retrieved, but that it does not go far enough. They suggest that there are at least three more memory fields: *action, geographic,* and *person.* We may deal briefly with these fields inasmuch as families of concepts organized into hierarchies, taxonomies, part–whole relations, and other arrangements may also be related to the memory fields.

Persons have motor skills along with knowledge that the skills may be used in particular situations. Knowing how to sign one's name and to be able to call forth this action does not fit the characteristics of either episodic or semantic memory. Rather, psychomotor skills and related knowledge are stored in and retrieved from *action memory*.

Episodic memory is characterized by the time dimension. We remember events according to the time at which they occurred. We may also store and retrieve events according to the place in which we experience something or the place where something is located. Thus, we might recall where a book we checked out from the library was stored or where a particular river is located. Place information is stored in *geographic memory*.

We spend much time in thinking about and interacting with other persons. We have information about individuals and groups of persons, and we also have attitudes toward them as individuals or groups. This kind of information is located in *person memory*.

As indicated earlier, percepts and concepts are the two main products of experience that are stored in secondary memory. Contextual information associated with a percept or concept may also be stored. This contextual information is not a defining attribute of the particular percept or concept; for example, one may recall where a book was seen or whom a person was with at a certain time. However, the contextual information may be used in recognizing an object or quality as the same one experienced earlier.

Remembering and Other Fundamental Operations

Miller and Johnson-Laird (1976) use the terms *perceive, intend, remember, know*, and *feel* to indicate the fundamental operations by which the human being relates to the external and internal environments. (The CLD operations of attending and discriminating are analogous to perceiving.) According to Miller and Johnson-Laird, to know something is an outcome, or product, of intending, perceiving, and remembering. To know is the primary function of the information-processing system. Relations among the fundamental operations of perceive, intend, and remember and of related internal control instructions and

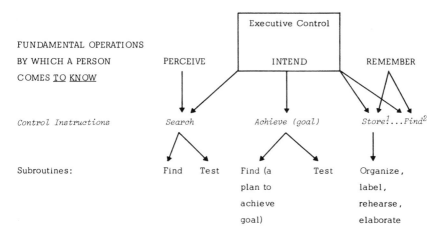

FUNDAMENTAL OPERATIONS
BY WHICH A PERSON
COMES <u>TO</u> <u>KNOW</u>

Control Instructions

Subroutines:

[1]Produce in secondary memory a representation of information currently in primary memory.

[2]Produce in working memory a pointer to the target in secondary memory.

Figure 4.2. Possible relations among perceiving, intending, and remembering. (Based on Miller & Johnson-Laird, 1976.)

subroutines are shown in Figure 4.2. The feel operation is not dealt with in any detail by Miller and Johnson-Laird, but it is thought to influence the intend operation directly and thus indirectly the perceive and remember operations.

Input of information to the human information-processing system is accomplished through perceiving. A memory system is required for changes in knowledge and other products of experience to become permanent. The outputs of the system in terms of overt actions and products of thought are directed and controlled by intending. Though conscious perceiving and remembering are controlled by intend, not all perceiving and storing of information is done consciously. Rather, there is some perception and storage of information of which the person is unaware.

According to Miller and Johnson-Laird, the individual generates internal control instructions that are directly related to intend. In connection with perceiving, the instruction is "to search" the environment. This instruction is further delineated "to find" something in the environment and to continue to search until a test shows that what is sought is found. In the operation of remembering, information may be processed and then stored in secondary memory; the secondary store may be searched so that particular information is found and brought to working memory for processing. Finding desired information in secondary memory is thought to be simplified if incoming information is stored in the five domains previously mentioned, namely episodic, semantic, action, geographic, and person. Both the storing and retrieving of information are controlled by intend instructions, although with varying levels of consciousness on the part of the individual.

At times persons intend to achieve goals without securing further information either by attending to the environment or by searching memory. To achieve a goal, it is necessary either to generate a new plan or to find and retrieve a plan that was generated in the past. In some cases, the goal achievement is carried out through motor actions; in other cases, only mental actions are involved. The intention to carry out the plan is continued until a test shows the plan to be completed.

Memory Search

Miller and Johnson-Laird (1976) describe how human beings generate control instructions and related routines analogous to the programs developed for controlling information processing in the computer. These instructions and routines enable secondary memory to be searched and the information to be found and retrieved so that it may be processed.

Natural language is presumed to be used by human beings in generating instructions and routines. One remaining theoretical problem is to determine whether, and possibly how, routines stated in natural language are translated into the language of the central nervous system. The reader may find it fruitful to review the work of Miller and Johnson-Laird, who indicate how yes–no questions, statements in present progressive, commands, and declarative sentences are translated into natural language routines and how these routines are used to retrieve information and also to test the retrieved information against a current perception or an internally generated question. One illustration may prove instructive.

Translating as part of human information processing is described as devising a "program of instructions" from the input. For example, an input to a person in the form of question "Is the plant in your front yard a *tree* or a *shrub?*" is translated into a *program* of search and recognition. Let us consider the search first. When executed, the program of search activates the *routine* "find," which specifies the description of the target and its location in secondary memory to be searched. One *subroutine* is to find in geographic memory the representation of the "tree or shrub in your front yard." (In this example, we are assuming that the person is not within viewing distance of the front yard.) Two other subroutines are to find in semantic memory the concepts *tree* and *shrub*: (1) Find the concept *tree* in semantic memory, and (2) find the concept *shrub* in semantic memory. This search program and routine → subroutines, which may be either heuristic or algorithmic, are controlled by the executive decision maker.

The second aspect of the program of search and *recognition* involves carrying out tests in short-term memory in order to answer the question. The nature of the test is predetermined by the context provided by the speaker who raised the question. The plant retrieved from geographic memory will be tested for type of plant (i.e., "tree or shrub"), rather than location ("yard"), possession ("your"), or existence (" is a tree or shrub there?"). In order to determine whether the plant is a "tree" or "shrub," two subroutines are executed: (1) Test whether the plant is a tree, and (2) test whether the plant is a shrub. The representation of the specific plant in the yard retrieved from geographic memory is tested against the information retrieved from semantic memory, specifically, against the defining attributes that are needed to discriminate trees from shrubs (the critical attribute is a single main stem). The subroutines and related tests can be carried out in parallel or in succession.

In general, there are three means of testing: (1) through comparison of information held in memory, as in the example above, where information stored in geographic memory is tested against information stored in semantic memory; (2) through comparison of a phenomenal perception with information held in memory, where what is perceived in the environment is tested against a percept or concept stored in memory; and (3) through logic, where a problem is solved or a conclusion is deduced through inference. The translating mechanism accepts externally and internally originated inputs in generating programs → routines →· subroutines for both searching and testing.

MEMORY AND CONCEPT ATTAINMENT LEVELS

Memory is an essential operation at all levels of concept attainment. In treating memory at the various levels we shall use the term *image* to designate the internal representation at the concrete and identity levels and *trace* at the classificatory and formal levels.

The use of *image* implies that individuals generally attain the first two levels while quite young and do not use language extensively in storing the representation of the object attended to and discriminated. The use of *trace* implies that individuals generally have the name of the concept and possibly the names of some of its attributes at the time of initially attaining the classificatory level. At this initial attainment of the classificatory level, an image of an example of the concept, the name of the concept, and some aspects of the situation in which the examples were experienced may be stored as the classificatory-level trace. It is possible that a formal-level trace may include an image of some kind along with the names of the concept and its defining attributes and some contextual information.

Memory at the Concrete and Identity Levels

Attaining a concept at the concrete level involves attending to something—an object, event, quality, or relation—discriminating it from other objects, events, qualities, or relations, forming a representation of it, and storing it in secondary memory. (Hereafter we will usually use the term *object* rather than including all four terms or using the indefinite *something*.) Then, when the same object is experienced again, the stored representation is retrieved from secondary memory and used to test the incoming phenomenal representation as being the same or different. (This description implies that a time interval of at least a few seconds must elapse between the initial and second experience with the object.) The concrete-level representation of the object is presumed to be constructed by the individual, rather than being an automatically produced literal copy, photograph, or template. This view of the nature of the concrete-level representation is similar to that of Hebb (1968), Gibson (1969), Gibson and Levin (1975), and Miller and Johnson-Laird (1976), in presuming that the internal representation of an object results from selectively attending to and discriminating some features of the object.

Attaining the same concept later at the identity level for the first time requires having the concrete-level image stored in secondary memory. Then, when the same object is experienced again but from a different spatiotemporal perspective, in a different context, or in a different sensory modality, the phenomenal image, held briefly in working memory, is tested against the earlier concrete-level image. We may illustrate the test relationship between the concrete and identity levels. A given isosceles right triangular form with the 90-degree angle in the lower right portion of the field is seen a second time in the identical orientation and is recognized as the same form (concrete level). Later, the same form is seen with the right angle in the lower left portion of the field, in the apex of the field, or in some other orientation. The individual tests this new phenomenal image against the concrete-level image retrieved from secondary memory and evaluates them as the same form. The person has now attained the concept of *right isosceles triangle* at the identity level.

In the transition from the concrete to the identity level, three questions arise for which the answers are incomplete. What happens to the concrete-level image? What enables individuals to attain the identity level when earlier they could not? What is the nature of the image at the identity level?

Let us assume that an individual has a concrete-level image of an object in a typical orientation or context. Logically, this image might be expected to persist rather than, or along with, the image of the same object when experienced later in a less typical orientation or context. We have not found firm experimental evidence regarding the factors that determine which image might persist. It is possible also that individual preferences might contribute to the survival of either or both images.

According to CLD theory, persons are able to move from the concrete to the identity level as they become able to generalize across spatiotemporal perspectives, sensory modalities, and contexts. This ability emerges with maturation and learning. The maturing child becomes able to test, for example, the incoming phenomenal image of the right isosceles triangle against the concrete-level image and generalizes that the forms are the same. The same individual also becomes able to discriminate either more properties of the triangular form or some of its less obvious properties and also to ignore orientation and other contextual information. Some of the more obvious features are that the two forms have the same shape and are of the same size. Less obvious features, which we call defining attributes, are that the figure is closed, plane, simple, and three-sided, that one angle is 90 degrees and larger than the other two (which are always of equal size), and that one side is larger than the other two (which are always of equal length). Inability to discriminate some of these attributes would result in overgeneralizing, for example, to a four-sided figure, a three-sided open figure, an equilateral triangle, a non-isosceles right triangle, and others.

Miller and Johnson-Laird (1976) provide an informative account of the formation of percepts, corresponding to concrete- and identity-level images. They organize percepts into five major categories: objects, space, time, changes, and causes. They do not, however, deal with the change in the percepts of the same objects that occur from infancy onward until a relatively unchanging percept is formed. They do indicate, however, that the simplest perception of any concrete object seems to depend on a prior concept of object permanence and also that processes traditionally regarded as purely perceptual have an important interactive relationship with conceptual processes. Both of these views are incorporated in CLD theory.

Some research has been done on the development of memory per se, although this is a very new area of investigation (Flavell, 1977). Empirical results and theoretical views are now presented, particularly those which appear to be relatable to memory at the concrete and identity levels of concept attainment.

Steinberg (1974) studied encoding of information, recall of information, and transfer of learning in children 24–36 months of age. Three age groupings were studied: 24–27 months, 28–31 months, and 32–36 months. The other two variables accounted for were amount of time of the experiments and retention–transfer procedures. All children were taught to discriminate one of three farm animals presented in the form of three-dimensional objects—a cow, a horse, and a pig. The various treatment groups were then tested for the ability to retain the discrimination and also to transfer this ability to pictorial representations of the animals. If they could recall but not transfer, it was assumed that they had formed a percept (corresponding to a concept at the concrete level); if they could recall and transfer, it was assumed they had formed a concept of the animal (analogous to a concept at the identity level). At the end of the discrimination task, the child was also asked to name the animals.

It was concluded that children after 28 months, but not before, were able to respond with recognition to a previously discriminated stimulus in the face of perceptual transformation; whereas children younger than 28 months easily remembered and recognized a re-presented stimulus for as long as 45 minutes. But they did not transfer their recognition response to an altered version. The evolution of symbolic processes during the third year of life affects the coding of information, not the retention. Younger children code perceptual characteristics of the stimuli, and older children conceptual.

Experiments by Russian psychologists (reported by Zaphorozhets, 1965) also indicate developmental differences in object recognition. In one set of experiments, the eye movements of children of different ages were recorded while they were viewing unfamiliar figures of irregular form. Each figure was projected on a screen for 20 seconds and the children were instructed to look at the screen attentively so that they could recognize the figures among other figures later. Eye movements of 3- and 4-year-old children were not numerous; they tended to fixate for longer periods between movements than did older children. The movements were within the figure and no attempt was made to move the eye around the edge of the figure. The children's technique of studying the object is very primitive at this age, and their subsequent recognition of the figures was very low. In children 4–5 years of age, the number of eye movements was twice as great as for the younger group. The movements were mainly inside the figure and many appeared to trace the length of the figure. There were no movements tracing the outline of the figure, but movements were noticed between fixation points that occurred at specific features (e.g., an angle) of the form. The attentional responses of these children resulted in a more highly differentiated image than for the younger group, as inferred from their much better recognition performances. Children 5–6 years of age began tracing the outline of the figure, but usually looked at only part of the outline. With 6- to 7-year-old children, the eye movements followed, for the most part, the outline of the figure as if modeling its form. Recognition performance for these children was 100% correct.

Other Russian experiments have dealt with exploratory tactual responses as well as visual perceptual responses and later recognition of objects. The results are similar to those just cited. That is, with age the perceptual activity of the child (both tactual and visual) becomes increasingly attuned to discriminating more features and the less obvious features of objects. As a consequence, the images formed become more accurate in terms of representing the features of the object, and recognition is enhanced.

Shepard and Metzler (1971) demonstrated that imagery was used in mentally rotating representations of three-dimensional objects, and Huttenlocher and Presson (1973) found that rotation problems involving perspective were easier when the observer moved with respect to an array rather than when the observer remained fixed and moved the array. Cooper and Shepard (1973) also showed that subjects were able to rotate figures mentally in order to compare them with figures presented in unexpected orientations.

In summary, as children mature they are able to discriminate more attributes and less obvious attributes of objects. The images formed and stored are more accurate representations of the objects; also, more objects are represented. The ability to retrieve an image from secondary memory and to manipulate it in primary memory to test incoming phenomenal information also seems to improve as mental rotation of images emerges. It remains unclear, however, precisely how the transition from memory at the concrete level to the identity level occurs.

Children also acquire language and may associate the name of the object with the object and store both the object representation and the name, as will be discussed in Chapter 5. However, as Gibson (1969), Gibson and Levin (1975), and Paivio (1974) point out, naming and verbal coding are not essential for object recognition.

Memory at the Classificatory Level

Attaining a concept at the beginning classificatory level, in comparison with the identity level, presumes that persons become able to attend to and discriminate more attributes and also attributes that are less obvious. They also are able to form more highly differentiated yet generalized representations and store and hold them in secondary memory. Further, they become able to generalize across at least *two different examples* of the same concept that necessarily have the same common defining attributes but that also have one or more different variable attributes. To do this, they must already have formed a concept of one of the examples at the identity level and must be able to do so for the other, so that each of the examples is recognized as the same across the different spatiotemporal orientations or contexts in which it may be experienced, or across the different sensory modalities, as the case may be. It is probable that concepts of at least two examples have been formed at the identity level before the beginning classificatory level is attained.

Drawing upon the example of the right isosceles triangle used earlier, suppose that the identity level is attained for a triangle of a given size with the right angle first in a lower left orientation and later in a lower right orientation. This identity-level image, or both images, and possibly elements of the context are stored in secondary memory. Suppose the identity level of a second isosceles right triangle is attained next, but it is larger and the right angle is first in the lower left position and later at the vertex. An identity-level image of this larger triangle is formed and held in secondary memory. In first attaining the classificatory level, both identity-level images presumably are retrieved from secondary memory and are tested for likenesses in working memory. Here a sufficient number of the defining attributes are present and recognized so that the two forms are generalized as being examples of the same class; orientation, size, and irrelevant contextual information, if held in working memory along with the identity-level image or images, is ignored, or judged to be nondefining.

Children form many concepts at the beginning classificatory level before Grade 1, as indicated in Chapter 3, possibly before they have acquired the labels for the concept or any of its attributes. Many are still at the classificatory level years later, not having attained the formal level, at which time they may have some or all of the labels. When a label is available for a concept at the classificatory level, it may be stored initially as part of the trace along with an image of a typical example and contextual information. Also, other concepts will probably have been formed that are part of the same taxonomy, hierarchy, or other family of concepts; and their traces will be stored in secondary memory in an appropriate field such as semantic or episodic, as mentioned earlier. We shall not attempt to indicate the many changes that probably occur in the classificatory-level concept trace from the beginning classificatory level when words do not yet represent the concept, through the phase at which only the word for the concept is used in thinking and in oral or written discourse. Rather, we shall sketch the role of memory at the formal level, since CLD theory specifies that having the name of the concept and the names of its attributes is one of the prerequisites of attaining the formal level. In Chapter 5 a more complete account of the relationship between language and concept attainment will be given.

Memory at the Formal Level

Attaining a concept at the beginning formal level has several prerequisites. The person will readily be able to categorize newly encountered instances as members of certain concepts and therefore as nonmembers of other concepts. Also, the person will be able to discriminate the defining attributes of the particular concept. Another prerequisite is that the person will have the names of the defining attributes and also of the concept itself. The primary test of whether the concept has been attained at the formal level is whether the person, when encountering examples and nonexamples of the concept, can evaluate them as examples or nonexamples on the basis of the presence or absence of the defining attributes of the concept. We may illustrate with the concept *tree*. When a person encounters two instances of a plant, one of which is a tree and the other a shrub, the person must first identify one properly as a tree, and then indicate why it is so categorized on the basis of the defining attributes of tree. To do this a considerable amount of information must be retrieved from secondary memory as the basis against which to test the incoming phenomenal traces held in primary memory.

Assume that the individual retrieves from secondary memory the classificatory-level trace for tree, including the key critical attribute, namely one, woody stem. This is the critical attribute for discriminating trees from the two coordinate classes, shrubs and herbs. The trace retrieved may be only the words for one or more of the critical attributes of tree, one or more words and an image of a "typical" tree, or words and an image of the critical attribute, namely one, woody stem. Testing the incoming trace against the retrieved trace leads to correct identification of the tree. Assume, too, that the incoming trace of the shrub is tested against the retrieved classificatory-level trace of tree.

Here, the critical attribute "one" woody stem is not found in the shrub; rather, it has two or more woody stems. Let us assume next that the person now uses the word *tree* and other words to indicate that one is a tree because it has one woody stem and the other is not a tree because it has, in this case, two or more woody stems. If the person is simply making this kind of analysis independent of other persons, nothing further occurs. On the other hand, if the individual had been responding to another person's question, "Are both of these trees?," a verbal response to elaborate the analysis would be forthcoming.

The reader will recognize that being able to identify trees and shrubs and to explain why each is so categorized may be of little importance, except perhaps to landscapers, foresters, and some property owners. We point out, however, that the operations at the formal level apply to all kinds of concepts. An obstetrician examines newborn infants and evaluates them as normal by testing their attributes against attributes of abnormalcy. A psychologist studies different theories of development and evaluates the validity of their constructs against a concept of psychological theory. The practical importance of correct categorizing and the related decision making based on correct categorizing are dealt with in some detail by Bruner (1973).

Before proceeding further, it is important to recognize that images may play a more important role in memory of concepts for which there are perceptible examples, drawings, or three-dimensional models than has often been thought. Paivio (1974), who formulated a dual-coding theory of information processing and memory, expressed this point of view. The four major propositions of the theory and related evidence supporting the theory follow.

One proposition is that verbal and nonverbal types of information are represented and processed in distinct but interconnected symbolic systems. Though the two systems are functionally independent, they are partly interconnected, and activity in one system can initiate activity in the other. A second proposition is that the nature of the symbolic information differs qualitatively in the two systems. The imagery system is specialized for representing and processing information concerning nonverbal objects and events in a rather direct, analog fashion. The verbal system is specialized for dealing with linguistic units and generating speech. The qualitative distinctions between the two systems involve the organization of information. In the imagery system elementary images are organized into higher-order structures so that the informational output of the system has a synchronous or spatial character. In the verbal system linguistic units are organized into higher-order sequential structures.

A third major proposition is that both systems are capable of functioning in a dynamic and flexible way to reorganize, manipulate, or transform cognitive information. Dynamic visual imagery involves transformations of such visual and spatial attributes as size, location, and orientation of imagined objects, whereas verbal transformations involve sequential rearrangements of words and other linguistic units.

Various kinds of evidence support the proposition that the two kinds of coding are independent. Milner and Teuber (1968), Gazzaniga (1970), Sperry (1973), and Kimura (1973) have shown that the two halves of the brain differ in their ability to deal with verbal and nonverbal material. Memory of linguistic information and the processing of that information is localized in the left hemisphere for most people, whereas certain kinds of spatial and nonverbal memory skills are specific to the other hemisphere, usually the right. This supports the idea that verbal and nonverbal types of information are stored and processed independently to a significant degree.

The nature of individual differences in human abilities also provides evidence for independent symbolic systems. Guilford (1967) and Di Vesta, Ingersoll, and Sunshine (1971) have demonstrated that verbal and nonverbal abilities are factorially independent when measured by relevant tests. This general independence of verbal and nonverbal abilities indicates that the two kinds of knowledge are not represented in a common symbolic format.

A third kind of evidence consistent with a dual-coding theory comes from studies showing that performance on a perceptual task can interfere with a memory task, or vice versa, if the two involve the same perceptual–motor system (Brooks, 1968; Byrne, 1974; Klee & Eysenck, 1973). However, little interference between the two tasks is observed if they involve different systems (e.g., visual and auditory). The different perceptual and memory channels are functionally independent insofar as memory activity can go on in one channel in the form of visual imagery, for example, while the other is at the same time engaged in perceptual activity such as listening to speech. However, the same channel cannot efficiently carry on both perceptual and memory processing.

Paivio inferred qualitative differences between imagery coding and verbal coding. In one experiment (Paivio, 1974), drawings of pairs of animals, an animal and an object, and a pair of objects were presented. In some pairs of drawings, the size of an animal (e.g., a zebra) and of an object (e.g., a lamp) were congruent according to their actual sizes, the zebra being larger than the lamp. In other pairs they were incongruent, the drawing of the lamp being larger than that of the zebra. In other pairs they were equally small or large. Words naming the animals and objects were paired in the same four ways: equally small-sized letters, equally large-sized letters, congruent size, or incongruent size. The reaction time required to view the stimulus material and to indicate which of the animals or objects in each pair was larger was the dependent variable. Paivio reasoned that if the size comparison involved a visual memory system, the reaction times would be faster with the drawings than with the words, on the assumption that the words which named the animals or objects would have to be read and converted to analog representations of the animals and objects to preserve their relative size. Another prediction was that reaction time would be faster for the congruent than for the incongruent pairs of drawings because of the conflict between the tendency to respond to the perceptual representations as provided and the memory representations when the drawings were incongruent. A third prediction was that this effect would be less for incongruent word pairs than for pairs of drawings because the words had to be read first and the images retrieved before the sizes could be compared. Reaction times were found to be faster for the drawings than for the words; reaction times were also significantly faster for the congruent than for the incongruent drawings but not for the words. Paivio interpreted these results as supporting the construct of qualitative differences between imagery and verbal coding.

Bird and Bennett (1974) gave recognition tasks to children of age 4, 6, 8, and 10 years involving orally presented words that were examples of concrete nouns or abstract nouns and black and white drawings of concrete nouns. The drawings were recognized significantly better than both concrete and abstract nouns by children of ages 4 and 6, and significantly better than abstract nouns only at ages 8 and 10. The authors interpreted this finding as supporting Paivio's hypothesis regarding dual encoding. No significant difference was found at any age between the recognition of abstract nouns and that of concrete. The authors suggest that this finding cannot be accounted for by dual encoding theory.

Paivio also identified three possible relationships between imagery and abstract knowledge as follows. One possibility is that some highly abstract concepts are processed entirely verbally, with little involvement of the imagery system. A second possibility is that, within limits, images might be abstract and schematic rather than analog in the sense that the representation of a class of things includes only an image of the defining attributes. Another possibility is that concretized images of examples of a concept might be held in secondary memory. Rosch (1974) found that people represent conceptual categories in terms of analog prototypes that are the best examples of the categories. Anderson and McGaw (1973) concluded similarly that people use images of highly probable exemplars to represent the meanings of general terms.

CONDITIONS OF LEARNING AND MEMORY REQUIREMENTS

In the previous section we have indicated how memory may function at the four different levels of concept attainment. The initial conditions of learning influence both the form in which information is stored and the memory requirements. Two significant accounts of the influence of conditions of learning are represented in theory and research dealing with strategies of learning concepts inductively and with meaningful reception learning. It will be recalled that these are the two means specified by CLD theory for attaining concepts at the formal level. We shall draw upon the theoretical propositions in discussing these areas rather than reporting the substantial number of empirical studies on which each theory is based.

Strategies in Attaining Concepts Inductively

Bruner (1973) and Bruner, Goodnow, and Austin (1956) reported the strategies that persons use in attaining concepts inductively. A strategy is defined as a pattern of decisions in the acquisition, retention, and utilization of information that serves to meet certain objectives, that is, to ensure that concepts or some other outcomes of learning are attained. A strategy is an intentional, consciously formulated, and organized plan of attack. One objective of a strategy for attaining concepts is to minimize the amount of strain on memory; however, before dealing with memory and strategies, we shall consider the experimental procedures by which strategies are inferred. This is done in some detail inasmuch as one means of attaining concepts at the formal level, according to CLD theory, involves an inductive approach.

The pioneering experimental procedures used by Bruner et al. (1956) have several important features. First, a universe of concepts is created and displayed to the subject in the experiment and is usually made of geometric forms. The universe of concepts is created in such a way that the instances can be grouped into different rule-related, inclusive–exclusive classes, each class being defined by one or more of the values of one or more of the attributes that define the universe of concepts. For example, a universe of eight concept instances might be created so that each instance is definable by one of two values of each of three attributes: size—large or small; color—red or green; and shape—triangle or circle.

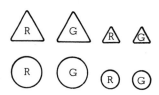

The principles for combining the attributes to form concepts also may vary—for example, a principle may be conjunctive or inclusive–disjunctive. Illustrative conjunctive two-value concepts are figures that are small and red, figures that are large and green, figures that are triangular and red, figures that are circles and green, etc. Illustrative inclusive–disjunctive concepts are figures that are either green or triangles, figures that are either small or circles, etc. (In order to test hypotheses regarding memory of adults, displays having 128 instances or more may be constructed by increasing the number of attributes, the number of values, or both.)

A second feature is the two distinct ways in which the subject can get information while attaining a concept. In the selection-type experiment, the subject successively selects and tests one figure, or instance, after another for its possible membership in a class that the subject hypothesizes. In the reception-type experiment, the experimenter presents the instances, often successively, and the subject again tests membership in the hypothesized class. In both sets of experimental conditions, the experimenter provides feedback to the subject that enables the subject to determine whether the instance is or is not a member of the target concept the experimenter has in mind and that the subject is trying to identify. The third feature of this experimentation is that the target concept can be identified only through an inductive process. A fourth feature is that the concept to be attained is defined by one or more values and a principle for joining them. A final feature is that by studying the pattern of instances used by the subject in identifying the concept, including the hypotheses made, the experimenter can infer which of four ideal selection strategies, or which of two ideal reception strategies, the subject's strategy approximates. The four ideal selection strategies described by Bruner et al. (1956) are simultaneous scanning, successive scanning, conservative focusing, and focus gambling. The two ideal reception strategies are wholist and partist. These are "ideal" strategies in the sense that able persons can be taught what each one is and can use it in attaining concepts drawn from a particular population of concepts. Uninstructed college students in Bruner's experiments tended to adopt a strategy that closely resembled one or another of the ideal strategies. However, their strategies were less than "ideal" in that they often did not secure as much information from each instance as they might have and they sometimes shifted from one strategy to another while attempting to attain a particular concept. Let us consider the strategies used by subjects in the selection-type experiments.

Some subjects who adopted a scanning strategy formed several hypotheses, or predictions of the target concept, each of which included all the attribute values of each hypothesized concept. For example, hypotheses might have been the concept *figures that are small and red, figures that are large and green*, etc. The subject then selected instances successively and, with each instance, concurrently tested more than one hypothesis. Feedback from the experimenter following each instance enabled the subject to determine that the particular hypotheses tested were incorrect, or that one of the hypotheses was correct. This strategy, called "simultaneous scanning," requires the subject to formulate all the potential concepts, to attempt to test more than one with each instance selected, to remember which ones were tested and rejected with each instance selected, to remember the attribute values of the instances that resulted in rejecting hypotheses, and finally to remember hypotheses that have not yet been tested. An alternative strategy, "successive scanning," involves offering and testing only one hypothesis with each instance selected. The successive scanning strategy also requires the subject to remember each hypothesis tested and rejected, the information contained in each instance that resulted in rejection of an hypothesis, and also the hypotheses that have not yet been tested.

The focusing strategies are quite different from the scanning strategies. Subjects who used a focusing strategy in the selection experiments hypothesized the possible attribute values that might define the concept, rather than hypothesizing a number of different concepts. In their successive selection of instances for testing as members of the concept, they eliminated the nondefining values and thus arrived at the ones that defined the concept. Conservative focusing involved selection of successive instances, each of which varied in only one attribute value from the focus instance given by the experimenter. Focus gambling involved selection of successive instances, each of which varied two or more values from the focus instance. Conservative focusing assures that some useful information can be gained on each successive choice. Focus gambling does not, for if two values are varied and the chosen instance is not a member of the concept, one does not know whether one, the other, or both values may be the defining one. On the other hand, had the chosen instance been a member, one would have had useful information regarding both values varied; therefore, the term *gambling*.

The conservative focusing strategy reduces to a minimum the task of processing information, storing it in secondary memory, and retrieving it. One is not required, as in the scanning strategies, to formulate, test, and remember a large number of hypothesized concepts or the attribute values of the particular instances tested. Essentially, all the subject has to remember is the hypothesized attribute values tested and the outcomes of each test, that is, whether the value is a defining one or not.

In the reception experiments, the subjects were not free to choose instances to test; they were, however, free to formulate their hypotheses. Subjects tended to use either of two types of reception strategies. The "wholist strategy" is a focusing strategy. The subject recognizes that the focus instance contains all the defining values as well as those that are not; the first hypothesis, then, contains all values of the focus instance. As each successive positive instance is presented, the subject's hypothesis retains only those values which the focus instance and each positive instance have in common. This wholist reception strategy, like the conservative focusing selection strategy, requires a minimum amount of information storage.

The second type of reception strategy that subjects employed was the "partist strategy," a variant of scanning. Here the subject, with each successive instance presented, hypothesizes the target concept. In turn, this strategy requires memory of each hypothesis tested, the information contained in the instance used for testing, and the hypotheses not yet tested.

All these ideal strategies are logical and were used by at least some of the college-age students, according to Bruner et al. (1956). Some subjects used the focusing and wholist strategies, which eliminate the need for continuous storing and retrieving specific information about each instance tested and also about the hypotheses tested and others to be tested. Other subjects used the scanning and partist strategies, which have heavier memory requirements.

A series of experiments conducted at the Wisconsin Research and Development Center during the period 1960–1964 (Klausmeier, Harris, & Wiersma, 1964) and 1964–1967 (Klausmeier, Harris, Davis, Ghatala [Schwenn], and

Frayer, 1968) extended the pioneering work of Bruner *et al.* (1956), and also provided some of the experimental base of the initial CLD theory (Klausmeier, 1971; Klausmeier, Ghatala, & Frayer, 1974). The key experiments are summarized in the 1974 book. We, as well as Johnson (1971) and Miller (1971), were not able to replicate the ideal strategies completely.

In dealing with memory requirements during inductive concept learning, we concluded that, without instruction concerning strategies, some persons do use strategies approximating the ideal conservative focusing strategy; other persons use guessing strategies that are not close approximations of the ideal scanning strategies. The various strategies do place unequal demands on memory. Thus, the role of memory in inductive concept learning must take into account the strategies individuals employ.

We also found that we could teach subjects the conservative focusing strategy and also a principle for getting a maximum amount of information from both examples and nonexamples (Klausmeier & Meinke, 1968). The instruction markedly facilitated their attainment of concepts. The facilitation is accomplished through more efficient information processing combined with less storage and retrieval of information. As will be pointed out later in Chapter 10, the results from this line of experimentation have been incorporated into a design for developing instructional materials to teach concepts by a combination of meaningful reception learning and induction.

Meaningful Reception Learning

Textbooks, reference works, sound films, and other instructional materials are used extensively to teach concepts. When students study the new material presented, relate the new information to what they already know, and organize it into a more complete cognitive structure, they are engaging in meaningful reception learning, according to Ausubel's theory (Ausubel, 1963; Ausubel, 1977; Ausubel & Robinson, 1969).

Two dimensions of learning processes are fundamental in this theory. One dimension deals with the two ways by which knowledge to be learned is made available to the learner. These two ways are reception learning and discovery learning. The second dimension indicates the two ways by which learners may incorporate new information into their existing cognitive structures. These two ways are described as meaningful and rote. The theory assumes that the two dimensions are relatively independent. Therefore, four basic kinds of learning are proposed: meaningful reception, rote reception, meaningful discovery, and rote discovery.

In reception learning the entire content of what is to be learned is given in its final form in expository and other material. If the learner attempts to retain the new information by relating it to what is already known, meaningful learning occurs. If the learner attempts merely to memorize the new information, rote learning occurs.

In discovery learning not all that is to be learned is presented in final form. The learner gets some information independently through attending to and searching the environment or by searching memory. This information is then integrated into the existing cognitive structure and reorganized or transformed to produce a new or modified cognitive structure. Presumably, meaningful discovery learning requires less use of rehearsal strategies or other memory strategies than does reception learning, since the learner controls the information input more fully during discovery learning than during reception learning and also identifies the relationships among items rather than being presented them. By definition, rote learning requires the use of rehearsal or other memory strategies.

According to CLD theory, concepts are not acquired by rote processes; but they may be attained by either inductive or reception processes. The inductive process as described in the previous section of this chapter is probably used as persons attain concepts independent of instruction and use of instructional materials. However, most concept learning at the formal level occurs as a form of meaningful reception learning at the upper elementary school level, high school level, and college level. According to Ausubel, the primary means of reducing memory load is to organize instruction so that a general and more inclusive concept or proposition is learned at a beginning level prior to receiving information about less inclusive concepts and other information that may be part of the same taxonomy, hierarchy, or topic. The more inclusive concept provides a structure for relating and organizing the new information. A more complete explanation in the terminology of CLD theory is that knowing the defining attributes of the more general or supraordinate concept provides the basis for relating the more specific critical attributes that define the subordinate classes, including those that are coordinate to one another. The more complete this conceptual core is the easier it is to learn new information that may be related to it.

To summarize the memory requirements associated with inductive and reception strategies, Bruner has shown that persons may use different strategies in attaining concepts inductively. The memory load is least when a conservative focusing strategy, rather than a scanning strategy, is used in selection situations, and a wholist strategy, rather than a partist, is employed in reception situations. According to Ausubel, memory requirements, not in terms of the amount to be remembered but as related to the use of memory strategies, are lower under meaningful discovery learning than under meaningful reception learning and much lower under meaningful learning than under rote learning. Though neither the theory nor the related empirical evidence may be as definitive as desired, it is clear that memory requirements for concept attainment, particularly at the classificatory and formal levels, are related to the external conditions of learning that individuals experience. Also, the requirements vary greatly among individuals, both in informal and formal educational settings.

FOR FURTHER STUDY

Bruner, J. S. *Beyond the information given*. New York: W. W. Norton & Company, Inc., 1973. Pp. 131–185.

Chapters 8 and 9 of this book are reprints of Bruner's pioneering publications dealing with the process of concept attainment and the use of selection and reception strategies in attaining concepts.

Coltheart, M. Contemporary models of the cognitive processes, I. Iconic storage and visual masking. In V. Hamilton & M. D. Vernon (Eds.), *The development of cognitive processes*. London: Academic Press, 1976. Pp. 11–42.

Coltheart discusses the processes and relationships involved among the sensory register, short-term memory, and long-term memory (a) in the initial learning of something and (b) in the recognition or identification of something learned previously. The identification of words as is done in reading is used for illustrative purposes.

Estes, W. K. (Ed.). *Handbook of learning and cognitive processes: Attention and memory* (Vol.4). New York: John Wiley, 1976.

Modern developments in cognitive psychology are presented with the focus on models, theories, and methods pertaining to attention and short-term memory. The following chapters are of particular interest: Introduction to Volume 4, W. K. Estes; Ch. 3, The Concept of Primary Memory, Fergus I. M. Craik and Betty Ann Levy; Ch. 4, Capacity Limitations in Information Processing, Attention, and Memory, Richard M. Shiffrin; Ch. 5, Perceptual Learning and Attention, David LaBerge; and Ch. 6, Auditory Information Processing, Dominic W. Massaro.

Flavell, J. H. *Cognitive development*. Englewood Cliffs, New Jersey: Prentice-Hall, Inc., 1977. Pp. 183–218.

Chapter 6 provides a basic and well-organized treatment of the recent and complex literature on memory development, not readily available elsewhere. Major theoretical ideas are presented and summarized.

Ghatala, E. S., & Levin, J. R. Children's recognition memory processes. In J. R. Levin & V. L. Allen (Eds.), *Cognitive learning in children: Theories and strategies*. New York: Academic Press, 1977. Pp. 61–100.

These authors relate and explain the processes involved in recognition memory to frequency theory. Accounting for changes in recognition memory is of much significance to developmental theory.

Kail, R. V., Jr., & Hagen, J. W. *Perspectives on the development of memory and cognition*. New York: Halstead Press, 1977.

The first section of this volume is concerned with the development of basic memory processes; the second with memory development as a major component of cognitive development.

Miller, G. A., & Johnson-Laird, P. N. *Language and perception*. Cambridge, Massachusetts: Harvard University Press, 1976.

These authors provide the foundation for a new theory regarding the meaning of words, called psycholexicology. The relationships among perception, conception, and word meaning are dealt with at the level of single words, sentences, and complete structures of knowledge. The developmental aspects of language and perception, however, are referred to only incidentally. Familiarity with psychology, artificial intelligence, linguistics, philosophy, and social anthropology aids in understanding the arguments and theory.

Olson, G. M. Developmental changes in memory and the acquisition of language. In T. Moore (Ed.), *Cognitive development and the acquisition of language*. New York: Academic Press, 1973. Pp. 145–158.

Research is reviewed suggesting that increases in length of utterance cannot be explained and understood in terms of corresponding age-related increases in short-term memory span. Rather, improvements with increasing age in immediate memory span and language acquisition both reflect complex changes in the child's information-processing capacities, including ability to encode and recode, monitor, and integrate the processing and retrieval of information.

Peterson, L. R. Verbal learning and memory. In M. R. Rosenzweig & L. W. Porter (Eds.), *Annual review of psychology* (Vol. 28). Palo Alto, California: Annual Reviews Inc., 1977. Pp. 393–415.

Peterson reviews the experimental literature regarding verbal learning and memory. He gives particular attention to auditory memory, visual memory, phonemic memory, and the levels of processing information.

5

Language and Concept Attainment

Natural languages have two key aspects: structure and meaning. The structural aspect may be divided into the sound system, or phonology; the rules for the formation of words from sounds, or morphology; and the rules for combining words into phrases and sentences, referred to as syntax, or grammar. The semantic aspect of language deals with the use of words to represent the meanings associated with the individual members and classes of objects, events, and processes and the qualities and relations thereof.

Semantics plays a very important role in communication. Just as concept attainment requires empirical knowledge of the physical and social world, so also forming and comprehending spoken and written sentences demand it. Thus, it is important to try to determine the relationship between the semantics of language development and the four levels of concept attainment, which is the main emphasis of this chapter.

Describing the course of language development from infancy into adulthood is far beyond the scope of this chapter. Accounts of various aspects of language development can be found in Beilin (1975), Brown (1973), Carroll and Freedle (1972), Dale (1976), and Miller and Johnson-Laird (1976).

THE LINGUISTIC-RELATIVITY HYPOTHESIS

The relationship between language, understanding, and behavior is of high interest because of its importance in communication among people at all levels, including across national and cultural groups. Languages differ in their structure and vocabulary; the concepts symbolized by the form classes and constructions of one language often do not have exact counterparts in other languages. Does this mean that the vocabulary and the structure of the language we speak affect our perceptions of the world and our actions in it in a way that would be different if we happened to speak another language? This question is at the heart of the linguistic-relativity hypothesis, which has been most strongly stated by Whorf (1956). The hypothesis in three parts states that the vocabulary and the structure of the language one speaks control the way in which one perceives the world and how one acts, that thought is relative to the language in which it is conducted, and that a particular language implies a unique "world view," or *weltanschauung,* for those who speak it.

Bourne, Ekstrand, and Dominowski (1971) and Dale (1976) present excellent analyses of the linguistic-relativity hypothesis. The interested reader is referred to these sources for a more detailed discussion. Bourne *et al.,* following Fishman (1960), divided the linguistic-relativity hypothesis into four separate levels, each one dealing with a different aspect of the possible effects of language on behavior. The four levels result from separating language into vocabulary and grammar and inquiring about the effects of both on either world view or nonverbal behavior.

Level 1 of the analysis concerns vocabulary differences and world view. Here the hypothesis is that the differences in vocabulary among languages produce differences in the world outlooks of the people speaking them. Level 2 concerns vocabulary effects on nonverbal behavior. The linguistic-relativity hypothesis states that differences among languages in vocabulary are associated with differences in behavior, including how one classifies and also relates objects, events, qualities, feelings, and relations. Level 3 concerns linguistic structure and world view. This level is much like Level 1, which deals with vocabulary and world view, except that at this level it is asserted that the linguistic structure of a language determines the speaker's perception of reality or world view. Level 4 of the linguistic-relativity hypothesis concerns the relationship between grammatical structure and nonverbal behavior and implies that behavior is affected by grammatical structure.

After reviewing the available evidence, Bourne *et al.* (1971) found only meager support for the second level of the analysis and none for the other three, and concluded that "We do think about things in words and these words encode information—but it is the information, or knowledge, that is primarily responsible for the success of our problem-solving efforts and not the language which conveys this knowledge [p. 300]."

Dale (1976) characterizes the Whorf hypothesis as a grand and sweeping statement and the related reasoning as not very convincing. The experimental evidence regarding it is disappointing and not generally confirming, as Bourne *et al.* also concluded.

CULTURE, CONCEPTS, AND LANGUAGE

Bruner (Bruner et al., 1966, Bruner, 1973) also studied language from a cross-cultural perspective and arrived at conclusions quite different from those in Whorf's linguistic-relativity hypothesis. According to Bruner, variability among languages in the amount of vocabulary is not as critical as is implied by the hypothesis. Rather, of crucial importance are differences in the concepts, represented by words, that cultural groups do and do not attain, and especially the cultural differences in organization of concepts into supraordinate–subordinate or other systematic relations, also represented by words. Syntax is important to the extent that it permits the expression of inclusive–exclusive and other relationships among concepts.

One of the main sources of information was Bruner's study in Senegal of Wolof monolinguals, Wolof bilinguals who spoke their native language and French, and French monolinguals of elementary school age, approximately Grades 1–6. The Wolof monolinguals did not attend school whereas the other two groups did. In the Wolof language, unlike French or English, there is neither the word *color* nor the word *shape*. There are, however, words for the different colors, such as yellow and orange, and for the different shapes, such as round and not-round. Bruner's experimental tasks were arranged so that on the first of two trials the child could group on the basis of either a single color or a single shape; on the second trial the child could group on the basis of a different color or a different shape. There was a total of six trials. The monolingual Wolof, who did not have the supraordinate terms *color* and *shape*, formed their first grouping on the basis of a single color or a single shape (more often color) and then tended to group on the same color or shape for all six trials. The bilingual Wolof children, who had the supraordinate words in their French vocabularies, also grouped on a a single color or shape and tended to maintain the single basis of grouping. In contrast, each monolingual French child changed the basis of grouping at least once across the six trials. Bruner concluded that access to the conceptual hierarchies involving color and shape was available only to French monolinguals who had mastered all the semantic implications of the hierarchies. The Wolof bilinguals, who had the terms *color* and *shape* in their French vocabulary, seemed not to have acquired the concepts and relations of the hierarchical structures as had the French monolinguals. Basing his observations on this study and other cross-cultural studies, Bruner concluded that no matter how many words may be available to describe a given domain, they are of limited use as instruments of thought if they are not organized into a hierarchy that can be activated in totality. Further, the hierarchy is not merely the labels or words; rather, it is the inclusive–exclusive and other relationships of the hierarchy that are included in the meanings of the words. Thus, the Wolof bilinguals had the term *color* in their

French vocabulary but apparently did not fully comprehend how the coordinate subclasses of yellow, orange, and red were related to one another and to color.

Bruner also gathered evidence concerning the semantic aspects of grammar by asking the children at the end of each trial to give the basis of the groupings formed. Three main types of responses were made: pointing and giving no verbal response, giving the word only without including a verb in the utterance, or using a sentence. No pointing was done by French monolinguals, even those in the first grade. Some pointing was done by both the young unschooled Wolof monolinguals and Wolof bilinguals, particularly those bilinguals who had not yet started school. The pointing disappeared in both groups with advancing age. The infrequent use of sentences did not change with increasing age among the unschooled Wolof monolinguals and remained at a constantly low level; however, it increased among both the bilinguals and the French monolinguals with increased years of schooling. The greatest contrast was between the monolingual unschooled Wolof children and the bilingual Wolof children attending school. About 90% of the 11- to 13-year-old Wolof unschooled monolinguals used only words; about 90% of the Wolof bilingual sixth-graders doing the experiment in the French language used sentences.

Bruner also examined whether there was a relationship between grammatical structure and conceptual structure by observing the extent to which the supraordinate and subordinate terms appeared in the sentences that the children used and also in the nonsentences, either a word or two words that did not include a verb. From this analysis, he inferred a relationship between the language usage of the three groups and the hierarchical conceptual cores related to color and shape that the children did or did not have. Having or not having the hierarchical conceptual core was found to be positively correlated with the use of sentences in which the supraordinate term appeared.

Bruner's final conclusion was that it is schooling, or the lack of it, more than differences between languages in grammar and amount of vocabulary, that influence behavior. The categorizing behavior and skills of the schooled Wolof children by Grade 6 were far more like those of schooled children in Mexico, Alaska, and continental United States than like those of the unschooled Wolof children of Senegal. Bruner (1973) concluded:

> We may hypothesize that it is the fact of being a written language that makes French such a powerful factor in the cognitive growth of the children we have studied. For all of the semantic and syntactic features that we have discussed in relation to concept formation—a rich vocabulary that is hierarchically organized, syntactical embedding of labels, and so on—become necessary when one must communicate out of the context of immediate reference. It is precisely in this respect that written language differs from spoken. But school itself provides the same opportunity to use language out of context—even spoken language—for, to a very high degree, what one talks about are things not immediately present [p. 389].

Bruner's conclusions regarding the effects of schooling on conceptualizing behavior have been submitted to further inquiry, as shown in a review by Ginsburg and Koslowski (1976). For example, Cole and Scribner (1974) suggest that although there are multiple and interrelated effects of schooling, it is difficult to generalize across all groups and situations. They indicate that, at a minimum, schooling may promote verbalization concerning one's cognitive activities. They propose further that unschooled populations tend to solve problems singly, each as a new problem, whereas schooled populations tend to treat them as instances of classes of problems that could be solved by a general rule. Nelson and Klausmeier (1974), in accordance with Bruner's view, found that changes in the mathematics curriculum influenced the conceptualizing skills that students developed and also their level of concept achievement.

WORDS, WORD MEANINGS, AND CONCEPTS

In attempting to relate the semantic aspect of language development to conceptual development across the school years, it would be advantageous if one could clearly specify the meaning of the word for any particular concept that an individual might have at each of the four levels of attainment. This is not possible for many concepts because the conditions of learning of a particular concept and also of acquiring the words for the concept and its defining attributes vary so greatly among concepts. The name of concepts such as *cup* may be learned at about the same time that the concept is attained at the concrete level. Other concept names, such as crustacean, may not be learned until the classificatory level. There is not a one-to-one correspondence between the acquisition of words and word meanings and words and concepts for all concepts for all individuals. However, the concept (mental construct) held by a person at any level of attainment—concrete, identity, classificatory, formal—is regarded as the core of the meaning of the particular word employed by the person for the concept. Further, an individual's meaning of a word at the formal level of attainment, by definition of the formal level, closely approximates the societally accepted meaning. In this manner, the levels of attainment, words, and word meanings are relatable.

Carroll (1964a) provided a meaningful analysis of the relationship among words, meanings, and concepts as follows:

> Perhaps it is useful to think of words, meanings, and concepts as forming *three* somewhat independent series. The words in a language can be thought of as a series of physical entities—either spoken or written. Next, there exists a set of "meanings" which stand in complex relationships to the set of words. These relationships may be described by the rules of usage that have developed by the processes of socialization and communication. A "meaning" can be thought of as a standard of communicative behavior that is shared by those who speak a language. Finally, there exist "concepts"; the classes of experience formed in individuals either independently of language processes or in close dependence on language processes.

> The interrelations found among these three series are complex: almost anyone can give instances where a word may have many "meanings," or in which a given "meaning" corresponds to several different words. The relationship between societally-standardized "meanings" and individually-formed "concepts" is likewise complex, but of somewhat different nature. It is a question of how well each individual has learned these relationships, and at least in the sphere of language and concepts, education is largely a process whereby the individual learns either to attach societally-standardized words and meanings to the concepts he has already formed, or to form new concepts that properly correspond to societally-standardized words and meanings. A "meaning" of a word is, therefore, a societally-standardized concept, and when we say that a word stands for or names a concept it is understood that we are speaking of concepts that are shared among the members of a speech community [pp. 186–187].

Carroll in 1964 employed Skinnerian principles in explaining how words, word meanings, and concepts are learned and related. Miller and Johnson-Laird (1976) also offer an explanation of the relationship among words, word meanings, and concepts in dealing with perception and language. They reject Skinnerian principles in favor of information theory and regard their 1976 formulations as the first phase in building a semantic theory of language.

Whereas most linguists and many psycholinguists have concentrated first on syntactic relations and have worked from them toward semantic relations, Miller and Johnson-Laird start with word meanings, fully recognizing that the meanings of words must be compatible with the meanings of sentences in which the words are used. However, the individual's strategies for constructing sentences and interpreting them must dovetail and be integrated with procedures for developing and expressing the meanings of the words employed in the sentences. These authors suggest that this new approach to psycholinguistics, which starts with a conceptual theory of meaning, may lead to a quite different view of the relation between meaning and syntax and also more generally of the study of connected discourse. Their views are presented first and are followed by a discussion of word meanings at the four levels of concept attainment. It may be helpful to review some of the main aspects of their theory as given earlier in Chapter 4.

Lexical Concepts and Word Meanings

The meaning-conveying element of connected discourse is words and the relationships among them. For sentences to convey meaning the words and the relationships among the words must convey meaning. Every word expresses a lexical concept, which is defined as anything capable of being the meaning of a word. Lexical concepts are organized into semantic fields. Each semantic field is based on a conceptual core. In other words, lexical concepts and semantic fields are related to the real world first by means of perception and then by the subsequent organization of percepts and concepts into conceptual cores.

What is the meaning of a word, that is, a lexical concept shared by adults who speak the same language? According to Miller and Johnson-Laird (1976) there are five elements of a word meaning. However, not all words incorporate all the elements.

1. "The meaning of a word can tell you what is, and what is not, an entity that can be labeled with that word [p. 702]." For example, having the meaning of the word *tree* permits a person to identify examples of trees. The meaning includes the intrinsic attributes of a class. The word for which the meaning is held can be used as part of a person's internal, natural language instructions to search and to find (e.g., "Is this object a tree?"). This makes it possible to retrieve from secondary memory perceptual and other information to test an incoming perception in working memory. The term *natural language instructions* will be shortened hereafter to *programmatic instructions* to convey the idea of Miller and Johnson-Laird that persons use their natural language to generate computer-like instructions in the form of programs and routines to direct other internal mental operations, including the retrieval of information from secondary memory. For example, when someone asks the question "What is space?" the question is translated into natural-language programmatic instructions to find the perceptual and conceptual information stored in secondary memory regarding *space*.

The organized perceptible intrinsic attributes that are used to identify entities as belonging to the same class comprise only a partial description of the class. This partial description is designated a *perceptual paradigm* by Miller and Johnson-Laird.

2. "The meaning can tell you the function or purpose of the entity that the word labels [p. 702]." The intrinsic attributes are not sufficient for identifying the members of some concepts reliably; the inferred or stated functional attributes also must be known. For example, knowing the intrinsic attributes of *table* and *stool* does not permit reliable differentiation of all the members of both classes; knowing both the intrinsic and the functional attributes of each class does. According to Miller and Johnson-Laird, the perceptual paradigm, as noted in the preceding paragraph, along with the functional attributes, constitutes the *schema* for the particular class. A word with meaning, when used as part of internal programmatic instructions, makes possible retrieval of the schema from secondary memory by which to test incoming perceptual or verbal descriptive information. The schema is used to identify the members of the class it represents.

3. "The meaning can lead you to all you know about the entity. It has access to encyclopedic information in long-term memory [p. 702]." Objects, events, properties, and relations are experienced in contexts—that is, at particular places and particular times and under certain internal and external conditions. These kinds of contextual information that are stored may be retrieved as well as the schema.

4. "The meaning can tell you about relations between what the word labels and what other words label. The schema underlying the meaning of any word is integrated with schemata represented by other words, a part of a conceptual

system that captures conceptual relations between words [p. 702]." The schemata are organized and comprise the *conceptual core* of a semantic field. The conceptual core, which includes the critical attributes of sets of related concepts, serves as a kind of decision table that is used to test newly encountered instances as examples of the different concepts of the set.

Central to this element of meaning is knowledge of the attributes of objects, events, properties, and relations that may be related to one another in a taxonomy or hierarchy involving location, part–whole, and class inclusion. Words related in this manner to a conceptual core may be called a *semantic field*. In a taxonomy attributes of the generic class are common to all members of the taxonomy, whereas there are critical attributes that are unique to the members of each coordinate subclass. Knowledge of the critical attributes makes it possible to discriminate between members of the different coordinate subclasses, each of which is represented by a contrastive word. For example, green plant is the generic class and three coordinate subclasses are tree, shrub, and herb.

5. "The meaning of a word can tell you about what other sorts of words can occur with it in sentences. It can place syntactic and semantic constraints on other words [p. 702]." The relations among words involved in forming sentences—that is, the rules of syntax—are also an element of the meaning of a word. Children of social groups who speak the same language seem to learn these rules and relations almost effortlessly; however, explaining scientifically the relations of word meaning to syntax and syntax to word meaning, as noted earlier, is still in its infancy.

Lexical Concepts and Levels of Concept Attainment

The preceding elements of societally accepted word meanings both as separate elements and in totality may be related to ideas regarding concepts as mental constructs of individuals and as societally accepted meanings of words, to the levels of concept attainment, and to the uses of concepts.

Miller and Johnson-Laird outline a sequence of sensation → perception → concepts and the parallel labels → words as lexical concepts; they do not deal with attainment of concepts developmentally or with the development of increasingly comprehensive and valid meanings. They treat words as either labels having no meaning or as lexical concepts having full meaning as defined by the five elements. The meaning of a word as defined by the preceding five elements refers, then, to a societally accepted meaning, not to the meaning that different individuals may have who speak or hear the word, except as those individuals also have the societally accepted definition. However, persons who have not attained the concept at the formal level may also have not attained the societally accepted meaning of the word or words expressing the concept.

We should be aware that Miller and Johnson-Laird use a procedural approach to semantics that draws heavily on computer simulation for the verification of the theoretical formulations. Words and the societally accepted meanings of words are not organized and stored by a person in the manner of an unabridged dictionary. The human organization is more like that of *Roget's Thesaurus* (1962) of English words and phrases. In the *Thesaurus* many separate words are related to eight supraordinate classes. Each class has a conceptual core, organized into four hierarchical levels. In the total system the lowest levels are represented by a total of 1040 words representing the same number of mutually exclusive subclasses. Almost any word in a person's spoken vocabulary can be related to these 1040 subclasses, which in turn are related to the successively higher classes of each of the eight primary classes. To use the *Thesaurus,* one goes to an alphabetized list of words and word phrases, finds a number, and uses this number to find the word in the main part of the *Thesaurus,* where it is related to the 1040 subclasses. This kind of strategy for gaining access to the content of the *Thesaurus* bears some resemblance to retrieving information from the conceptual cores in the five memory locations identified by Miller and Johnson-Laird.

ELEMENTS OF WORD MEANING AND CLD THEORY

Miller and Johnson-Laird treat a label as a name for something that has no meaning; however, as noted in the previous section, they regard a word as a lexical concept, the societally accepted meaning of the word. In CLD theory four levels of attaining the same concept are indicated. A word that any person may have for expressing the concept at each of the four levels has a meaning corresponding to the level of the concept attained, the formal level corresponding to the societally accepted meaning. Once learned, concepts are used in three main ways but the uses are not included as part of the societally accepted definition, as indicated by Miller and Johnson-Laird. These kinds of differences are now examined in more detail.

According to Miller and Johnson-Laird, a label may be stored along with the percept of the particular object, event, quality, or relation. The label, though having no meaning but having been stored with the percept serves, when heard later and translated as part of internal instructions, to retrieve the percept from secondary memory.

A young child might attain a concept at either the concrete or identity level, hear the word spoken when the particular object or property is experienced, and store the label with the percept, or image, of the object along with other contextual cues. When the label is heard subsequently in the absence of the same object, the label might be used in retrieving the percept from secondary memory. As indicated earlier, a label is not essential for attaining a concept at the concrete or identity level. However, when the word is acquired simultaneously with the concept at these two lower levels and functions in this manner to retrieve a concrete- or identity-level image from secondary memory, it is no longer a meaningless label. Rather, the word carries a low level of meaning corresponding to the level at which the concept has been attained. That is, the word represents the individual's meaning of the particular entity that has been discriminated from other entities in the environment.

If the word is in the speaking or reading vocabulary of the person who has attained a concept at the classificatory level, the word then has a meaning that in turn enables the individual to identify members, or examples, comprising the class and to discriminate these from members of other classes. Some, but not necessarily all, of the intrinsic and functional defining attributes of the class are incorporated in the meaning of the word corresponding to the classificatory level.

The meaning of the word accompanying a person's attainment of a concept at the formal level includes the first three elements of the lexical concept definition—that is, the meaning includes the intrinsic and functional attributes of the concept and other contextual information, enabling the person to identify members of the class of concepts and also to evaluate newly encountered instances as members or not members of the class in terms of the absence or presence of the defining attributes.

The fourth element of word meaning stated by Miller and Johnson-Laird is that a word's meaning can tell you about relations between what the word labels and other words label. Its schema is integrated with schemata represented by other words. In the CLD formulation, this element is not included directly in the meaning of a word that parallels attainment of the concept at the formal level inasmuch as the use of a concept in understanding taxonomic and other hierarchical relations is not considered as part of the concept. Instead, the concept at the formal level, as well as at the classificatory level, serves as a tool of thought to be used in understanding taxonomic and other hierarchical relations. Moreover, when an individual has formed a comprehensive cognitive structure corresponding to a complete taxonomy or other hierarchy, any single word meaning that is part of the structure may be related to the meaning of every other word meaning of the complete structure.

Having the meaning of the words representing the concepts included in principles and in hierarchical and other structures of knowledge is prerequisite for understanding the relations among them, but it is not sufficient. Feldman (1974) tested the sufficiency hypothesis in connection with the understanding of principles. Even though students had attained all the key concepts of the principle, they did not fully understand the principle, apparently because understanding the relationship among the concepts requires a higher level or different kind of thought. We will see in Chapter 8 also that, in general, mastery of the uses of concepts follows mastery of the formal level.

As a person attains concepts at the classificatory and formal levels that are represented by words called *nouns, verbs,* etc., the accompanying meanings may also then place syntactic and semantic constraints on the other words in sentences, the fifth element of a lexical concept as defined by Miller and Johnson-Laird. This aspect of word meaning and cognitive development was not investigated specifically as part of the longitudinal study or in any of our controlled experimentation. It is presumed, however, that developmentally, as a word with increasing meaning is heard being used in sentences, constraints concerning its use and meaning in the sentence are also learned. Tiemann, Kroeker, and Markle (1977) and Markle (1977) report that some college students have not developed this aspect of meaning of many relatively simple words that are used to express supraordinate and subordinate relationships.

DEVELOPMENTAL LEVELS OF WORD MEANING

Imagine that a young child is attending to an object that has been placed on the table near a plate. While the child attends to the object, the parent says, "knife." The word *knife* heretofore has had no meaning to the child, even though it may have been experienced before as an aural sensation. At this point, however, there are simultaneously two phenomenal patterns held in the child's working memory. One is the visual image of the knife and of elements of the context in which it is experienced; the other is the oral presentation of the spoken word *knife*. The child stores the image, contextual cues, and word in secondary memory. Assume that the child attends to other things for a short time and cannot see the knife. The word *knife* is now heard and attended to. It elicits the image and contextual cues. The visual image, plus any contextual elements, is the child's meaning of the word *knife,* not as a percept, but as an object of permanence, identifiable by the features included in the image and by the contextual cues.

Let us assume now that a child says the word *knife* on the next experience with knife in the same situation. Assume also that the child already has learned that words are used as names for objects and qualities and that the word *knife* names the object being experienced. If these assumptions are met, then the child's spoken word *knife* also has the meaning corresponding to the concrete-level concept just discussed. Recall that it is not essential to have the word for the object in the speaking or listening vocabulary in order to attain a concept at any level except formal, but that the word may be in the listening vocabulary, speaking vocabulary, or both at any level, including concrete, identity, and classificatory.

Assume that some time later the child experiences the same knife in different orientations and contexts and, as outlined in Chapter 4, organizes and stores the images and elements of the context. This is the identity level of attainment. At this level, the meaning of the word *knife* is increased above that of the concrete level to include object permanence across orientation and context and also any other attributes of the knife that may have been discriminated, patterned, organized, and stored in secondary memory. As shown in Chapter 3 in discussing developmental trends, there is a regular progression in the ability to attend to and discriminate the attributes of concepts as the number of examples and nonexamples to attend to increases and as the objects become increasingly alike.

Assume that some time later the child has attained the identity level of two different knives, recognizes their common defining attributes, and treats the two knives as members of the same class. The child has formed a concept of *knife* at the beginning classificatory level. The word meaning now consists of the defining attributes, including functional, that have been discriminated, patterned, and represented internally, any contextual cues that may have been stored, and any other iconic or semantic content that may have been related to the concept *knife*. As the child subsequently has more experience with knives and other objects, qualities, etc., and more language experiences, a more accurate and inclusive classificatory-level concept will be formed. When the child is asked, "What is a knife?" the classificatory-level trace retrieved from secondary memory will probably include a visual image of knife; one or more of the words that indicate such attributes as *sharp, to cut with, smooth edge;* and other information, including the different contexts in which the individual has used knives and seen others using knives. Concepts of other eating tools, including *spoon* and *fork*, and of other *cutting tools,* including *file* and *saw,* will also have been attained. Visual and semantic information regarding these concepts may also be retrieved and included, not directly in the meaning of *knife* but as part of the conceptual core for the taxonomy *cutting tools,* or *things used to cut.* At this level the words representing some of the defining attributes and their meanings will also have been learned.

The formal level of attainment by definition requires having the words for the concept and for the defining attributes. At this level, as at the classificatory level, that part of the formal-level secondary trace that includes any image and some of the defining attributes is probably all that is required to discriminate between frequently encountered examples and nonexamples. Additional information is useful in relating the concept to the conceptual core and also in using the concept in the three ways indicated. The formal-level trace of the particular concept is presumed to be organized as part of the conceptual core of the taxonomy or hierarchy that enables a person to differentiate between the members of two or more coordinate classes and to handle inclusion relations in supraordinate classes.

The preceding description of the development of word meaning is based on an extension and synthesis of perceptual theory as formulated by Gibson (1969), semantic theory of Miller and Johnson-Laird (1976), and analysis of the tasks employed in our experiments with children of school age. As we shall now see, recent experiments and theorizing provide interesting accounts concerning the early learning of concepts, words, and word meanings.

Nelson and Bonvillian (1973) carried out a 6-month longitudinal study of young children's acquisition of words for different experimental objects. Five boys and five girls and their parents participated in the study. The age of the children ranged from 16.2 months to 17.5 months at the commencement of the study.

The 16 two-syllable words introduced as part of the experiment were noun names that no child had used at the start of the study. Words such as *barrel, pulley, silo,* and *whetstone* were used. The objects or referents for the 16 words, used only in the experimental sessions, either did not typically appear in the homes of the children, or the parents agreed not to speak the words or use the referents of the words in the child's presence except during the experimental sessions involving the mother and the child.

Six objects for each word and the 16 words were introduced to the child in the first two experimental sessions. Each mother was instructed to employ whatever method she judged natural to draw her child's attention to the objects in these two experimental sessions and to teach the child the appropriate words for the experimental objects in the later sessions. One constraint was that, throughout the study, half of the objects should be used in teaching the names and the other half not used; a second constraint was that the mother should provide no corrective feedback to the child. There were 16 experimental sessions, one per week, in which the mother proceeded in this manner. Audio tapes were used to record the results of each session. The child's manipulation of the objects was also observed and inferences were drawn concerning correct and incorrect naming of the objects. If the child properly associated two or more of the six objects with the name, it was concluded that a concept had been formed (corresponding to the beginning classificatory level).

Three conclusions were drawn. First, the children learned both the concepts and the words that named the concepts, despite the fact that there were relatively few encounters with the concept examples, few adult demonstrations of how the objects should be named, and virtually no corrective feedback.

The second conclusion was that the routes to word acquisition and word meaning in the sense of giving the correct names to the objects varied markedly among the children. Surprisingly, the most common route, accounting for over two-thirds of the cases of concept attainment, was applying the word correctly to new examples of the concept, those not used by the mother in her informal teaching. A second route involved initially focusing on one feature of an object and then on another, apparently unsystematically, but subsequently focusing on one or more defining attributes.

A third alternative involved shifting systematically from initial naming, based only on the most obvious and general features of the objects—as, for example, when the word *pulley* was applied to all the objects that had a similar shape to pulley—to naming based upon more of the defining attributes of pulley, and finally to naming based on one or more specific perceptible or functional attributes. Thus, the early overgeneralizing disappeared.

A final path preceding correct naming was to use the word initially in a consistent but overrestricted manner (undergeneralization), basing the naming on one or more specific features or functions of the objects. For example, only one attribute of an object, such as *brown*, was attended to and the name of the object, such as *pulley*, was applied to the brown pulleys only.

The authors could not determine the reason for the variability among the children in employing these different routes that preceded correct naming and classifying. They were especially impressed that about two-thirds of the children neither overgeneralized nor undergeneralized; results of prior research might have led to an opposite conclusion.

A final conclusion was that children varied greatly in their conceptualizing and naming abilities. The individual differences were sharp. Of the objects named by the mother, the range in correct naming by the child ranged from a mean of .4 for the boys to 19.6 for the girls; the similar range for the objects not named by the mother was from .2 for the boys to 8.4 for the girls.

K. Nelson (1974) (one of three Nelsons cited in this chapter) formulated a conceptual model to explain the formation of concepts by the preverbal child and the relation of concept formation to language development, particularly the acquisition of vocabulary and the beginnings of syntax. Her model is a synthesis and extension of concept formation theory, semantic feature theory, and Piagetian theory.

According to Nelson, individual objects are perceived as wholes and are conceptualized by infants as early as 12 months of age, prior to the age at which they have acquired comprehensible vocabulary or object permanence. (We would treat this as the forming of a percept, not a concept at the concrete level.)

A major proposition of the model is that at about 12 months of age the preverbal child starts to translate the dynamic functional relations of objects experienced in the immediate environment into conceptual "core" meanings. It is to these primitive core meanings that identificational features of concept instances, and also words, are later attached. The conceptual core for any concept or set of concepts continuously enlarges.

According to the theory, the preverbal child forms concepts of separate objects before learning that objects have permanence. Further, the concept is not represented internally as an image of the object but as a core meaning, consisting of dynamic functional relationships arising through the interaction of the child with the object. Attending to and discriminating features or attributes of the object, which are essential to subsequently recognizing the object as the same object over time and then later to classifying similar objects, follow from and after the core meaning. The process of concept formation, starting with acquiring the initial core meaning, or primitive concept, and leading to being able to classify two objects as belonging to the same class may be illustrated with *ball*.

Imagine that Billy focuses his attention upon a not previously conceptualized object, a ball, which serves as a center for his interaction with the ball in situations with his mother. Out of this interaction certain actions and relationships emerge. In the living room and on the porch, Billy sees Mother throw, pick up, and hold the ball. Billy throws, picks up, and holds the ball. The ball rolls, bounces on the floor, under the couch, etc. The core meaning of this object, ball, based on these interactions with Mother and ball across time consists of relations of the ball to self, to Mother, to the place where the interactions occur, and to the actions and the effects of the actions. This ball now exists for Billy only phenomenally in one of these relations in the specific situation, not outside of them. To form a concept of this ball (at what we would call the identity level), Billy must synthesize over time the various relations into which the ball enters. This functional synthesis is the core of Billy's concept, his core meaning of ball.

Once functional synthesis has taken place with regard to this ball—that is, once a core meaning has been established—other balls may be grouped within the same functional synthesis. For example, Billy may see "Boy" on a playground throw or catch another ball. That ball rolls and bounces over the ground, under a fence, etc. Certain functions and relations in this situation are the same as those for the first ball: the ball rolling and bouncing, someone throwing. Here the relations involving location and actor are different, but the actions are the same. Boy in this second situation stands in the same relation to the movements of ball (i.e., rolling, bouncing) as do "Mother" and "I" in the first situation. Nelson labels the relationships in the two situations as follows:

> Location of activity: living room, porch, playground
> Actor: Mother, I, boy
> Action: throw, pick up, hold, catch
> Movement of ball: roll, bounce
> Location of object: on floor, under couch, under fence, etc. [p. 277].

Nelson indicates that to recognize new instances of ball outside the context of its core movements and its relationships to persons and places, the child must depend upon additional identifying information. Billy needs to be able to pick out a ball from other objects when the balls are not in action or being acted on. In order to do this, he needs to attend to and discriminate one or more of the distinctive features of balls. Billy will probably attend to and discriminate some salient features, such as color or form. Nelson assumes that this process may begin shortly after the initial core meaning is formed. Attending to and discriminating distinctive features is not discontinuous with the "core" primitive concept formation process.

With further interactions in various situations, Billy's internal representation of the concept *ball* contains the perceptual–descriptive information as well as the earlier-mentioned functional–relational information. Billy, in these interactive situations, may also hear words that represent the agent of action—*ball, baseball*; the actor—*I, Mama*; the action—*throw, pick up, catch, hold*; movement of the ball—*roll, bounce*; nonfunction features of the balls experienced—*red, round, large, small*; locations where the interactions occurred—*living room, basement, street*; and locations of the ball—*in the air, on the ground, on the floor, behind the couch*. Nelson outlines how various words come to have meaning—that is, to express the object of action, the action, features, etc.—and also relates this to the child's learning of syntax, starting with sentential relations incorporated in single words.

Nelson's theory describes concept formation and the development of word meaning in the absence of informal or formal instruction. Strongly emphasized is the idea that it is the functions of the objects and the child's actions on them, not the static features of the objects, that serve as the basis of primitive concept formation. To these functional core relationships and relations involving the actor and location, the descriptive features and the names are added. As we have seen in the work of the coauthors K. E. Nelson and Bonvillian (1973), both acquiring names and classifying proceed very rapidly in children 18–24 months of age when the parent names and points to objects in the presence of the child. Nelson's (1974) theory does not account for this later development.

These promising beginnings in the description and explanation of the relationship between concept formation and the semantic and syntactical aspects of language development, if continued with older children in both informal and formal educational settings, should greatly extend our knowledge of this most critical area of human cognitive development.

Word Meanings, Concepts, and Sentence Meanings

Learning and communication are heavily dependent upon a person's being able to comprehend the meaning of sentences. In turn, comprehending a sentence requires having the meanings of the words in the sentence and also understanding the relationship among the words; in other words, comprehension involves understanding the semantic content of the sentence and also its grammatical structure.

Carroll (1968) analyzed what was involved in understanding the simple sentence "Robins fly north in the spring." Understanding the sentence involves perception of the separate base structures that can be roughly indicated as:

> *robins fly*
> *fly north*
> *north in spring* (as opposed to *south in fall*)

[p. 6]

Comprehension of the sentence organized into base structures in this manner depends at least upon the following recognitions:

(1) The lack of a determiner shows that robins are spoken of as a generic class (contrast *The robins . . . ; Some robins . . .*).
(2) *Robins* are birds (contrast *The [people named] Robbins fly north in the spring [by airplane]*).
(3) *Fly* is a verb (contrast *The robin's fly*) and because of (2) probably implies a kind of self-locomotion characteristic of birds. Contrast with *Flags fly on Flag Day; Boys fly kites*. But consider also the possible question *Do robins fly kites?*
(4) The verb tense indicates "usual or customary action" as contrasted with what would be implied by *Robins are [unexpectedly] flying south this spring.*
(5) *North* is a direction of the compass and indicates the direction of motion when used

in association with a verb of motion. Contrast *Robins invade the north in the spring,* which shows the force of the determiner *the*.

(6) *Spring* is a season of the year. At least, this is the obvious interpretation. Conceivably, *spring* might be a spirally-coiled mechanical device in the interior of which robins could fly; or it might be a source of water, as in *Robins bathe in the spring.* Thus the sentence might appear ambiguous to a computer translation program [p. 7].

Though it is essential to have word meanings to comprehend sentences, it also is true that contextual cues are provided in the sentence to help identify the specific meaning a word may have. Without the contextual cue, the person does not comprehend some of the words that may be used in the sentence. The word *fly* may be used as a noun or as a verb; in the preceding example the syntax indicates that it is a verb. Similarly, because one knows the attributes of robins as birds, one recognizes that *fly* implies self-locomotion.

A single sentence is a meaningful unit of communication. Most information, however, is communicated not in a single sentence, but in a series of sentences. Printed instructional material can be written to present information to teach concepts in a precise manner, as we shall see in Chapter 9.

FACILITATIVE EFFECTS OF LANGUAGE AND CONCEPT ATTAINMENT

Although having the names of the concepts is not essential for attaining the first three levels, it is facilitative; also, it is prerequisite for attaining the formal level. Using the names in sentences when communicating with and instructing children and youth facilitates all levels of attainment under appropriate learning conditions. This was reported in some detail in the earlier account of the relationships between language and concept attainment by Klausmeier, Ghatala, and Frayer (1974). Some representative studies from the earlier work, more recent studies, and the main conclusions follow. We found it useful to combine the concrete and identity levels inasmuch as research on verbal cuing and object recognition cannot be clearly differentiated according to these two levels.

Language and the Concrete and Identity Levels

Language in the form of verbal instructions giving the name of the concept facilitates attending to objects (Staats, 1971). For example, the individual's attention is directed toward an object by such instructions as "look at the cup" and "here is the cup." In the case of young children with a limited listening and speaking vocabulary, physical actions such as pointing may also be necessary to supplement the verbal commands. Does having the names for objects, qualities, and actions also help one discriminate and remember them? It is clear that having the appropriate labels does not alter one's absolute capacity to discriminate among things when they are perceptually very similar (Carroll, 1964a). The detection of a small difference between things, as in a psychological experiment, appears to be a function of sensory ability and is little affected by verbal labeling. However, there is evidence that learning distinctive labels for objects and qualities facilitates later acquisition of discriminative responses to the stimuli.

Norcross (1958) demonstrated that children who learned distinctive labels for faces (e.g., *wug, kos*) showed better transfer to a task in which they learned to push a particular button for each face than children who learned similar names (e.g., *zim, zam*) for the faces. Thus, having distinctive names for things facilitated discriminative responding to them.

G. K. Nelson (1976) studied children's attainment of concepts at the concrete, identity, and classificatory levels. The experimental materials were geometric blocks. The five experimental conditions consisted of (1) visual inspection of the blocks one at a time, (2) visual inspection plus motor training consisting of free haptic play and tactile–kinesthetic exercises guided by the experimenter, (3) visual inspection plus verbal-orienting instructions consisting of giving the child the names of some of the perceptible defining attributes, (4) visual inspection plus motor plus verbal-orienting instructions, and (5) unrelated play activity. The amount of time for each condition was held constant. Fifty children at each of two age levels, 3 and 5 years, were tested on a variety of recognition and classification tasks and on transfer tasks immediately after the training session. The three combinations of visual with verbal and motor instruction (conditions 2, 3, and 4) were equally effective and significantly more effective than the visual only or the unrelated play for both the 3-year-old group and the 5-year-old group. Under all five conditions the 5-year-olds performed significantly better than the 3-year-olds, and they profited relatively less from the motor training in attaining concepts at the classificatory level. Apparently, motor training facilitated discriminating the attributes of the concept examples and the 3- and 5-year-old children therefore attained the concepts at the concrete and identity levels as well as when verbal instruction was added. At the classificatory level, the verbal instruction was more facilitative for the 5-year-olds, who were also more capable of classifying than the 3-year-olds. In the next section of this chapter, we shall see that other experimenters have also found that verbal cuing aids learners when the classificatory-level task is not too easy or too difficult. In the Nelson study it was too difficult for the 3-year-olds.

Let us now turn to the question of whether having names for things enhances memory for them. It would seem that attaching distinctive labels to things should facilitate recognition memory. The evidence on this matter is not clear-cut. Paivio (1971) reviewed the experiments dealing with effects of labeling pretraining on the subsequent recognition memory for nonverbal (visual) material. His summary statement gives perhaps the clearest picture regarding this issue:

> verbal labels do not consistently facilitate recognition memory for nonverbal stimuli, although such labels can be helpful under certain conditions. The general nature of those conditions can be inferred from some of the findings. Klapp (1969) found that codability of colors correlated highly with recognition memory for the colors in the case of subjects with poor visual memory but not subjects with good visual memory. Amount or pretraining with distinctive labels had no effect in the Vanderplas and Garvin (1959b) study, in which the labels were meaningless trigrams, whereas practice was effective (especially with more complex stimuli) in the Ellis and Muller (1964) study, in which the labels were meaningful words. Finally, Clark found that reported coding predicted recognition accuracy for complex forms but not for simple forms. The emerging pattern is that verbal coding may be effectively used when such codes are readily available and when the subjects find it difficult to store the nonverbal information in memory either because they have poor visual memory or because the stimulus is complex. However, verbal coding need not be resorted to if (a) the subject has good visual memory, (b) the stimuli are simple shapes or familiar objects that can be stored as uncoded images, or (c) the verbal code (e.g., a nonsense syllable) is not readily available in the subject's response repertoire [p. 189].

The conclusion appears to be that though having the names of objects *can* enhance recognition memory in certain situations, it is not a necessary condition.

Language and the Classificatory Level

The facilitative effects of being instructed regarding the names of the concepts to be learned at the classificatory level are generally recognized. The facilitating effects have been interpreted as due to mediating between the environmental input and the individual's responding (Kendler, Glasman, & Ward, 1972); enhancing the distinctiveness of the concept examples (Cantor, 1965; Miller & Dollard, 1941); and enhancing the individual's sensitivity to the defining attributes of the concepts (Tighe & Tighe, 1968). It is probable that in different real-life situations as well as under a variety of experimental conditions, all of these and other interpretations are plausible. For example, Osler and Madden (1973) carried out a series of experiments with kindergarten and second-grade children to ascertain more definitively the role of verbal labels and perceptual cues in children's attainment of concepts at the classificatory level. They found that direct verbal cuing and perceptual training equally facilitated classifying. The perceptual training involved practice in visually matching the defining attributes without any naming. The verbal cuing consisted of directly telling the child every 16 trials to look for things red, blue, round, or square—the four attributes that defined the single-attribute concepts used in the experiment. Since the effects of the verbal cuing and perceptual training were equal, the verbal labels were inferred not to have served as verbal mediators; also they did not have the other two effects. The verbal labels and the perceptual cues facilitated classifying because they aided the individuals to divide the complete set of instances into the subsets or classes that in turn were correlated with the classifying they learned to do.

Along similar lines, Carey and Goss (1957), Goss and Moylan (1958), and Dietze (1955) also found facilitative effects of giving names of concepts. The main conclusion of these studies was that having the names of different categories results in increased intracategory similarity and decreased intercategory similarity, which in turn facilitates placement of things into their proper categories.

The effects of verbal cuing on attaining concepts at the classificatory level appear to be related to the individual's level of classifying ability. Landau and Hagen (1974) studied the effects of verbal cuing on concept acquisition and retention in normally developing and mentally retarded children. The cuing in each trial consisted of the experimenter's selecting one of six three-dimensional blocks used in the classification task, giving one of the block's defining attributes, and asking the child to find other blocks like it. Children at an intermediate level in conceptualizing ability profited from the cuing, whereas those more advanced, who could readily group and regroup the blocks, and those least advanced did not.

Wagner (1975) carried out a study to determine the effects of labeling on short-term memory rather than on classifying. Overt verbal labeling facilitated recall in younger children of age 7–11 by focusing attention on the relevant items; however, it impeded rehearsal in older individuals of age 13–21. Despite the fact that overt labeling impeded rehearsal, short-term memory was still better for the older students than for the younger ones.

To conclude, giving students the names of concepts and other verbal cues facilitates attainment of concepts at the classificatory level when the children are capable of using the labels and when the task is not so easy that verbal labels or other cues are not helpful. There is no substantial agreement among experimenters concerning the internal mechanisms that might explain the facilitative effects. Explanation in terms of increasing intraclass similarity and decreasing interclass similarity appears plausible.

Language and Hypothesizing Behavior at the Formal Level

Earlier, in Chapters 1 and 3, the inductive approach to concept attainment at the formal level was explained as formulating and evaluating hypotheses and inferring the concept. Language, including having the names of the defining attributes, is essential for the effective formulation of hypotheses. It also facilitates the evaluation of hypotheses. Evaluation of hypotheses involves (1) processing a current hypothesis against evidence in order to classify members of a concept population, and (2) utilizing information concerning the correctness of the classification to modify the current hypothesis if it is not correct. The first step in evaluating an hypothesis, using a focusing strategy as explained in Chapter 4, can be represented as a sequence of decisions involving tests of the hypothesized individual attributes (or values of the same attribute). Thus, attribute by attribute, individuals check their successive choices of instances against their hypotheses. Persons can be viewed as "asking themselves questions" concerning the correspondence between the current hypothesis and the instance. Moreover, these "questions" are asked in sequential fashion, and whether or not a next question is asked depends upon the outcome of the preceding question. For example, if the hypothesis of *equilateral triangle* is "a plane closed figure with three sides of equal length," the decision is made whether or not to classify figure X as an example of the concept by asking, "Is it a plane figure?" If the answer is yes, then the person asks, "Is it a closed figure?" If the answer to successive questions regarding attributes continues to be yes, then the testing continues. If the answer to any question is no, then no further questions are needed—the figure is classified as "not an equilateral triangle." The preceding is an example of serial processing of information. Verbal codes are especially adapted for carrying out tasks involving serial processing (Paivio, 1971). This is not to say that visual images could not also be used in processing hypotheses. The contention is that verbal codes are more efficient for this type of mental operation than are other types of codes.

The second step in evaluating hypotheses is utilizing informative feedback following each successive choice of instances to modify one's current hypothesis. It appears that persons who are efficient concept learners utilize logical rules of inference when forced to modify a current hypothesis. An example of the use of a logical rule of inference might be the following: "If this large figure and this small figure are both members of the class, then size is not a defining attribute." Again, logical reasoning of the kind just cited may be facilitated with the use of visual images. It would appear, however, that such "if-then" reasoning involves proper ordering or sequencing of ideas for which verbal codes are highly efficient. Marliave (1976) found that pretraining in formulating and evaluating hypotheses facilitated attainment of concepts at the formal level but that it was not sufficient. Being able to synthesize and to infer are apparently also necessary.

Language and Inferring a Concept Definition

In an inductive approach at the formal level of concept attainment, the learner infers and states the definition of the concept in terms of its defining attributes. In order to accomplish this, the learner must have language competence sufficient for the formulation of statements that will be accepted and understood by the particular speech community. In addition, formulation of societally accepted definitions often requires the acquisition of new terminology or a different use of terminology that may already have been acquired.

Persons typically learn to classify correctly some members of concepts before being able to provide societally accepted definitions of the concepts. These persons have attained the concepts at the classificatory but not the formal level. Johnson and O'Reilly (1964) speculated that children's ability to give acceptable definitions may well be increased by practice in defining concepts verbally. The two conditions of the Johnson and O'Reilly study that are directly relevant to the preceding hypothesis are now described.

A concept-identification task was administered to children (11–12 years of age) under a reception paradigm. The children were shown pictures of birds that varied on three attributes: wing color (red, yellow, or blue), tail color (orange, green, or black), and beak conformation (short and pointed, long and pointed, or hooked). The children were told that they were to learn the difference between a "gunkle bird" and a "bunkle bird" and that the differences consisted of a single thing rather than a combination of things (e.g., all gunkle birds had black tails). The children were then presented with pictures one at a time and required to guess whether each was a bunkle or a gunkle bird. This classification training continued until 10 consecutive correct responses were made. Following classification training, all the children were given the defining test—they were asked to state how to tell a gunkle bird from a bunkle bird.

During classification training, one group of children was given practice in defining. After each five pictures, these children were asked to guess how to tell a gunkle bird from a bunkle bird. No evaluation of their answers was given. The other group of subjects was not given practice in defining the concept. The results were that the children given practice in defining gave almost twice as many acceptable definitions, as determined by independent judges, as did children not given such practice. This result occurred despite the fact that the children in the defining group were not given feedback on their definitions. The authors concluded that even a small amount of practice in formulating verbal definitions without knowledge of results improves performance on a defining test.

Language and Reception Learning at the Formal Level

For most children formal schooling marks the point at which oral and written language begin to be used extensively to communicate in the absence of direct experiencing of concept examples and nonexamples. As children progress further into their school years, concepts are learned to the successively higher levels increasingly by verbal means. In a parallel manner, there is less inductive inferring of concepts solely through experiences with examples and nonexamples and more reception learning in which information is provided orally and in written form, supported with actual examples, verbal examples, drawings, or other representations of the concept and its attributes. We do not suggest that most concept learning is solely inductive or reception; rather, it is usually more one or the other. In reception learning, most of the information is provided to learn the concepts; however, the learners must transfer their knowledge in order to identify and evaluate instances as examples or nonexamples and also to use their concepts in understanding principles and in solving problems. Some inductive learning is necessarily involved in the transfer process.

Information to teach concepts may be presented orally or in written language and also by means of audiovisual aids of many kinds. A design for preparing written instructional materials to aid students to move from the classificatory to the formal level is given in Chapter 9. The research on which the design is based is also presented there, including experiments dealing with the effects of presenting a societally accepted definition of the concept to be learned, the use of advance organizers, and a variety of commonly used verbal methods of instruction.

Language and Strategies for Acquiring and Remembering Information

One powerful role of language in concept attainment at the classificatory and formal levels involves the retrieval of conceptual cores from secondary memory, relating information to the core, and organizing all the information to form a more comprehensive core. Ausubel (1963, 1968, 1977) gives one explanation of how this occurs by means of derivative, correlative, and combinatorial subsumption. This use of language in attaining concepts is thus directly related to the knowledge one has already acquired and one's means of relating new experiences to the existing knowledge. The means may be called a strategy, in this case, a relating–organizing strategy.

Language is also used in an elaborative way. Elaboration as defined by Rohwer (1973) is less comprehensive than the relating–organizing strategy. In elaboration, two or more things may get connected or differentiated in some way. For example, a person might raise a question mentally or read a statement concerning a likeness or difference between mollusks and reptiles. This information could be used in attaining a more exact concept of mollusk and reptile at the classificatory or formal level. Elaboration, as relating and organizing, also requires a knowledge base so that new information can be related to it.

Rehearsal involves the repetition of items. Young children in particular frequently repeat words they have heard, whereas older children and adults repeat nonmeaningful series of items, such as telephone numbers, addresses, names, and other items they want to remember.

Although these three strategies may involve nonverbal images, particularly by younger children, persons use verbal strategies increasingly as their language competence increases. Flavell (1977) suggests that rehearsal probably precedes elaboration ontogenetically.

DEVELOPMENTAL TRENDS IN ACQUIRING CONCEPT DEFINITIONS
AND NAMES OF CONCEPTS AND DEFINING ATTRIBUTES

Acquiring Definitions

Definitions of the concepts *cutting tool, tree, equilateral triangle,* and *noun* were formulated as part of a concept analysis used in the longitudinal study. Definitions stated in nontechnical vocabulary were used as the correct choices in a multiple-choice item to measure students' attainment of the definition. The nontechnical vocabulary was employed so as not to penalize students with a limited vocabulary. The definition items for *noun* and *tree* follow to illustrate the students' task:

Which of the following is the definition of noun?

a. a word that indicates one action or being

b. a word that indicates one or more actions or beings

c. a word that names one person, place, or thing

d. a word that names one or more persons, places, or things

e. I don't know.

Which of the following is the definition of tree?

a. any living thing with leaves

b. a plant that lives for many years and has a single main stem that is woody

c. a plant that lives one year and has a single main stem that is nonwoody

d. any plant that grows well in a forest

e. I don't know.

More sensitive items could have been constructed that would have called for recognition of the critical attributes of each concept—for example, those that are needed to discriminate between trees and plants of the two coordinate classes (i.e., shrubs and herbs). Use of more technical terms would have been required. The decision was made, therefore, to include all the defining attributes of *tree* in the correct choice and not to include the critical attributes of each shrub and herb in other choices. Retrospectively, it might have been effective to construct and use both kinds of items and also to have had at least 10 items dealing with definitions. However, the amount of testing time required of the participating students and the related disruption of their class activities were already great.

The smoothed curves portraying students' rate of acquiring the definitions of

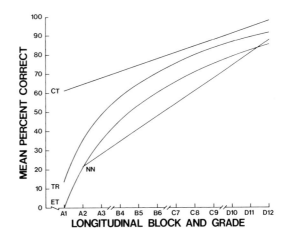

Figure 5.1.   Development related
to acquiring concept definitions.

cutting tool, tree, equilateral triangle, and *noun* are given in Figure 5.1. The mean score of the students of Longitudinal Block A when in Grade 1 was 61% for *cutting tool.* The rate of increase across the grades within this block and across the other blocks was uniform, and the students of Block D when in Grade 12 scored 98% correct. There was a rapid increase in the acquisition of the definitions of *equilateral triangle* and *tree* by the students of Longitudinal Blocks A and B and then a decelerating rate of increase by the students of Blocks C and D. The mean percentage correct for *equilateral triangle* was 86 in Grade 12. Acquisition of the definition of *noun* started at 22% correct in Grade 2 (a chance level) the first year this test was administered. There was a uniform increase across the grades thereafter. In Grade 12 the mean percentage correct was 88. From Grades 3 through 11 the order of acquiring the definitions, from highest to lowest percentage correct, was *cutting tool, tree, equilateral triangle,* and *noun*; at most grade levels the difference between the percentages correct for the four concepts was quite large.

We may conclude that acquiring the definitions of concepts starts for some children during the primary school years and continues for some students throughout the high school years. The development of lexical concepts, as defined earlier by Miller and Johnson-Laird, proceeds quite slowly throughout the school years. The difference in the rate at which the definitions of different concepts are acquired is quite large until the senior high school years. This difference among the concepts is attributed primarily to the two conditions discussed earlier in Chapter 3—that is, the concrete–abstract dimension of the concept examples and the informal experiences and formal education of the students with the definitions. Judging from the mean performances of the students when in Grade 12, we conjecture that some students will not develop mature lexical concepts of *noun* and *equilateral triangle* (and of many other equally important concepts) under present conditions of schooling.

Names of Concepts and Defining Attributes

The list of names for each of the four concepts and their defining attributes follows: *cutting tool*—tool, blade, toothed blade, smooth blade; *tree*—green plant, stem, woody stem, perennial, roots, seeds, leaves, broad leaves, needles, flowers, cones, deciduous, coniferous; *equilateral triangle*—triangle, equal, angle, side, closed, plane, simple; and *noun*—word, proper noun, common noun, subject of sentence, direct object, object of preposition, possessive, plural. One item used to test a function attribute of *noun* as a direct object follows.

Group 1	Group 2
I gave him the <u>ball</u>.	She ate in the <u>morning</u>.
We ate <u>dinner</u>.	Dick went to <u>school</u>.
Tom will play <u>golf</u>.	A prize was given to the <u>girls</u>.

What one name <u>best</u> fits all the underlined words in the sentences in Group 1 but does not fit the underlined words in the sentences in Group 2 ?

    a. appositives

    b. direct objects

    c. object complements

    d. indirect objects

    e. I don't know

Figure 5.2 shows the smoothed curves for acquiring the names of the concepts and of the defining attributes of the four concepts. The mean percentage correct for the students of Longitudinal Block A when in Grade 1 for *cutting tool* was 87. This was followed by a uniform rate of increase, and the students of Block D when in Grade 12 had 97% correct. The names related to *tree* were also acquired at a uniform rate, starting at 37% correct in Grade 1 and ending with 93% in Grade 12. Students of Blocks A and B acquired the names of the concept and of the defining attributes of *equilateral triangle* and *noun* at rapid rates; there was a gradual decelerating rate of acquisition by the students of Blocks C and D. The differences among the four concepts in all longitudinal blocks and grades were surprisingly large. For example, the percentages correct for *cutting tool* and *noun* were 91 and 43 in Grade 6 and 97 and 70 in Grade 12. We may conclude that there is a large difference among concepts. Also, despite the fact that children acquire a relatively large speaking vocabulary prior to entering school at age six, they are still acquiring the relatively simple

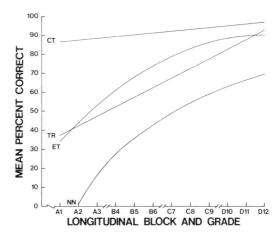

Figure 5.2. Development related to acquiring names of concepts and names of attributes.

names of key mathematical and English concepts and attributes, such as those related to *equilateral triangle* and *noun*, during their senior high school years.

FOR FURTHER STUDY

Brown, R. *A first language: The early stages.* Cambridge, Massachusetts: Harvard University Press, 1973.

Brown reports studies involving the conversational performances of three young children. Both the semantic and grammatical aspects of their language development are presented. These findings are compared with the recent work of others in psychology and linguistics.

Bruner, J. S. *Beyond the information given.* New York: W. W. Norton & Conpany, Inc., 1973. Pp. 368–396.

Chapter 21 of this book is a reprint of a treatise on culture and cognitive growth. Bruner reports his own studies and also other studies which lead him to attach much importance to language and education in cognitive development.

Carroll, J. B., & Freedle, R. O. (Eds.). *Language comprehension and the acquisition of knowledge.* Washington, D.C.: Winston & Sons, 1972.

Various authors present chapters dealing with different aspects of language comprehension. Theoretical views regarding language comprehension as well as practical applications dealing with controlling and measuring the degree of comprehension in both spoken and written discourse are included.

Clark, E. V. What's in a word? On the child's acquisition of semantics in his first language. In T. Moore (Ed.), *Cognitive development and the acquisition of language.* New York: Academic Press, 1973. Pp. 65–110.

After reviewing and critiquing several theories of semantic development, Clark outlines an hypothesis for explaining how word meanings develop in language acquisition. Initially full word meanings are unknown; early semantic features of words, usually based on perceptual attributes of the referent, are few and so the child overextends the use of the word. As the child correctly perceives additional features, the word meaning gradually approaches adult (mature) meaning.

Research findings supporting the hypothesis are presented, although the author acknowledges the need for further elaboration and testing.

Dale, P. S. *Language development: Structure and function* (2nd ed.). New York: Holt, Rinehart, and Winston, 1976.

A comprehensible, lucid account of language development is provided in this textbook. Different models and theories regarding language development are presented in a scholarly manner.

Macnamara, J. (Ed.). *Language learning and thought*. New York: Academic Press, 1977.

This book has chapters by a number of different authors from the fields of developmental psychology, artificial intelligence, linguistics, anthropology, and philosophy. The following chapters are of particular interest: Chapter 8, The Conceptual Basis for Naming, by Katherine Nelson; Chapter 10, Problems about Concepts, by John Macnamara; Chapter 11, Strategies and the Mapping Problem in First Language Acquisition, by Eve V. Clark; Chapter 13, The Contexts of Language Acquisition, by David R. Olson; and Chapter 17, Semantics and Miniature Artificial Languages, by Shannon Moeser.

Price-Williams, D. R. Cross-cultural differences in cognitive development. In V. Hamilton and M. D. Vernon (Eds.), *The development of cognitive processes*. London: Academic Press, 1976. Pp. 549–590.

This single chapter is an excellent survey of cross-cultural research in several areas of cognitive development. Similarities and differences across cultures are discussed, as well as many of the conceptual and methodological problems that must be considered in conducting and interpreting cross-cultural research.

Seymour, P. H. K. Contemporary models of the cognitive processes, II. Retrieval and comparison operations in permanent memory. In V. Hamilton & M. D. Vernon (Eds.), *The development of cognitive processes*. London: Academic Press, 1976. Pp. 43–110.

After reviewing the recent research and theory, Seymour proposes a division of secondary memory into independent lexical and pictorial systems which are interrelated by an overlying semantic system. The semantic component is viewed as a system for classification of characteristics of objects and object classes.

Vygotsky, L. S. *Thought and language*. Cambridge, Massachusetts: The M. I. T. Press, 1962.

Vygotsky presents the Russian view regarding the relationship between thought and language, a contrasting view to that of Piaget. The translation is easy to read and understand.

6

The Invariant Sequence in Attaining Four Successive Levels of Concepts: Longitudinal–Cross-sectional Results

In Chapters 3 and 5 some findings of the longitudinal–cross-sectional study were presented. Normative development of children and youth related to the operations of discriminating objects, discriminating the defining attributes of concepts, generalizing, and evaluating examples and nonexamples of concepts was described in Chapter 3. In Chapter 5 developmental trends related to understanding concept definitions and acquiring the names of concepts and their defining attributes were presented.

In this chapter and Chapters 7 and 8, results from the longitudinal–cross-sectional study are presented that deal with other dimensions of cognitive development. In this chapter results related to the sequence in attaining the four successive levels are presented. The rate and pattern of attaining the four levels and of understanding principles, taxonomic relations, and problem solving are presented in Chapter 7. Chapter 8 is devoted to individual differences in rate of cognitive development.

INVARIANT SEQUENCING

Understanding invariant sequencing in development requires knowing both what is meant by *sequencing* and what is implied by *invariance*. First of all, let us consider the notion of cognitive developmental sequences.

A number of important theories have employed constructs that represent development as progressing through a series of qualitatively different and increasingly complex steps, or phases. The most typical construct is that of developmental stage. Stages describe a developmental progression because they emerge sequentially over time. Piaget's six stages of the sensorimotor period, for example, describe an orderly progression in early cognitive development. Other examples of stage-sequential approaches are Kohlberg's (1969) six-stage theory of moral development and Erikson's (1959) theory of personality development. Stage theories, however, have many other formal properties in addition to the notion of developmental progressions or sequencing. A comprehensive discussion of stage theories is beyond the scope and intent of this chapter. Extensive material on stages and stage theories can be found in recent sources (e.g., Flavell, 1971, 1972, 1977; Flavell & Wohlwill, 1969; Van den Daele, 1969; Wohlwill, 1973).

Several theorists have proposed developmental sequences without invoking the stage construct or aspiring to meet the qualifications demanded by a "true" stage theory. That is, they have some, but not all, attributes of a stage theory. McNeill's (1970) treatment of language development and the enactive–ikonic–symbolic progression for modes of representation delineated by Bruner et al. (1966) also describe sequences in the growth of language and cognition. In a less formal way, developmental progressions such as these simply describe an orderly developmental sequence with respect to the emergence, extension, and refinement of a cognitive process, structure, or combination of processes and structures. Sequencing, then, implies that cognitive growth proceeds in an orderly manner. *Orderly* is a key word that brings us to the closely related idea of invariance.

Any proposed developmental sequence usually implies a specific temporal order of emergence. The successive parts of a complete sequence do not emerge at random—sometimes in one order and sometimes in another—but are assumed to appear in a fixed, constant progression. For example, if X, Y, and Z are identified as three hypothetical cognitive acquisitions in an invariant developmental series, then X must appear in every individual before Y, and Y must occur before Z. The sequence in attaining X, Y, and Z does not vary among individuals; it is invariant. However, the rates at which X, Y, Z emerge may vary among individuals. Although the invariant sequence itself should not be altered by differences in environmental conditions of the population to whom the sequence purportedly applies, the onset of a particular part of the sequence may be facilitated or retarded depending on each individual's experiences.

Flavell (1972) has observed that not all developmental sequences need be invariant and not all invariant sequences need be of interest to the developmentalist. He points out that a sequence may show a great deal of regularity but defy any meaningful, theoretical–conceptual interpretation. For example, the acquisition of object permanence (X) may regularly precede the acquisition of a sex-role concept (Y), but, as a developmental sequence (X→Y), the two cognitive acquisitions could only be related by recourse to a complicated chain of mediation that would not be especially productive conceptually or theoretically. Other developmental sequences might be bidirectional or reciprocal (X→Y *and* Y→X), rather than unidirectional and invariant.

Assuming that a conceptually meaningful, invariant developmental sequence is proposed, the basis of the invariance should be explicable on conceptual or logical grounds. Flavell (1972) has suggested three possible types of explanation for invariant ordering. The first is structure of the organism: The invariant sequence is determined by biological maturation (e.g., the development of locomotion). The second is structure of the environment: The sequence is explicable in terms of regularities and universal conditions in the environmental milieu that are typically perceived and experienced by individuals (e.g., the development of role-taking skills). Finally, an explanation for invariance may be found in the structure of the cognitive acquisitions comprising the sequence. The nature of the acquisitions X and Y may be such that X→Y is logically (and psychologically) necessary; but the possibility of Y→X must be eliminated purely on logical grounds. As an example, in Piaget's system concrete operations must logically appear before formal operations because the latter are defined by cognitive acts upon the former and the reverse sequence is logically impossible.

It is certainly likely, however, that no one of these three types of explanation may explain independently the invariance for a given developmental sequence. That is, the invariance of many developmental progressions is probably a product of the interaction of biological maturation with the regularities that individuals experience in their physical and social environments.

If an invariant developmental progression is postulated, empirical validation is usually sought. According to Flavell, however, if the logical structure of the cognitive acquisitions explains the invariance, then empirical testing of the invariance itself is superfluous. However, empirical research might still seek to verify developmental priority of an earlier over a later acquisition versus the possibility of concurrence in development. In general, if an invariant developmental progression is predicted, then empirical results should demonstrate a high degree of sequential regularity across individuals. Invariant sequences subjected to empirical tests may not hold up well. For example, consider Kohlberg's (1969) theory, which holds that the growth of moral reasoning proceeds through an invariant sequence of six qualitatively different stages in which the sixth represents the most advanced, mature level. From their evaluation of existing empirical evidence, Kurtines and Greif (1974) concluded that there was very little support for the postulated developmental sequence or the idea that individuals proceeded through the six stages in a fixed order. Cross-sectional and longitudinal data indicated that stage four was predominant across ages (late adolescence to early adulthood), that college students frequently obtained lower scores than they had in high school, and that a considerable amount of "stage-skipping" and "back-sliding" occurred. These empirical findings do not preclude the possibility of an invariant sequence in the development of moral reasoning, but they do suggest that Kohlberg's six-stage theory (or the measuring instruments) may require substantial modification. The important point is that although a developmental theory that postulates invariant sequencing may have intuitive appeal and heuristic value, empirical testing enables the sequence to be either validated or modified and improved.

CROSS-SECTIONAL RESULTS

Attaining the four successively higher levels of a concept—concrete, identity, classificatory, and formal—is predicted to occur in an invariant sequence. Mastery of each successively higher level requires mastery of the prior level, the use of at least one new mental operation, and the continuing use of the operations of the prior level, with content of increasing quantity and complexity encountered in a greater variety of contexts. The ability to learn a concept at each level is determined not only by emergence of the requisite mental operations, but also by external conditions of learning. That is, in the absence of the opportunity to learn concepts, particularly at the classificatory and formal levels, the new operations will not emerge or at least they will not function in the acquisition of the higher level. Invariance is therefore attributable to the biological characteristics of the human species and to their informal and formal learning experiences with similar objects, events, relations, and processes in their physical and social environments.

In order to determine whether the concept levels are attained in an invariant sequence, we must first examine the kinds of performances that are consistent with the prediction. Recall that the four concept batteries were administered at 1-year intervals in 1974, 1975, and 1976 to the 62, 77, 80, and 73 students composing the four longitudinal blocks. The obtained scores were evaluated as showing either full attainment or nonattainment of the concrete, identity, classificatory, and formal levels of each of the four concepts. As seen earlier in Table 2.1 the criterion of full attainment, or mastery, of the level, was set at 80–85% correct, to the nearest whole test item (e.g., 4 of 5 items correct, 7 of 8 items correct, 12 of 15 items correct). The one exception was the test for the classificatory level of *equilateral triangle*. Here there were 3 items, and 3 was set as the mastery criterion.

Five of 16 possible patterns of fully attaining (A) or not attaining (N) the four successively higher levels are consistent with an invariant sequence; 11 are not. The five patterns that are in accord with an invariant sequence are (1) failing to attain all four levels (NNNN); (2) attaining the concrete level, but not attaining the three higher levels (ANNN); (3) attaining both the concrete and identity levels, but not the two higher levels (AANN); (4) attaining the concrete, identity, and classificatory levels, but not the formal (AAAN); and (5) attaining all four levels (AAAA).

There are 11 possible patterns of attainment and nonattainment that do not

conform to an invariant sequence of attaining the four levels. In each nonconforming pattern, a higher level is attained although a lower one is not. For
example, an individual attains the concrete and identity levels, does not attain
the classificatory level, and goes on to attain the formal level. This person
falls into an AANA pattern that is not consistent with the invariant sequence.

The empirical question is this: Are the levels of the four concepts attained by
normally developing children and youth in the predicted invariant sequence?
More specifically, what are the results of the analysis of the conforming–
nonconforming patterns of attainment?

Conformity to the Invariant Sequence

Table 6.1 gives the percentage of students in the four longitudinal blocks
whose pattern of fully attaining the levels conformed to the predicted invariant
sequence. The information is presented for each concept, for each of the four
longitudinal groups of students—A, B, C, D—and for the three different grades
at which each group was assessed: A—Grade 1, 2, 3; B—Grade 4, 5, 6;
C—Grade 7, 8, 9; and D—Grade 10, 11, 12. Scores based on each annual
administration of the four test batteries to the students of each longitudinal
block were analyzed separately in deriving the percentages for each grade.

**TABLE 6.1   Cross-sectional Results: Percentage of Students Whose Patterns of Concept
Attainment Conformed to an Invariant Sequence**[a]

Block and grade	Conforming patterns					Total percentage	Total N
	NNNN	ANNN	AANN	AAAN	AAAA		
A1 (N = 62)							
CT	—	—	3	52	40	95	59
TR	—	3	35	61	—	100	62
ET	3	2	27	68	—	100	62
NN	26	52	23	—	—	100	62
A2 (N = 62)							
CT	—	—	6	56	32	95	59
TR	2	2	13	73	2	90	56
ET	—	2	8	90	—	100	62
NN	3	8	77	11	—	100	62
A3 (N = 62)							
CT	—	—	—	45	53	98	61
TR	—	2	6	81	8	97	60
ET	—	—	3	94	3	100	62
NN	3	3	44	47	—	97	60
B4 (N = 77)							
CT	—	—	6	44	47	97	75
TR	—	—	12	73	13	97	75
ET	—	1	6	75	4	96	74
NN	—	3	79	18	—	100	77

(continued)

TABLE 6.1   (Continued)

Block and grade	NNNN	ANNN	AANN	AAAN	AAAA	Total percentage	Total N
			Conforming patterns				
B5 (N = 77)							
CT	—	—	1	29	70	100	77
TR	—	1	6	47	35	90	69
ET	—	—	6	66	17	99	76
NN	—	—	47	52	1	100	77
B6 (N = 77)							
CT	—	—	—	17	83	100	77
TR	—	—	4	58	38	100	77
ET	—	—	3	45	52	100	77
NN	—	—	43	56	1	100	77
C7 (N = 80)[b]							
CT	—	—	6	33	60	99	79
TR	—	—	14	34	51	99	79
ET	—	—	11	50	35	96	77
NN	—	—	36	60	4	100	80
C8 (N = 80)							
CT	—	—	3	30	68	100	80
TR	—	—	1	41	58	100	80
ET	—	—	5	39	50	94	75
NN	—	—	25	53	21	99	79
C9 (N = 80)							
CT	—	—	—	11	89	100	80
TR	—	—	—	23	78	100	80
ET	—	—	—	25	75	100	80
NN	—	—	11	54	35	100	80
D10 (N = 73)							
CT	—	—	3	12	84	99	72
TR	—	—	1	10	88	99	72
ET	—	—	4	26	67	97	71
NN	—	—	19	49	32	100	73
D11 (N = 73)							
CT	—	—	—	14	84	97	71
TR	—	—	3	12	82	97	71
ET	—	—	3	23	71	97	71
NN	—	—	19	30	47	96	70
D12 (N = 73)							
CT	—	—	—	5	89	95	69
TR	—	—	—	14	86	100	73
ET	—	—	—	21	74	95	69
NN	—	—	1	36	62	99	72

[a] A dash (—) indicates no student showed this pattern.

[b] Grades 7–12 were not administered the concrete and identity levels because prior research showed 100% attainment by students in these grades; therefore, full attainment of these two levels was assumed (Grade 7 students were administered concrete and identity tests of *noun*).

Percentages are reported because there were different numbers of students in each longitudinal block.

Table 6.1 shows that 95% of the children of Block A when in Grade 1 had patterns of attainment conforming to the predicted invariant sequences for *cutting tool* and 100% for *tree, equilateral triangle*, and *noun*. When in Grade 2 and 3, between 90 and 100% of the children of Block A had fully attained the levels of each of the four concepts in accord with the predicted invariant sequence. At each year of testing, 94–100% of the students of Blocks B, C, and D had patterns of attaining the levels of the four concepts that conformed to the principle of invariance.

These results are so consistent that we shall not offer comparisons for concepts or for grades. Minor differences among the 3 years and among the four concepts will become apparent as we discuss the few cases of nonconforming patterns in the next section of this chapter.

We reiterate that these results are based on the evaluation and analysis of each student's scores on each concept assessment battery each year. The same students' scores across the 3 years are not included. In the last part of this chapter, we shall present the analysis of the longitudinal data in which we trace each individual's pattern of attaining the successively higher levels across the 3 years of testing. We may now consider the results related to seven patterns of nonconforming, the 3 years of testing, and the four concepts.

Deviation from the Invariant Sequence

There were 66 instances of nonconforming patterns, as shown in Table 6.2. Summing the last column of Table 6.1 results in 3438 instances of conforming to the invariant sequence. There were 3504 instances possible: Each student each year contributed four instances of conforming, not conforming, or a combination of these patterns. Forty-three of the 66 *nonconforming patterns* of attaining the four levels involved AANA—that is, fully attaining the concrete level, fully attaining the identity level, not fully attaining the classificatory level, but fully attaining the formal level. Eighteen of the remaining 23 instances involved not mastering the concrete or the identity level or both but mastering the classificatory level, the formal level, or both. The remaining five instances of nonconformity were NANN. These patterns of not mastering a lower level but mastering a higher level were probably due to error of measurement, combined with the criterion of mastery that was set for each level. These matters will be discussed more fully after all the results are presented.

The instances of nonconformity for the *years of testing* were 19 for Year 1, 33 for Year 2, and 14 for Year 3. The corollary instances of conformity were 1149, 1135, and 1154. The slightly higher incidence of nonconformity during Year 2 was probably due to errors of measurement that may have been associated with an influenza epidemic in 1974–1975, which resulted in considerable absenteeism and subsequent re-scheduling of tests. The physical health of the

TABLE 6.2 Cross-sectional Results: Number of Students in Patterns of Concept Attainment Not Conforming to an Invariant Sequence

Nonconforming pattern	Cutting tool (N = 292)				Tree (N = 292)				Equilateral triangle (N = 292)				Noun (N = 292)				Total by pattern
	Year: 1	2	3	Total	Year: 1	2	3	Total	Year: 1	2	3	Total	Year: 1	2	3	Total	
AANA	6	3	5	14	3	3		6	6	8	4	18		4	1	5	43
NAAN	1	1		2		2	1	3	2			2					7
NNAN		1		1													1
NANN					1	2		3							2	2	5
ANAN						7	1	8									8
ANAA						1		1									1
NAAA						1		1									1
Total instances of nonconformity each year[a]	7	5	5	17	4	16	2	22	8	8	4	20	0	4	3	7	66

[a] No student demonstrated any of the four remaining nonconforming patterns that are not listed.

142

students and related attention and ability to perform may have contributed to lower performance during the regular testing or the makeup testing. Unfortunately, students' records of absenteeism were not available to test this hypothesis.

The instances of nonconformity for the *concepts* were 17 *cutting tool,* 22 *tree,* 20 *equilateral triangle,* and 7 *noun.* Though not included in Table 6.2, the instances of nonconformity for each of the four *longitudinal blocks* were 17 for A; 16, B; 11, C; and 22, D. The relatively small differences in the instances of nonconformity among the different concepts and the longitudinal blocks are interpreted as resulting from errors of measurement primarily associated with differences in the attentiveness of the students and other conditions at the time of testing. The different batteries necessarily were administered at different times within the same year; and there were administrations in three different years.

Despite the fact that there were very few instances of nonconformity in comparison with conformity, each instance of nonconformity was studied further inasmuch as any exception to the postulated invariant sequence must be taken seriously. Therefore, the test protocols of the students who contributed the instances of nonconformity to an invariant sequence were examined to deal with matters of error of measurement more precisely and to identify the extent to which the same students may have been involved across the 3 years of testing.

Let us consider illustrative data for *equilateral triangle.* Twenty instances of nonconformity—8 in Year 1, 8 in Year 2, 4 in Year 3—were observed (there were 856 instances of conformity). There were 18 occurrences of the AANA pattern (fully attaining formal but not fully attaining classificatory) and two occurrences of the NAAN pattern (attaining identity and classificatory but not attaining concrete). The 20 instances of nonconformity were produced by 19 different individuals; one student showed the AANA pattern in 2 consecutive years. The 19 students who deviated from the predicted sequence came very close to meeting the full-attainment criterion for the level that should have been attained, missing it by either one or two items.

Similar analyses of the test protocols were conducted on the instances of nonconformity involving the other three concepts. Individuals exhibiting a nonpredicted sequence did so as an isolated event; only two cases occurred in which any individual followed a nonconforming pattern in two consecutive years. Also, those children who deviated from the predicted sequence on *cutting tool, noun,* and *tree* usually missed the mastery criterion for the level not attained by only one or two items.

We might also inquire about the frequency with which individuals who followed a nonconforming pattern on one concept in a given year also showed a nonconforming pattern on one or more of the other concepts in the same year. A high degree of independence prevailed; in a given year only two children had nonconforming patterns on more than one concept.

In summary, the instances of nonconformity to the sequence can be accounted for primarily if not entirely by inevitable errors of measurement, including those associated with test reliabilities that are relatively low for making decisions about individual, as opposed to group, performances. As we shall see in the discussion of the invariant sequence based on the longitudinal data, the error of measurement of each test was quite large when we consider that a change in test score of one or two items in a negative direction produced a nonconforming pattern.

Influence of Retesting and Cohort on
Conformity to the Invariant Sequence

Each participating student of each longitudinal block was tested annually across three successive grades of school. Did repeated testing influence conformity to the five predicted sequences of concept attainment on any of the four concept assessment batteries? (See Chapter 2 for details regarding the control groups for the effect of repeated testing and cohorts.)

Chi-square tests ($p < .05$) computed on the frequencies of individuals following predicted patterns in the retest control groups and in the longitudinal samples at each year of assessment showed no significant retesting effects. Receiving the same tests three times apparently had no effect on students' conformity to the invariant sequence.

Did the year of birth influence conformity to the predicted sequence? For each concept assessment battery, chi-square tests were computed on the frequencies of students following conforming patterns in the cohort control groups and in the longitudinal blocks at each year of assessment. This statistical procedure again yielded no statistically significant differences between the students of the four longitudinal blocks and their control groups. Cohort control groups, whether born 1 year or 2 years later than the students in the four longitudinal blocks, did not differ from them in the frequency with which their patterns conformed to the predicted sequence.

LONGITUDINAL AND COMBINED
LONGITUDINAL–CROSS-SECTIONAL RESULTS

The analysis of the cross-sectional data indicated very high conformity to the predicted invariant sequence. Despite this high consistency within and across each longitudinal block of students, one questions whether each of the 292 students either mastered a successively higher level of each concept each successive year or maintained the highest level mastered the prior year. Answering this question requires that each student's score on each test of each level of each concept be evaluated in terms of the mastery criterion each year and that the resulting patterns of attainment–nonattainment for each student be analyzed between Years 1 and 2 and between Years 2 and 3. By this procedure, we can determine whether every individual attained the successively higher levels of each of the four concepts in an invariant sequence. If the students of all the longitudinal blocks performed in much the same way, then we may generalize across the longitudinal blocks and across the years of schooling, Grade 1–Grade 12.

Conformity to the Invariant Sequence across Three Years

In the three left columns of Table 6.3 are given the sequences of full attainment of the levels of each concept during Years 1, 2, and 3 that are consistent with the principle of invariance (deviations are treated later). The percentage of students of each longitudinal block who followed each particular sequence across the 3 years is shown in the right columns and the total percentages and also the total numbers conforming are also given. The conforming patterns, or "routes," for each concept are presented according to the levels: first the year-to-year patterns concluding with full attainment of the formal level in Year 3, the final year of assessment; next, those patterns ending with full attainment of the classificatory level in Year 3; and finally, those ending with identity, concrete, or no level. To illustrate, an individual whose highest attainment level in Year 3 was formal might have arrived at that level via a number of different routes, all consistent with the principle of invariance: formal→formal→formal (i.e., maintaining full attainment of the level); classificatory→formal→formal; identity→classificatory→formal; and so on. In fact, for each concept there are 15 possible Year 1→2→3 routes leading to full attainment of the formal level that are in accord with an invariant progression; there are 10 possible Year 1→2→3 routes for the classificatory level, 6 for the identity level, and 3 for concrete. Only those routes observed in students' performances are shown in Table 6.3. The information on each individual summarized in this manner permits us to pinpoint the specific patterns of conformity for each concept and for each longitudinal block of students. The primary results are presented according to the four concepts.

For the concept *cutting tool*, many students in all four longitudinal blocks conformed to the predicted sequence and mastered either the formal level or the classificatory level during Years 1→2→3. The percentage mastering the formal level in the predicted sequence by the five routes combined was 38 for Block A, 82 for Block B, 82 for Block C, and 88 for Block D. The corresponding percentages for the classificatory level were 12 for Block A, 7 for Block B, 9 for Block C, and 3 for Block D. The total percentages with conforming patterns for attaining the successive levels of *cutting tool* were 48 for Block A, 88 for Block

TABLE 6.3 Longitudinal Results: Percentage of Students Who Attained the Concept Levels in an Invariant Sequence

Highest level of attainment			Grade block[a]				
Year 1	Year 2	Year 3	A (N = 62)	B (N = 77)	C (N = 80)	D (N = 73)	Mean total percentage (N = 292)
			Cutting tool				
FO	FO	FO	6	38	53	78	45
CL	FO	FO	15	30	14	5	16
CL	CL	FO	15	10	10	4	10
ID	FO	FO	—	1	1	—	1
ID	CL	FO	2	3	4	1	2
CL	CL	CL	10	4	8	3	6
ID	CL	CL	2	3	—	—	1
ID	ID	CL	—	—	1	—	<1
	Total percentage		48	88	90	92	81
	Total N		30	68	72	67	237
			Tree				
FO	FO	FO	—	9	41	78	33
CL	FO	FO	2	14	13	5	9
CL	CL	FO	3	10	14	—	7
ID	FO	FO	—	2	—	—	1
ID	CL	FO	2	1	4	—	2
ID	ID	FO	—	—	1	—	<1
CO	CL	FO	2	—	—	—	<1
CL	CL	CL	45	32	6	3	21
ID	CL	CL	26	5	9	—	9
ID	ID	CL	3	1	—	1	1
CO	CL	CL	2	—	—	—	<1
ID	ID	ID	3	1	—	—	1
	Total percentage		87	78	88	88	85
	Total N		54	60	70	64	248
			Equilateral triangle				
FO	FO	FO	—	3	31	56	23
CL	FO	FO	—	13	23	15	13
CL	CL	FO	3	22	11	3	10
ID	FO	FO	—	4	4	—	2
ID	CL	FO	—	4	3	—	2
ID	ID	FO	—	1	—	—	<1
CO	CL	FO	—	1	—	—	<1
CL	CL	CL	60	27	13	7	25
ID	CL	CL	24	4	5	3	8
ID	ID	CL	—	4	—	1	1
CO	CL	CL	2	—	—	—	<1
No Levels	CL	CL	2	—	—	—	<1
No Levels	ID	CL	2	—	—	—	<1
ID	ID	ID	2	—	—	—	<1
	Total percentage		94	83	89	85	87
	Total N		58	64	71	62	255

(continued)

TABLE 6.3   (*Continued*)

Highest level of attainment			Grade block[a]				
Year 1	Year 2	Year 3	A (N = 62)	B (N = 77)	C (N = 80)	D (N = 73)	Mean total percentage (N = 292)
				Noun			
FO	FO	FO	—	—	3	25	7
CL	FO	FO	—	—	21	18	10
CL	CL	FO	—	1	6	8	4
ID	FO	FO	—	—	1	5	2
ID	CL	FO	—	—	4	3	2
ID	ID	FO	—	—	—	1	<1
CL	CL	CL	—	5	24	11	11
ID	CL	CL	3	31	19	4	15
ID	ID	CL	10	16	5	5	9
CO	ID	CL	19	—	—	—	4
CO	CL	CL	2	—	—	—	<1
No Levels	CL	CL	2	—	—	—	<1
No Levels	ID	CL	13	—	—	—	3
ID	ID	ID	8	22	8	—	10
CO	ID	ID	19	3	—	—	5
CO	CO	ID	5	—	—	—	1
No Levels	ID	ID	6	—	—	—	1
No Levels	No Levels	ID	2	—	—	—	<1
CO	CO	CO	2	—	—	—	<1
No Levels	CO	CO	2	—	—	—	<1
No Levels	No Levels	No Levels	2	—	—	—	<1
Total Percentage			94	78	90	81	85
·Total N			58	60	72	59	249

[a] A dash (—) indicates no individuals observed in that sequence.

B, 90 for Block C, and 92 for Block D. (These percentages vary from the totals derived by adding the column entries because of rounding off the separate column entries.) No data are presented in Table 6.3 for the concrete and identity levels of *cutting tool* because these levels were already mastered by the students when in Grade 1. The reader may wish to summarize this same information for the other concepts.

The percentages of all 292 students fully attaining the successive levels of *cutting tool, tree, equilateral triangle,* and *noun* in the predicted sequence during Years 1→2→3 by the various routes are given in the right column of Table 6.3 and are readily interpretable by visual inspection. The number and percentage of students of each longitudinal block that conformed to the predicted sequence are given in the last two rows for each concept. These percentages are noted now inasmuch as they also imply the amount of nonconformity. The percentages of conformity for each block and concept were *cutting tool*: A—48, B—88, C—90, D—92, total—81; *tree*: A—87, B—78, C—88, D—88, total—85; *equilateral triangle*: A—94, B—83, C—89, D—85, total—87; *noun*: A—94, B—78, C—90, D—81, total—85.

Some of the commonalities of the patterns across the four concepts merit attention and are readily inferrable from comparison of the percentages given in the right column. A substantial percentage of the students maintained either the formal level or the classificatory level across the 3 years, but only a few maintained the identity or concrete level. The other conforming patterns involved fully attaining one or two next higher levels each successive year (e.g., CL→FO; ID→CL between any 2 years). The percentage of students advancing according to these patterns for *cutting tool* was 34 for Block A, 47 for B, 30 for C, and 10 for D. The corresponding percentages for *tree* were 40, 33, 41, and 6; for *equilateral triangle*, 33, 53, 46, and 22; and for *noun*, 83, 51, 56, and 44. There was no progression from the concrete to the identity level for any concept except *noun*; most students of Block A had fully attained the identity level of the other concepts when in Grade 1.

Exceptions to the Invariant Sequence across Three Years

We may first review the differences in the total number of exceptions based on the cross-sectional data and the longitudinal data. The percentage of students whose patterns of full attainment longitudinally conformed to the predicted invariant sequence was quite high, as shown earlier in Table 6.3: *cutting tool*, 81; *tree*, 85; *equilateral triangle*, 87; and *noun*, 85. The percentages based on the analysis of the cross-sectional data as presented earlier in Table 6.1 were substantially higher, ranging from 90 to 100.

It is crucial to recognize that the nonconforming exceptions for Year 2 and for Year 3 are cumulated in the nonconforming exceptions group for each longitudinal block of students. That is, any student who did not maintain mastery of the highest level of any of the four concepts between Years 1 and 2 or between Years 2 and 3 is included in the exception group in the longitudinal data analysis. For example, if in a group of 70 students 7 students deviated from a conforming pattern between Year 1 and Year 2, the percentage conforming to the invariant sequence would be 90.

If in the third year when followed again, 7 different students did not conform for any one concept, the percentage not conforming to the predicted sequence would drop to 80 since 14 of the 70 students would show nonconforming patterns. However, had the same students been responsible for the exceptions in Year 3 as in Year 2, the percentage would remain at 90. Thus, testing the prediction by this analysis of the longitudinal data is exceptionally rigorous.

Table 6.4 presents for each concept the number of students in each longitudinal block who did not maintain their mastery of a level either in Year 2 in comparison with Year 1 or in Year 3 in comparison with Year 2. Four patterns accounted for the exceptions to the invariant sequence: (1) attaining the formal level and then dropping to the classificatory level the next year (FO→CL); (2) attaining the classificatory level and dropping to the identity level the subsequent year (CL→ID); (3) attaining the identity level and dropping to the concrete level the following year (ID→CO); or (4) dropping more than one level between successive years. The total exceptions presented in Table 6.4 will be examined for these four patterns for the four concepts, the years of testing, and the longitudinal blocks.

The total number of exceptions was 179, or 15%. (As may be derived from Table 6.3, there were 989 instances of conformity to the invariant sequence for the four concepts.) The frequency of exceptions varied substantially among the four patterns—FO→CL, 104; CL→ID, 65; and ID→CO, 2. Eight students dropped more than one level during their 3 years of testing.

The number of exceptions varied somewhat for the four concepts: 55 for *cutting tool*, 44 for *tree*, 37 for *equilateral triangle,* and 43 for *noun*. In contrast with other concepts and patterns, a large number of exceptions occurred related to the FO→CL pattern of *cutting tool* (49) and the CL→ID pattern of *noun* (36). These two areas alone accounted for 85 of the 179 exceptions.

The exceptions for Year 1→2 (129) greatly exceeded those for Year 2→3 (50). The differences between Year 1→2 and Year 2→3 for the four concepts were *cutting tool,* 45 versus 10; *tree,* 29 versus 15; *equilateral triangle,* 32 versus 5; and *noun,* 23 versus 20. The two very large differences here were *cutting tool,* FO→CL (39 versus 10), and *equilateral triangle,* CL→ID (16 versus 1).

The number of exceptions occurring within each longitudinal block were 48(A), 56(B), 35(C), and 40(D). Block B had a large number of exceptions (30) involving the CL→ID pattern, mainly for *equilateral triangle* and *noun*. The exceptions for Block A students were primarily contributed by the FO→CL pattern of *cutting tool* (28).

As noted earlier, the preceding exceptions were somewhat higher than might have been expected in view of the cross-sectional results; but more important, the principle of invariance may be questioned if the exceptions cannot be accounted for satisfactorily.

Examination of the students' records showed that students involved as exceptions between Year 1 and Year 2 were totally different from those involved between Years 2 and 3. This suggested that small variations in performance from one year to the next might be responsible for many exceptions. Logical

TABLE 6.4 Longitudinal Results: Exceptions to an Invariant Sequence[a]

Concept and block		FO→CL		CL→ID		ID→CO		Loss of more than one level		Totals	
	Years	1–2	2–3	1–2	2–3	1–2	2–3	1–2	2–3	1–2	2–3
CT	A	20	8	2	—	—	—	2	—	24	8
	B	8	—	1	—	—	—	—	—	9	—
	C	7	—	1	—	—	—	—	—	8	—
	D	4	2	—	—	—	—	—	—	4	2
Total		39	10	4	—	—	—	2	—	45	10
TR	A	—	—	5	—	1	—	1	1	7	1
	B	3	10	3	—	—	—	1	—	7	10
	C	7	3	—	—	—	—	—	—	7	3
	D	7	1	—	—	—	—	1	—	8	1
Total		17	14	8	—	1	—	3	1	29	15
ET	A	—	—	3	—	1	—	—	—	4	—
	B	2	1	9	1	—	—	—	—	11	2
	C	4	1	3	—	—	—	1	—	8	1
	D	8	2	1	—	—	—	—	—	9	2
Total		14	4	16	1	1	—	1	—	32	5

NN										
A	—	—	—	3	—	—	—	1	—	4
B	—	1	3	13	—	—	—	—	3	14
C	—	—	8	—	—	—	—	—	8	—
D	3	2	9	—	—	—	—	—	12	2
Total	3	3	20	16	—	—	—	1	23	20
Total Concepts	73	31	48	17	2	—	6	2	129	50
Totals Blocks										
A	20	8	10	3	2	—	3	2	35	13
B	13	12	16	14	—	—	1	—	30	26
C	18	4	12	—	—	—	1	—	31	4
D	22	7	10	—	—	—	1	—	33	7

[a] A dash (—) indicates no students observed in this pattern of loss.

analysis indicated that the largest determinant of the exceptions was associated with a combination of three closely related matters: test reliabilities of less than 100%, a stringent criterion of full attainment, and regression to the mean. This may be illustrated in connection with the formal level tests.

The Hoyt reliability coefficients and the related standard errors of measurement were given in Table 2.3. The 12 reliability coefficients for the formal-level test of each of the four concepts for each of 3 years were uniformly and moderately high: .77, .74, and .81 for *cutting tool*; .91, .86, and .92 for *tree*; .84, .82, and .83 for *equilateral triangle*; and .85, .92, and .87 for *noun*. The number of items in the test and the errors of measurement for the 3 years were: *cutting tool*—18 items, 1.38, 1.34, and 1.08; *tree*—35 items, 2.09, 2.08, and 2.07; *equilateral traingle*—18 items, 1.62, 1.60, and 1.34; and *noun*—25 items, 2.07, 1.91, and 2.06. The probabilities are .67 and .95 that a student's true score on any test will fall within ±1 or ±2 units of the standard error of measurement of the test, provided the test was not exceptionally easy or difficult for the student who took it. In regard to the formal-level test of *cutting tool* for Year 1, the probability is .67 that a student's true score in any year fell within ±1.38 points of the observed score and .95 that it fell within ±2.76 points of the observed score. Stated differently, the probabilities are 33 in 100 and 5 in 100 that a student's score on any test administration may have varied this much because of error of measurement of this magnitude.

The criterion of mastery for all the formal-level tests was 80–85% correct to the nearest item: 15 of 18 items for *cutting tool,* 28 of 35 items for *tree,* 15 of 18 items for *equilateral triangle,* and 20 of 25 items for noun. As may be inferred, a change in score in a positive direction of one or two items because of measurement error (e.g., from 13 or 14 to 15 for *cutting tool* and *equilateral triangle,* 18 or 19 to 20 for *noun,* and 26 or 27 to 28 for *tree*) would result in meeting the full attainment criterion. A similar change in a negative direction would result in not maintaining the formal level. We may raise the question as to whether the direction would more likely be positive or negative. In terms of regression to the mean, a positive direction is more likely for scores below the mean and a negative direction for scores above the mean. For the mastery criterion, the regression would be in the negative direction for scores at or above the cutoff score for full attainment. However, the higher the score is above the criterion, the lower is the probability of falling below the criterion (and thereby failing to maintain the highest level across 2 years).

The question might also be raised as to whether more students within each block fully attained the formal and classificatory levels during the first, second, or third year they were tested. As shown in Table A.4, the percentage of the students who mastered the levels of each concept was higher each year, and as shown in Table A.2, the mean scores for each level tended to be higher each successive year. As the students' scores went farther above the mastery criterion, there was less probability of failing to maintain the level. In actuality, many more exceptions involving not maintaining the formal level occurred between Years 1 and 2 (73) than between Years 2 and 3 (31). In line with the preceding discussion, the larger number of exceptions between Years 1 and 2 (42) is probably attributable solely to error of measurement, and the other 31 exceptions between Years 1 and 2 and the 31 between Years 2 and 3 may also be in part. A similar interpretation holds for the exceptions involving the classificatory level: 48 between Years 1 and 2 versus 17 between Years 2 and 3.

Concrete illustrations of the preceding are drawn from the complete analyses conducted on all the test protocols of the students with nonconforming patterns. Twenty-two of the 39 students who attained the formal level of *cutting tool* in Year 1 but not in Year 2 missed the mastery criterion in Year 2 by one or two items. In Block A specifically, 15 of the 20 students scored 15 in Year 1; in Year 2, these same 15 students missed the mastery criterion by one or two items. Eleven of the 17 Block B, C, and D students who fully attained the formal level of *tree* in Year 1 but not in Year 2 failed in Year 2 by one or two items. A final illustration involves failure to maintain mastery of the classificatory level of *equilateral triangle*. There are three items in this classificatory test, and three of three items, or 100%, was set as the mastery criterion. Thirteen of the 16 students who fully attained the classificatory level of *equilateral triangle* in Year 1 but not in Year 2 missed the criterion by one item.

A few specific examples of the types of errors made by students might merit attention. A number of Block A students attained the formal level of *cutting tool* in Year 1 but not Year 2, as we have just seen. One Block A student who showed this pattern of loss fully attained the formal level in 1974, although 1 item constructed to measure the ability to discriminate a defining attribute and 2 items constructed to measure the ability to evaluate examples and nonexamples were missed (15 of 18 items correct are required for mastery). The following year, this student missed 4 items on the formal test and consequently did not meet the mastery criterion. The same item to measure ability to discriminate a defining attribute missed in 1974 was responded to incorrectly again in 1975, and one additional discriminating attribute item was also missed. The following item was answered incorrectly both years.

Below are four things. Put an X on the one that has a hard edge.

As shown, the student placed an X on the hammer, when the paring knife should have been selected.

This discriminating attribute item was missed only in 1975:

Below are four things. Put an X on the one that has a sharp edge.

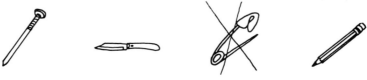

The student placed an X on the safety pin rather than on the paring knife. At a speculative level, it is possible that this student did not attend properly to both words *sharp edge,* which together are a defining attribute of *cutting tool.* Similarly, in the previous item missed both years, *hard* may have been attended to rather than the complete defining attribute *hard edge.* Insufficient attending or perhaps impulsiveness probably account for errors such as these. That is, the item may have appeared very easy to the student so that *hard* and *sharp* were focused on while *edge* was ignored.

Another type of error causing loss of a level between successive years is illustrated by a Block C student who missed one of the eight classificatory items of *noun* in 1974 and consequently met criterion for mastery, but did not meet mastery criterion the following year.

These are the two items missed in 1975:

Put an X on the things below that name one or more persons, places, or things.

tent   go   rob   Dick   when

Put an X on the things below that name one or more persons, places, or things.

brother   Russia   particularly   made   able

fallen   cannot   teacher   Johnny   beautiful

As shown in the first item, *rob* was marked and should not have been; other responses were correct. In the second item, the student failed to mark *brother,* although all other choices were correct. Speculatively again, both of these errors might be attributed to lack of attention since most responses were correct.

As a final example, we illustrate a typical error on the classificatory test of *equilateral triangle* that caused a drop from classificatory to identity level attainment between successive years. Three items are included on this test; all three must be answered correctly to meet the criterion for full attainment. A

Block B student who fully attained the classificatory level in 1974 missed one item in 1975:

Put an X on the drawings on the right that have exactly the same shape as the one on the left. (The letters R, Y, and B indicate that each figure was red, yellow, or blue.)

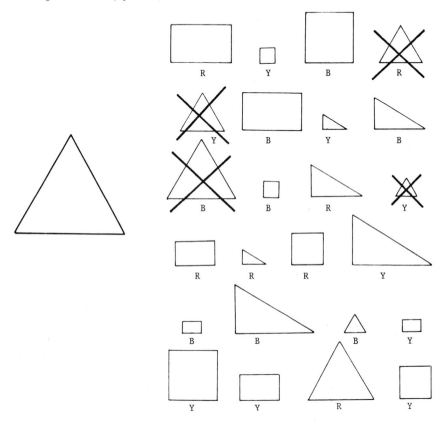

As shown, this student failed to mark two equilateral triangles, one in each of the two bottom rows of figures. These errors probably resulted from inadequate attentiveness to the complete array of 24 choices when the test was taken in 1975. Year-to-year variation in attention and persistence might be due to many individual, environmental, and test-taking conditions.

To summarize, the exceptions to invariance are based on a student's failure to maintain the highest level mastered during the prior year. Though the majority of these exceptions could be accounted for by error of measurement, the possibility also remains that some of the exceptions represent a real failure of an individual to perform as well on a particular level in a subsequent year as in a prior year. Some individuals may have fully mustered their intellectual resources in Year 1 or Year 2 and barely met the mastery criterion. In the following year, they could not carry out the same operations on the particular content included in one or more test items of the particular levels, or they could not retrieve a necessary bit of information from memory. As we shall see in Chapter 8, each individual's cognitive growth appears to be quite regular and consistent but some individuals experience occasional plateaus and even losses over short time periods. The biological inheritance of individuals and their environmental interactions vary so widely that we should probably not expect every individual to conform to any invariant sequence of intellectual development. Despite this possibility, the high proportion of direct instances of conformity to the invariant sequence and the number of exceptions that are probably attributable to error of measurement enable us to conclude that the vast majority of school-age students acquire the successively higher levels of concepts in an invariant sequence.

DISCUSSION

The invariant sequence in attainment of concepts at four successively higher levels has been supported empirically. We account for this invariant developmental progression in terms of the conditions that are necessary and sufficient for it to occur.

According to Flavell (1977), a specific factor may bear a necessary, sufficient, necessary and sufficient, or neither necessary nor sufficient relation to a given cognitive outcome. How do these differ? Suppose B will develop if, and only if, A_1 occurs. A_1 is then necessary and sufficient to B. On the other hand, suppose A_1 must occur, but so must A_2, A_3, etc., if B is to develop. A_1 is then necessary but not sufficient to B. If A_1 or A_2 or A_3 can each independently produce B, then A_1 is sufficient but not necessary to B. Finally, if B can develop without A_1 and A_1 cannot alone produce B (but may aid in B's development, along with other factors), then A_1 is neither necessary nor sufficient to B.

What conditions are necessary and possibly sufficient to explain the invariant sequence in full attainment or mastery of the four levels? Mastery of each successively higher level requires (1) mastery of the prior level, (2) functioning of at least one new mental operation in combination with the continuing operations, (3) functioning of the operations of the prior level, with content of increasing quantity and complexity encountered in a greater variety of context, (4) intending to attain the next higher level, and (5) persisting until it is attained. The necessary external conditions of learning include experience and practice with examples and nonexamples of the particular concept.

Other analyses of cognitive–developmental sequences have been suggested in an attempt to explain many kinds of developmental sequences. Flavell (1972) proposed a classification of five different relationships or processes to account for all types of developmental sequences. If X is a cognitive item that always precedes Y in a developmental sequence, the relation between X and Y is one of addition, substitution, modification, inclusion, or mediation. Each of the five accounts for a different kind of developmental progression, but as Flavell takes care to note, deciding which type of relationship best explains a particular sequence may not always be a clear-cut task. We will briefly review each of the five types and suggest which of Flavell's general categories fits with the invariant sequence in levels of concept attainment. We hasten to point out that the order of these relationships has no bearing on their cognitive–developmental importance.

Developmental sequences in which the items are related by addition are those in which the developmentally later item supplements or is added to the earlier item; it does not replace or eliminate it. Although Y regularly develops later than X, X continues to be available for use. It coexists and may alternate with Y, and may undergo further refinement as the individual matures. According to Flavell, Bruner's enactive–ikonic–symbolic sequence of modes for representing experience is a developmental sequence related by the addition process. Although it occurs earlier in development, the ikonic mode continues throughout life to play a viable role in the way the individual codes information.

In a substitution sequence, a developmentally later item entirely replaces the earlier item in the sequence. In an X→Y progression, once Y develops, X is extinguished. Substitution sequences are probably relatively rare and may overlap with the addition or modification categories. Flavell finds one example of a substitution sequence in Piaget's research on children's beliefs about dreams. The belief that dreams are real, physical entities is replaced by the belief that dreams are subjective, internal events.

If a developmentally later item represents a differentiation, generalization, or stabilization of an earlier item, the sequence is described by a modification process. If X is the developmentally earlier item and Y the later, the two are not so distinct as in addition or substitution sequences; rather, Y appears more as an improved, perfected X. Differentiation is a particularly common type of modification sequence. Much of cognitive development proceeds through the differentiation of more diffuse cognitive items, as well as through the generalization of cognitive items as they undergo extension and breadth of application. The development of object permanence provides an example of generalization; over the six stages of the sensorimotor period the search strategy for a hidden object progresses from one that is highly restricted to one that is increasingly generalized.

In an inclusion sequence the earlier cognitive item becomes incorporated into the later. In the X→Y sequence, X becomes included as an integral part of Y much as a subroutine becomes part of a computer program. Piaget's concrete operations→formal operations sequence provides a good example of the inclusion relation in a developmental progression. Similarly, Gagné's cumulative learning hierarchy is best described as an inclusion sequence. Each higher skill in the hierarchy depends upon and includes the acquisition of lower-order skills.

Finally, a mediation sequence is one in which a developmentally early item provides a bridge to a later one. In many ways, the mediation sequence is similar to an inclusion sequence. But in contrast to it, in an X→Y mediation sequence, X facilitates formation of Y but does not become an integral part of Y. Much more apparent discontinuity may exist between X and Y in mediation than is usual in inclusion and modification. For example, an infant's ability to crawl probably mediates development of many new sensorimotor skills; ability to read mediates a host of new and complex cognitive acquisitions. Some mediation sequences may be fairly indirect but, nonetheless, developmentally important. A great many developmental progressions would seem to be due, at least in part, to mediation.

Which of these five types of relationships might account for the invariant sequence in the four successively higher levels of concept attainment? In order for concept learning to proceed from the concrete to the identity, the classificatory, and finally the formal level, the individual must acquire the use of at least one new mental operation. We have stated that attainment of each higher level requires mastery of the prior level, the use of at least one new cognitive operation, and continuing the operations of the prior level but on content that increases in scope and complexity and is less context-bound. That is, the mental operations required at the identity level, for example, after reaching a sufficient level of maturity, are maintained and become part of a larger unit of cognition at the classificatory level. We cannot conceive of classificatory level attainment without its identity level components. Consequently, the inclusion relation proposed by Flavell appears to account for the invariant sequence in attainment of the four levels. However, the invariant sequence proscribed by CLD theory also describes a developmental pattern whereby a relatively low-order cognitive skill (e.g., discriminating an object from other objects) develops to the point where it paves the way for higher-order processes. Although the cognitive operation of discriminating at the identity level becomes subsumed or included as a subroutine within the higher classificatory level, it has also become a more refined and extended cognitive operation. This example points up the fact that the invariant progression in concept attainment illustrates more than one type of relationship. For example, the individual's ability to discriminate progresses from the identity level to that required at the classificatory and formal levels. This could be explained as a modification process (as cognitive operations become increasingly differentiated, extended, and stabilized), and probably as a mediation process as well (since cognitive acquisitions at an earlier level facilitate development of those required by the next higher level). Nevertheless, because individuals form concepts through such cognitive operations as attending, discriminating, and remembering, the relation between these operations and levels of concept attainment appears best interpreted by an inclusion process.

FOR FURTHER STUDY

Brainerd, C. J. The stage question in cognitive-developmental theory. *Brain and Behavioral Science,* 1978, *1,* no. 1.

Brainerd examines the various uses of the stage concept: as metaphor and description, and as an explanation of age-related changes in behavior. Focusing on Piaget's theory of cognitive development, Brainerd concludes that the stage concept falls short of true explanation and is primarily descriptive. The author also notes that this issue is relevant to educational practice. The explanatory status of Piaget's stages is critical to instruction that has been designed according to Piagetian theory if it is assumed children should never be taught material that is beyond their "current stage."

Flavell, J. H. Stage-related properties of cognitive development. *Cognitive Psychology,* 1971, *2,* 421–453.

In order to understand better the typical course of cognitive development, Flavell examines four critical components of the concept *cognitive developmental stage* and evaluates how closely each actually fits with developmental reality. Highly recommended to the advanced student who has some background in Piagetian theory.

Flavell, J. H. An analysis of cognitive-developmental sequences. *Genetic Psychology Monographs,* 1972, *86,* 279–350.

In this important monograph, Flavell examines many types of cognitive–developmental sequences. He proposes a classification of five kinds of relationships that describe a variety of sequences and also offers several possible explanations for sequencing in cognitive development. A significant theoretical monograph highly recommended to the advanced student.

7

Rate and Form of Cognitive Development across the School Years: Longitudinal–Cross-sectional Results

Gesell spent the major portion of his professional life studying and charting the course of human growth from infancy through age 16. The results appeared in three books, one treating the years of infancy (Gesell & Ilg, 1943), another the years from 5 to 10 (Gesell & Ilg, 1946), and the final one the years from 10 to 16 (Gesell, Ilg, & Ames, 1956). One feature of Gesell's work was to describe the typical behaviors for each year of age rather than the rate and form of the various dimensions of development or related interindividual and intraindividual differences.

The preceding books report the most recent comprehensive longitudinal study of human development, infancy to age 16, in America. However, the influence of these studies already had waned markedly by the late 1960s. At that time Rohwer (1970) indicated that the contribution of developmental psychology to educational practice was slight. Mussen (1970) pointed out that developmental psychologists of the 1960s were less concerned than the prior generation of psychologists both with precise descriptions of children's capabilities at various ages and with the reliable determination of age changes in psychological functions. Mussen called for more accurate and detailed descriptions of many aspects of development, particularly of cognitive functions and of social and emotional behavior.

This kind of precise descriptive information is helpful, probably essential, in diagnosing an individual child's current status and in understanding the child's pattern of growth across longer time intervals. The medical profession relies heavily upon precise descriptive information in the diagnosis and prognosis of many dimensions of physical growth, vitality, and health throughout the life span.

Wohlwill (1973) also stressed the need for both descriptive and correlational studies of the many dimensions of human development, studies of individual differences in development, and continuing theory formulation. He outlined procedures for describing the course of developmental change along scalar dimensions. He proposed that any dimension or function of development should be identified and described according to its form, its rate, the values of maxima, minima, and terminal levels, and the age corresponding to specified points of the development.

In the present study, seven developmental dimensions were identified for each of the four concepts, namely, the four levels of attainment—concrete, identity, classificatory, and formal—and understanding of principles, understanding of taxonomic relations, and problem solving. Tests were constructed to measure each student's performance related to the 28 dimensions.

As noted in Chapter 2, mean scores were obtained for each of the 28 measures at the grades where they were administered. These mean scores were changed to percentages to make it possible to compare development across the dimensions. (Not all tests have the same number of items.) The mean percentages were then changed to predicted mean percentages according to procedures outlined in Chapter 2. Smoothed curves connecting the predicted percentages were then developed. The smoothed curves tend to eliminate rises and dips that may result from repeated testing effects, cohort effects, and measurement error, also discussed in Chapter 2. They permit estimations of true development, not only for each of the four groups of students followed longitudinally, but also across the four successive blocks. The curves presented in this chapter are the best estimates of both the form and the rate of development of each of the dimensions, that is, the levels and the uses of the concepts. The beginning and end points of these curves merit further discussion related to minimal and maximum performances.

Each test was constructed to be scored from 0 to 100%; however, in line with the original objective the study was carried out not from infancy into adulthood but with four groups of children of school age, Grades 1–3, 4–6, 7–9, 10–12. It was expected that the Grade 1 children might score 100% on a concrete level test and 0 on a formal level test. Therefore, the beginning point could not be ascertained for some dimensions. Similarly, some mean scores of the students when in Grade 12 were less than 100%. In these cases the age of full attainment, or mastery, could not be ascertained. To determine ages corresponding to beginning and mastery performances for all the dimensions, younger children and older individuals would also need to be studied. (Matters of test reliability as noted in Chapter 2 also pose a problem for establishing the age of true beginning performance.) The curves presented in this chapter are based on the mean predicted scores. No attempt is made to extrapolate to earlier or later years. As we shall see in Chapter 8, these curves provide useful information for interpreting the development of individual students.

As indicated earlier, Wohlwill (1973) calls for identifying the ages that correspond to specified points in development—beginning, ending, maximal. Identifying the grade at which the students fully attained the same levels of the different concepts was carried out in this study to estimate the extent to which mastery of the various dimensions may have varied for the four different concepts. Substantial variability in the mastery of any level of the four different concepts—for example, the classificatory level—would imply that ability to perform the mental operations essential at this level is not independent of the content of the four different concepts.

In addition to this very important matter concerning the rate of development and the determination of beginning and ending points for the concept levels and uses, it is helpful to know which level of concept attainment is necessary, sufficient, or facilitative of learning the uses (Flavell, 1977). Gagné (1977), for example, proposed that concepts are necessary for learning rules and rule using is necessary for solving problems. Resnick, Wang, and Kaplan (1973) attempted to identify learning hierarchies in reading and mathematics. In the present study, predictions were related to the facilitative effects of full attainment at each of the four levels in understanding principles of which the concept is a part, in understanding taxonomic relations involving the concept, and in solving problems. Moreover, it may be assumed that if the facilitative effects hold in the same way for the four concepts used in the present study, they will also hold for other similar concepts.

The developmental curves presented in this chapter and those in Chapters 3 and 5 are drawn to the same scale to permit accurate comparisons of the curves presented in the different figures.

In this chapter normative cognitive growth within the longitudinal blocks and across the 12 school grades will be described first. Next, results related to two predictions regarding cognitive development are presented. One prediction is that maturing individuals master the levels of the different concepts at different ages, corresponding to grades of school. For example, more students of Longitudinal Block A, Grades 1–3, will master the formal level of *cutting tool* than the formal level of *noun*. Another prediction is that the attainment of concepts at the successively higher levels is accompanied by increased ability to understand principles, to understand taxonomic relations, and to solve problems. For example, more students of any grade in school who have fully attained the formal level of *noun* will also understand principles and taxonomic relations than will those whose highest level of attainment is the classificatory level.

We shall at times refer to the "uses" tests rather than mentioning the tests by name (e.g., understanding taxonomic relations). Separate tests were constructed to measure understanding principles, understanding taxonomic relations, and problem solving involving each concept, *cutting tool, tree, equilateral triangle,* and *noun.* However, they measure more than transfer of the concept in that attainment of the concept, though necessary, is not sufficient for understanding the several principles or taxonomic relations included in each test. Therefore, the description of normative development, based on the test results of the students within and across the longitudinal blocks, pertains to growth in understanding principles, in understanding taxonomic relations, and in problem solving per se, rather than to the transfer of a single concept.

DEVELOPMENTAL NORMS RELATED TO ATTAINING THE LEVELS OF EACH CONCEPT

Concrete, Identity, Classificatory Levels

Figure 7.1 contains the smoothed curves for the concrete, identity, and classificatory levels of certain concepts. The longitudinal blocks and related grades are shown and also the predicted mean percentages of the items correct. The curves are presented only for the levels in which the obtained mean percentage correct was 90 or less for the children when in Grade 1.

Five curves are given in Figure 7.1: one for the concrete level of *noun*, another for the identity level of *noun*, and one for the classificatory level of each *tree, equilateral triangle,* and *noun.* Curves are not presented for the concrete and identity levels of the other three concepts inasmuch as the students of Longitudinal Block A in Grade 1 had mean percentages correct above 90. Also, the mean percentage correct for the classificatory level of *cutting tool* was 95 for the Block A students when in Grade 1.

Figure 7.1 shows that the mean percentage of items correct on the concrete level of *noun* was 90 for Grade 1. When in Grade 3, these same Block A

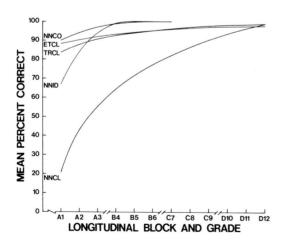

Figure 7.1. Normative development related to attainment of the concrete and identity levels of *noun* and the classificatory level of other concepts except *cutting tool.*

students had 97% correct. The curve for the identity level of *noun* begins at 67% for Grade 1, substantially lower than the curve for concrete. By Grade 3, however, the mean was 94%, and starting with Block B, Grade 4, the mean was 98% or more for both the concrete and identity levels.

Visual inspection of Figure 7.1 shows consistent growth by the students of Block A in attaining the classificatory level of the concepts *equilateral triangle, tree,* and *noun.* The students of Block B showed a decelerating rate of increase for the classificatory level of the three concepts. Longitudinal Blocks C and D maintained a very high percentage correct from Grade 7 through Grade 9 and Grade 10 through Grade 12, respectively, for the classificatory level of *equilateral triangle* and *tree.* They continued to attain *noun* at a fairly rapid rate from Grades 7 through 9 and Grades 10 through 12, respectively.

We may summarize attainment of the concrete, identity, and classificatory levels of the four concepts. The children of Longitudinal Block A had fully attained the concrete, identity, and classificatory levels of *cutting tool* and the concrete and identity levels of *tree* and *equilateral triangle* prior to Grade 1. They made much progress toward full attainment of the classificatory level in Grade 1, and by Grade 3 near full attainment of the classificatory level of *tree* and *equilateral triangle* had occurred. Children of Longitudinal Block A attained the classificatory level of *noun* at a very rapid rate from Grade 1 through Grade 3; a less rapid rate of increase was shown by the three older groups of students until full attainment was reached in Grade 12.

Formal Level

Figure 7.2 depicts normative development related to the formal level for all four concepts. The test of the formal level for *noun* was not administered to Longitudinal Block A students when they were in Grade 1, but it was in Grade 2; therefore, the curve for *noun* starts in Grade 2.

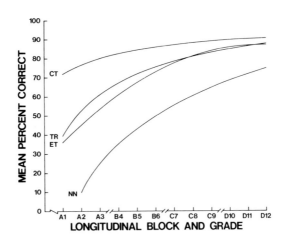

Figure 7.2. Normative development related to attainment of the formal level of concepts.

A highly consistent pattern of growth by each longitudinal block of students is reflected in the four curves of the formal level. The rate of increase is related to the level of performance on the first test administration. In Longitudinal Block A at the time of the first test administration, the percentage correct for the various concepts was as follows: 72%, *cutting tool*; 39%, *tree*; 36%, *equilateral triangle*; and 10%, *noun*. The corresponding percentages in Grade 12 were 91%, *cutting tool*; 88%, *tree*; 87%, *equilateral triangle*; and 75%, *noun*.

It will be recalled that the formal level has four subtests that measure subjects' discrimination of the defining attributes (Chapter 3), acquisition of the names of concepts and of defining attributes (Chapter 5), recognition of the definition of concepts (Chapter 5), and evaluation of examples and nonexamples of the concept on the basis of the presence or absence of the defining attributes (Chapter 3). Smoothed curves based on each of these subtests for each concept were presented in the chapters noted above.

The four smoothed curves for *equilateral triangle* are presented in Figure 7.3 to illustrate the timing and rate at which these aspects of the formal level were attained. As may be noted in Figure 7.3, the order of attainment from earlier to later by the students of Longitudinal Blocks B, C, and D was discriminating the attributes, acquiring the names, acquiring the definition, and evaluating examples and nonexamples. The order of the last two was reversed for Longitudinal Block A.

Development regarding the formal level of concept attainment may be summarized as follows. Children and youth attain the formal level of concepts throughout the school years at a consistent rate. The temporal order of attaining the formal level is related to the concrete–abstract dimension of the examples of the concepts discussed earlier in Chapter 3. The formal level is attained earlier for concepts for which there are concrete examples or pictured representations (i.e., *cutting tool*, *tree*, and *equilateral triangle*), than for concepts that can be experienced only in oral or written form (i.e., *noun*). During the

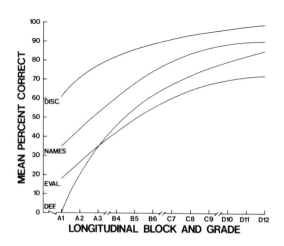

Figure 7.3. Smoothed curves for four subtests of formal level of *equilateral triangle*: discriminating defining attributes, acquiring names of concepts and of defining attributes, acquiring concept definition, and evaluating examples and nonexamples.

elementary school years children make rapid progress related to the two prerequisites for attaining the formal level: discriminating the defining attributes and acquiring the names of the concept and the defining attributes. Being able to define the concept and to evaluate examples and nonexamples follow after discriminating and naming.

DEVELOPMENTAL NORMS RELATED TO UNDERSTANDING PRINCIPLES, UNDERSTANDING TAXONOMIC RELATIONS, AND PROBLEM SOLVING

As part of each concept assessment battery, one test was developed to measure understanding of principles, understanding of taxonomic relationships, and ability to solve problems (see Chapter 2). In Chapter 1, we described these products of learning in some detail and stressed the enormous power they provide the individual in organizing, predicting, explaining, and learning independently.

Understanding Principles

Figure 7.4 includes four smoothed curves that depict development related to understanding principles based on the mean percentage of the items correct, changed to predicted true scores. The curves show development both within the four longitudinal blocks and also across them.

For Longitudinal Block A the curves start in the grade at which the particular test was first administered: *cutting tool*, Grade 1; *tree*, Grade 2; and *equilateral triangle* and *noun*, Grade 3. It may be recalled that these tests were composed of multiple-choice items and that students on a chance basis would get approximately 25% of the items correct. One may infer, then, that the students were essentially functioning at a chance level in Grade 3 for the concepts *noun* and *tree*, but above the chance level for the other two concepts.

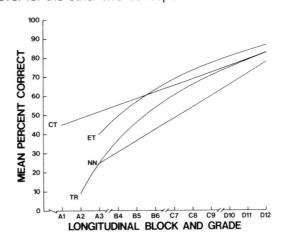

Figure 7.4. Normative development related to understanding principles.

From Grades 4 through 12, the students of Longitudinal Blocks B, C, and D developed an understanding of principles related to *cutting tool* at a uniform rate of increase. The same three groups of students developed an understanding of principles involving *tree* at a rapid but decelerating rate of increase. The principles involving *equilateral triangle* were also understood at a rapid but decelerating rate of increase. The understanding of *noun* increased at a uniform rate.

We may conclude that the understanding of principles, except those related to some concepts that have many concrete examples in the immediate environment (e.g., *cutting tool*), are not understood well by children of primary school age. Progress in understanding principles occurs at about the same rate during the intermediate, junior high school, and senior high school years. When in Grade 12, the mean achievement is still relatively low, ranging from 78 to 87% correct.

The importance to the individual of understanding principles may be inferred from the illustrations that follow, one for each of the four concepts. The principle is stated and a test item to measure understanding is given. The test item samples the many situations a person may experience and interpret correctly if the principle is understood.

Principle for <u>cutting tool</u>: A large cutting tool accomplishes a greater amount of cutting than a small cutting tool of the same kind.

Test Item:

Knife X

Knife X is larger than Knife Y. Knife X and Knife Y have equally sharp blades. Knife X will cut through a large piece of meat _____ Knife Y.

Knife Y

a. more quickly than

b. less quickly than

c. as quickly as

d. It is impossible to tell without trying them out.

e. I don't know.

Principle for <u>tree</u>: New trees develop from seeds.

Test Item: This tree developed from _____.

    a. a trunk
    b. a leaf
    c. a seed
    d. a root
    e. I don't know.

Principle for <u>equilateral triangle</u>: The perimeter of an equilateral triangle is three times the length of any side.

Test Item:

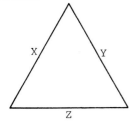

This is an equilateral triangle with sides <u>x</u>, <u>y</u>, and <u>z</u>. Its perimeter is _____.

    a. three times the length of side <u>x</u>, or <u>y</u>, or <u>z</u>.

    b. three times the length of the sum of sides <u>x</u>, <u>y</u>, or <u>z</u>.

    c. two times the length of sides <u>x</u>, <u>y</u>, or <u>z</u>.

    d. I don't know.

Principle for <u>noun:</u> A noun may be used in a sentence as the direct object of a verb.

See the sentence below with the word underlined.

        "John hit the <u>ball</u>."

In the sentence above, the word <u>ball</u> is used as:

a. the subject of the sentence

b. the direct object of the verb

c. an appositive

d. an object of a preposition

e. I don't know.

Understanding Taxonomic Relations

Figure 7.5 contains the smoothed curves portraying development related to understanding taxonomic relations. These curves are to be interpreted in the same manner as the curves for understanding principles. The course of development within and across the longitudinal blocks is now described.

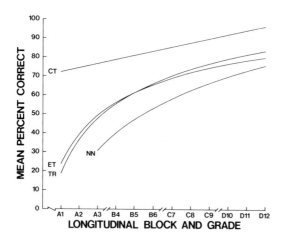

Figure 7.5. Normative development related to understanding taxonomic relations.

Understanding of taxonomic relations related to *cutting tool* proceeded at a uniform rate of increase within and across the four longitudinal blocks. Development related to understanding the taxonomic relations involving *equilateral triangle* and *tree* proceeded at a rapid rate of increase from Grade 1 to Grade 2, and the rate of increase decelerated slowly thereafter. Understanding of the taxonomic relations related to *noun* proceeded at a fairly uniform rate of increase from Grade 3 through Grade 12. It may be observed that taxonomic relations were understood somewhat better than principles during the early grades, but at Grade 12 understanding principles related to *equilateral triangle* and *noun* was slightly better than for understanding taxonomic relations.

In summary, the understanding of taxonomic relations increases quite rapidly throughout the elementary school years; for the four concepts students when in Grade 6 ranged from 53 to 83 in mean percentage correct. The rate of increase in understanding taxonomic relations is low during the junior and senior high school years. Students when in Grade 12 had mean percentages correct for the four concepts ranging from 76 to 96.

Examination of printed textbook and curriculum guides indicates that structures of knowledge, such as taxonomies and other hierarchies, are often not taught explicitly. Apparently curriculum developers and teachers infer that students will integrate separate items and relate them independently. Also, the taxonomies and related material that are included in textbooks and guides seem to imply that students should learn where the classes are located in the taxonomy but that the attributes that indicate the supraordinate, subordinate, and coordinate relations need not be understood. This would result in rote learning of the location of classes within the taxonomy, rather than understanding of relationships as well as of the location of the classes in the taxonomy.

The power gained by the individual through understanding taxonomic relations in terms of relating phenomena in the physical and social world may be inferred from the four statements of taxonomic relations and an example of each.

Relation: Some but not all members of a supraordinate class belong to a given subclass. Example for *cutting tool*: Some but not all cutting tools have a blade that is smooth.

Relation: All members of a subclass belong to a higher class. Example for *tree*: All trees are plants.

Relation: The sum of the members of the subclasses equals the sum of the members of the supraordinate class. Example for *equilateral triangle*: Equilateral triangles, right triangles, and other kinds of triangles equal all triangles.

Relation: The members of one coordinate class are not members of another coordinate class. Example for *noun*: No proper nouns are common nouns.

Problem Solving

Figure 7.6 gives the four smoothed curves depicting development related to problem solving, based on the predicted mean percentage of items correct. The problem-solving tests for *cutting tool* and *tree* were first administered in Grade 1; those for *equilateral triangle* and *noun* were administered for the first time in Grade 3.

The ability to solve problems involving *cutting tool* increased markedly between Grades 1 and 2 and it increased at a gradually decelerating rate

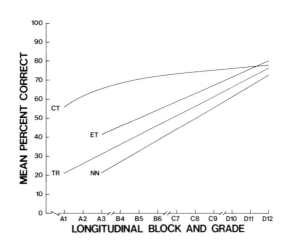

Figure 7.6. Normative development related to problem solving.

thereafter through Grade 12. Problem solving involving *equilateral triangle, tree,* and *noun* showed a uniform rate of increase.

A visual comparison of Figures 7.4 and 7.6 indicates that the students of Longitudinal Blocks A and B tended to solve problems somewhat better than they understood the related principles; however the reverse was true for the students of Longitudinal Blocks C and D. This may be interpreted in terms of our intention to have the problem-solving exercises range in difficulty in order to ascertain whether students who had mastered only the concrete or identity level could solve easy problems. Items to measure the understanding of the principles did not employ a criterion of difficulty.

To summarize development related to problem solving: The ability to solve problems shows a consistent and uniform pattern of increase between consecutive grades throughout the school years. Children of primary school age are able to solve some problems, particularly if the relations among the elements and the solutions are perceptibly obvious. Students throughout the school years develop continuously but relatively slowly in their problem-solving skills. The level of performance throughout the school years is quite low, as indicated by the percentages correct in Grade 12: 78 for *cutting tool*, 76 for *tree*, 80 for *equilateral triangle*, and 72 for *noun*.

Being able to solve complex problems is one attribute of an independent learner, one who can learn without assistance from others. Having attained concepts at the classificatory or formal level and understanding principles involving the concepts facilitates, but is not sufficient for, problem solving. The four exercises that follow illustrate the kinds of performances sampled by the problem-solving tests. The four items involve use of the four principles given earlier in this chapter.

Problem-solving item for <u>cutting tool</u>:

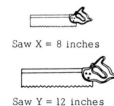

Saw X = 8 inches

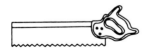

Saw Y = 12 inches

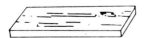

Saw Z = 16 inches

Imagine that Saw X has a sharp blade and is eight inches long. Imagine that Saw Y has a sharp blade and is twelve inches long. Imagine that Saw Z has a sharp blade and is sixteen inches long.

Which saw should be used to cut through the large piece of wood most quickly?

a. Saw X

b. Saw Y

c. Saw Z

d. It is impossible to tell without tryinc them out.

e. I don't know.

Problem-solving item for <u>tree</u>:

Suppose that you had an apple tree and wanted to grow other trees like it. What would you plant from this tree?

a. the roots
b. the seeds
c. the branches
d. any of these
e. I don't know

Problem-solving item for <u>equilateral triangle</u>:

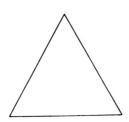

Suppose that one side of this equilateral triangle is 2 inches long. The perimeter of the triangle would be _____.

a. 12 inches

b. 6 inches

c. 3 inches

d. It is impossible to tell without measuring.

e. I don't know.

Problem-solving item for <u>noun</u>:

See the sentence below.

"He hit the _____."

What should be added to complete the sentence above?

a. the word <u>ball</u> used as the subject

b. the word <u>ball</u> used as a predicate nominative

c. the word <u>ball</u> used as a direct object

d. the word <u>ball</u> used as a helping verb

e. I don't know.

DEVELOPMENT RELATED TO ATTAINING THE CLASSIFICATORY AND FORMAL LEVELS COMBINED AND THE THREE USES OF THE CONCEPTS COMBINED

We have examined normative development related to attaining the levels of concepts separately and understanding principles, understanding taxonomic relations, and problem solving. We are now ready to examine normative development based on the classificatory and formal levels combined and on understanding principles, understanding taxonomic relations, and problem solving combined. This will permit comparing the developmental rates for the levels and uses within and across the longitudinal blocks in which all of these tests were administered. The test reliabilities are higher for the combined tests than for the single tests (see Table 2.2); therefore, a more accurate estimate of these two aspects of development is obtained. Also, we shall see in Chapter 8 that a factor was found for each concept battery but not for each level or use separately. Therefore, combining test scores within a battery appears to be an appropriate means for describing these particular aspects of cognitive development.

Figure 7.7 presents eight smooth curves. There are two for each concept: one for the combined levels and one for the combined uses. Visual examination of Figure 7.7 shows that the percentage correct on the combined levels for the students in Longitudinal Block A was higher than on the combined uses. The comparable percentages at Grade 3 were as follows: *cutting tool*—85 for levels, 63 for uses; *tree*—63 for levels, 32 for uses; *equilateral triangle*—59 for levels, 41 for uses; *noun*—34 for levels, 28 for uses. Thus the students of Block A during their primary school years consistently attained the levels somewhat earlier than they were able to use the concepts in understanding principles, in understanding taxonomic relations, and in solving problems involving the particular concepts.

This trend persisted through Longitudinal Blocks B, C, and D. However, as a higher percentage correct was achieved, the size of the difference between the levels and the uses decreased. By Grade 12 the differences between the percentage correct on the levels and the uses were small; in all cases, however, performance on the levels was still higher than on the uses.

Earlier we saw that the separate levels were attained consistently in the following order from highest percentage correct within each longitudinal block to lowest percentage correct: *cutting tool, tree, equilateral triangle,* and *noun.* We also observed that the relative placement of *tree* and *equilateral triangle*

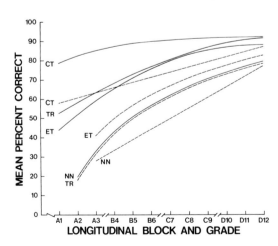

Figure 7.7. Normative development related to attainment of the classificatory and formal levels combined (solid line) and understanding principles, understanding taxonomic relations, and solving problems combined (broken line) based on mean percentage of items correct.

was reversed related to the uses except in understanding taxonomic relations. As might be expected, the same trend is observed in the combined levels and combined uses as depicted in Figure 7.7.

There is remarkable consistency in the rate of development of the levels and the uses of the concepts. For example, a gain from 79 to 93% is shown in the levels for *cutting tool* from Grade 1 to Grade 12 and a gain from 58 to 87% in the uses for *cutting tool* from Grade 1 to Grade 12. The smoothed curves for *tree* and *equilateral triangle* indicate that after rapid development in the students of Longitudinal Blocks A and B there is a gradual decelerating rate of increase in the students of Longitudinal Blocks C and D. The uses of *noun* were attained at a uniform rate.

This difference in the form of the curve for *noun* between the combined levels and the combined uses is not regarded as of much practical significance; however, the students in Longitudinal Blocks A and B acquired the levels more rapidly than in Blocks C and D, where a decelerating rate of increase was observed.

The curves of normative development presented in this chapter are based on the mean scores of the four longitudinal blocks of students. As we shall see in Chapter 8, the curves differ in form from those of individual children and youth. The normative curves provide useful information for interpreting each individual's rate of development.

DIFFERENCE AMONG CONCEPTS IN TERMS OF THE AGE AT WHICH STUDENTS ATTAIN THE CLASSIFICATORY LEVEL AND THE FORMAL LEVEL

One important prediction of CLD theory is that the same level of the different concepts will be fully attained by the individual at different ages. This prediction is based on a substantial amount of research showing that concepts that have many concrete examples widely distributed in the environment are attained earlier than are concepts that can be experienced only verbally. This has been referred to earlier as the concrete–abstract dimension of concept examples. Individuals are able to perform the mental operations earlier on the concepts with the concrete examples.

Figure 7.8 shows the obtained percentages of students in Grades 1, 3, 6, 9, and 12 who fully attained each concept at the classificatory level and at the formal level. Summary information for these 5 grades is presented here and later in the chapter and is regarded as sufficient for drawing conclusions across all 12 grades. The massive amount of detailed information for each grade is presented in various tables of the Appendix. These percentages are not predicted percentages as reported in the prior sections of the chapter, nor are they the mean scores changed to percentages; rather, they indicate the percentages of the students of the four longitudinal blocks who fully attained the level,

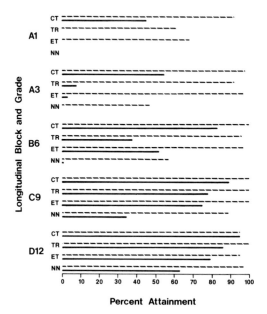

Figure 7.8. Percentage of students in Grades 1, 3, 6, 9, and 12 who mastered each concept at the classificatory level (broken line) and the formal level (solid line).

based on the mastery criterion of 80–85% correct to the nearest item. As shown in Table A.4, a very high percentage of Longitudinal Block A students when in Grade 1 fully attained the concrete and identity levels of the four concepts except *noun*; therefore, it is not possible to present *differences* among the concepts in mastery of these two levels. Instead the classificatory level is considered first.

The percentage of the students of Longitudinal Block A in Grade 1 who mastered the classificatory level of the four concepts varied markedly: *cutting tool*, 92; *tree*, 61; *equilateral triangle*, 68; and *noun*, 0. The difference in mastery of this level did not vary much for *cutting tool, tree,* and *equilateral triangle* in Grades 3, 6, 9, and 12; in all cases 92% or more of all students achieved mastery. The results for *noun*, however, were quite different. In Grade 3 the percentage of mastery was 47%; in Grade 6, 57%; and in Grade 9, 89%. Thus, across Longitudinal Blocks B and C, many fewer students mastered the classificatory level of *noun* than of other concepts; and it was not until Grade 12 that the percentage of mastery was about the same for all concepts.

The differences among the concepts in mastery of the formal level were pronounced within and across all of the longitudinal blocks, as is also shown in Figure 7.8. For example, in Grade 9 the percentages were *cutting tool*, 89; *tree*, 78; *equilateral triangle*, 75; and *noun*, 35. In each grade except 6 the order of mastery from highest to lowest was *cutting tool, tree, equilateral triangle,* and *noun*. In Grade 6 a higher percentage of the students mastered the formal level of *equilateral triangle* (52%) than of *tree* (38%).

The large differences in full attainment of the formal level of the different concepts is of importance both theoretically and practically. In terms of theory of cognitive development, we recognize that the time at which individuals become capable of performing the various operations necessary to master the formal level is highly dependent upon the concrete–abstract dimension of the examples of the concept. Apparently we can carry out the inductive and deductive operations of the formal level more effectively on nonverbal content with which we have experience in informal learning environments outside the school setting. As we saw in a preceding section of this chapter, attainment of concepts at the formal level precedes acquiring an understanding of principles in which the concept is embedded, understanding taxonomic relations of which the concept is a part, and solving problems in which the concept is involved. In the area of formal education, it would appear that more effort might be directed toward helping students acquire concepts at the formal level as early as possible. More explicit information regarding this implication is presented in the next section of the chapter.

RELATIONSHIP BETWEEN MASTERY OF EACH CONCEPT LEVEL AND MASTERY OF THE RELATED PRINCIPLES, TAXONOMIC RELATIONS, AND PROBLEM SOLVING

One of the major propositions of CLD theory is that understanding a principle, understanding taxonomic relations, and solving problems are related to the level at which the concepts are attained. More specifically, a concept attained only to the concrete or identity level can be used only in solving simple problems of a perceptual kind and in cognizing simple perceptual relations among concepts—tasks that can be accomplished without symbolic thinking. When a particular concept and also the other concepts that may be involved in the principle or taxonomy have been attained at the higher levels, however, they can be used in understanding taxonomic and other hierarchical relationships, in understanding principles involving cause-and-effect and other relations among concepts, and in solving problems. Moreover, attainment of concepts at the formal level in comparison with attainment at the classificatory level further facilitates concept utilization.

To test these predictions, each student's score on each test was evaluated in terms of fully attaining or not fully attaining each of the four levels and mastering or not mastering each of the three uses. The number of students who fully attained each level and the instances of mastery of each use are given in Appendix Table A.6. (The term *instances* is used because one individual who mastered a level of any concept may also have mastered as many as three uses of the same concept.) Within each longitudinal block at each grade the highest level that a student had fully attained was identified and then that student's records were examined to find which uses the student had also mastered.

In Table 7.1 summary information for Grades 1, 3, 6, 9, and 12 is presented

TABLE 7.1 Number of Students Fully Attaining Each Concept Level and Instances of Mastery of Understanding Principles, Understanding Taxonomic Relations, and Problem Solving[a]

Block and grade	Concrete/identity					Classificatory					Formal												
	CT	TR	ET	NN	Total	CT	TR	ET	NN	Total	CT			TR			ET			NN			Total
											PR	TAX	PS	PR	TAX	PS	PR	TAX	PS	PR	TAX	PS	
A1																							
N att. level	2	24	18	46	90	32	38	42	0	112	28			0			0			*			28
Instances/uses mastery	2	0	0	*	2	27	0	0	*	27	0	13	16	0	0		0			*	*	*	29
A3																							
N att. level	0	5	2	31	38	28	52	58	29	167	34			5			2			0			41
Instances/uses mastery	0	0	0	0	0	18	11	28	3	60	2	25	17	0	1	0	0	1	1	0	0	0	47
B6																							
N att. level	0	3	2	33	38	13	45	35	43	136	64			29			40			1			134
Instances/uses mastery	0	0	3	4	7	11	18	35	12	76	37	58	43	5	24	9	17	29	31	1	0	0	254

178

															Total
C9															
N att. level	0	0	0	9	9	9	18	20	43	90	71	62	60	28	221
Instances/ uses mastery	0	0	0	4	4	9	19	17	26	71	40 64 52	24 58 43	37 49 47	15 23 21	473
D12															
N att. level	0	0	0	1	1	4	10	15	26	55	69	63	58	46	236
Instances/ uses mastery	0	0	0	1	1	3	5	18	17	43	44 65 51	34 52 51	48 42 51	32 31 38	539
Total															
N att. level	2	32	22	120	176	86	163	170	141	560	266	159	160	75	660
Instances/ uses mastery	2	0	3	9	14	68	53	98	58	277	123 225 179	63 135 103	102 121 130	48 54 59	1342

[a] Asterisk indicates test not administered.

for the concrete and identity levels combined of each of the four concepts and the three uses combined, for the classificatory level and the three uses combined, and for the formal level and each use separately.

As may be observed in Table 7.1, the number of individuals who fully attained the concrete or identity level as their highest level of attainment when in Grade 1 was *cutting tool*, 2; *tree*, 24; *equilateral triangle*, 18; *noun*, 46. Of these students who mastered the concrete or identity level as their highest achievement in Grade 1, there were only two instances of mastery of any use and that was for *cutting tool*. Across the five grades and four concepts, a total of 176 students mastered either the concrete or identity level of one of the concepts as their highest achievement. There was a total of only 14 instances of mastery of understanding principles, understanding taxonomic relations, and solving problems.

Another prediction of CLD theory is that full attainment of the classificatory level will facilitate understanding of principles, understanding of taxonomic relations, and problem solving. In Table 7.1 we see that substantial numbers of students fully attained the classificatory level as their highest level of achievement. The proportion of instances of mastery of the uses in relation to the number of students mastering the levels was 277/560, or .49. The number of instances of mastery of the uses in relation to the number of students who mastered the classificatory level increased at each successively higher grade. There was great variability among the four concepts in the number of students mastering the classificatory level and the relative number of instances of mastery of the uses. The proportion of instances of mastery of the uses in relation to the number of students mastering the classificatory level was from highest to lowest: *cutting tool*, *equilateral triangle*, *noun*, and *tree*.

The number of students who mastered the formal level and the instances of mastery of each of the three uses of each of the four concepts are given in Table 7.1. Having the information for each of the uses of each of the four concepts permits comparing the facilitative effects of fully attaining the formal level on each use of each concept.

As can be seen in Table 7.1, the number of students who fully attained the formal level of the various concepts increased consistently from Grade 1 through Grade 12. The proportion of instances of mastery of the uses (total 1342) in relation to the number of students mastering the level (total 660) was much higher than was found for the classificatory level. Further, the proportions were quite high for all four concepts and all five grades.

Adding across the instances of uses in Table 7.1 shows that full attainment of the formal level was associated with mastery of the uses from highest to lowest as follows: taxonomic relations, problem solving, and principles. One might speculate that many individuals who have mastered a concept at the formal level have also formed a conceptual core, or semantic field, that includes other supraordinate and coordinate concepts of the taxonomy. On the other hand, understanding the more complex relations among the concepts embodied in principles requires a higher level of cognitive functioning.

In summary, substantial numbers of students when in Grades 1, 3, and 6 fully attained the concrete or identity level as their highest achievement but they rarely mastered understanding principles, understanding taxonomic relations, or problem solving. Substantial numbers of students in Grades 1, 3, 6, 9, and 12 mastered the classificatory level of three or four concepts as their highest achievement. The instances of uses mastered in relation to the numbers mastering the classificatory level increased across the grades. The ratio of the total instances of mastery of the uses to the total number of students who mastered the classificatory level was 277/560, or about .49 to 1.00.

Relatively few students through Grade 3 fully attained the formal level of any concept except *cutting tool*, and in Grade 6 only one had fully attained the formal level of *noun*. Full attainment of the formal level of the concepts was associated with substantial mastery of understanding taxonomic relations, problem solving, and understanding principles. The ratio of the total instances of mastery of the uses to the total number of students who mastered the formal level of one or more concepts was 1342/660, or about 2.03 to 1.00. (The maximum ratio possible is 3.00 to 1.00.) Clearly, understanding principles, understanding taxonomic relations, and problem solving are facilitated by full attainment of concepts at the formal level more than at the classificatory level.

DISCUSSION

In the preceding pages, normative growth curves have been presented that portray the course of development in attaining the four levels of concepts, in understanding principles and taxonomic relations, and in problem solving. What do the smoothed curves imply regarding the course of cognitive development during the school years? What is their relevance for some of the important issues concerning the nature of cognitive growth?

Let us first clarify certain matters related to the beginning point, ending point, and form of the curves. Figure 7.9 shows the curves for the four levels of *noun*. The form of the concrete and identity curves is quadratic, whereas those for classificatory and formal are natural log. Near 100% correct was attained for the first two levels prior to Grade 6, whereas in Grade 12 the percentage correct had not yet approached 100%. Since there was an increase between Grades 11 and 12 for the classificatory and formal levels, further increase might be expected. The form of the curve might also then change to quadratic if near 100% correct was attained. Similarly, if the younger children had been studied earlier, a sharper rise might have occurred during the two or three earlier years for the concrete and identity levels but the form would still probably have been quadratic. Other curves for which the beginning points were above 20–25%

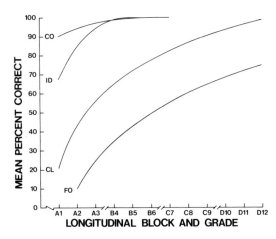

Figure 7.9. Normative development related to attainment of the concrete, identity, classificatory, and formal levels of *noun*.

correct in Grade 1 or rising between Grades 11 and 12 are to be interpreted in a similar manner. The fact that the beginning points of some curves and the ending points of others were not found is taken into account in the remainder of this discussion.

Flavell (1971, 1977) and Wohlwill (1973) present some of the major questions that continue to persist in regard to describing the course of cognitive development: Do all individuals progress through the stages, levels, or phases in the same invariant sequence? Do the items of a stage or level reach mature functioning abruptly in a short period of time or gradually over a long time interval? Do the items or dimensions within an area develop in a synchronous manner or in an asynchronous, concurrent pattern? Items that develop in "pure" synchrony start functioning and reach full maturity at the same time and their developmental curves are of identical rates and forms. Items may, however, begin functioning and reach full functioning at the same or different times and also progress at somewhat different rates. We use the term *concurrent* to indicate this pattern, and the smoothed curves indicate the years during which two or more items are developing concurrently.

In Chapter 6 the evidence is clear that the large majority of students of school age master the four successively higher levels of the same concept in an invariant sequence. We may now examine the continuity and synchrony attributes of development.

Figure 7.10 shows the form of curves for depicting abrupt and synchronous development such as occurs in the stages of metamorphosis of the frog or butterfly. At the beginning of each stage all the functions of which the organism at that stage is capable are mature, and new functions and a different structure emerge at the beginning of each stage (see Flavell, 1972, for a more complete discussion). Clearly, attainment of the four successive levels as shown in Figure 7.9 does not emerge in this kind of pattern. Rather, there is concurrent development of the first three levels in Grades 1, 2, and 3; neither the concrete nor the

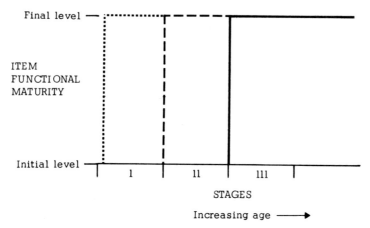

Figure 7.10.   Metamorphosis analogy to stages of cognitive development. (Based on Flavell, 1971, p. 426.)

identity level has reached its maximum level when attainment of the classificatory level begins. There is a similar amount of concurrence of the identity, classificatory, and formal levels. Development of the classificatory level continues throughout the school years, and the formal level has not reached full maturity in Grade 12. Thus, there is continuous, gradual, and concurrent development of the levels rather than discontinuous, abrupt, and synchronous development. The gradual and continuous nature of this development is explained in terms of information presented in earlier chapters: (1) the emergence of the new operations necessary for attaining each successive level; (2) the increasing ability to attend to, discriminate, process, and store more information and also more complex information; (3) increasing language competence; (4) increasing knowledge, including the attainment of the prior levels, that enables more effective relating and organizing; and (5) effective strategies for securing, processing, and remembering information.

We now turn to the curves for understanding principles, understanding taxonomic relations, and problem solving that were presented in this chapter. It will be recalled that an invariant sequence was not assumed for these three dimensions of development. Also, the mental operations that might be involved in learning these products were not specified.

Growth in problem solving progresses at a uniform rate throughout the school years (straight line), whereas understanding taxonomic relations progresses rapidly during the earlier years and less rapidly in successively later years (quadratic curve). Growth in understanding principles proceeds at a uniform rate for certain concepts and progresses rapidly during the earlier years and less rapidly during successively later years. As noted earlier in this discussion, the form of the straight curves might have become quadratic had the Grade 12 students been followed until they reached near 100% or had there been no further increase after Grade 12. Careful examination of the curves for these three dimensions of cognitive development also implies continuity and gradualness for each dimension and concurrent development of the three dimensions. The gradual and continuous nature of this development is explained in terms of (1) sequentially attaining concepts to successively higher levels, (2) the ability to attend to, discriminate, process, and store more information and also more complex information, (3) increasing language competence, and (4) more effective strategies for securing, processing, and remembering information.

FOR FURTHER STUDY

Bayley, N. Development of mental abilities. In P. H. Mussen (Ed.), *Carmichael's manual of child psychology* (Vol. 1). New York: John Wiley & Sons, Inc., 1970. Pp. 1163–1209.

After briefly discussing theories of intelligence and the measurement of mental abilities, Bayley summarizes the findings of several longitudinal studies. A number of indivdual and group curves, based on Berkeley Growth Study data, illustrate the growth of intelligence from birth to adulthood. Comparisons of Bayley's curves with our curves is of some interest, although the former were derived from standardized intelligence tests. The classic longitudinal studies of mental development of the past half century relied almost exclusively on the use of infant scales and either the Stanford-Binet or the Wechsler scales.

Brainerd, C. J. *Piaget's theory of intelligence*. Englewood Cliffs, New Jersey: Prentice Hall, 1978.

Piagetian theory is presented as a system of hypotheses that should be submitted to scientific test. Research that supports or refutes the hypotheses is included. Separate chapters are given to each of the four stages. Key metatheoretical concepts including stage, structure, and schema are treated in objective and neutral language. Education based on Piagetian theory is discussed.

8

Interindividual and Intraindividual Differences in Cognitive Development: Longitudinal–Cross-sectional Results

In Chapters 6 and 7, several important dimensions of cognitive development during the school years were clarified. Because of their significance for the complete picture that emerged from the study, some of the primary conclusions may be reviewed before proceeding to results presented in this chapter.

In Chapter 6, we observed that the four successively higher levels of concepts are attained in an invariant sequence. The consistency of the results across the four concepts and within the longitudinal blocks supports a powerful principle of development, namely, that the new mental operations essential for attaining each successively higher level of a concept emerge successively with learning and maturation.

In Chapter 7, the rate at which the levels of concepts, the understanding of principles, the understanding of taxonomic relations, and problem solving develop across the school years was depicted in smoothed curves. In general, there is a rapid rate of increase during the first year or two during which any of the four levels is being attained. This is followed by a decelerating rate of increase and then a plateau as attainment approaches 95% correct. The consistency of this pattern for all levels and all concepts is remarkable. Understanding taxonomic relations for most concepts proceeds in the same manner as the levels; however, problem solving shows a uniform rate of increase throughout the school years. Understanding principles also progresses consistently throughout the school years; for some concepts growth proceeds at a uniform rate of increase and for others at a rapid rate of increase followed by a decelerating rate. More important than the form of the curves is the consistent development throughout the school years.

The four levels and the three uses of *cutting tool* were mastered first and of *noun* last., This finding supports a basic proposition that the same mental operations are performed earlier on concepts with three-dimensional examples that can be experienced directly rather than only verbally.

Another important dimension of cognitive development clarified in Chapter 7 is that as concepts are attained to the successively higher levels, they can be used with increasing effectiveness in understanding taxonomic relations, in solving problems, and in understanding principles. Mastery of only the concrete or identity level is accompanied by practically no mastery of any use; mastery of the formal level is associated with much greater mastery of the uses than is mastery of the classificatory level. We digress momentarily to emphasize how important it is to the individual to master the formal level as early as possible.

In this chapter, we portray interindividual differences and intraindividual differences in development. How much variability in performance might a teacher or other person expect among students in any grade who are of approximately the same chronological age? Results based on the percentage of students who did and who did not master the levels and the uses of concepts are presented to answer this question. Should we expect students to be equally high, middle, or low in their performances across the four concepts? Differences within individuals in their patterns of attaining the four concepts as inferred from factor analysis are presented to clarify this facet of development.

Some of the most interesting findings concern interindividual differences in cognitive development. Curves depicting the individual performances of a few of the most rapid and a few of the least rapid developers underscore the presence of wide individual differences in cognitive growth. Because large differences were found among individuals, conditions in the student, the home, and the school that may have contributed to the differential rates of development were identified. These findings are presented in the last part of the chapter.

INTERINDIVIDUAL DIFFERENCES IN FULL ATTAINMENT OF THE CONCEPT LEVELS AND IN MASTERY OF THE USES WITHIN AND ACROSS GRADES

Eighty–85% correct to the nearest whole item was established as the criterion for full attainment of each concept level and use, except for the classificatory level of *equilateral triangle*, where the criterion was 100%, or three of three items. Each student's performance each year was evaluated against this criterion of full mastery. Appendix Table A.4 gives the complete results of this evaluation, part of which is included in this section to illustrate the extent of interindividual differences in mastery of the concept levels and uses across longitudinal blocks and grades. Examination of Table A.4 shows that a large percentage of the students of Longitudinal Block A had mastered the concrete, identity, and classificatory levels of the four concepts, except *noun*, in Grade 3 or earlier; however, only a small percentage had mastered the formal level of any concept, except *cutting tool*, or the understanding of principles in Grade 3. Also, less than 100% of the students in Longitudinal Block D had mastered the formal level and understanding of principles in Grade 12. Therefore, from the large amount of available information, mastery of the formal level of the four concepts and of understanding the related principles was selected to illustrate the differences among students' performances within grades and across the four longitudinal grade blocks. As may be noted in Appendix Table A.4, the percentage of students in Grades 1–12 who mastered the understanding of taxonomic relations and problem solving was, in general, slightly higher than for principles but substantially lower than for the formal level.

Table 8.1 gives the percentage of students of Grades 1, 3, 6, 9, and 12 who did and did not attain the formal level of each concept and who did and did not attain mastery of each principle. Examination of Table 8.1 reveals a wide range of individual differences both within each grade and across the four longitudinal blocks. For example, the percentages of students who did and did not attain the formal level of *cutting tool* were as follows: Grade 1—45 and 55; Grade 3—55 and 45; Grade 6—83 and 17; Grade 9—89 and 11; and Grade 12—95 and 5. The comparable percentages of mastery and nonmastery of the principles for *cutting tool* were Grade 1—2 and 98; Grade 3—3 and 97; Grade 6—49 and 51; Grade 9—50 and 50; and Grade 12—60 and 40. Further examination of the table reveals the large differences within each grade in students' mastery of the formal levels and of the principles of the other three concepts.

The differences across the longitudinal blocks are even more dramatic, as may be illustrated by comparing performances related to *equilateral triangle*. The percentage of students mastering and not mastering the formal level are Grade 3—3 and 97; Grade 12—79 and 21. What do these percentages reveal in terms of variation across these two widely separated grades? They indicate that 3% of the Grade 3 children in the study performed better, in terms of full attainment of the formal level, than did 21% of students in Grade 12. In understanding principles related to *equilateral triangle*, 38% of the Grade 6 students attained mastery but 27% of the twelfth-graders failed to reach the mastery criterion.

What do these findings imply? Clearly, there are very wide differences among students within grades and across grades in their levels of cognitive development. It is difficult to visualize what would be involved in attempting to arrange instruction that would take these differences into account. To illustrate, although 52% of the Grade 6 students had attained the formal level of *equilateral triangle*, among the 48% who had not, one would expect 21% still not to have done so in their last year of high school as instruction was carried out for these students.

TABLE 8.1 Percentage of Students Who Did and Did Not Fully Attain the Formal Level of Each Concept and Who Did and Did Not Master the Related Principles[a]

Block and grade	Formal level								Principle							
	CT		TR		ET		NN		CT		TR		ET		NN	
	A	NA	A	NA	A	NA	A	NA	A	NA	A	NA	A	NA	A	NA
A1	45	55	0	100	0	100	*	*	2	98	*	*	*	*	*	*
A3	55	45	8	92	3	97	0	100	3	97	2	98	0	100	2	98
B6	83	17	38	62	52	48	1	99	49	51	6	94	38	62	1	99
C9	89	11	78	22	75	25	35	65	50	50	31	69	51	49	25	75
D12	95	5	86	14	79	21	63	37	60	40	47	53	73	27	49	51

[a] * indicates test not administered at this grade.

INTRAINDIVIDUAL DIFFERENCES IN PATTERNS OF ATTAINING THE CONCEPT LEVELS AND USES

In the prior section of this chapter, we noted the wide differences found among individuals within the same grade and among individuals across grades in their mastery of the concept levels and uses. In this section, intraindividual differences in attaining the levels and uses of the four different concepts are presented; the related prediction of CLD theory is that individuals will not perform equally well across all four concepts. This prediction is based on the premise that persons do not process different kinds of content equally effectively—for example, the mathematical content of *equilateral triangle* and the verbal content of *noun*. Factor analytic methods and tabulating a sample of students' quartile scores were used to identify and describe the intraindividual differences.

Results of Factor Analysis

Correlations were run among all the test scores obtained at each grade level. The resulting matrices were analyzed by three methods of factor analysis: the principal components method, the R–S² method as developed by Harris (1962), and the unrestricted maximum likelihood method of factor analysis (UMLFA) of Jöreskog (1967). Both orthogonal and oblique rotations were performed on the raw factor matrices, yielding six different factor solutions.

The number of factors identified by each of the six solutions was determined objectively by ceasing to derive additional factors when the eigenvalue of the next factor was less than 1.00. That is, the eigenvalue of the last factor obtained was always 1.00 or larger. Each common factor was determined by identifying the tests that loaded .30 or higher (absolute value) on the same factor in four or more of the six solutions. These criteria for objectively determining the number of factors and also for identifying the common factors were employed by Harris and Harris (1973). The primary merit of employing the comparable factor strategy is that neither a single method nor a single rotational procedure, in isolation, can account for a variable's acceptance or rejection on a common factor.

In Table 8.2 the four factors identified for Grade 6 are indicated. The related correlation matrix is presented in Appendix Table A.7. We shall use the results from Grade 6 to illustrate the intraindividual differences. Intraindividual differences for Grades 1–5 vary somewhat from the factors identified from Grade 6 because more and somewhat different factors were found in Grades 1–5. Essentially the same factors were found in Grades 7–12 as in Grade 6. A complete report of the factors identified in each grade is presented in Klausmeier and Associates (in preparation).

For Grade 6, one factor was found for each of the four concepts: *cutting tool, tree, equilateral triangle,* and *noun*. As shown in Table 8.2, three tests of the

TABLE 8.2 Common Factor Results for Grade 6 Based on Three Methods of Analysis and Orthogonal and Oblique Rotation Procedures[a]

	Orthogonal			Oblique		
	P	M	H	P	M	H
Comparable Common Factor 1						
CTTAX	57	33	63	62	64	73
CTPR	79	89	35	55	33	37
CTPS			73	80	100	85
Comparable Common Factor 2						
TRTAX	79	72	68	69	84	74
TRPR	64	60	72	81	75	75
TRPS	50	42	61	63	69	72
TRCL	65	51	52	74	53	56
TRFO	71	72	45	45	45	47
Comparable Common Factor 3						
ETTAX	73	72	68	78	63	67
ETFO	77	66	63	74	69	67
ETPR	62	45	71	73	72	72
ETPS	70	62	45	62	43	44
Comparable Common Factor 4						
NNFO	56	69	64	69	65	66
NNPS	61	63	61	43	63	57
NNCL	69	47	56	74	44	55
NNTAX	44		67	60	69	65
TRCL	−36			−56	−45	−47

[a] Includes values greater than .30. Decimals have been omitted.

cutting tool battery—understanding taxonomic relations, understanding principles, and problem solving—had loadings of .33 or higher in six, six, and four of the solutions, respectively. This factor may be designated cutting tool. The tests of the classificatory level and the formal level did not appear in four of the six solutions. Five tests of the *tree* battery loaded .42 or higher in all six solutions of the next factor, called tree. Here the tests of the classificatory and formal levels loaded on this factor in all six solutions, as did the other three tests. On Factor 3, equilateral triangle, the formal-level test and the other three tests loaded .43 or higher in all six solutions. The fourth factor, noun, had loadings very like those for equilateral triangle. We point out that although both the concrete-level and identity-level tests for all four concepts were administered in Grade 6 (but not in Grade 7 and thereafter), students scored 100% correct on these tests; therefore, loadings for these tests were absent from any factor obtained by any of the six procedures.

It is clear from the preceding that attainment of the concepts and their uses by sixth-grade students is related to the content of each concept. The operations involved in attaining the classificatory and formal levels and the related uses of each concept appear to be content related. This finding has considerable importance for CLD theory and also for instruction, especially since it parallels the results of a comprehensive study dealing with students' achievement of concepts that were taught to them as part of the schools' curricula.

Harris and Harris (1973) analyzed the results of achievement tests of 30 different concepts drawn from each of four curricular areas—mathematics, science, language arts, and social studies—that were administered to 200 boys and 200 girls who had recently completed Grade 5. They obtained one language arts concept–achievement factor, one mathematics factor, and one science factor. The social studies factor tended to be related also to science.

The cutting tool factor identified in the present study merits further discussion. It may be recalled that the concept *cutting tool* was selected for this study as the one concept that is not normally taught in school as a part of any curricular area. We saw also in Chapter 7 that the classificatory and formal levels of this concept are attained by students at a younger age than are any of the other concepts. It is possible that this factor may represent the effects of both earlier learning and informal learning rather than later learning that occurs with formal instruction in school.

Tabular Presentation of Results

The structure of concept attainment abilities differentiated according to the separate concepts implies that students do not score at the same level on the same tests of the different concepts. To illustrate this, five boys and five girls were drawn at random from the Grade 6 sample of boys and girls. Their *total scores* on five tests were obtained: classificatory level, formal level, principles, taxonomic relations, and problem solving. These scores were changed to quartile scores, based on the total distribution of Grade 6 scores. The quartile scores are plotted for each of the four concepts in Table 8.3.

As may be observed in Table 8.3, Student Number 1 was in the top quartile, the fourth quartile, on all four concepts. Three students had scores in two adjacent quartiles. These students are numbered 2, 5, and 9. Three students, namely, Numbers 3, 7, and 8 had quartile scores in three adjacent quartiles. Two students, Numbers 6 and 10, had scores in three quartiles, but not adjacent quartiles, namely quartiles 4, 3, and 1 and 4, 2, and 1, respectively. One student, Number 4, had scores in four different quartiles.

In summary, we infer from the factor analytic results and the tabular illustration that individuals vary within themselves with respect to their performances on different concepts. Cognitive growth is not unitary or global, a kind of growth characterized by equally high or low performance related to all concepts. Students vary within themselves in the rate at which they grow in different content fields.

TABLE 8.3   Patterns of Grade 6 Students' Attainment of Four Concepts Based on Quartile Scores[a]

Top	CT	TR	ET	NN
Quartile 4	1 2 3 4	1 5 6	1 10	1 2 3 5 7
Quartile 3	5 6	2 3 7 8	2 5	4 6 8
Quartile 2	7	4 10	3 7 8	9
Quartile 1	8 9 10	9	4 6 9	10
Bottom				

[a] The five boys (numbered 1, 3, 5, 9, 10) and five girls (numbered 2, 4, 6, 7, 8) were selected at random from the 77 Longitudinal Block B students.

DIFFERENCES IN INDIVIDUALS' RATES OF COGNITIVE DEVELOPMENT

Earlier in this chapter we saw that there were very wide differences in the performances of students of the same grade. These wide variations reflect differences among the students in the rates at which they have learned and matured cognitively up to the particular grade level. We also saw that individuals vary within themselves in their performances related to the four different concepts. We shall now deal with individuals' rates of cognitive development. To illustrate maximum differences in rate of cognitive development, eight individuals were identified in the following manner. Using only the data from the last year of testing, a total test score on each battery was obtained for all students in each longitudinal block (Grades 3, 6, 9, and 12). These scores were changed to percentile scores. One student among those scoring in the highest quartile and one student among those scoring in the lowest quartile across all four assessment batteries were selected at random from each grade block.

For each of the eight students, scores on the classificatory and formal levels of each concept were combined, as were scores on the three uses of each concept. This procedure ensured reasonably high reliability of the test scores, which is critical when examining the rates of individual students. The highest scorers and the lowest scorers—selected on the basis of their performances in 1976—were expected, however, to show considerable variability across the 3 years of testing related to the different concepts. A substantial amount of intraindividual variability was demonstrated in the preceding section. Similarly, smooth curves should not be expected across 3 years for the same individuals because of the relatively small number of items in the combined tests and the relatively large error of measurement in relation to the total number of items.

To depict the rates of the eight individuals, their combined classificatory and formal-level scores on each concept, changed to percentages, were plotted, as were the scores for the combined uses. The smoothed developmental curves based on the mean scores of each longitudinal block were included in the figure depicting the individuals' rates. This permits observation of the eight individuals' rates, comparison among them, and also comparison with the developmental curve obtained across all 12 grades. It may be recalled (see Chapter 2) that the smoothed curves take into account possible distortions due to the effects of repeated testing, cohort differences, and possible low reliability of scores due to ceiling effects and conditions of test administration. The eight individuals' curves do not, since they are based on the actual scores obtained.

Figure 8.1 shows the curves for the combined classificatory and formal levels related to *cutting tool* for four rapid and four slow developers. The rapid and the slow developer in Longitudinal Block A show different levels of performance and also rates of development. The rapid developer was at 100% correct in Grade 1, then dropped in Grade 2, and went to 92% correct in Grade 3. On the other hand, the slow developer was at 54% correct in Grade 1, went up to 58% in Grade 2, and to 77% in Grade 3. The smoothed curve for the entire group of students in Longitudinal Block A shows that the mean was 79% in Grade 1 and 85% in Grade 3.

The rapid and the slow developer in Longitudinal Block B had similar rates of development, but their levels of performance were quite different. The difference in the level and the form of the curves between the rapid and the slow developer is very great in Longitudinal Block C. The level of performance and the rate also vary greatly for the rapid developer and the slow developer in Longitudinal Block D.

As the reader can observe in this and the next seven figures, the difference in

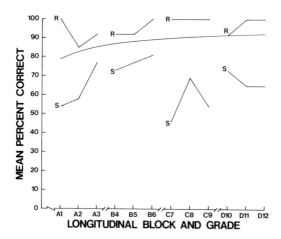

Figure 8.1. Rates of rapid (R) and slow (S) developers within each grade block: classificatory and formal levels combined—*cutting tool.*

the level of attainment between the rapid and the slow developer tends to increase with each successive longitudinal block. Also there is a tendency for the slow developer in Grade 12 to perform less well in Grade 12 than in Grade 10. And finally, the scores of the slow developers tend to vary more from one year to the next than do those of the rapid developers, even though the rapid developers are near the ceiling on many tests. A brief interpretation of the main trends follows.

Figure 8.2 shows the rate of development related to principles, taxonomic relations, and problem solving combined for the concept *cutting tool*. The curves are for the same eight individuals as discussed in the prior paragraph. The large differences between the rapid and the slow developers of Longitudinal Blocks C and D are immediately apparent.

Figure 8.3 shows the rates of the four rapid and four slow developers related to the classificatory and formal levels combined of the concept *tree*. Figure 8.4

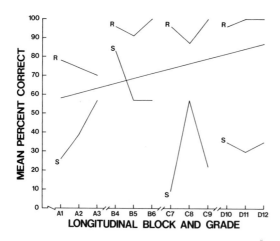

Figure 8.2. Rates of rapid (R) and slow (S) developers within each grade block: principles, taxonomic relations, and problem solving combined—*cutting tool.*

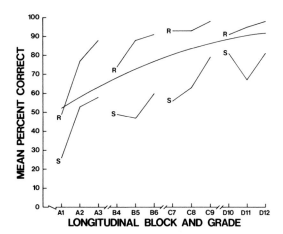

Figure 8.3. Rates of rapid (R) and slow (S) developers within each grade block: classificatory and formal levels combined—*tree*.

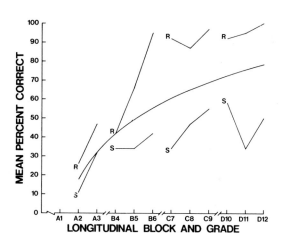

Figure 8.4. Rates of rapid (R) and slow (S) developers within each grade block: principles, taxonomic relations, and problem solving combined—*tree*.

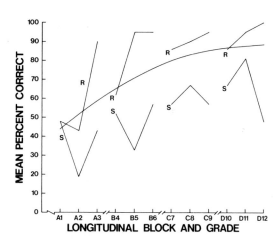

Figure 8.5. Rates of rapid (R) and slow (S) developers within each grade block: classificatory and formal levels combined—*equilateral triangle*.

presents similar information for the combined principles, problem solving, and taxonomic relations tests. The rates of the rapid and the slow developers here are much the same as they are for the combined classificatory and formal levels. One observable contrast is that the differences in the level of performance finally attained by the rapid and the slow developers of Blocks C and D are somewhat greater than for those of Blocks A and B.

Figure 8.5 gives the results for the classificatory and formal levels combined for *equilateral triangle*. The rapid developers in Longitudinal Blocks A and B showed a rapidly accelerating rate of development. The rapid developers of Blocks C and D showed a much lower rate of acceleration. The curves for the four slow developers are typical of the slow developers generally in that their performances from one year to the next are erratic. Figure 8.6 portrays the rates related to principles, problem solving, and taxonomic relations combined. The patterns are much the same as for the levels.

Figure 8.7 presents the patterns for the classificatory and formal levels for *noun*. The rapid developer of each longitudinal block shows a consistent increase from the first year to the last year of testing. (It will be recalled that the formal level of *noun* was not administered in Grade 1.) The slow developers show an inconsistent pattern. Similar patterns are indicated in Figure 8.8 for principles, problem solving, and taxonomic relations combined. There is some variability among the rapidly developing students and an erratic pattern in the rate of development and also in the level of performance of the slow developers.

The graphic displays of eight individuals' rates of cognitive development provide some indication of the uniqueness of human cognitive growth. Three generalizations may be inferred from analysis of the eight individuals' patterns. First, the rate of growth is more consistent for rapidly developing individuals than it is for slowly developing individuals. Second, the difference in final level of performance between the rapid and slow developer tends to increase across

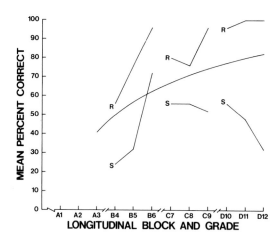

Figure 8.6.   Rates of rapid (R) and slow (S) developers within each grade block: principles, taxonomic relations, and problem solving combined—*equilateral triangle*.

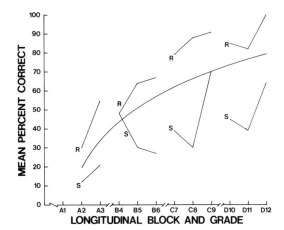

Figure 8.7. Rates of rapid (R) and slow (S) developers within each grade block: classificatory and formal levels combined—*noun*.

the successive longitudinal blocks from A to B to C to D. Finally, there is a possibility that cognitive growth actually stops for slow developers in Grades 9 and 10, as suggested by the consistently lower performance of the slow developer of Block D across the concept levels and uses in comparison with the performances of the slow developers of Longitudinal Block B and Longitudinal Block C. (Table A.3 shows that the mean percentage scores of students tended to rise slowly if at all between Grades 10–11 and 11–12 on a number of the tests, even though well below 90%.)

It may be instructive to conjecture concerning the apparent losses that occurred between consecutive years of testing, particularly as they occurred for the four slowly developing students. On a post hoc basis, these losses may be attributed to a number of possible conditions: unidentifiable variations in test administrations across the 3 years of testing, unidentifiable variations in the student's test motivation, health, and other conditions at the time of testing

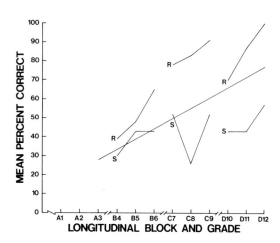

Figure 8.8. Rates of rapid (R) and slow (S) developers within each grade block: principles, taxonomic relations, and problem solving combined—*noun*.

across the 3 years, and actual losses of knowledge. The apparent losses by the students of Longitudinal Blocks A, B, and C are most likely to have resulted from the unidentifiable differences in testing conditions and motivational and other conditions of the student. The consistent lack of increase by the student in Longitudinal Block D may reflect an actual loss.

CONDITIONS CONTRIBUTING TO RAPID AND SLOW COGNITIVE DEVELOPMENT

An intensive study of six rapid and six slow developers was undertaken when the students of Longitudinal Blocks B and D were in Grades 6 and 12 (Mize & Klausmeier, 1977). Grades 6 and 12 were selected because these are the terminal grades of elementary and secondary schooling and because relatively complete school records were available for the prior 6 years. (These rapid and slow developers are not the same students as those whose performances were described in the preceding section.)

One purpose of the study was to identify conditions related to each student's individual and personal characteristics, school and education, and home and family that might contribute to rapid or slow cognitive development. The hypothesis was that one pattern of conditions might be identified as contributing to rapid development and another to slow development. Should this hypothesis prove correct, a second objective was to determine which conditions associated with slow development might be ameliorated or possibly prevented.

Comprehensive information was gathered on each of the 12 children in order to answer the following questions:

1. Do students of rapid and slow conceptual development differ in
   a. Intellectual abilities?
   b. Self-esteem and perceptions of self?
   c. Self-directedness of behavior?
   d. Peer relations?
   e. Educational aspirations and life goals?
   f. Attitudes toward school and teachers?
   g. Rapport with teachers?
   h. Attributions of responsibility for academic performance?
   i. Use of leisure time (e.g., television viewing, reading, interests)?
   j. Home orientation, responsibilities, and perceptions of family?
2. Do parents and families of students of rapid and slow conceptual development differ in
   a. Demographic characteristics (e.g., divorce, education, number of children)?
   b. Family structure and family life (e.g., cohesiveness)?
   c. Attitudes and perceptions of the child?

    d. Attitudes toward children and child rearing?

    e. Attitudes toward school, teachers, and education?

    f. Values, goals, and aspirations for the family and for their child?

3. Do the school programs and educational backgrounds of students of rapid and slow conceptual development differ in

    a. Schools attended?

    b. Courses taken?

    c. Activities pursued?

    d. Grades made?

    e. School attendance?

    f. The teacher's perceptions of the student's attitudes toward school and education, achievement motivation, school behavior, self-esteem and self-perceptions, peer relations, and values and goals? (Mize & Klausmeier, 1977, p. 3)

Tests, structured interviews, and examination of school records were employed to secure information as follows: (1) Primary Mental Abilities Test—total IQ score, verbal meaning, number facility, reasoning, and spatial relations (Thurstone, 1963); (2) Coopersmith Self-Esteem Inventory—general self, social self-peers, home–parents, school–academic (Coopersmith, 1967); (3) Intellectual Achievement Responsibility Questionnaire—self-responsibility total, self-responsibility for successes, self-responsibility for failures (Crandall, Katkovsky, & Crandall, 1965); (4) School Sentiment Index—respondent's perceived feelings and attitudes toward teachers, school subject matters, learning experiences, social structure and climate of school, peers, and schooling generally rather than toward specific school environment (Instructional Objectives Exchange, 1972); and (5) Subject Area Preference Index—relative preferences for different academic subjects (Instructional Objectives Exchange, 1972).

Structured interviews were conducted with each student individually, with one or both parents, and with one or more of the child's teachers. The interview with the student was directed toward securing information about the student's educational history and aspirations, school attitudes, school and extracurricular activities, family activities, and school, family, and social–affective perceptions. The interview with the parent dealt with parental and family demographic information; parental educational attitudes and aspirations held for their child; family activities; child activities; parental supervision and direction, and parental affective attitudes toward school, education, child rearing, and child development. The interview with the teacher had open-ended questions focusing on the teacher's perception of the student's educational history; school attitudes and school behavior; self-concept; and achievement motivation; and any known family, home, or school factors that might have some bearing on the child's present school attitudes and performance.

Each student's school records were examined for information such as courses taken, grades earned, and absenteeism. The courses taken and grades received by one slow developer, presented in Table 8.4, illustrate the change in kinds of courses and grades received between the junior and senior high school years, Grades 7, 8, 9 and Grades 10, 11, 12.

Information from all the preceding sources was evaluated and synthesized, first for each individual and then for the rapid and slow developers in Grades 6 and 12. The judgment as to whether a certain condition was or was not associated with rapid and slow development is presented in Table 8.5.

TABLE 8.4 Courses Taken by a Grade 12 Slow Developer[a]

Grade 7		Grade 8	
English	C	English	B
Mathematics	C	Mathematics	C
Science	C	Science	C
Social Studies	C	Social Studies	B
Physical Education	C	Physical Education	B
Physical Education	B	Industrial Arts	C
Industrial Arts	C	Band	C
Speech Arts	C		
Art	B		
Band	C		

Grade 9		Grade 10		
English	D	English	D	
General Mathematics	D	Biology	C−	
World Civics	D	Physical Education	C	
Physical Education	C	Art	C	
Elementary Words	C+	Typing	W	F
R.O.T.C.	B	Cabinet Making	A	
		Drivers Education	C	

Grade 11			Summer School—Grade 11	
English—Writing it Right	F		Problems in Democracy	D
English— Man and His World	F		U.S. History	D
English— Business World	D		Grade 12	
English— Mastery of Mystery	F		English— Basics and Spelling	D
Physical Science	D	F	English— Man and His World	F
American Civics	F	F	English—Death	F
Physical Education	S	S	English— Mastery of Mystery	F
Carpentry	D	D	Advanced General Science	F
Automobile Mechanics	F	F	Government	D
Drivers Education	S		Physical Education	S	S
			Mythology	F
			Heroes	F
			Metals	D−	F

[a] From Klausmeier, 1976a.

TABLE 8.5   Variables Associated with Rapid and Slow Cognitive Development[a]

Variables	Sixth grade	Twelfth grade
Self		
IQ Score	Yes	Yes
Self-Esteem	Yes	Yes
Internalized Responsibility for Learning	No	No
Attitudes toward School	Yes	Yes
Attitudes toward Curriculum	Yes	Yes
Achievement Motivation	Yes	Yes
Self-Directedness of Behavior	Yes	Yes
Peer Relations	No	Yes
Attitudes toward Parents–Home	No	Yes
School/education		
Absenteeism	Yes	Yes
Grades (A–F)	Yes	Yes
Curriculum (Courses Taken)	No	Yes
School Involvement–Activities	No	Yes
Extracurricular Activities:		
TV	No	Yes
Reading	Yes	Yes
Sports	No	No
Hobbies	Yes	Yes
School Structure[b]	No	No
Classroom Structure[b]	No	No
Home–School Interaction	No	Yes
Rapport with Teachers	No	Yes
Home/family		
Demographic:		
Socioeconomic Status of Parents	Yes	Yes
Marital Status of Parents	No	No
Number of Children in Family	No	No
Parental Attitudes toward School–Education	Yes	Yes
Parental Expectations for Child	Yes	Yes
Parental Involvement with Child	No	Yes
Parental Supervision–Control of Child	No	Yes
Intellectual Climate of Home	Yes	Yes
Child's Home Responsibilities	No	No
Parental Child-Rearing Attitudes	No	No

[a] Based on Mize and Klausmeier, 1977, p. 220.

[b] The rapid and slow developers in each grade group went to the same schools and also had their instruction in the same or similar classroom arrangements.

Eight of the 31 variables were judged not to be useful for differentiating rapid and slow developers at either grade level. Fourteen were judged to differentiate between rapid and slow developers at both grades. Nine variables discriminated between the two developmental extremes at Grade 12, but not at Grade 6.

This difference between the students in Grades 6 and 12 appeared to be interpretable as follows. The self-concept, school–education, and home–family variables differentially associated with rapid and slow cognitive development in Grade 12 had become more stable and also more sharply differentiated than they were in Grade 6. The Grade 6 students were still developing cognitively and socially and some of their self, school–education, and home–family attitudes and behaviors were not yet crystallized and integrated. For example, Grade 6 students whose school achievements were relatively low and whose rate of cognitive development was slow nevertheless demonstrated peer relationships, attitudes toward parents and home, involvement in school activities, rapport with teachers, and other variables shown in Table 8.5 similar to those of the rapid developers.

The contributions of the various variables to rapid and slow cognitive development at each grade level may be summarized succinctly. The rapid concept attainers have above-average IQ scores, good school achievement, and high grades. They have a low rate of school absenteeism and pursue an academic curriculum in high school. They enjoy reading and manifest strong achievement motivation, self-esteem, and positive attitudes toward school, education, and teachers. They actively engage in school activities and hold positive attitudes toward parents, family. and home, and their social skills with peers and adults are good. More often than not they come from upper-middle- or middle-class homes characterized by a good intellectual climate. Their parents have completed high school and possibly some college, have high aspirations and expectations for their child, show a great deal of involvement with their child, hold positive attitudes toward school and education, and are concerned and actively interested in their child's school, teachers, and curriculum.

Slow concept attainers, in contrast, have average or below average IQ scores and make low grades in school. They have a high rate of school absenteeism and pursue nonacademic subjects in high school. They are not interested in reading but depend on television for sedentary recreation. They have low self-esteem, poor motivation for learning, and negative attitudes toward school, education, and teachers. They do not engage in extracurricular school activities regularly. They have less positive attitudes toward family and home and poor social skills and peer relations. Slow concept attainers are more likely to come from a lower-middle-class home with an impoverished intellectual climate and parents who did not complete high school. The parents or guardians have low expectations for their child, show little involvement with the child, express negative attitudes toward school and education, and exhibit little understanding of or interest in their child's school, teachers, and curriculum. This description of the slow concept attainer is even more negative at the high school level.

It should be pointed out that the slow concept attainers identified in this study in Grade 12 undoubtedly represent the high end of the range of slow conceptual learners at the high school level. These seniors were all sufficiently successful to complete 4 years of high school and receive a diploma. Other students who dropped out of school before their senior year could not be included in the present study.

Many of the conditions associated with slow development are probably preventable if changes can be made, starting during the primary school years, in the home and family situation, in the school curriculum and instruction of the child, and in the relations among teachers, parents, and the student. School absenteeism, lack of interest in reading, and low self-esteem and achievement motivation would appear to be among those variables associated with slow cognitive development that could be prevented or remedied in order to alter the alarming downward course of cognitive development observed in some of these Grade 12 students.

To test these views, a doctoral study was conducted by Mize (1977). An intervention program was carried out that included children, their parents, the children's teachers, and two school psychologists. The main intervention effort was directed toward involving the parents in understanding the instructional programs of their children and in spending time at least twice a week with the child in activities closely related to the child's instruction in reading. The intervention, carried out over 7 weeks, had four main aspects: The parents attended three inservice sessions conducted by the school psychologist; the parents worked with the child at least twice a week carrying out the adult–child conference procedures in reading outlined by Klausmeier, Jeter, Quilling, Frayer, and Allen (1975); there were weekly written communications from the teacher to the parents, supplemented with periodic conferences and telephone calls; and finally the teachers systematically encouraged the child and reinforced incidences of desired overt and verbal behavior in the school setting. The latter was also done for the control children.

Thirty-four children in Grades 3 and 4 enrolled in four elementary schools participated in the study. All were assessed as manifesting a low rate of cognitive development. Half of the 34 were assigned at random to the experimental group to receive the intervention procedures and the other half to a control group. The intervention process itself resulted in more parent–teacher interactions and parent involvement in the child's educational and other activities in the home for the experimental group than for the control group. Results from structured interviews indicated that the parents' attitudes toward the child, teachers, and school in general improved markedly. The statistically significant test results favored the experimental group of children with regard to self-esteem; motivation to learn; attitudes toward learning, peers, and teacher authority and control; attitudes toward reading; and reading achievement itself. The cooperative relationship established between the home and the school and the interested, helping relationship between the parent and the child were judged to have positive effects on the variables associated with the rate of cognitive development.

DISCUSSION

Exceedingly large differences across grades were found in the number of students who did and who did not master the formal level of the various concepts and the understanding of related principles. In fact, these differences were somewhat greater in magnitude than might be expected from studying secondary sources on individual differences—for example, Buss and Poley (1976), Messick and Associates (1976), and Tyler (1974). They provide a challenge to replicate this study, to carry out research dealing with other dimensions of cognitive functioning, to find causes of the large differences, and to change schooling conditions so that instruction may be better adapted to the individual student. Chapters 9 and 10 deal with these concerns.

The intraindividual variability in attaining concepts was sharply delineated. A separate factor was identified for each of the four concepts—*cutting tool, tree, equilateral triangle*, and *noun*. Identifying the last three factors was expected in view of findings of other researchers. Harris and Harris (1973) studied the concept achievements of Grade 5 students and found separate factors for mathematics, language arts, science, and social studies. The achievement tests used in the study sampled concepts that were in the school's curriculum. Shaycoft (1967) found four major group factors in Grade 9 and Grade 12— mathematics, English, technical information, and spatial relations. Tests measuring knowledge in the fields of the physical, biological, and aeronautical sciences contributed to the technical information factor.

The important conclusion from the longitudinal study and these studies is that there is substantial intraindividual variability that is directly relatable to the different subject fields. Instruction should be arranged that takes into account this intraindividual variability.

Large differences in the rate of learning were observed between the pairs of rapid and slow developers of the four longitudinal blocks. The rate of increase across the years was greater and the form was more regular for the rapid developers. We may examine data from another study where the form of the developmental curve was of interest.

Bayley (1970) followed a group of individuals from birth to 36 years of age and identified five males and five females who scored highest and lowest on IQ tests during most of the school years. The scores for the five females at age 4–18 are shown in Figure 8.9. The scores are standard scores, based on the mean scores and standard deviations of all of Bayley's sample. The median standard score, 50, is also shown. Had each individual's IQ score remained constant from age 6–18, straight lines would have extended from the left to the right side for each individual. The forms of the curves of these five individuals during age 6–18, corresponding to Grades 1–12, resemble those of the rapid and slow cognitive developers. There are sharp ups and downs between successive measurements, including during ages 12–18, and the high individuals show somewhat more stability than the low ones. Bayley interpreted

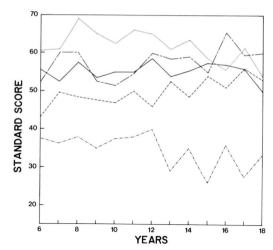

Figure 8.9. Individual curves of relative intelligence (standard deviation scores) of five females, ages 6–18, Berkeley Growth Study cases. (From Bayley, 1970, p. 1175.)

the observed changes from one test to the next as real changes in IQ. Our inclination is to treat the drops of our students during successive years as resulting mainly from error of measurement rather than as representing real changes in performances. However, an actual loss in cognitive functioning could be responsible for a few drops. For example, the performance of the slowly developing Block D student who scored lower in Grades 11 and 12 than in Grade 10 may reflect actual lower cognitive functioning.

What may have contributed to the very large interindividual differences? Assuredly, they can be attributed to large differences in students' self-esteem and perceptions of self, relations with others, attitudes toward teachers and parents, and interests; school attendance, courses taken, participation in school activities, and rapport with teachers. They are also associated with the family's socioeconomic status, parents' attitudes toward school and their expectations for the student, and the intellectual climate of the home.

FOR FURTHER STUDY

Buss, A. R., & Poley, W. *Individual differences: Traits and factors.* New York: John Wiley, 1976.

The polar and controversial views of various scholars on many issues regarding the extent and determinants of individual differences are discussed in a manner which assumes considerable scientific sophistication. Factor analytic approaches to identifying and explaining differences are featured.

Harris, M. L., & Harris, C. W. *A structure of concept attainment abilities.* Madison, Wisconsin: Wisconsin Research and Development Center for Cognitive Learning, 1973.

The scholar interested in intraindividual differences will find the factor analytic procedures and results of much interest. The primary mental abilities found to underlly concept achievement in boys and girls of elementary school age, as well as the organization of the achievements according to subject fields, is of general interest and of high theoretical and practical significance.

Horn, J. L. Human abilities: A review of research and theory in the early 1970s. In M. R. Rosenzweig & L. W. Porter (Eds.), *Annual review of psychology* (Vol. 27). Palo Alto, California: Annual Reviews Inc., 1976. Pp. 437–485.

Horn reviews recent research and theory regarding different categories of abilities and also the development of abilities in infancy, childhood, and adulthood.

Tyler, L. E. *Individual differences: Abilities and motivational directions*. Englewood Cliffs, New Jersey: Prentice-Hall, 1974.

This textbook provides a readable, comprehensible introduction to individual differences.

9

Instructional Design

Some of the conclusions regarding cognitive development expressed earlier in this book may be recalled as a prelude to considering an instructional design. The instructional design is intended for use by teachers and other persons when preparing materials to teach concepts, and by teachers to guide their instructional practices.

One principle central to the design of instruction is that children and youth attain the four levels of the same concepts in an invariant sequence. Closely related to this principle is the generalization that concepts attained only at the concrete and identity levels cannot be used in understanding principles, in understanding taxonomic relations, or in solving problems. Attainment at the formal level, in comparison to the classificatory, greatly facilitates the use of a concept.

What do these principles imply for instructional design? Instructional materials should be designed that enable students to attain the successive levels of individual concepts and related groups of concepts and also to use the concepts in the three ways indicated.

A second generalization: The levels and the uses of different concepts, the understanding of related principles and taxonomies, and the acquisition of problem-solving skills that involve the concept are mastered by students at different ages. Concepts such as *cutting tool* and *tree*, which have examples that are directly observable as objects in the environment, are attained earlier than are concepts such as *noun*, whose examples are words or other symbols that stand for individual objects, persons, events, processes, relations, and qualities, or classes of them. Developers of instructional materials, as well as teachers, may be able to profit from the study of a design that takes this knowledge into account.

Intraindividuality in patterns of cognitive development is related to the subject fields in which knowledge is organized, including language arts, mathematics, science, and social studies. Most students as individuals do not acquire knowledge in these different areas at the same rate. Intraindividual variability in cognitive functioning is an important variable to consider in a design for instruction.

Interindividual differences in the rate of attaining concepts, in understanding principles and taxonomic relations, and in solving problems are exceedingly large. Some school children at age 9 are more advanced in these dimensions of cognitive functioning than are some high school seniors at age 18. The differences are so large that any single piece of instructional material, such as a film, filmstrip, or chapter of a book, cannot possibly be used effectively with an unselected group of students of the same chronological age. Any oral interactive instruction designed to teach the same content to an unselected group of 25–40 students also will surely fail with some of the students. Instruction can be designed to provide for interindividual differences in rate of development.

Three kinds of analyses are carried out as part of the instructional design reported in this chapter. A *content analysis* is performed to identify the information or substance related to the concepts that will be taught. A *behavioral analysis* identifies the behaviors, operations, or skills that students must demonstrate in order to learn the substance. An *instructional analysis* identifies the instructional principles that may be followed in attaining the desired objectives. The first two analyses were performed on the concepts used in the longitudinal study and also in the controlled experiments in school settings that are reported in this chapter.

CONDUCTING A CONCEPT ANALYSIS

Concepts are attained to successively higher levels, and attaining concepts at the classificatory and formal levels is essential for understanding principles, acquiring structures of knowledge, and solving problems. This suggests that the teacher, curriculum designer, and materials developer should identify the specific concepts that are to be taught, the level at which they will be taught, principles involving the concepts, problems involving the concepts, and also the taxonomy, other hierarchy, or theory of which the concepts are a part. The process of concept analysis has been formulated for this purpose and includes the following activities:

1. Outlining the taxonomy, other hierarchy, or theory of which the target concept is a part

2. Defining the concept in terms of its attributes
3. Specifying the defining attributes and some of the variable attributes of the concept
4. Indicating illustrative examples and nonexamples of the concept
5. Identifying illustrative principles in which the concept is incorporated
6. Formulating illustrative problem-solving exercises involving use of the concept
7. Developing a vocabulary associated with the concept and its defining attributes

Procedures for carrying out Steps 2, 3, and 4 are based on the pioneering work of Markle and Tiemann (1969), whereas the other steps are related directly to the principles of conceptual learning and development as presented in earlier chapters of this book.

Our experiences[1] in conducting concept analyses as a basis for preparing lessons for use in experiments at the elementary and high school levels indicate that the analysis should be directed toward the formal level of attaining the concept, and that the complete analysis should be expressed in terminology appropriate for teaching senior high school students. The concept analyzer needs the knowledge at least at this level, even though the instruction may be directed subsequently to a lower level. Some persons may prefer to analyze the concept at a higher level, using examples and nonexamples and terminology that experts in the field would use. What is eventually included in a particular set of instructional materials or oral instructional activities must be related to the level of concept attainment to be taught, and to the level of vocabulary and other characteristics of the target population of students. A description of a concept analysis follows, using as examples information pertaining to the concepts *equilateral triangle* and *observing scientifically*. Each step of the analysis is described in some detail because a concept analysis provides much of the information needed to develop instructional materials, plan oral instructional activities, and construct tests of the kind used in the longitudinal study.

Outlining a Taxonomy or a Hierarchy

A starting point for the analysis of a concept is outlining the taxonomy, other hierarchy, or theory of which the concept is a part. A taxonomy involves

[1] Recognition is given to the following graduate advisees of the first author and to research associates who served as members of research teams and participated in developing concept analyses used in theses and dissertations that also were published as technical reports of the Wisconsin R & D Center for Cognitive Learning: Michael E. Bernard, Kathryn V. Feldman, Dorothy A. Frayer, Richard M. Gargiulo, Linda J. Ingison, Selena E. Katz, Richard S. Marliave, Nancy E. McMurray, Barbara A. Nelson, Gordon K. Nelson, Winston E. Rampaul, Joan M. Schilling, Thomas S. Sipple, James E. Swanson, Keith M. White, and Suzanne P. Wiviott.

inclusive–exclusive relationships among classes of things, whereas a hierarchy implies relationships among things ordered by some principle, such as importance, priority, or dependency. A learning hierarchy, as defined by Gagné (1962a, 1968, 1970, 1974), implies that there is only one sequence in which a set of skills can be mastered. (Gagné classifies concepts and other outcomes of learning as skills.) In this sense, taxonomies as structures of knowledge in various subject matters are clearly not learning hierarchies. It is essential, therefore, to differentiate the relationships in a learning hierarchy, a taxonomy, and other hierarchies that are not learning hierarchies as defined by Gagné.

A learning hierarchy results from an analysis of a learning task. Gagné analyzes a learning task into its prerequisite skills. An analysis is begun by asking the question: "What skills must individuals possess to perform the task successfully?" Answering this question yields the hierarchy of skills that are prerequisite to eventually performing the final task, which is also a skill. The hierarchy of skills obtained by the analysis provides the basic information needed to sequence instruction, either in instructional materials or by a teacher. Throughout an instructional sequence, one hierarchical skill is built successively upon another. Three assumptions underlying this kind of analysis, and the concept of learning hierarchy, are that the learning tasks can be analyzed into hierarchical sets of skills, the prerequisite skills must be learned in order to learn the next successively higher skill, and the same sequence of instruction will facilitate all persons learning the successive skills.

Figure 9.1 is a learning hierarchy resulting from an analysis of the task of subtracting whole numbers (Gagné & Briggs, 1974). It shows the intellectual skills that are essential for performing the task of subtracting whole numbers. A teacher or writer of instructional materials would teach the skills in the order shown in the hierarchy. The learning hierarchy also indicates explicitly the internal conditions that are prerequisite and essential for learning the successive skills. For example, being able to perform the simple subtraction facts, Skill I, is the primary internal condition necessary for being able to learn and master Skills II and III.

For Gagné (1968, 1970, 1974), the learning hierarchy is the building block in developing an instructional sequence to teach any particular task. Students are placed in an instructional sequence to start the first skill or coordinate set of skills that they have not yet mastered, and they continue through the sequence at their individual rates until the final task is performed successfully. Gagné presumes that most learning tasks can be analyzed into learning hierarchies.

Taxonomic relationships differ from hierarchical relationships. This is reflected in the network of defining attributes of the classes comprising a particular taxonomy and also in the pattern of inclusive and exclusive relationships among the classes comprising a taxonomy. As may be inferred from examining the taxonomy that follows for *equilateral triangle* (from Klausmeier, 1976b), a supraordinate concept includes all members of all classes subordinate to it.

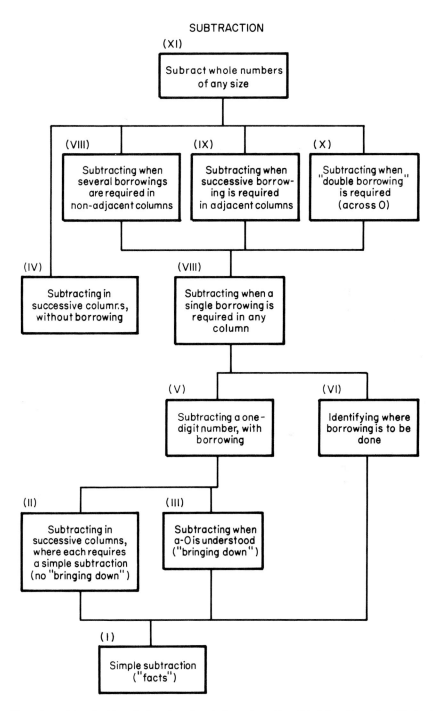

Figure 9.1. A learning hierarchy for subtracting whole numbers. (From *Principles of Instructional Design* by Robert M. Gagné & Leslie J. Briggs. Copyright © 1974 by Holt, Rinehart and Winston, Inc. Reprinted by permission of Holt, Rinehart and Winston.)

Taxonomy for Equilateral Triangle:

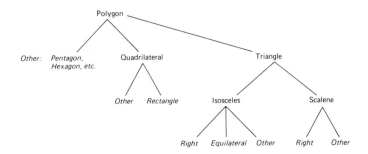

Illustrative taxonomic relations involving *equilateral triangle* follow:

1. Some, but not all, isosceles triangles are equilateral triangles.
2. All equilateral triangles are isosceles triangles.
3. The sum of all right, equilateral, and other triangles is equal to the total possible number of isosceles triangles.
4. Right triangles are not equilateral triangles.

The concepts that are coordinate are at the same level of specificity, and the members of any coordinate class are not members of any other coordinate class. Concepts that are coordinate—for example, *isosceles triangle* and *scalene triangle*—may be either supraordinate or subordinate to other classes, depending on their location in the particular taxonomy. Concepts of a taxonomy—for example, *quadrilateral* and *triangle,* subordinate to a given supraordinate concept, *polygon*—have all of the defining attributes of the supraordinate concept but require at least one additional attribute to define them. *Polygon,* the generic concept for all classes of figures of three or more sides, is defined by the attributes *plane, simple,* and *closed*; and all of its subordinate classes, which are also polygons, include the same three attributes. Concepts that are coordinate may or may not have the same number of defining attributes, depending upon the particular taxonomy of which they are a part.

Tiemann, Kroeker, and Markle (1977) and Markle (1977) present both a rationale and strategies for the analysis and teaching of coordinate concepts at the classificatory level. Their research indicates that many students of college age have not learned the relationships among the concepts of common taxonomies. Apparently students learn isolated concepts but not the more powerful structures that include the relationship among the concepts.

A hierarchy of concepts is shown in Figure 9.2, but it is not a learning hierarchy as defined by Gagné. It was developed for 13 process-concepts: *observing scientifically, inferring, classifying,* etc. The concepts are drawn from *Science . . . A process approach* (AAAS Commission on Science Education, 1967); however, the figure itself is not. Arrows indicate prerequisite relationships among processes, solid lines connect coordinate or closely related pro-

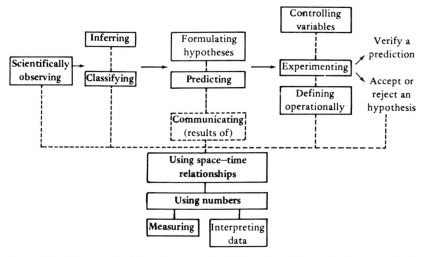

Figure 9.2. Hierarchy involving observing scientifically. (From Klausmeier, Swanson, & Sipple, 1976.)

cesses, and dashed lines indicate that communicating the results from performing the processes is itself an integrative process. Although there are prerequisite relations, they are not invariantly sequenced as in a learning hierarchy.

These are the process-concepts that, in this curriculum, students should learn during the elementary school years. It is not assumed that the terminal process, experimenting, is mastered during the elementary school years. Also, as indicated, some of the relationships are prerequisite and others are coordinate. For example, observing scientifically is prerequisite for inferring and classifying; inferring and classifying are coordinate processes.

Some of the knowledge of a subject field may be organized in statements of related principles as well as in taxonomies or other hierarchies. These principles and the related information may be considered as a theory. As an example, the interpretation of cognitive development during the school years is synthesized in the principles treated in Chapters 6, 7, and 8 of this book.

Bruner (1960) made a useful distinction between subject-matter structures as organized by experts and those which are learnable by students. However, the latter cannot be derived by a concept analyzer without the former. Without knowledge of the structure formulated by scholars, one cannot proceed intelligently in subsequently formulating an instructional analysis, or in actual teaching.

At present, some of the substance of school subject matters that could be organized into taxonomies, hierarchies, or other structures is not available in the textbooks or other materials used in the schools, or in college courses to prepare teachers, or in college courses such as history or English. In the absence of this kind of information, the structures are developed by using the best available printed materials and also by securing assistance from persons with expertise in the particular subject matter. The taxonomy and the hierarchies presented in this section were formulated in this manner.

We should make clear the differences between Gagné's analysis of learning tasks and the analysis of concepts involving taxonomies and other structures of knowledge. The latter is an information-processing approach that takes into account the substance as well as the processes of learning and is consistent with the views of Ausubel (1963, 1968) regarding cognitive structure, Bruner (1960) regarding the structure of knowledge, and Miller and Johnson-Laird (1976) regarding conceptual cores and memory locations. Memory locations include not only action but also semantic, episodic, person, and geographic locations. Gagné's analysis of learning tasks has a strong behavioristic flavor and is patterned after the systematic analysis of training tasks employed in man–machine systems (Gagné, 1962b, 1970); his preference for explicitly stated, detailed performance objectives is similar to that expressed by Mager (1962). Carrying out a complete information analysis, rather than a task analysis of a single terminal skill, assures that one knows how the particular concepts of interest are related to a more comprehensive structure of knowledge.

Defining the Concept

The person conducting an analysis must know or arrive at a societally accepted definition of the word representing the concept even though it may be inappropriate to teach it to younger children. Further, so that examples and nonexamples may be identified for use in teaching and testing, the meaning of the word should be stated in terms of the defining attributes of the concept. As indicated in Chapter 1, a defining attribute may be an intrinsic property of the concept examples, a function performed on or by the concept examples, a relation between concepts, such as prerequisite, or any other invariant of two or more objects, events, persons, processes, relations, or qualities.

Not all concepts have examples that can be experienced by the sense organs. Many such concepts are important in our daily lives. Here verbal descriptions, metaphors, analogies, line drawings, physical models, and context are used in attempting to provide a definition and examples.

Not all concepts have societally accepted definitions. Where experts disagree on the meaning of a word, such as *intelligence, career education, religion,* or *the origin of the earth,* the concept analyzer does well to identify the definitions of different experts and arrive at a synthesis, if possible, or include the different definitions as part of the analysis.

An acceptable definition of a concept that is part of a taxonomy states (1) either the name of the supraordinate generic concept or the defining attributes of the generic concept, and (2) the attributes that are common to all examples of the concept and that distinguish its examples from those of other concepts. In most cases, the name of the concept immediately supraordinate is included as part of the definition. When the supraordinate name does not convey the defining attributes of the supraordinate class (which are also defining attributes of the target concept), it is more appropriate to specify a more inclusive concept name. For example, *geometric figure* may be a more appropriate supraordinate concept than either *isosceles triangle* or *polygon* for the subordinate concept *equilateral triangle*.

Definitions of *equilateral triangle* and *observing scientifically* follow. The five intrinsic attributes of *equilateral triangle* are boldface, as are the three operations that together make possible observing scientifically.

> *Equilateral triangle*   A **plane, simple, closed** figure with **three equal sides** and **three equal angles.**

> *Observing scientifically:*   **Using one or more of the senses** in critically **examining** objects or events and precisely **recording data** about those objects or events.

The reader will recognize that *observing scientifically* might be treated as a concept that can be understood by a person without being performed, as a process that can be performed, or both. We treat it as both. A classroom experiment showed that teaching students to understand it as a process transfers to their being able to observe objects and events included in their regular science instruction (Klausmeier, Sipple, Swanson, & Schilling, 1976).

Different words with identical spellings—for example, *bear*—may represent different concepts; therefore, one decides the target concept in advance of defining it. Word definitions that include the defining attributes of concepts frequently are not given in dictionaries. Definitions given in abridged dictionaries are usually synonyms, examples, or uses of the word in context. These also appear in unabridged dictionaries but have limited value in determining the defining attributes (Markle, 1975). In arriving at the defining attributes of most concepts the concept analyzer, if not expert in the particular subject matter, uses authoritative printed materials and also may seek the assistance of subject-matter experts.

Specifying the Defining Attributes

The concept analyzer specifies the defining attributes of the concept in order to identify sets of teaching examples and nonexamples (Markle & Tiemann, 1969) and also to teach students an algorithmic strategy for evaluating instances as examples and nonexamples of the concept (to be explained and illustrated later). Those attributes which are present in every example of a concept and therefore are also essential for distinguishing the concept examples from examples of all other coordinate concepts are called the *critical attributes*. Other attributes of the generic concept combined with the critical attributes comprise the *defining attributes*.

The name of the generic concept or its attributes is included in the defining attributes of subordinate concepts so that a subordinate concept may be learned even when the supraordinate concept is not. Establishing the defining attributes of the concept and arriving at a definition of the word representing the concept proceed simultaneously during the concept analysis. We note again that the attributes of a concept may be intrinsic, functional, or relational.

The defining attributes of *equilateral triangle* and *observing scientifically* follow:

> Defining attributes of *equilateral triangle* in the form of intrinsic and perceptible properties of examples: (1) plane, (2) simple, (3) closed, (4) three equal sides, and (5) three equal angles.

> Defining attributes of *observing scientifically* in the form of subprocesses: (1) using one or more of the senses, (2) examining, (3) recording data. (Not all experts agree that recording the data should be considered as part of observing.)

Specifying the Variable Attributes

Examples of the same concept vary in their nondefining attributes. For example, reptiles are of different colors and sizes; fish also vary in some of the same colors as reptiles and in size. The nondefining attributes that members of the reptile class and members of the fish class have in common, and that therefore may hinder persons in discriminating between the members of the two classes, are called variable attributes. (In much previous literature, starting with Bruner, Goodnow, & Austin [1956], they have been included as irrelevant attributes.) The variable attributes of the concept are not defining and are identified to facilitate the later selection of examples and nonexamples.

The first rule for identifying variable attributes is to identify those that are common to the examples of coordinate concepts, that is, members of the coordinate classes. It is these nondefining attributes that are present in both the examples and nonexamples of a particular concept that often lead to errors in classification. The second rule is to identify the nondefining, variable attributes that may be present in both the target concept and either its supraordinate or subordinate concepts.

Examples of variable attributes identified for two concepts follow:

> Variable attributes for *equilateral triangle*: (1) size—small, medium, large, (2) orientation in space.

> Variable attributes for *observing scientifically*: (1) the kinds of objects or events being observed, (2) the sense or senses being used, (3) the place or situation in which objects or events are being observed, (4) the methods of recording data.

Selecting Illustrative Examples and Nonexamples

Examples and nonexamples of the concept are needed in teaching the concept and in assessing students' attainment of the concept. At least one set (a rational set, as will be described later) of examples and nonexamples is identified during the concept analysis in such a way as to ensure that errors of undergeneralization, overgeneralization, and misconception by the learner will be avoided (Markle, 1975; Markle & Tiemann, 1969). Undergeneralization occurs when examples of a concept are encountered but are not identified as examples. Undergeneralization results when the examples provided in instruction are not sufficiently different from one another in the variable attributes. For example, the child who has experienced only large dogs such as collies may not identify miniature poodles and other small dogs as dogs.

Overgeneralization occurs when examples of other concepts are treated as members of the target concept. For example, a right isosceles triangle is treated as an equilateral triangle. The primary cause of overgeneralization is that the learner does not experience a sufficient number of nonexamples that have nearly the same defining attributes as the target example.

Misconceptions occur when both kinds of errors are made; some examples are treated as nonexamples and some nonexamples are treated as examples. For example, a misconception of chickens occurs when brown chickens are classified as chickens, white chickens are classified as turkeys, and brown pheasants are treated as chickens. Here the brown color is treated incorrectly as a critical attribute.

When coordinate concepts of the same taxonomy are taught, the examples of any one concept are in reality nonexamples of the other concepts. Using examples of different concepts of coordinate classes for nonexamples permits the critical attributes to be excluded meaningfully from the nonexamples and the variable attributes to be included meaningfully in both the examples and the nonexamples. One can deal with examples and nonexamples of concepts in taxonomies more systematically than in other hierarchies since there are clearly delineated supraordinate, coordinate, and subordinate concepts. Descriptions of possible examples and nonexamples of *equilateral triangle* and *observing scientifically* follow:

> Examples of *equilateral triangle*:   drawings of equilateral triangles of various sizes in various spatial orientations.
>
> Nonexamples of *equilateral triangle*:   drawings of open, nonsimple, nonplane figures and of right triangles and quadrilaterals of various sizes in various orientations.
>
> Example of *observing scientifically* (a verbal description in which all three defining attributes are included):   Bill looked at a marshmallow carefully, felt it, tasted it, and smelled it. Then he put it over the flame of a Bunsen burner and watched as it turned from white to

black. He smelled it as it burned. After it cooled, he felt it and noticed that it felt crisp. He tasted it and thought that it tasted like charcoal. He recorded these things in his report book. (This event could also be demonstrated by the teacher or a student.)

Nonexample of *observing scientifically* (a verbal description in which two of three defining attributes are not included): Cecil saw the mailman deliver a box to the principal. Cecil thought to himself, "The principal said he was going to order a new microscope for the school." Cecil saw his friend, Jim, and told him that the new microscope had arrived.

Identifying Illustrative Principles

Concepts are useful to an individual in several ways, as indicated earlier in this book. One especially important use of concepts is in understanding the principles that incorporate the concepts. Understanding principles involving cause–and–effect, correlational, and other relationships among concepts in turn makes it possible to understand and explain many events and also, in some cases, to predict and to control. Understanding principles facilitates the solution of problems. It is useful, therefore, to identify illustrative principles of which the target concept is a part and subsequently to teach the principle in order to promote transfer of concept learning to the understanding of principles. Further, understanding the principle enables the learner also to learn a new relationship among the concepts, thereby extending understanding of the component concepts. Illustrative principles related to *equilateral triangle* and *observing scientifically* follow.

Illustrative Principles Involving Equilateral Triangle:

1. All equilateral triangles are similar in shape. (*Similar* here is synonymous with *identical* in the sense of having three equal angles and three sides of equal length.)
2. If the three angles of a triangle are equal in the number of degrees, the sides of the triangle are of equal length.
3. If the three sides of a triangle are of equal length, the angles of the triangle are equal in the number of degrees.
4. A line that bisects any angle of an equilateral triangle forms two equal angles (and lines) when it intersects the opposite side.
5. The perimeter of an equilateral triangle is three times the length of any side.

Illustrative Principles Involving Observing Scientifically:

1. Observing objects and events is a prerequisite for drawing inferences regarding them.
2. Using more than one of the senses in observing objects and

events increases the probability of gaining more precise information.

3. Quantitative observation permits drawing more precise inferences than does qualitative observation.

Examination of the preceding principles indicates that each one expresses a relationship between the target concept and another one in the taxonomy or hierarchy, between the target concept and one or more of its defining attributes, or between the target concept and a less closely related concept. There appear to be no rules for arriving at a set of illustrative principles. However, once principles are identified, sets of applications and misapplications of the principles, corresponding to rational sets of examples and nonexamples of concepts, can be identified and used successfully in teaching the principles (Feldman, 1974; Katz, 1976).

Formulating Illustrative Problem-Solving Exercises

As part of a concept analysis, problem-solving exercises are formulated, the solutions of which presumably are facilitated by understanding the target concept and applying knowledge of a principle or a combination of principles. No attempt is made to make the problem-solving exercises of equal difficulty. On the contrary, a range of difficulty is preferable in the analysis so that additional examples of an appropriate level of difficulty can later be prepared for a particular target population of students.

Problem-solving exercises for *equilateral triangle* and for *observing scientifically* follow (from Klausmeier, 1976b):

Illustrative Problem for Equilateral Triangle:

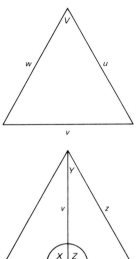

Sides u, v and w are of equal length. How many degrees are in angle V?

a. 60°
b. 90°
c. 120°
d. It is impossible to tell without measuring.
e. I don't know.

Line v bisects the upper angle of this equilateral triangle. Suppose that side z is 2 inches long. How many degrees are in angle Y?

a. 30°
b. 60°
c. 90°
d. It is impossible to tell without measuring.
e. I don't know.

Illustrative Problem for Observing Scientifically:

Below are drawings of a growing plant. It was marked on Day 1 and again on Day 3.

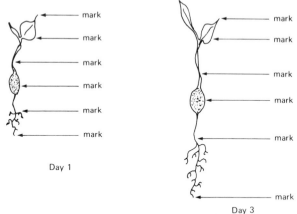

Day 1

Day 3

Which part grew the most in the two days: (a) the leaf, (b) the stem, (c) the part of the root close to the seed, or (d) the part of the root near the end or tip?

Developing a Vocabulary List

The rule for generating a vocabulary list as part of a concept analysis is to include the name of the concept and the key terms of the defining attributes. The extent to which the terms will be used in teaching a particular concept varies according to the level of attainment desired. None of the vocabulary may be used at the concrete level; all of it must be used at the formal level. Students' knowledge of the name of the concept and the names of its defining attributes has shown a high, positive correlation with the level of concept attainment and also with the uses of concepts (Klausmeier, Sipple, & Allen, 1974a, b). The lists for *equilateral triangle* and *observing scientifically* follow:

Vocabulary for *equilateral triangle*:   angle, side, equal, equilateral, triangle, figure, closed, plane, simple.

Vocabulary for *observing scientifically*:   observing, scientifically, senses, critically, examine, record, accurately, data, information, precisely.

CARRYING OUT A BEHAVIORAL ANALYSIS

The mental operations presumed to be essential for attaining concepts at each of four successively higher levels, as given in earlier chapters, were identified initially through a behavioral analysis of concept learning tasks and a review and synthesis of research related to the learning of concepts. Results from subsequent controlled experiments and from the longitudinal study as reported in the earlier chapters of this book tend to confirm the results of the behavioral analysis.

The operations are presumed to be the same for all concepts, however, the age at which the operations can be performed on different concepts by the same individual varies markedly. Students are able to perform the operations earlier on concepts for which there are concrete examples in the environment—for example, *cutting tool* and *tree*—and later for concepts with examples that are represented in drawings or by words—for example, *equilateral triangle* and *noun*. (See Chapters 6 and 7.)

The internal conditions of learning regarded as necessary and sufficient for attaining the successively higher levels of a concept are as follows: (1) mastery of the prior level, (2) functioning of at least one new mental operation in combination with the continuing operations, (3) functioning of the operations of the prior level with content of increasing quantity and complexity experienced in a greater variety of contexts, (4) intending to attain the next higher level, and (5) persisting until it is attained. In addition, being able to discriminate the defining attributes of the concept and to name the concept and the defining attributes is necessary for carrying out the new operations at the formal level. The specific mental operations for each level are given later when discussing instructional conditions so that the internal conditions pertaining to the levels may be related to the instructional conditions for the same levels. The necessary external conditions of learning include experience and practice with the content of the particular concept as represented in examples of it and in examples of related concepts. The amount and kind of experience and practice vary according to both concepts and the four levels of attainment.

PERFORMING AN INSTRUCTIONAL ANALYSIS

An instructional analysis is conducted to identify the instructional conditions that facilitate student learning. In the analysis, the main variables considered are the characteristics of the learners, the level at which the concept is to be attained, the instructional materials, and the amount of teacher guidance to be provided. Results of relevant research, as well as analyses of learning situations, are incorporated in an analysis. In this section, instructional conditions that facilitate student attainment of successively higher levels are described. The teacher necessarily does the analysis with particular students and particular concepts in mind. Similarly, the curriculum designer and materials developer delimit their analyses.

Concrete and Identity Levels

Attaining a concept at the concrete level involves attending to an object, discriminating that object from other objects, and subsequently recognizing the object as the same one experienced before. At the identity level, the object is generalized as the same thing when experienced in a different spatiotemporal perspective or context or when sensed in a different modality. Acquiring the name of the concept and associating the name with the object may come almost simultaneously with learning the concept at these levels.

As we are aware, children form many concepts at these levels and also acquire the names of the concepts through informal experiences in the home and neighborhood prior to starting school. The following instructional conditions facilitate attainment of concepts at these two levels:

1. Present the actual item—inanimate object, animate object, perceptible event or process, quality or condition, or a pictorial representation of it—and also one or two nonexamples of it.
2. Give the name of the item and aid the learner to associate the name and the item.
3. Provide for immediate informative feedback regarding correct identification of the item and also for correct naming.
4. Present the item later and determine whether the child recognizes it.
5. Repeat the preceding sequence as necessary.

Persons who have seen "Sesame Street" recognize that the preceding conditions have been incorporated into this television program. In "Sesame Street," many fundamental concepts including numerical concepts, the letters of the alphabet, relations such as *above* and *between*, and examples of qualities such as *red* and *soft* are taught in a delightful manner. Examples are always given, and the name of the concept is given orally or in written form almost simultaneously with the presentation of the examples. Nonexamples of other concepts are used, for example, of *over* and *under*, *near* and *far*, *one* and *two*, *a* and *e*. There is feedback to the viewers so that they can determine whether their covert mental responses, or their overt responses if made, are correct or incorrect. "Sesame Street" provides for a great deal of surprise, fun, repetition, and practice.

Beginning Classificatory Level

The lowest attainment of a concept at the classificatory level is inferred when a person recognizes two different things as being equivalent in some way. Persons are still at the classificatory level when they can properly identify many instances as examples and nonexamples but cannot state explicitly the basis of their categorizing in terms of the presence of the defining attributes in the examples and the absence of one or more of the defining attributes in the nonexamples. The new operation involved in attainment at the classificatory level is generalizing that two or more different instances are equivalent in some way. As shown in earlier chapters, students form the classificatory level of many concepts, especially of concepts for which there are concrete examples, prior to the first grade. But for many other concepts, such as *equilateral triangle* and *noun*, many errors are made by many first-graders. To facilitate attainment of concepts at the beginning classificatory level:

1. Assure that the concept has been attained at the identity level and that the student is capable of attaining it at the classificatory level.
2. Present at least two examples and one or two nonexamples of the concept.
3. Give the name of the concept along with the concept examples and aid the learner to associate the name of the concept with the examples. (This applies only to concept names that the learner already has in the speaking vocabulary or can learn to pronounce readily.)
4. Using an inductive method, supplemented with an expository method as necessary, aid the learner to discriminate and name some of the defining attributes of the concept. (This applies only if the attribute names can be learned readily or are already in the speaking vocabulary.)
5. Using an inductive method, supplemented with an expository method as necessary, aid the learner to define the concept. Being able to define the concept is not essential, but it is helpful to the extent that the words used are comprehended. Committing a definition to memory in a rote fashion without understanding is probably harmful and is clearly a waste of time.
6. Provide for informative feedback.
7. Arrange for use of the concept in recognizing newly encountered things as examples or nonexamples.
8. Repeat the preceding sequence as necessary.

With many concepts, several years elapse between the time that children first attain a concept at the beginning classificatory level and the time at which they are capable of all the operations essential to attaining the same concept at the formal level. The kind of instruction that aids students to move from the immature to the more mature phase of the classificatory level through use of printed instructional materials, along with oral instruction and other techniques, is described next.

Mature Classificatory Level and Formal Level

Printed instructional materials for teaching concepts can be prepared and used effectively with students who can read and who have already attained the target concepts at the beginning classificatory level. The materials may be used to aid students to classify more correctly and extensively at the classificatory level, to attain a beginning formal level, and to attain an adult formal level, as research by graduate students and other project staff working with the first author at the Wisconsin Research and Development Center for Cognitive Learning has demonstrated. In one controlled classroom experiment that employed two experimental groups and two control groups, McMurray, Bernard, and Klausmeier (1975) prepared and used two lessons to teach fourth-grade students the concept *equilateral triangle*. Each lesson required about 35 minutes to complete. Of the two experimental groups that received the lessons, 60% and 64% attained the formal level, whereas only 7% and 11% of two control groups did. Two months later, the experimental group had maintained this high level of attainment, and the control groups had increased their level of attainment only slightly. The achievement of the two fourth-grade experimental groups compared favorably with that of sixth-grade students participating in a longitudinal study who had not received the lessons (Klausmeier, Sipple, & Allen, 1974a, b). Klausmeier, Schilling, and Feldman (1976) conducted a similar experiment using two lessons dealing with the concept *tree*. The two experimental groups of second-semester, third-grade students performed significantly higher than two control groups.

Bernard (1975b) prepared and used three lessons to teach high school seniors a set of eight concepts at the formal level; the concepts were organized in a taxonomy dealing with behavior management. These lessons incorporated the seven guidelines presented later in this section. In addition, an advance organizer and within-text questions were used in the experimental lessons. A control group in this study not receiving instruction on the concepts scored 30% correct on the dependent measures; the students receiving the most powerful lesson—one incorporating all the variables mentioned—scored 70%. The taxonomy and excerpts from the lessons are presented and discussed in the last section of this chapter.

Sufficient knowledge has accrued from the preceding studies and from others so that the following guidelines for instruction are regarded as validated, and they can be applied in developing printed materials. Whether teachers can base their instructional procedures on the guidelines without the support of carefully prepared printed materials has not been determined.

1. *Establish an intention to learn concepts.* An intention to learn concepts is developed before the student tries to learn a particular concept. This is done by means such as telling the students that they will be learning concepts, by pointing out important features of concept learning, or by describing the concept population comprising the taxonomy or hierarchy. Amster (1966), Fredrick and Klausmeier (1968), Kalish (1966), Laughlin, Doherty, and Dunn (1968), and Osler and Weiss (1962) have all reported facilitative effects from instructions designed to establish an intent to learn concepts. Ausubel (1968) has demonstrated the facilitative effects of advance organizers on learning various kinds of new materials, and Bernard (1975b) has shown the facilitative effects of an advance organizer on learning concepts specifically.

Establishing an intention to learn concepts (as opposed, for example, to establishing a set to memorize a definition) activates several operations essential to attaining concepts at the classificatory and formal levels. First, such instructions may alert the learners that they should attend to and discriminate the attributes of instances. Second, such instructions may engage the learners in an active search for the attributes that distinguish instances from noninstances. At the outset, then, the learner is engaged actively in searching behaviors directed toward learning the particular concept or concepts at a higher level of attainment.

2. *Elicit student verbalization of the concept name and the defining attributes*. To accomplish this, a vocabulary list is presented at the beginning of a series of lessons and the students are taught to recognize the words. Having the concept and attribute labels greatly facilitates carrying out both inductive and reception operations at the formal level of attainment, including formulating, remembering, and evaluating hypotheses and assimilating and processing information that is presented verbally in an expository approach to instruction. Linguistic codes are maximally efficient for carrying out the sequential information processing that is involved in inferring concepts from examples and nonexamples inductively—and also for assimilating the information as presented in a definition, a set of verbal examples and nonexamples of the concepts, and verbal explanations or descriptions. Clark (1971) reported facilitation of concept attainment through giving the label of the concept and/or the labels of its defining attributes. When printed material is used, the students must be able not only to use the terms orally but also to read them.

3. *Present a definition of the concept in terms of defining attributes, stated in vocabulary appropriate to the target population*. Providing students with the concept definition eliminates the operations involved in identifying the defining attributes of the concept and inferring the concept from experiences with examples and nonexamples of the concept. However, simply presenting students with the concept definition does not ensure concept attainment—the students may merely acquire a string of words memorized by rote. To ensure that the students acquire a concept and not a string of words, at a minimum they must also be presented with concept examples and nonexamples to classify. Correct classification requires that the students differentiate examples from nonexamples on the basis of the defining attributes contained in the concept definition. Thus, both discriminating the attributes of instances and evaluating instances to determine whether or not they exhibit the defining attributes contained in the definition are operations that the students should perform after they are given the concept definition.

The facilitative effect of a definition is a function of several variables, including the number of rational sets of examples and nonexamples presented. In a controlled experiment with fourth-grade students Klausmeier and Feldman

(1975) found a definition to have about the same amount of facilitation as one rational set of examples and nonexamples. A definition combined with one rational set was more effective than a definition or a rational set alone; and a definition combined with three rational sets showed greatest facilitation.

A definition must be stated in appropriate terminology. Feldman and Klausmeier (1974) found a common-usage definition to be more effective than a technically stated definition with fourth-graders, whereas the technically stated definition was more effective with eighth-graders. Markle (1975) and Merrill and Tennyson (1971) also reported a facilitative effect for definitions.

4. *Present at least one rational set of properly matched examples and nonexamples of varying difficulty level.* Markle and Tiemann (1969) outlined one use of critical and variable attributes for identifying a rational set of examples and nonexamples of a concept. A slightly different procedure specifies an example and a nonexample to be used for each defining attribute (Klausmeier & Feldman, 1975). Each nonexample should have at least one defining attribute of the target concept and may have all the defining attributes except one. Each example has at least one variable attribute that is also present in one or more nonexamples of the concept. When coordinate concepts are being taught, the examples of one coordinate concept are nonexamples of another coordinate concept (e.g., a tree, a shrub, and an herb; a noun, a verb, and an adjective). Examples of concepts lower in a hierarchy are nonexamples of concepts higher in the same hierarchy (e.g., in Guilford's [1967] structure of intellect examples of units of information are nonexamples of classes of information). Using real examples and nonexamples in this manner facilitates the identification of rational sets to be used in teaching or in preparing instructional materials. In this approach to identifying examples and nonexamples, one example and one nonexample are first identified for each critical attribute; a decision may also be made to include one example and one nonexample for the attributes that define the generic concept. Regardless of the specific procedure followed, a sufficient number of rational sets should be included in an instructional sequence so that students learn the concept to the level desired.

In presenting each rational set, each example should be matched with a nonexample having the same variable attribute or attributes. The difficulty level within a set should range from easy to difficult and yet be appropriate to the target population of students. The use of rational sets effectively reduces and eventually eliminates errors of undergeneralization, overgeneralization, and misconception (Feldman, 1972; Klausmeier & Feldman, 1975; Markle & Tiemann, 1969; Merrill & Tennyson, 1971; Swanson, 1972; Tennyson, 1973; Tennyson, Woolley, & Merrill, 1972).

5. *Emphasize the defining attributes of the concept by drawing the students' attention to them.* Giving students the names of the defining attributes of the

concept in the concept definition is insufficient for teaching them to discriminate the defining attributes and to use them subsequently in differentiating examples from nonexamples of the concept. Frayer (1970) found that emphasizing the defining attributes by verbal cues improved immediate concept learning and later transfer and retention.

Merrill and Tennyson (1971) compared the effects of a concept definition, a definition that gave the attributes of the concept, a rational set of examples and nonexamples, and attribute prompting singly and in various combinations. Attribute prompting was found to be more facilitative than a definition of the concept or definitions of the attributes. The most effective condition included all four variables. Clark (1971) reported that a large majority of researchers obtained beneficial effects by directing the students' attention to the concept attributes and/or the conceptual rule; also, pointing out the attributes and rules to the students yielded better results than permitting the students to discover them themselves.

6. *Provide a strategy for differentiating examples and nonexamples.* Bruner, Goodnow, and Austin (1956) described various reception and selection strategies that students learn incidentally, without instruction concerning the strategies. They showed that certain strategies were more effective than others in terms of reducing the memory load and also the requirements for inferring. Fredrick and Klausmeier (1968) and Klausmeier and Meinke (1968) reported the facilitative effects of teaching students a conservative focusing strategy for attaining concepts. This strategy is the one that most effectively reduces the demands on memory and inferring. Bernard (1975b), McMurray, Bernard, and Klausmeier (1975), and Klausmeier, Schilling, and Feldman (1976) incorporated the same strategy for evaluating instances as examples or nonexamples in experimental lessons with excellent results.

Teaching the efficient strategy in the printed material ensures that this strategy is learned, and it also eliminates much trial–and–error learning of the concepts. Prompting the students to use the strategy in identifying examples and nonexamples and providing feedback promotes active learning of the strategy.

7. *Provide for feedback concerning the correctness and incorrectness of the responses.* Clark (1971), Frayer and Klausmeier (1971), Markle (1975), and Sweet (1966) report the desirable effects of feedback to students. Clark, for example, reported that concept attainment improved as the frequency of feedback increased. Frayer and Klausmeier in their survey of research found that feedback should be provided after every response, but that it is most important after an incorrect response. Feedback that not only tells the students that a response or hypothesis is wrong but also enables them to infer *how* it is wrong and how to correct it is particularly helpful.

ILLUSTRATIVE LESSONS

Excerpts from lessons used in experiments on concept learning follow. The excerpts and the accompanying narrative are intended to make clear how the preceding guidelines were used in preparing printed, illustrated instructional material. The first set of lessons was used in teaching a single concept, *equilateral triangle*, and the last set a taxonomy of eight concepts dealing with behavior management.

Single-Concept Lessons: Equilateral Triangle

Two instructional lessons were developed dealing with the concept *equilateral triangle* for use in an experiment involving fourth-grade children from two elementary schools (McMurray, Bernard, & Klausmeier, 1975). In the first lesson the children were taught to recognize the words in the vocabulary list and to discriminate and label the defining attributes of the concept. The word list contained all of the words used in the defining attributes and a few others: *equilateral, triangle, definition, attributes, angle, length, equal, plane, closed, simple, straight, figure, connect.* Teaching the students to discriminate the attributes and to learn the labels followed this sequence: First, the preceding word list was read aloud; second, each word representing an attribute was defined and illustrated through the use of examples and nonexamples of the defining attributes; third, the children represented each attribute by connecting dots placed on a page; and fourth, the children were shown drawings of figures and were instructed to indicate whether each figure had a particular defining attribute. Immediate feedback was provided in the material that indicated to the children whether their answers were correct as well as giving the rationale behind the answer.

The beginning of the second lesson was devoted to a review of the previous day's material, after which a definition of the concept was presented and explained. The children were then instructed to draw several equilateral triangles using the defining attributes presented in the definition. Part of a page of a lesson follows to illustrate how the definition was presented (from Klausmeier, 1976b):

In this lesson you will learn about a special kind of figure. It is called an equilateral triangle. These figures are equilateral triangles:

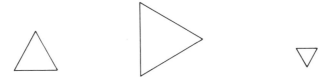

You will learn five important things about equilateral triangles. Equilateral triangles have

1. three straight sides of equal length
2. three equal angles

They are

3. plane
4. closed
5. simple

You will learn about these five things by looking at some figures. You will draw some figures that are outlined in dots. You will also draw some figures by following the numbered dots. You will need to learn and REMEMBER the names of the five important things about equilateral triangles.

To start the second lesson, a review of the five defining attributes of *equilateral triangle* was presented. The material used in the review follows (from Klausmeier, 1976b):

Yesterday you learned some things about figures. You learned that some figures have *three straight sides of equal length.*

yes   no

You also learned about angles:

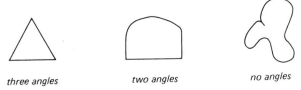

three angles   two angles   no angles

Some angles are the same size. They are equal angles.

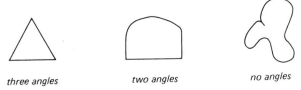

equal   not equal

You learned that some figures have *three equal angles.*

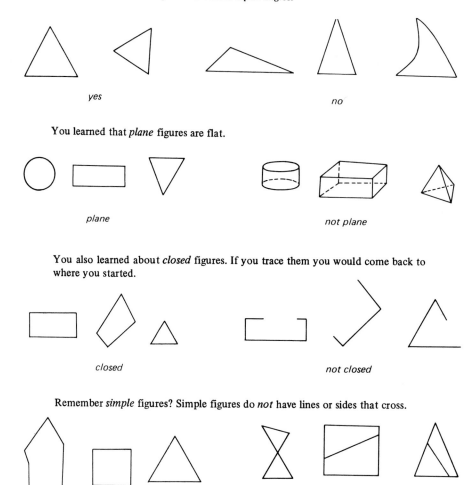

You learned that *plane* figures are flat.

You also learned about *closed* figures. If you trace them you would come back to where you started.

Remember *simple* figures? Simple figures do *not* have lines or sides that cross.

You learned five important things about a special figure. Say the five things to yourself. What is the name of the figure?

three straight sides of equal length + three equal angles + plane + closed + simple = **equilateral triangle**

Finally, the children were taught the strategy for evaluating examples and nonexamples in terms of whether all five defining attributes were or were not present in the instance given in the exercise. Teaching the strategy involved presenting blocks of material, each block having an example or a nonexample and six questions. The children answered the questions in order to evaluate whether or not the given figure was an *equilateral triangle*. One block of material follows (from Klausmeier, 1976b):

Remember, your job is to tell if the figure is an equilateral triangle. Be sure to circle yes or no to each of the five questions. Then circle yes or no after the question: Is it an equilateral triangle?

1.	Does it have three straight sides of equal length?	Yes	No
2.	Does it have three equal angles?	Yes	No
3.	Is it a plane figure?	Yes	No
4.	Is it a closed figure?	Yes	No
5.	Is it a simple figure?	Yes	No
6.	Is it an equilateral triangle?	Yes	No

Multiple-Concept Lessons: Behavior Management

Bernard's (1975b) study had two basic objectives. The first was to determine whether the instructional principles and procedures found effective in teaching single, subject-matter concepts would facilitate the attainment of a group of concepts organized in a taxonomy. The principles and procedures were those explained earlier in this chapter. The second objective was to determine the effects of advance organizers and within-text questions on students' attainment of concepts, understanding of taxonomic relations, and knowledge of relative position in a taxonomy. Two levels of advance organizers were studied: presence or absence. The advance organizer was an overview of the taxonomy of concepts. Two types of within-text questions were of concern: *Attribute-prompting questions* that directed the learner's attention to the presence or absence of the defining attributes of the concepts, and *relational questions* that asked the learner about relationships among the concepts within the taxonomy (taxonomic relationships). Both kinds of questions were presented within the lessons following the relevant instructional material. The taxonomy of concepts is shown in Figure 9.3.

The participating students were twelfth-grade high school students drawn from 10 classrooms in four midwestern high schools. The students in each classroom were assigned at random to one of six treatment groups in a 2×3 factorial design having two levels of advance organizers (present and absent) and three levels of within-text questions (attribute prompting, relational, and no questions). A seventh group, a control group, received placebo material and was compared apart from the other six groups.

Three instructional lessons designed to teach the different behavior management concepts were developed. All of these instructional lessons contained, at a minimum, material incorporating the single-concept instructional vari-

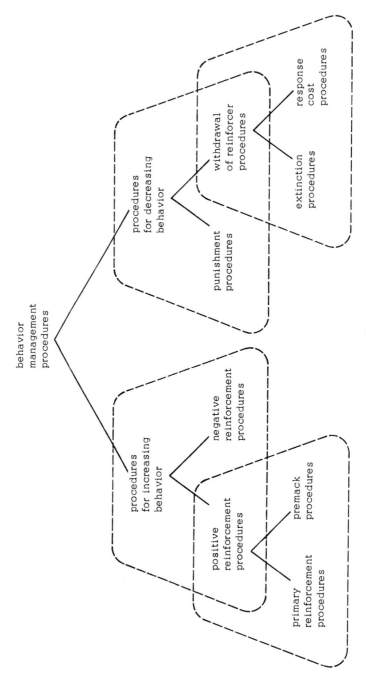

Figure 9.3. Taxonomy of behavior management showing the supraordinate–coordinate–subordinate units within the concept taxonomy. (From Bernard, 1975b.)

ables. The independent variables of advance organizers and within-text questions were systematically varied across and incorporated within the instructional lessons according to the requirements of the design. Where present, a different advance organizer preceded each of the three instructional lessons. Three placebo lessons dealing with nonrelated psychological material were also prepared for use with the control group.

The study was conducted over 4 consecutive days. Each student studied the three lessons on 3 successive days. On the fourth day, all students received three different multiple-choice tests. The first, Concept Mastery Test, was constructed to assess mastery of each of the eight concepts. The second, Understanding Relationships Test, assessed understanding of the taxonomic relationships among the concepts. The third, Concept Taxonomy Test, was constructed to determine how well subjects could identify the position of each concept within the taxonomy.

The mean scores and the standard deviations related to the experimental treatments are given in Table 9.1. The highest mean scores are directly relatable to the experimental treatments. Students receiving the advance organizer and the attribute-prompting questions in their lessons had the highest mean score (26.46) on the Concept Mastery Test. The attribute-prompting questions apparently aided them in mastering the concepts at the formal level. Students receiving the advance organizer and the relational questions had the highest mean score on the Understanding Relations Test (17.73) and also on the Concept Taxonomy Test (4.89). Questions focusing on the taxonomic relations aided students in learning the taxonomic relations and in locating the concepts

TABLE 9.1 Mean Scores and Standard Deviations for Experimental Groups Receiving Multiple Concept Instruction

Experimental group	Concept Mastery Test (34 items)		Understanding Relations Test (24 items)		Concept taxonomy (6 items)	
	M	S.D.	M	S.D.	M	S.D.
Advance organizer	23.17	5.48	15.41	4.35	4.49	1.59
No advance organizer	20.58	5.92	13.35	4.16	2.94	1.49
Advance organizer and attribute-prompting question	26.46	5.30	15.00	3.67	4.58	1.50
Advance organizer and relational questions	22.35	4.72	17.73	4.26	4.89	1.56
No advance organizer and no inserted questions	17.54	5.50	11.27	4.06	2.50	1.56
Placebo	10.12	3.95	6.31	3.22	1.88	1.18

in the taxonomy. It is clear that these lessons were prepared with precision to teach important outcomes effectively.

A comparison of the achievements of the group receiving the placebo lessons, the group getting the concept lessons but without an advance organizer or inserted questions, and the highest groups mentioned earlier is most revealing. The mean scores, changed to percentages, for these groups on the three tests follow: Concept Mastery: 30, 52, and 78; Understanding Relations: 26, 47, and 74; Concept Taxonomy: 33, 42, and 83. Through three lessons, high school seniors were brought from a near chance level of functioning to a relatively high level of performance related to three important areas of cognitive functioning.

Excerpts from the lessons used in the experiment follow. The advance organizer for the first lesson is given first and is followed by the opening of the first lesson that includes an explanation of property (attribute), the definition of positive reinforcement procedures, examples of the four properties (attributes) of positive reinforcement, one example, one nonexample, and related information.

Advance Organizer:

A taxonomy is a way of distinguishing, ordering, and naming groups of related things or ideas. The following is an example of a taxonomy of all things in the world.

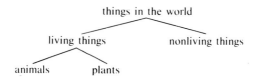

This taxonomy shows that living things and nonliving things are subsets of all things in the world. Plants and animals are subsets of living things.

In taxonomies, the things or ideas that are lower down in the taxonomy are also examples of things higher in the taxonomy. All animals are also living things. All nonliving things are also things in the world. Make sure you understand what has been said before going on.

There are two subsets of *behavior management procedures* that people use. They are presented in the taxonomy below.

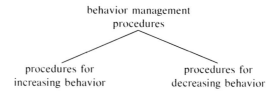

One subset is *procedures for increasing behavior*. They are used by a person to increase the number of times a person's behavior occurs. Examples of particular behavior that people want to increase are "making one's bed," "handing in assignments on time," and "getting a friend to keep a promise."

The other subset is *procedures for decreasing behavior*. These *behavior management procedures* are used to decrease the number of times a person's behavior occurs. A teacher may think that smoking pot before class is a behavior that ought to be stopped. A girl may be making herself "overly attractive" to boys and her friends may want to eliminate what they consider to be a problem behavior.

In the following lesson, you will learn about a subset of *procedures for increasing behavior* called *positive reinforcement procedures*. All *positive reinforcement procedures* are also *procedures for increasing behavior*.

You will also learn about a subset of *positive reinforcement procedures* called *primary reinforcement procedures*. All *primary reinforcement procedures* are also *positive reinforcement procedures*.

Both *positive reinforcement procedures* and *primary reinforcement procedures* are added to the *behavior management* taxonomy.

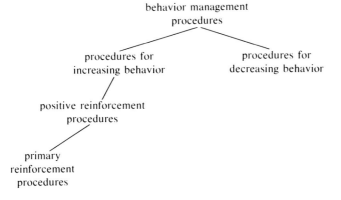

Study this taxonomy carefully. It will help you in understanding and remembering procedures you are about to learn.

Now turn to Lesson 1.

In this lesson you will learn about two procedures that can be used to increase the number of times a person's behavior occurs. First, there are a couple of terms that you should become familiar with.

The first term is *important property*. All objects, events, and just about anything you can think of have important properties. Important properties are characteristics of things that define what they are. The important properties of "chair" are (1) it has a back, (2) it is a single-person seat, and (3) it has a rigid seat. All chairs have these three important properties. If an object has a back, a single-person seat and a rigid seat it is an example of a chair.

Anything that has the three important properties of chair is called an *example* of chair. Examples have all the important properties of the thing you are talking about. "Triangles" have five important properties. All triangles (1) have three straight sides, (2) have three angles, (3) are plane figures, (4) are closed figures, and (5) are simple figures. Any geometric form that has all of these five important properties is an example of triangle.

A *nonexample* lacks one or more important properties. A "stool" is a nonexample of "chair" because it does not have a back. A "square" is a nonexample of "triangle" because it lacks the two important properties of having three sides and having three angles.

Another term that will be used in this lesson is *reinforcer*. A *reinforcer* is any object or event that a particular person likes, such as a hug, money, praise, or food. It is any object or event that a person will work for. Examples of a *reinforcer* will be presented in this lesson.

The two procedures that can be used to increase the number of times a person's behavior occurs are called *positive reinforcement procedures* and *primary reinforcement procedures*. A definition as well as the important properties of each procedure will be presented. Examples and nonexamples of each procedure will help show how each procedure is used.

A definition of *positive reinforcement procedures* is provided in the box below:

Positive reinforcement procedures: A person is given a reinforcer immediately after and every time the person's behavior occurs. This procedure is used to increase the number of times a person's behavior occurs.

Positive reinforcement procedures have four important properties.

1. The procedure is used to increase the number of times a behavior occurs.

   There are many times we want someone to do something for us. You may want a friend to lend her car to you. You may want your teacher to get off your back and be a little more friendly. *Positive reinforcement procedures* can be used to increase the number of times each of these behaviors occurs.

2. A person is given a reinforcer.

   As was mentioned earlier, a reinforcer is something that a person likes. It is something that a person will work for. Suppose that you know that a certain teacher likes to be told that she is doing a good job, is explaining things clearly, etc. By telling a teacher these things, you are giving her a reinforcer. A reinforcer for the friend whose car you want to borrow might be letting the friend use something that you have. If you have an electronic calculator that you know your friend likes to use, letting your friend use the electronic calculator would be a reinforcer.

3. A reinforcer is given immediately after the person's behavior occurs.

   If you wanted a friend to lend you a car, you would give the person a reinforcer (use of the calculator) immediately after the person lends you the car. If you wanted a teacher to be more friendly, you would give the teacher a reinforcer (telling her she's doing a good job) immediately after the teacher does something friendly. A person is given a reinforcer immediately after a behavior occurs; not at the end of the day or week.

4. A reinforcer is given every time the person's behavior occurs.

To get the friend to lend you a car more often, you must lend the person your calculator every time you are permitted to borrow the car. The teacher must be told each time that she is doing a good job, or explaining things clearly if you want her to increase the number of times she is friendly.

Now you will be presented with an example and a nonexample of a *positive reinforcement procedure*. The example will have all four important properties. The nonexample will lack one or more of the important properties.

This is an example	a. Jack liked to drive around town but didn't own a car. His folks would rarely lend him theirs. His friend Marge would sometimes let him borrow hers. To get Marge to lend him her car more often, he suggested the following. He knew that Marge enjoyed playing music on his stereo. He told her that every time he borrowed her car she could come right over and play whatever music she wanted. The number of times Marge lent Jack her car increased over the following months.

This is a nonexample	b. Claire loved to drive around town after dinner, but unfortunately, she didn't own a car. Her friend Bill would sometimes lend her his. To get Bill to lend her his car more often, she told him that every time she borrowed his car, he could come over *sometime* when she was free and use her stereo. Even though Bill really liked playing music on Claire's stereo, he did not increase the number of times he lent Claire his car.

"a" is an example because it contains all four important properties. The procedure is used to *increase* a behavior (Marge's lending Jack her car). A person (Marge) is given a *reinforcer* (use of Jack's stereo). The reinforcer is given to Marge *immediately after* every time she lends Jack her car.

"b" is a nonexample because it lacks one important property. The reinforcer (letting Bill use stereo) is not given by Claire immediately after Bill lends his car. It is given "sometime when she was free." For *positive reinforcement procedures* to work, the reinforcer must be given immediately after the behavior occurs.

The preceding lessons illustrate how knowledge gained from experiments on concept learning and instruction and from carrying out concept analyses, behavioral analyses, and instructional analyses has been applied in developing instructional materials to supplement classroom instruction. The materials have proved to be effective in aiding students who can read to attain a more mature classificatory level of concepts and to move from the classificatory level to the formal level. The effectiveness of the materials results from the precision with which the learning process is guided throughout the lessons. Our knowledge base, though incomplete, is sufficient that cognitive learning can be facilitated markedly over short time periods.

FOR FURTHER STUDY

Merrill, M. D., & Tennyson, R. D. *Teaching concepts: An instructional design guide*. Englewood Cliffs, New Jersey: Educational Technology Publications, 1977.

This is a how-to-do-it textbook that presents instructional strategies for teaching concepts. The primary emphasis is given to teaching single concepts rather than related sets of concepts that form structures of knowledge.

Wittrock, M. C., & Lumsdaine, A. A. Instructional psychology. In M. R. Rosenzweig & L. W. Porter (Eds.), *Annual review of psychology* (Vol. 28). Palo Alto, California: Annual Reviews Inc., 1977. Pp. 417–459.

Wittrock and Lumsdaine review the recent research and theory in instructional psychology, including the design of instruction and means of improving instruction. Research and theory regarding attention, motivation, learning and memory, and instruction and teaching are included.

10

Nurturing Cognitive Development through Instructional Programming for the Individual Student

In Chapter 9, a design for instruction was presented that takes into account principles of cognitive development. The principles were elaborated in the earlier chapters of the book. They are restated here to provide an introduction to instructional programming for the individual student.

Children and youth attain the four levels of the same concepts in an invariant sequence. Concepts attained only at the concrete and identity levels cannot be used in understanding principles, in understanding taxonomic relations, or in solving problems. Concepts when attained at the classificatory level can be used to a limited extent but when attained at the formal level are used much more effectively. Attaining groups of related concepts at the formal level, such as those forming taxonomies, enables the individual to develop conceptual cores corresponding to the powerful structures of knowledge that are used to organize knowledge within and across subject fields.

The levels and the related uses of different concepts are mastered by students at different ages. The four levels and the uses of concepts with examples that can be experienced as objects in the environment are attained earlier than are the levels and uses of concepts with examples that are words or other symbols. Many high school students do not master the formal level or any of the uses of concepts that have only verbal or other symbolic examples.

Intraindividuality in patterns of cognitive development is related to the structures of knowledge that scholars have organized according to subject fields, including language arts, mathematics, science, and social studies. Most students as individuals do not acquire knowledge in these different subjects at the same rate. Further, the differentiation is well advanced by age 9.

There is great variability among individuals in the rate of attaining concepts, in understanding principles, in acquiring structures of knowledge, and in solving problems. Some children at age nine have advanced to a higher level of cognitive functioning than have some high school seniors at age 18. Some of the many conditions associated with slow cognitive development, particularly during Grades 9–12, could probably be prevented through appropriate interventions involving the school and the home during the elementary school years.

In this chapter, a model of instructional programming for the individual student is presented as a framework for nurturing the cognitive development of the individual student. It takes into account the preceding principles of cognitive development and instructional design as explained in Chapter 9. The model cannot be used effectively in most schools as they are currently organized and administered. The schools must change first. An overview of Individually Guided Education (IGE) is described first in this chapter to indicate the kind of school in which instructional programming for the individual student is proceeding effectively. The last part of the chapter is devoted to a longitudinal study to indicate how the principles of cognitive development and instructional design were employed in IGE schools in teaching children basic process concepts of science.

The view expressed in this chapter is that major changes must be made from familiar, traditional forms of schooling in order to nurture properly the cognitive development of individual children and youth. The most committed and able teachers who fully understand principles of development and instructional design cannot be as effective as they wish in ensuring normal cognitive development of the individual student. The probable cause of this lack of transfer is that our familiar forms of age-graded group instruction do not permit teachers to apply their knowledge and skills in adapting instruction to the developmental characteristics of the individual student. The age-graded elementary school in which one teacher instructs 25 to 40 children as a classroom group in all curricular areas is clearly no longer effective (Klausmeier, 1975; Klausmeier, Rossmiller, & Saily, 1977). The typical age-graded high school in which each teacher instructs four to six classes of 20 to 40 students as classroom groups in separate subject fields is failing to aid many students to make a successful transition from childhood to adulthood (Gibbons, 1976). The widespread failure of the high schools is documented in the work of an outstanding national commission (Wirtz, 1977).

CHANGING THE SCHOOL TO NURTURE INDIVIDUAL STUDENT DEVELOPMENT

Rohwer (1970) indicated that the most powerful theories of development and learning were having relatively little impact on improving the quality of education. A main obstacle is that in our familiar age-graded schools students continue to be taught as classroom groups. Also, teachers, parents, and students cannot share in making decisions about the student's instruction as they should. Changes must be made so that the individual student rather than the classroom group is the focus of instruction.

Three recent responses to the need for more effective individualization of instruction have risen above faddism (Talmage, 1975). They are Individually Guided Education (IGE), Adaptable Environments for Learning (AEL, an extension of the initial system referred to as Individually Prescribed Instruction), and Planning for Learning in Accordance with Needs (PLAN). Though the three approaches have similar goals, the main difference between IGE and the other two is that IGE is a total system of schooling. It was developed as an alternative to age-graded elementary schools, departmentalized high schools, unstructured open education, and a variety of alternative schools that function outside the established tax-supported structure of public schools. Most of the materials and strategies now associated with Adaptive Environments for Learning are compatible with Individually Guided Education.

New strategies of instruction and new patterns of human associations are integral aspects of IGE. Chase (1976) emphasized the strategies as follows:

> Individually Guided Education (IGE) is a system of many interrelated components; but it is also a strategy, incorporating many tactics for attaining educational objectives; and when fully implemented, it takes on an institutional character as a new kind of school. It offers distinctive patterns for the organization and management of instruction and learning environments; it fosters new sets of relationships to other education agencies and to the supporting community; it incorporates coordinated strategies for continuing evaluation, refinement, and renewal; and it stimulates staff development and curricular innovation. Moreover, IGE stands out as one of the more widely adopted and better implemented of educational innovations which took shape in the '60s. The indications are that IGE may take its place among the more constructive of American contributions to the advancement of education [p. 196].

Smith (1977) focused on the human associations, social context, and teacher education aspects of IGE:

> Any field of study advances by increments of information—facts, concepts, techniques, procedures, and materials, each one of which may appear in isolation to be of little significance. Education, like other fields, tends to become saturated with pieces of information and materials which seem to bear little relation to one another. A significant breakthrough occurs when someone seizes upon a set of pieces, puts them together, adds a few pieces and forms a new cluster of relationships that renders teachers and other school personnel more effective. Individually Guided Education is such a breakthrough. . . . Starting with teaming arrangements, new concepts and practices were added to create novel forms of human organization to facilitate the adjustment of instruction to the learner.
>
> These new forms represent perhaps the first comprehensive restructuring of school management and teaching operations in this century. They consist of new relationships among school personnel, parents, and community representatives at different levels of responsibility. They put flexibility in the rigid hierarchical structure and replace the

self-contained classroom, age-grade classification, and the isolated teacher. The primary purpose of these new forms of association is to increase the achievement of children by helping them to learn in their own way and at their own rate. [pp. 1–2].

Instructional programming for the individual student is the means toward more effective instruction in IGE. It is most effective when changes are made in the organizational–administrative and other components of familiar age-graded schools.

Organizational–Administrative Arrangements

New organizational arrangements for instruction and administrative structures and processes have been invented to produce an environment in a school that facilitates instructional programming for the individual student (Klausmeier, 1975; Klausmeier & Pellegrin, 1971). These processes and structures at the elementary school level are shown in Figure 10.1. Lipham (1977), in a review of 15 research studies, found that the arrangements had proven effective in promoting shared decision making, building staff morale, promoting communication among teachers and between teachers and administrators, and contributing to the attainment of desired educational objectives in terms of student development in the cognitive and affective domains.

The organizational–administrative arrangements consist of interrelated groups at three distinct levels of operation: the Instructional and Research Unit at the child–teacher level of elementary and middle schools, and the Instructional and Advisory Unit at the student–teacher level of junior and senior high schools; the Instructional Improvement Committee at the building level of elementary and secondary schools; and the Systemwide Program Committee or a similar administrative arrangement at the school district level. As we shall see, these arrangements call for cooperative team efforts and shared decision making.

The nongraded Instructional and Research Unit and the Instructional and Advisory Unit include the students and their cooperative instructional team. Depending upon the developmental level of the students and other factors, a unit has from 75 to 200 students and three to eight teachers and support personnel such as instructional aides. Each instructional team is headed by a unit leader who is a teacher. These units replace age-graded, self-contained classes in elementary and middle schools and age-graded departmentalized classes in junior and senior high schools. The main function of each cooperative team of teachers is to plan, carry out, and evaluate instructional programs for the students of the unit. Teachers in IGE schools spend less time teaching class-size groups and more teaching small groups of 8–20. Students spend less time listening to a teacher and more time in independent work and in small group activities. The flexibility associated with teaming and the use of paid and volunteer instructional aides permits the more effective use of small-group instruction and of adult-supervised independent study and small-group work.

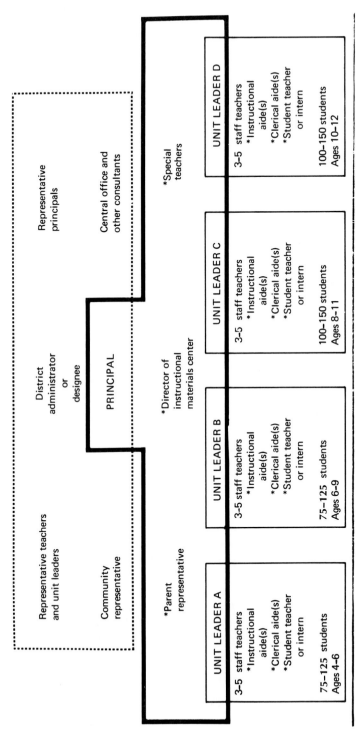

Figure 10.1. Organizational–administrative arrangements for IGE. (Thin line denotes Instruction and Research Unit; heavy line denotes Instructional Improvement Committee; broken line denotes Systemwide Program Committee; inclusion of persons marked with asterisks will vary according to particular school settings.) (Adapted from Klausmeier, Morrow, & Walter, 1968.)

The Instructional Improvement Committee is a new administrative arrangement in each school that becomes possible when schools are organized into units. The heads of the units are called unit leaders. They and the school principal form the Instructional Improvement Committee. This is the educational decision-making group in the school which enables teachers to share decision making with the principal and assistant principals. It is also a primary strength of IGE in comparison with other forms of schooling in which teachers do not share decision making with school administrators. Large schools have more than one Instructional Improvement Committee.

The four main functions for which the Instructional Improvement Committee takes primary initiative are formulating the general educational objectives and outlining the educational program for the student population of the school building or that part of it for which they are responsible; interpreting and implementing systemwide and statewide policies that affect the educational program; coordinating the activities of the different units; and arranging for the use of facilities, time, material, and the like that the units do not manage independently. One of the most important features of IGE is that teachers participate with the principal and others in making these very important decisions.

The Systemwide Program Committee is chaired by the superintendent of the school district and includes consultants and other central office staff, and representative principals, unit leaders, and teachers of IGE schools. Decision-making and facilitative responsibilities for which the Systemwide Policy Committee takes primary initiative include formulating district objectives and programs; recruiting personnel for IGE schools and arranging for their inservice education; providing instructional materials and other material resources; and disseminating information about IGE within the district and the community. An arrangement other than a Systemwide Program Committee is used in some larger school districts. The primary strength of the arrangement is that principals, unit leaders, and teachers share in decision making and program development at the district level.

Unlike some differentiated staffing programs that call for a proliferation of new roles and titles for personnel, the IGE organizational–administrative pattern establishes only one new position, that of unit leader. Basic changes are made, however, in the roles of the principal, department head, teacher, and counselor. Also, other personnel, such as the teacher aide, instructional secretary, student teacher, teaching intern, and parent volunteer, become part of the staff of each cooperative instructional team. The unit leader leads the unit staff, is a teacher in the unit, and is a member of the Instructional Improvement Committee. The role is that of a career teacher.[1] This role has great appeal to

[1] The roles and relationships of personnel in *IGE elementary and middle* schools are described in books as follows: the role of teachers by Nussel, Inglis, and Wiersma (1976); unit leaders by Sorenson, Poole, and Joyal (1976); principals by Lipham and Fruth (1976).

many excellent teachers who prefer to continue as teachers rather than moving to administration, counseling, or other nonteaching activities.

Evaluation for Educational Decision Making

In IGE schools, evaluation is carried out to facilitate student learning, not for the purpose of grading, selecting, or classifying. As we shall see later in the explanation of instructional programming, evaluation is carried out prior to, during, and at the end of instructional sequences. The model to guide the evaluation process involves five steps directly related to instructional programming for the individual student: (1) Formulate instructional objectives and set related criteria of attainment → (2) Measure → (3) Relate measurement to criteria → (4) Judge → and (5) Act on judgment (Klausmeier & Goodwin, 1975).

Compatible Curricular Materials

To adapt instruction to the developmental and other characteristics of the individual student, instructional materials are needed that meet several criteria. They have clearly stated objectives that may be used to indicate to students what is to be learned and to teachers what is to be taught. There are accompanying evaluation tools and procedures directly related to each objective to aid teachers in their evaluation of student learning. There are both printed and nonprinted instructional materials that aid students to attain their objectives. Finally, suggestions are provided to teachers in a manual or resource guide concerning instructional activities that will enable them to vary the instructional activities to provide for individual students.

Many high-quality materials are needed to take into account differences among students in their rates and styles of learning. In Chapter 9, we saw that printed materials can be prepared to teach single concepts effectively and also multiple concepts and related taxonomies. This kind of material is urgently needed to replace the encyclopedic textbooks currently in vogue.

Home–School–Community Relations

A continuing problem of modern education is that the school staff is not sufficiently aware of and responsive to the educational expectations and available resources of the community, parents, and students. Similarly, the community, parents, and children are not sufficiently aware of and responsive to the school's educational programs and to the teachers' expectations and goals for the student. A model for developing a program of home–school–community relations that is intended to resolve the problem is shown in Figure 10.2 (Fruth, Bowles, & Moser, 1977). Its implementation is directly related to the

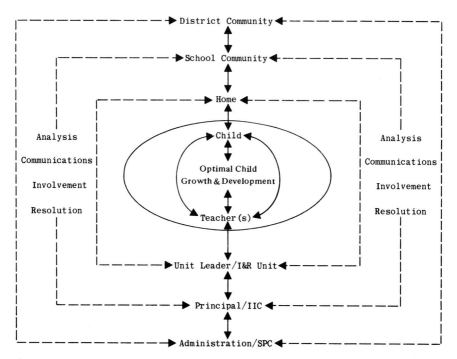

Figure 10.2. A model of home–school–community relations for IGE. (From Fruth, Bowles, & Moser, 1977.)

organizational–administrative arrangements shown earlier in Figure 10.1 and to instructional programming for the individual student, which follows later.

As we saw in Chapter 8, the key to better home–school–community relations is involvement of the parents in the education of their children. Teachers and parents learned to cooperate when school leadership and other conditions were provided. Children's cognitive development was nurtured far more effectively when there were more interactions and favorable attitudes among the teachers, the parents, and the child.

Community Learning and Work Experiences

In addition to an effective program of home–school–community relations in elementary and secondary schools, programs of community learning and work experiences are proving effective in many secondary schools. Prospective dropouts who work part time for pay and participate in nonpaid community activities often continue their high school education until graduation. More students need this opportunity as well as a chance to continue their education well beyond high school graduation. Programs such as these are needed to assure the development of cognitive functioning to a reasonable level of maturity.

ADAPTING INSTRUCTION TO NURTURE INDIVIDUAL
STUDENT DEVELOPMENT

A generic seven-step model of instructional programming for the individual student provides a theoretical framework for adapting instruction to meet individual student needs (Klausmeier, 1977c; Klausmeier, Sorenson, & Quilling, 1971). It should not be confused with programmed instruction of the 1960s or with Skinnerian principles of learning. However, knowledge accruing from studies of aptitude-treatment interactions (Cronbach & Snow, 1977) and learning styles (Messick & Associates, 1976) can be incorporated into it. After an explanation of its main features with examples drawn from several different curricular areas, a longitudinal intervention study will be reported demonstrating the application of instructional programming to teaching the basic process concepts of science.

Steps in Instructional Programming

The seven phases, or steps, in instructional programming are shown in Figure 10.3. Key terms referring to the organizational–administrative arrangements of individually guided elementary schooling and secondary schooling are italicized in the following discussion.

Step 1 involves setting general educational objectives to be attained by the student population of a school within a period of a year or longer. The initiative for setting these objectives is taken by the *Instructional Improvement Committee* of each school, with appropriate input from unit staff members, central office personnel, parents, and others concerned with the educational priorities of the school. As we shall see later, many objectives incorporate concepts.

Step 2 in instructional programming for the individual student requires identifying the instructional objectives that may be attainable by the students of each instructional unit. The initiative for this step is taken by the unit leader and staff teachers of each *Instructional and Research Unit* at the elementary school level and the *Instruction and Advisory Unit* at the secondary school level. Each unit staff must decide which objectives may be appropriate for the students of their unit so that they can later identify appropriate objectives for each student.

In Step 3 the teachers of the unit evaluate each student's level of understanding, skill, or attitudinal development by observing the student's performance or by administering tests. As an integral part of Step 3, an attempt is made to understand each student as an individual. Evaluative information is needed before starting each unit of instruction, but this may not always require *pretesting* of the student prior to beginning each unit of instruction. For example, when instructional programming is carried out in science, pretesting is done only at the beginning of each semester. Thereafter, evaluative information is gathered during each unit of instruction and at the end of the units.

Step 4 deals with setting instructional objectives for each student to attain

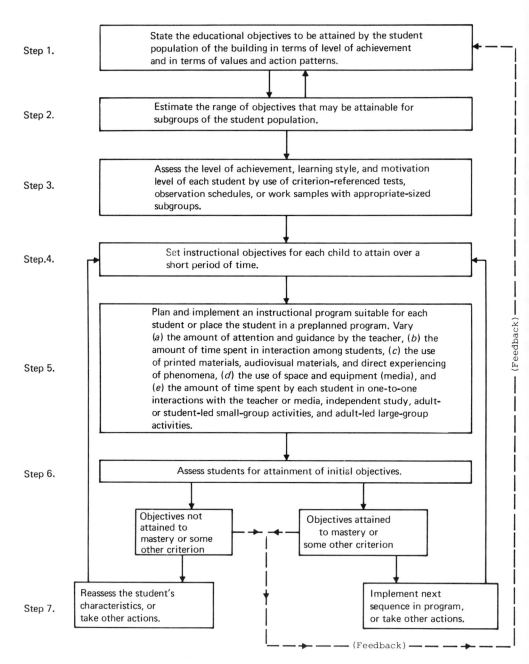

Figure 10.3. Model of instructional programming for the individual student. (Adapted from Klausmeier, Quilling, Sorenson, Way, & Glasrad, 1971.)

during the next instructional sequence, or unit of instruction. The particular objectives that the student has not yet attained to mastery or some other criterion set by the teachers become that student's instructional objectives. The length of time required to attain objectives varies according to the detail and specificity with which the objectives are stated.

Step 5 involves planning and implementing an instructional program through which the student attains the objectives. To provide for differences among students, the following are varied: (1) the amount of attention and guidance by the teacher; (2) the amount of time spent by the teacher in interaction with the student; (3) the use of printed materials, audiovisual materials, and direct experiences; (4) the use of space and equipment; and (5) the amount of time spent by each student in one-to-one interactions with the teacher or media, in independent study, in small-group activities, and in large-group activities.

Students may be instructed as individuals, in small groups, in large groups, or in combinations of these modes. Similarly, printed materials, audiovisual materials, and real objects may be utilized in instruction. The mode of instruction, the kinds of materials used, the amount of assistance by the teachers, and the amount of time given to instruction are important variables that are taken into account in carrying out instructional programs suited to each individual student.

Step 6 involves the teacher's assessment of the students to determine their attainment of objectives. Formative evaluation occurs during the instructional sequence and summative evaluation at the end of one or more sequences.

Step 7 deals with decision making. When students fail to attain an objective to the criterion that has been set, the appropriateness of the objective for the student along with readiness to attain it must be evaluated. Students who attain the instructional objectives move ahead to the next objectives in the sequence or to objectives in another area.

The application of this framework has been made to various subject fields at the elementary and middle-school levels: mathematics (Romberg, 1976), reading (Otto & Chester, 1976), science (Haney & Sorenson, 1977), and social studies (Bechtol & Conte, 1976). Results regarding its effectiveness in nurturing student development in the cognitive and affective domains are presented in Klausmeier et al. (1977).

Eight Patterns of Instructional Programming

Instruction dealing with closely related sets of objectives often is carried out for short periods of time, such as 3–6 weeks. It is convenient to designate the objectives, the materials and activities for attaining the objectives, and the tools and procedures for evaluating students' attainment of the objectives as a unit of instruction. A unit of instruction is defined as a grouping of objectives and related instructional materials and activities for which there is a beginning point and a terminal point. The instructional activities in units of instruction vary according to the objectives.

Three critical matters dealing with units of instruction are (1) whether the objectives are to be attained by all students enrolled in the school, (2) whether the desired level of attainment of the objectives is the same for all the students who are pursuing them, and (3) whether the units of instruction are to be taken in a fixed sequence. These three matters are handled differently both among various curricula and within the same curricular field. For example, in one strand of mathematics, namely arithmetic skills, attaining the same identical objectives may be required of all students; in another strand, probability and statistics, only some students may elect to attain the objectives. In the same way, the criteria that are established for attaining certain objectives in a curricular field may be identical for all students (for example, 80% correct on a test); the criteria for other objectives in the same curricular field may be stated variably in terms of each student's characteristics (for example, each student will participate successfully from 1 to 10 times monthly in activities related to the set of objectives). In a certain curricular field, the units of instruction covering one or more years of schooling may be invariantly sequenced, either because mastering each unit is prerequisite to starting the next one or because it is convenient to teach the units in an invariant sequence. In another curricular field, or in a different strand of the same curricular field, any unit of instruction may be started at any point in time during a given semester or school year, and starting one unit may not depend upon completing other units.

There are eight possible patterns of common or variable objectives, full mastery or variable attainment of objectives, and an invariant or variable sequence of instructional units, as shown in Figure 10.4. The staff of a school, taking into account state and school district policies and the needs of the students, should decide which of these patterns their students will pursue with regard to the various curricular areas and the areas of instruction within the same curricular areas.

The word *variable,* as used in the eight patterns, implies a range. For example, in connection with objectives it implies all the possibilities, ranging from most, but not all, the objectives being the same for many individuals to no objectives being the same for any two individuals. In connection with sequence, it implies, for example, that if there are six units of instruction undertaken during a year within one curricular area, the units may be taken in any order, or that only one of them may be taken out of a recommended sequence. Variable level of attainment means that students will attain a particular objective or set of objectives to a level appropriate for the student. Expected levels of attainment of objectives in the psychomotor and affective domains usually are variable. Examples of objectives indicating variable attainment are "Each student will hit from 2 to 8 out of 10 free throws, a number appropriate for the particular student," and "Each student will manifest a positive attitude (but

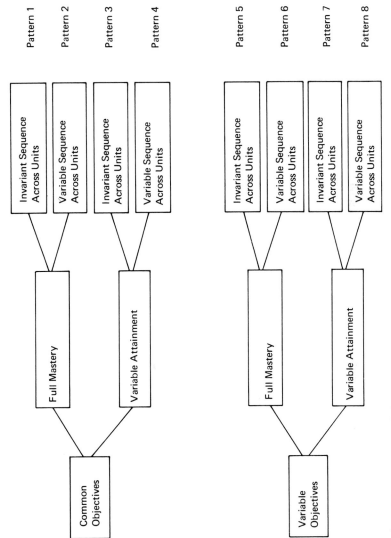

Figure 10.4. Patterns of objectives, criteria of attainment, and sequencing in instructional programming for the individual student. (From Klausmeier, 1977c.)

certainly not identically strong) toward other students, regardless of their ethnic group or socioeconomic status.''

Brief descriptions follow of the eight patterns of objectives, criteria of attainment, and sequencing of units of instruction.

1. *Common objectives, full mastery, and invariant sequence across units.* Instructional programming for the individual student may be organized so that all students proceed through the same sequence of units and attain the same objectives to the same criterion of full mastery. The objectives within the units of instruction may or may not be sequenced invariantly. Where this pattern is implemented properly, students master sets of objectives at their own rates. Instruction dealing with knowledge and skills organized in a hierarchical fashion, such as arithmetic skills and reading skills, may follow this pattern.

2. *Common objectives, full mastery, variable sequence across units.* Instruction may be organized so that all students pursue the same units of instruction to attain the same objectives incorporated in each unit to the same criterion of full mastery; however, mastering the objectives of one unit, though necessary for completing it, is not prerequisite for starting another one. Therefore, a student may start any one of the several units at any time during a semester or year. Students complete the units of instruction at their own rates; consequently, not all complete the same number of units during a particular time period, such as a semester; or they spend different amounts of time on the units during the semester.

3. *Common objectives, variable attainment, invariant sequence across units.* According to this pattern, all students pursuing a particular unit of instruction attain the same objectives to a level of achievement appropriate for each student. For convenience in managing instruction, or because of the hierarchical nature of the knowledge and skills, the units of instruction are sequenced invariantly during the school year. Students may go to the next unit whether or not they have mastered the objectives of the prior unit.

4. *Common objectives, variable attainment, and variable sequence across units.* Objectives required of all students in the affective domain and in expressive fields, such as art and dance, generally fall into this pattern. All students are to attain the same objectives incorporated in the units of instruction; they need not master them but should attain them to a level judged appropriate for each student. The units are not taken in a fixed sequence.

5. *Variable objectives, full mastery, invariant sequence across units.* Before dealing with this pattern, we should be aware that the four patterns involving variable objectives imply that students elect or are assigned to attain objectives that are different across curricular areas, within the same curricular area, or

both. For example, students may be assigned to, or choose from, several different course offerings, or within a course, be assigned to or choose the sets of objectives they will attain. Electives imply variable objectives; the same requirements for all students across curricular areas and within courses imply common objectives.

According to Pattern 5, instruction is arranged so that not all students attain the same objectives; however, sets of objectives in each unit of instruction taken by any student are attained to mastery, and the units of instruction incorporating the objectives are taken in an invariant sequence.

Instrumental music instruction may follow this pattern if not all students take instrumental music. Here the students who learn to perform on different instruments have different sets of objectives. However, those learning to play the same instrument are required to attain successive units in an invariant sequence and also to reach the same level of full mastery before proceeding from one unit of instruction to the next.

6. *Variable objectives, full mastery, variable sequence.* Instruction follows the same pattern here as in Pattern 5 except that the units are not sequenced. In connection with the previous example from instrumental music, the sequence of the units is not fixed but varies.

7. *Variable objectives, variable attainment, invariant sequence across units.* This pattern is uncommon because of the invariant sequence; however, some units of instruction of some curricular programs may follow it. Although no particular level of attainment of objectives is required, the invariant sequence presumes that some knowledge or skill (less than mastery, however) is needed before moving to the next unit of instruction.

8. *Variable objectives, variable attainment, variable sequence across units.* Not all students attending the same school are expected to pursue these units or courses, and those who do pursue the same units are not required to reach any specified level of knowledge or skill related to the objectives of the units. The units need not be taken in a specified sequence. Elective units of instruction in curricular areas and within-course enrichment are representative of this pattern.

From the preceding we infer that several different patterns of instructional programming for the students may be used in connection with their learning of concepts, principles, structures of knowledge, and problem-solving skills. The information presented in Chapters 6–8 suggests that there is much overlapping in attainment of the four levels. That is, the student has partially attained a higher level before fully attaining the two lower levels. A great deal of work must be done in each school and school district to determine when and whether to apply a mastery criterion or a variable criterion. Similarly, whether or not to follow an invariant sequence during a semester or a year requires the use of situational information. Our knowledge about the relationship between structures of knowledge, including taxonomies and learning hierarchies, and the sequencing of instruction is not sufficient to allow us to make judgments across subject fields and school situations. Wise decision making by informed practitioners is clearly needed.

MASTERY LEARNING AND INDIVIDUAL STUDENT DEVELOPMENT

Four patterns of instructional programming for the individual student involve mastery of objectives and four do not. The inclusion of mastery and nonmastery of objectives in the same theoretical framework is novel; however, the concept of mastery learning is not unique to instructional programming for the individual student. Morrison (1926) developed and applied a "mastery formula" to guide instruction in the Laboratory School of the University of Chicago and described the system in a widely used methods textbook. Washburne (1932) implemented a plan of differentiated instruction in Winnetka, Illinois, involving mastery and self-pacing by which each student mastered successive units of work at the student's own rate without being held back with slower students or being forced forward with faster children, as is done in age-graded classes. Other approaches to mastery learning were also formulated during the first half of this century. However, Carroll (1963) formulated an explicit theory of mastery learning. The main assumption of this theory is that, given enough time, every student can master any learning task. This assumption yielded the following equation:

$$\text{Degree of School Learning} = f \left(\frac{\text{Time Spent}}{\text{Time Needed}} \right)$$

That is, the degree of learning a school task is a function of the time spent in learning relative to the time needed to master the task. If the time spent is sufficient for mastery, then the degree of learning is 100%, or mastery.

Carroll hypothesized that the time spent and the time needed were influenced not only by learner characteristics but also by the characteristics of instruction. The time spent in learning is influenced by two factors: perseverance, defined as the amount of time a student is willing to spend actively engaged in learning, and opportunity to learn, defined as the classroom time allotted to learning. Three factors influence the time needed to learn: the student's aptitude for learning the task, the quality of instruction, and the student's ability to understand the instruction. The preceding equation restated in terms of the determinants of the amount of time spent and the amount of time needed follows:

$$\text{Degree of School Learning} = f \left(\frac{\text{1. Perseverance} \quad \text{2. Opportunity to learn}}{\text{3. Aptitude} \quad \text{4. Quality of instruction} \\ \text{5. Ability to understand instruction}} \right)$$

The extent to which a student masters a learning task is a function of perseverance and opportunity to learn relative to aptitude for the learning task, the quality of instruction, and the ability to understand this instruction. Carroll defined a learning task as going from ignorance of some specified fact or concept to knowledge or understanding of it, or as proceeding from incapability of performing some specified act to capability of performing it. The undefined element of the theory is the determination of the differential amounts of time—across both short time periods, such as a few lessons, and long time periods, such as the elementary school years—that different students might need to master the same tasks, such as learning to read at a level of functional literacy. It is also not clear that every student could master understanding of some abstract principles, such as relativity, or learn to solve complex problems, such as in astronomy or philosophy.

Bloom's (1968, 1976) theory of Learning-for-Mastery is an elaboration and application of Carroll's formulation. Using Carroll's conceptual model, Bloom hypothesized that if aptitude was predictive of the amount of time needed to learn, but not of the level of achievement (degree of learning), it should be possible to set the expected level of achievement at mastery. Then, by matching the opportunity to learn (time) and the quality of instruction, teachers should be able to ensure mastery by each student. When these two are matched properly, three variables, according to Bloom, should account for most of the variation among students in achievement: (1) their cognitive entry behaviors, that is, the extent to which the student has already mastered prerequisite knowledge and skills, (2) affective entry behaviors, that is, the extent to which the student is willing to engage actively in the learning process, and (3) the quality of instruction, the extent to which instruction is appropriate to the learner. According to Bloom, teachers in familiar age-graded self-contained schools and in departmentalized instructional arrangements can employ the mastery learning strategy to deal with these three variables effectively. Moreover, students can master the learning tasks, and the variability among students in levels of achievement can be greatly diminished.

Block (1974) and Block and Anderson (1975) set forth extensive elaborations of Bloom's mastery strategy. Their sequential steps, similar to those of instructional programming, are to identify objectives, designate the criterion of mastery, teach, test, arrange for enrichment and other activities for those who master the unit, arrange for corrective and remedial teaching of those who do not master, test, repeat if there are still nonmastery students, and start the next unit of instruction. They do not deal with objectives for which a mastery criterion is inappropriate nor do they indicate how the self-contained teacher can manage to provide for both the students who master early and for those who experience continuing difficulty in achieving mastery.

Peterson (1972) found support for the hypothesis that student achievement would be higher under a mastery approach than under nonmastery approaches in several research studies, all of which were carried out over very short periods of time, usually less than 4 weeks. However, the percentage of students who mastered the age-graded learning tasks varied considerably across the studies. The hypothesis that there would be less variability among the students in achievement was supported by the analysis of the posttests employed in the studies. Did this lower variability result from the higher achievements of the less rapid learners or from not permitting the more rapid learners to move ahead and attain more advanced objectives? These questions were not addressed in the experiments.

Block and Burns (1977) also found that mastery-taught groups achieved higher on posttests than did nonmastery groups in the large majority of the 24 studies reviewed. Likewise, the mastery-taught students performed better on retention measures. In fact, in every study where retention measures were gathered, the mastery-taught students did as well or better than the nonmastery students. The mastery-taught students also exhibited less variability than other students.

The majority of the studies reviewed by Block and Burns were conducted at the college level; however, 11 involved elementary school children. In only 1 of the 11 studies was the duration of instruction longer than 4 weeks, and in 9 of them the experimental instruction was only of 1–2 weeks duration. Block and Burns also found that the mastery approach to learning had a positive effect on students' interest in and attitude toward the subject matter learned, as well as on academic self-confidence, attitudes toward cooperation, attitudes toward instruction, and self-concept. Studies by Anderson (1976), Lee and others (cited in Bloom, 1976), and Poggio, Glasnapp, and Ory (1975) support this conclusion.

Although the mastery-learning strategy of instruction has been shown to attain desirable results in terms of higher mean achievement and desirable affective outcomes over short time periods, usually involving only one unit of instruction, it probably cannot be implemented successfully over long time periods in age-graded classrooms as recommended by Bloom (1976). Lower-aptitude students cannot be brought up to mastery by being given more time during the day or week without holding back higher-aptitude students who need less time to master the same objectives but then must wait, even though engaged in enrichment activities, to start the next set of objectives. Mueller (1976) evaluated Bloom's contention that mastery learning over long periods of time will maximize learning for individual students enrolled in our familiar age-graded schools as follows:

In traditionally organized schools, where learning is divided into grade levels and semesters, and where students are advanced together through these fixed-time instructional units, the mastery model cannot be used to maximize learning for all students. Since students learn at different rates, it is not legitimate for an instructor to expect all students to achieve the same level of performance (mastery) over the same amount of material in the same amount of time [p. 44].

The preceding conditions coincide with those we identified in the 1960s that led to the formulation of the model of instructional programming for the individual student and also to Individually Guided Education as an alternative to age-graded group instruction. Mastery of the same objectives by all students, as portrayed in Patterns 1 and 2 of the instructional programmming model, is facilitated when students are permitted and encouraged to proceed at rates suitable to the student across long time periods. When students, regardless of age or grade, are permitted to proceed in this manner, it is probable that differences among students in levels of achievement will be greater—rather than eliminated, as hypothesized by mastery learning theory—even though many more students will also achieve minimum levels of competency in basic skills at each successive level of schooling.

TEACHING PROCESS CONCEPTS OF SCIENCE: A LONGITUDINAL INTERVENTION STUDY

The application of instructional programming for the individual student to concepts, principles, structures of knowledge, and problem-solving skills is different from that to skills such as reading and arithmetic computations. Reading and arithmetic do not require the use of the same equipment and space by many students. On the other hand, the teaching of science concepts and principles usually requires all the students of an elementary school building to share a science laboratory and also a small amount of expensive science equipment. In order to use the space and equipment advantageously, considerable instruction must occur in the science laboratory that is arranged to accommodate 10–15 pairs of students, about 20–30 students. Within these groups, independent work, pairing of students, and small-group work as well as teacher demonstrations and other teacher-led activities directed toward the entire group are carried out.

Instructional programming for the individual student in science also differs greatly when a mastery criterion rather than a variable criterion is followed. Some schools follow a mastery pattern, others a variable pattern. In the science experimentation to be reported next, a mastery criterion was employed.

The longitudinal intervention study was carried out for 3 years in two IGE experimental schools and two IGE control schools of the same school district. The design of the study and the results of the first 2 years are reported in Klausmeier, Sipple, Swanson, and Schilling (1976). One key experiment during the third year of the study follows in some detail.

Purpose

One purpose of the experiments was to determine the effects of successively closer approximations of instructional programming for the individual student on the students' achievement of science objectives. The objectives were included as part of a published science program called Science . . . A Process Approach, or SAPA (AAAS Commission on Science Education, 1967). This program recommends that all students master consecutive sets of objectives. The objectives are incorporated into single lessons and related blocks of lessons for each of several basic process concepts of science. Single lessons involve three or more sessions of 25–30 minutes.

A second purpose was to determine the effects of lessons prepared by the project staff. These lessons were designed to facilitate each student's understanding of each of the process concepts associated with each block of lessons. The hierarchy of process concepts was given earlier in Figure 9.2. These lessons were prepared according to the design outlined in Chapter 9 and were based on the principles for preparing materials to teach concepts that are given in Chapter 9.

At least one experiment was carried out during each semester. Each successive experiment involved each of the following factors separately or in combination. First, the participating experimental teachers used the printed lessons developed by the project staff as advance organizers for each block of SAPA lessons. One of the printed lessons was used for each block of instruction dealing with a SAPA process concept. Second, the instructional procedure in the experimental schools was modified from group instruction of heterogeneous class-size groups to successively closer approximations of differentiated instruction that followed instructional programming for the individual student.

The studies were planned with the school staffs each year. During the first year only small-scale experiments were carried out in the experimental schools. Large-scale experiments involving minimum changes in the time allocated for science instruction were carried out during the second year. Experiments involving flexible allocation of time and more fully differentiated instruction were carried out during successive semesters of the third year. The teachers carried out all the instruction, the independent variable in the experiments, according to guidelines agreed upon by the project staff and the teachers.

Description of the Participating Schools and Students

The experiments were carried out in two pairs of experimental and control schools, matched on socioeconomic, ethnic, and general demographic characteristics of the students. The four schools were organized and administered in the IGE pattern. It was assumed that if the results were the same in the two pairs of schools, the results would be more applicable to IGE schools generally.

In the second year of the study, 216 children in their fifth year of schooling, corresponding to the fourth grade in traditional schools, and 230 children in their sixth year, corresponding to fifth grade, participated in the experiments. The fifth-year students were followed into their sixth year of schooling the third year; the sixth-year students were not followed into the third year of the experiment. However, the experimental sixth-year students served as a comparison group for the fifth-year students when they were in their sixth year.

Instructional and Data-Gathering Procedures

The instruction in the experimental and control schools and the data collection followed this pattern during the second-year experiments. At the beginning of each semester in both the control and the experimental schools, tests covering the objectives of the SAPA lessons that were taught during the semester were administered as a pretest to all students enrolled at Levels 5 and 6. The same tests were administered at the end of each semester as a posttest.

In the experimental schools, the students were organized for instruction into three groups, based on the pretest results: the top one-third, the middle one-third, and the bottom one-third in each school. In the control schools, the children were taught in heterogeneous, age-graded, classroom-size groups with some individualization. This was the manner in which teachers in the experimental schools carried out their instruction before the study started.

In the experimental schools, a process-concept lesson developed by the project staff was used at the beginning of each set of SAPA lessons dealing with the same process (e.g., inferring, measuring, predicting). The process-concept lessons were prepared to aid the students to understand the particular process concept, thus serving as an advance organizer for the block of lessons. The process-concept lessons were not used in the control schools.

In the experimental schools, provisions for differences among the students in their level of achievement were scheduled to be made at the end of each process block of SAPA lessons. The provisions were enrichment activities for the students who mastered the objectives, reteaching the near-mastery students, and a different kind of instruction for those who made little progress. However, as part of the experimental design for the second-year experiments, the amount of time given to instruction on the SAPA lessons was held constant in the experimental and control schools. The experimental schools used all the time for the initial teaching of the lessons, and no time remained for the further differentiation that was scheduled. Thus the main difference between the experimental and control schools was that the students in the experimental schools were instructed in groups formed on the basis of pretest scores, whereas those in the control schools were in heterogeneous groups of various entering achievement levels related to the science objectives. The teachers of all groups individualized instruction within their groups to the best of their ability.

Results of Second-Year Experimentation

At both Levels 5 and 6 in each semester and for the combined semesters, the children of the two experimental schools combined achieved significantly higher mean scores on the SAPA tests than did those of the combined control schools.

A test was developed for each process-concept lesson prepared by the project staff that was used in the experimental schools as an advance organizer for each SAPA block of lessons. The tests were administered at the end of each semester to the students in both the experimental schools and the control schools. The differences between the mean scores favored the combined experimental schools at Level 5 and were statistically significant for four of the five process-concept tests. The differences for the combined groups at Level 6 were significant for two of the five process-concept lessons but not for the other three.

Despite the substantial constraints put upon the experimentation in order to keep time for instruction constant, the results were generally supportive of the two interventions. The time constraint was especially crucial in the experimental schools inasmuch as a large amount of information was presented in the process-concept lessons that the control students did not receive. This information, combined with that in the SAPA lessons, may have caused some students in the experimental schools not to learn the substance in either set of materials well.

Results of Third-Year Experimentation

In this experiment, the amount of time was varied for the three groups, thereby allowing for more appropriate use of activities and materials in each group and enabling each group to proceed at a different rate. Only the fifth-year children were followed into their sixth year of schooling. The experimental groups in the two IGE schools included 135 children, and the control groups contained 124 children. Three lessons dealing with the process concept *inferring* were used in this experiment. The seven steps of instructional programming for the individual student as they were implemented in the experiment follow. (Except for the time variation, they were also implemented in the same manner during the second year.)

Step 1. Educational objectives were specified for the student population of the building. The schoolwide objectives were the objectives of the SAPA curricular program for kindergarten through sixth grade, modified slightly by the school district. Objectives within each set of process objectives were to be mastered in an invariant sequence, and each set in successive lessons and blocks of lessons in the same strand were to be mastered.

Step 2. The objectives that might be attainable for subgroups of the student population were determined. The objectives for science specified for the subgroup of the school population (Level 6) in both the experimental and control schools were the objectives of the three SAPA lessons used in the experiment.

Step 3. An assessment was made of each child's level of achievement. Each student's level of achievement related to these three SAPA science lessons was determined by pretesting prior to the beginning of instruction. (Students' learning styles and motivational levels were not evaluated or dealt with systematically as part of the experiment.)

Step 4. Instructional objectives were set for each child for a specified period of time. The same objectives of each SAPA science lesson were set for every child in the experimental and control schools for the period of time during which the lessons were taught. Further, school policies required that the same number of lessons should be completed each semester by all the students.

Step 5. An instructional program suitable for each student was planned and implemented. In the experimental schools, partial differentiation of instruction consisted of several elements. Three groups in each experimental school whose total scores on the pretests were in the upper, middle, or lower one-third of the distribution of the scores were formed prior to starting instruction on the three lessons dealing with the concept *inferring*. Each of these groups included from 18 to 24 students. The posttest scores of Lessons 1 and 2 were used in reforming groups for Lessons 2 and 3.

Instruction for the inferring block of lessons was approximately 6 weeks in length. The sequence of instruction for the first lesson as now illustrated was the sequence for all lessons. (Steps 6 and 7 are part of the sequence.)

Each high, middle, and low group in each experimental school received approximately 165 minutes of group instruction, primarily in the science laboratory, in groups of 18–24. Within each group, the teacher differentiated the instruction further in terms of the students' characteristics.

Step 6. The attainment of objectives was assessed. Upon completion of this initial instruction, a 10-item posttest covering the content of the lesson was administered and scored immediately by an instructional aide.

Step 7. Instructional decisions were made on the basis of the assessment. Based on the rank order of scores obtained on the posttest for each group, three new groups were formed for the purpose of reteaching and/or enrichment: the students who attained a posttest score of 8, 9, or 10 (mastery), those who achieved a score of 6 or 7 (near mastery), and the remainder of the students who scored in the 0–5 range. All the students moved into new groups of 18–24 on the basis of their posttest scores and for 15–30 minutes reviewed the lesson with the teacher. For another 60–75 minutes, the high-scoring students reviewed the lesson very briefly and proceeded to related enrichment activities (including tutoring a nonmastery classmate); students scoring in the middle range were instructed in the content they had not mastered; and low-scoring students received instruction on the lesson with supplementary activities either in the instructional materials center and/or with classmate tutors from the mastery group.

In the two control schools, the students were instructed in heterogeneous classes and spent approximately the same number of minutes in their science instruction as the students of the experimental schools did in the initial instruction prior to posttesting. Each of the control group classes contained between 25 and 29 students. The control groups received roughly 40 minutes more per lesson than did the experimental groups in initial instruction. The experimental groups spent approximately 60 minutes more per lesson, including the instruction after posttesting, than did the control groups.

The interval scores obtained from the posttests were analyzed using analysis of covariance, with the pretest score serving as the covariate. Also, the interval scores were translated from a numerical score to one of two categories: mastery or nonmastery. Mastery for these tests was defined as a score of 8, 9, or 10 and nonmastery as 7 or lower. A chi-square was calculated for the observed frequencies of mastery and nonmastery for each of the three lessons.

The students in the experimental schools combined scored significantly higher on the tests of *inferring* than did the students in the control schools combined; the differences between each pair of schools were also significant. Table 10.1 gives the mean raw SAPA pretest scores, the mean posttest scores,

TABLE 10.1   Mean Gain Scores in Science of Students in Experimental and Control Schools

	Tests E, F, G: Inferring
Experiment 1	
Pre	14.44
Post	23.73
Gain	9.29
Control 1	
Pre	13.16
Post	19.10
Gain	5.94
Experiment 2	
Pre	14.50
Post	22.47
Gain	7.97
Control 2	
Pre	13.32
Post	18.44
Gain	5.12

TABLE 10.2 Number of Students in Experimental and Control Schools Who Did and Did Not Master Science Objectives

Lesson 6

	E1	C1		E2	C2		E1, E2	C1, C2
M	24	2		25	5		49	7
NM	39	56		47	61		86	117
	.001			.001			.001	

Lesson 7

	E1	C1		E2	C2		E1, E2	C1, C2
M	46	17		46	7		92	24
NM	17	41		26	59		43	100
	.001			.001			.001	

Lesson 8

	E1	C1		E2	C2		E1, E2	C1, C2
M	48	36		45	24		93	60
NM	15	22		27	42		42	64
	.05			.01			.01	

and the mean gains for students in each of the experimental and each of the control schools. These mean scores are not adjusted by analysis of covariance. In all cases, the gains for the experimental schools were greater than for the control schools.

Table 10.2 presents a summary of the observed frequencies and of the chi-square tests for the mastery and nonmastery groups in the experimental and control schools. Of the nine obtained differences in numbers of mastery and nonmastery students, the results favored the experimental schools at the .05 level in one case, at the .01 level in two cases, and at the .001 level in six cases.

Chi-square tests for the mastery and nonmastery groups in these Level 6 experimental groups were compared with those of the Level 6 experimental groups of the prior year whose instruction had been less well differentiated because of time constraints. In all cases, the differences in the numbers of mastery and nonmastery students between the combined experimental and the combined prior comparison groups were significant at the .01 level, favoring the present experimental groups.

The time spent in instruction and the gains that accrued may be examined in Table 10.3 The experimental schools spent 39% and 25% more time than the control schools, and the gain scores were 56% greater in both cases. The increase in the percentage of students who achieved mastery was considerably greater than the increase in time. If it is assumed that performance, as measured by the tests, and time are linearly related, neither the mean gain increases nor the increase in percentage of students at mastery can be easily explained. However, the results are interpretable if the quality of instruction is assumed to interact with time spent. The greater amount of time used in the experimental

TABLE 10.3   Comparison of Amount of Instruction and Testing, Mean Gains, and Percentage of Students at Mastery Level

	C_1	E_1	Percentage of increase from C_1 to E_1	C_2	E_2	Percentage of increase from C_2 to E_2
Total minutes spent in instruction	610	850	39%	675	845	25%
Mean gains	5.94	9.29	56%	5.12	7.97	56%
Percentage of students at mastery on posttest	32%	62%	93%	18%	54%	200%

schools permitted better adaptation of instruction to meet individual student needs in accordance with instructional programming for the individual student.

A note is in order regarding the students who did not attain mastery, many of whom were in the lowest one-third on the pretests and posttests. It was the judgment of the participating teachers and the project staff that some of these students would not have attained mastery during the semester in which the experiment was conducted regardless of the amount of time that might have been given to instruction. Similarly, some students in the top one-third could have attained mastery in less time and could have proceeded directly to the next higher lessons dealing with *inferring* or to lessons dealing with other process concepts.

Instructional programming for the individual student was not completely implemented in this experiment. The students, regardless of their aptitude for learning science, started and completed the same number of lessons during each semester and year. Students must proceed at different rates through a sequenced series of lessons when a criterion of mastery is followed.

It was not agreed by the staff of the participating school district that all students should master the objectives of consecutive sets of lessons as recommended in the SAPA guides for teachers. It is possible that some students should be permitted to move ahead even though they do not achieve mastery of concepts if the same concepts will be taught again in later units of instruction. For example, when *inferring* is taught at 1- or 2-year intervals, students who, after reteaching, have made considerable progress might be permitted to move into the next unit with those who have mastered, assuming that with possible changes in motivation and level of cognitive development they will be able to attain mastery. Similarly, it is not clear which science concepts can and cannot be learned in an invariant sequence during a semester or year. Instructional programming to teach science concepts and other concepts can be carried out according to more than one pattern, and continuous research in school settings is needed to determine which pattern may achieve the best results with students of different learning characteristics.

FOR FURTHER STUDY

Bloom, B. S. *Human characteristics and school learning.* New York: McGraw-Hill, 1976.

Bloom presents the principles and rationale of mastery learning and proposes that differences among students in rate of learning can be greatly reduced or eliminated through this approach to education. Instructional programming for the individual student, explained in Chapter 10, includes mastery learning as one of several approaches to adapting instruction to individual student's learning needs and other characteristics.

Cronbach, L. J., & Snow, R. E. *Aptitudes and instructional methods: A handbook for research on interactions.* New York: Wiley, 1977.

Principles, methods, and theory regarding individual differences and instructional procedures are presented in a scholarly readable fashion. Chapter 1, "A perspective on aptitude and instruction" and Chapter 14, "What do we know about aptitude x treatment interaction? What should we learn?" provide an overview of the field.

Glaser, R. *Adaptive education: Individual diversity and learning.* New York: Holt, Rinehart, & Winston, 1977.

The inventor of Individually Prescribed Instruction describes the most recent version of this approach to providing for individual differences.

Klausmeier, H. J. Origin and overview of IGE; Instructional Programming for the Individual Student. In H. J. Klausmeier, R. A. Rossmiller, & M. Saily (Eds.), *Individually guided elementary education: Concepts and practices.* New York: Academic Press, 1977. Pp. 1–24; 55–76.

In Chapter 1 the author describes how and why IGE started during the 1960s and in Chapter 3 explains instructional programming for the individual student. The various modes of instruction that may be employed in meeting the learning needs of individual students are clarified.

Messick, S., & Associates. *Individuality in learning.* San Francisco: Jossey-Bass, 1976.

The focus is on styles of mental functioning rather than on either cognitive processes or the substance of thought. Styles are presumed to be more highly correlated with directions of achievement than with levels of achievement.

Talmage, H. (Ed.). *Systems of individualized education.* Berkeley, California: McCutchan Publishing Co., 1975.

Three widely practiced systems of individualized education are explained: Individually Guided Education, Adaptable Environments for Learning, an extension of Individually Prescribed Instruction, and Planning for Learning in Accordance with Needs. A historical and theoretical framework for understanding the three systems is provided.

11

Conclusion

In this book, results have been presented from three interrelated areas of research carried out by the first author and his research teams at the Wisconsin Research and Development Center for Cognitive Learning. One area had as its objective describing and explaining cognitive development during the school years (Chapters 1–8). Another area dealt with incorporating knowledge about cognitive learning and development into a design of instructional materials and classroom procedures for teaching concepts, principles, and structures of knowledge (Chapter 9). The third effort, which included persons of cooperating schools, state education agencies, and teacher education institutions, had as its objective changing schools to nurture the development of individual children and youth more effectively (Chapter 10). To bring results from the three areas into perspective, we offer some closing observations.

The cognitive structure of the individual at any point in time includes everything the individual has learned. The products of learning of particular interest are concepts, principles, structures of knowledge, and problem solving. It is the learning of these products during the school years that enables the individual to interpret the physical and social world and to continue to learn with increasing independence.

A concept is both a mental construct of the individual and the societally accepted meaning of one or more words that represent the concept. Concepts as mental constructs are the critical component of a maturing individual's continuously enlarging cognitive structure and serve as tools of thought. Concepts as societally accepted meanings of words comprise much of the subject matter that children and youth learn during the school years.

A principle may be defined formally as a relationship between two or more concepts. Understanding the concepts embedded in the principle is necessary but not sufficient for understanding the principle. Like a concept, a principle serves both as a mental construct of the individual and as the societally accepted meaning of the statement that expresses the principle. Principles are powerful tools of thought and are used in interpreting many events and conditions in the physical and social world and for solving problems.

Persons throughout the recorded history of humanity have been adding to their individual and collective knowledge, organizing it, and putting it into communicable forms, primarily symbolic. Taxonomies, other hierarchies, and theories are three important frameworks for organizing an individual's cognitive structure, and also for organizing the communicable knowledge of a group whose members share the same language and cultural experiences. Concepts and principles are the building blocks of these structures of organized knowledge.

The ability to solve problems is perhaps the most important product of learning inasmuch as a person, when capable of solving problems, can learn independently. The means of attacking problems and of acquiring, processing, and remembering information may be called strategies. Concepts, principles, and strategies are used in solving problems.

The importance of these products in our daily lives suggests that it would be advantageous to be able to describe and explain how they are learned during short time intervals and how they develop across long time spans, particularly during the school years. Added impetus for this work arose when not a single empirically based account of the cognitive development of children and youth across the school years could be found in the existing literature.

Psychologists employ many methods in their study of cognitive learning and development. We employed controlled experimentation in laboratories and in school settings in formulating principles of learning and instruction. Some of these experiments in school settings were described in detail in this book. We attempted to combine the best features of cross-sectional and longitudinal methods to describe cognitive development during the school years. The method was cross-sectional in that a group of students from each of four grades (1, 4, 7, and 10) was selected for inclusion in the study. These groups of students, stratified according to grade in school and sex, were drawn at random from the larger population of students of one school district. The method was longitudinal in that each of these four age groups was tested and studied annually during a 3-year period. This methodology permitted the charting of cognitive development across Grades 1–12 as well as the study of the growth patterns of the individuals of each group across 3 years.

Cohort control groups born either 1 or 2 years later than the students of each longitudinal block were included in the design to determine possible differences due to year of birth. Repeated testing groups were included to ascertain the effect on the longitudinal blocks of having received the same four batteries of tests three different times at 12-month intervals. The hypothesis was that the effects of year of birth and of repeated testing would not be significant. Some statistically significant effects, however, were found. In the second year, the majority of the significant cohort effects favored the longitudinal blocks over the cohort groups who were 1 year younger than the longitudinal blocks. In the third year, opposite effects were found; the mean scores of the cohort groups who were 2 years younger were significantly higher than the mean scores of the longitudinal blocks. The large majority of statistically significant repeated-testing effects favored the longitudinal blocks who were tested three times. The combined effects of being born 2 years later and of repeated testing resulted in some significantly higher mean scores for the younger students in their last year of testing when in Grades 3, 6, and 9 than for the older students in the first year of testing when in Grades 4, 7, and 10. Empirical curve fitting, based on the mean scores of the longitudinal blocks, was employed to take into account these statistically significant effects and also inevitable measurement errors.

The empirical curve fitting involved deriving predicted mean scores based on the obtained mean scores. It was employed only in one aspect of the study, namely in describing normative, or typical, development across Grades 1–12. The obtained scores were used in all other descriptions of cognitive development. The conclusions, based on both the obtained scores and the predicted scores, are regarded as generalizable to children and youth currently enrolled in American schools, Grade 1–Grade 12, where the dropout rate does not exceed 15–20%, where the mean school achievements are near the median of national norms, and where the population of the school reflects that of the nation in terms of racial mix and socioeconomic status. We may now consider some of the main conclusions regarding the course of cognitive development based on the actual scores made by the students and on the predicted mean scores derived by empirical curve fitting.

INVARIANT SEQUENCE

Sequential development implies orderly rather than random development with respect to the initial emergence and eventual mastery of the four successive levels of the same concept: concrete, identity, classificatory, formal. If the sequence is invariant, each prior level must be mastered before the next level is mastered. Further, once a level is mastered, it must be maintained. Each year the performance of every student on each test of each level of each concept was evaluated for mastery or nonmastery. In analyzing the resulting individual student protocols, we found that the vast majority of the students acquired the successively higher levels of the same concepts in an invariant sequence. This invariant developmental progression may be accounted for in terms of the conditions that are necessary and possibly sufficient for it to occur. What are these conditions?

Related to internal conditions of learning, the invariant developmental progression may be accounted for in terms of necessary conditions as follows: (1) mastery of the prior level, (2) functioning of at least one new mental operation in combination with the continuing operations, (3) functioning of the operations of the prior level with content of increasing quantity and complexity experienced in a greater variety of contexts, (4) intending to attain the next higher level, and (5) persisting until it is attained. In addition, being able to discriminate the defining attributes of the concept and to name the concept and the defining attributes is prerequisite and necessary for carrying out the new operations at the formal level. The necessary external conditions of learning include experience and practice with the content of the particular concept, as represented in examples of it, and with examples of related concepts. The amount and kind of experience and practice vary according both to concepts and to the four levels of attainment.

Some exceptions to the invariant sequence were observed. A small percentage of the students who mastered a particular level of one of the four concepts one year did not do so the following year. Also, a very small percentage of students mastered a higher level of one of the concepts but not the preceding lower level—for example, the formal level of *equilateral triangle* but not the classificatory level. The majority of these exceptions are accounted for by error of measurement. The possibility also remains that a few of the exceptions represent a true exception to an invariant sequence. The biological inheritance of individuals and their environmental interactions vary so widely that we should probably not expect every individual to conform to any invariant sequence in all the dimensions of cognitive development that were studied.

NORMATIVE DEVELOPMENT OF LEVELS

Sequence is one important aspect of development; rate is another. Empirical curve fitting was employed in charting the rate of development, Grades 1–12, based on each test of cognitive development that was administered. The resulting developmental curves have several uses as follows.

Differences in the rate of increase between annual measurements can be inferred by inspecting the form of the developmental curve across the years. Also, the beginning point and the ending point may be observed. An individual's performance on any item can be compared with the normative curve for the same item. Curves of two or more items, such as the four levels of concept attainment, may be compared to infer whether the items develop in a roughly parallel and concurrent pattern across 1 or more years or in a completely congruent and synchronous fashion from the beginning point to the ending point.

Children had fully attained the concrete, identity, and classificatory levels of *cutting tool* and the concrete and identity levels of *tree* and *equilateral triangle* prior to Grade 1. They made much progress toward full attainment of the concrete and identity levels of *noun* and the classificatory level of *tree* and *equilateral triangle* by Grade 3. They attained the classificatory level of *noun* at a very rapid rate from Grade 1 through Grade 3; a less rapid but continuous rate of increase was shown by the older groups of students until near full attainment was reached in Grade 12.

Children made much progress in attaining the formal level of *cutting tool* before and during the primary school years. Attainment of the formal level of the other three concepts progressed at a rapid rate during the intermediate school years and at a decelerating rate of increase thereafter. In Grade 12 the mean percentage correct remained quite low, ranging from 75 for *noun* to 91 for *cutting tool*.

Discriminating the defining attributes of concepts and acquiring the names of the concept and its defining attributes may occur with any of the first three levels of concept attainment. Both are necessary and prerequisite for carrying out the operations at the formal level by either an inductive or a meaningful reception strategy. Being able to evaluate examples and nonexamples of the concept in terms of the presence or absence of the defining attributes and acquiring a definition of the concept are other necessary operations for attaining the formal level. The emergence of these four operations from first to last was found to be in the temporal order just described. Development of the four operations was continuous from Grade 2 through Grade 12.

Growth in each of the four levels of concept attainment also may be characterized as gradual and continuous rather than discontinuous and abrupt. Development of three levels proceeds concurrently across 1 or more years, not in synchrony across several years. For example, neither the identity level nor the classificatory level is fully attained at the time initial attainment of the formal level begins. The gradual and continuous nature of development of the levels may be accounted for by individuals' increasing ability to attend to, discriminate, process, and store more information and also more complex information; increasing language competence; increasing knowledge including attainment of the prior levels that enables more effective relating and organizing of new information; and finally, more effective strategies for securing, processing, and remembering information.

NORMATIVE DEVELOPMENT RELATED TO UNDERSTANDING PRINCIPLES, UNDERSTANDING TAXONOMIC RELATIONS, AND PROBLEM SOLVING

Little understanding of principles occurred during the primary school years. Progress in understanding principles increased at about the same rate throughout the intermediate, junior, and senior high school years. In Grade 12, the mean achievement was still relatively low, ranging from 78 to 87% correct.

Understanding taxonomic relations increased substantially during the primary school years and continued to increase quite rapidly through the intermediate school years. The rate of increase was quite slow during the junior and senior high school years.

Children of primary school age were able to solve some problems, particularly if the relations among the elements and the solutions were apparent visually, as was the case for *cutting tool* and *equilateral triangle*. Students during the intermediate, junior, and senior high school years developed at a relatively slow rate in their problem-solving skills. The level of performance throughout the school years was quite low, with the percentages correct in Grade 12 ranging from 72 to 80.

Growth in understanding principles, understanding taxonomic relations, and problem solving is gradual and continuous across the school years. Development of the three items proceeds concurrently, not in synchrony, from Grade 4 through Grade 12. The gradual and continuous nature of this development may be accounted for by the students' sequentially attaining the concepts to successively higher levels; their ability to attend to, discriminate, process, and store more information and also more complex information; their increasing language competence; and their more effective strategies for securing, processing, and remembering information.

DIFFERENCES AMONG CONCEPTS IN AGE OF ATTAINMENT

The invariant sequence in mastering the successive levels of the same concept is accounted for in part by the emergence of one or more new operations necessary for attaining the successively higher levels. It is of major theoretical and practical significance to determine whether these necessary operations emerge at the same time for all concepts.

Large differences were found among the four concepts in the percentage of students of each grade who mastered the classificatory level and the formal level. Of the Grade 1 students 45% mastered the formal level of *cutting tool,* but only 35% of the Grade 9 students mastered the formal level of *noun.* Concepts that have many concrete examples in the immediate environment are mastered earlier than are concepts whose examples are represented only symbolically. The time at which individuals become capable of performing the operations and carrying out the other conditions necessary and sufficient to master the levels is related to the abstractness of the examples of the concept. Persons carry out the necessary operations years earlier on concrete, nonverbal content than on abstract, verbal content.

MASTERY OF CONCEPT LEVELS AND MASTERY OF USES

Ascertaining the prerequisites for learning principles and taxonomic relations is of continuing interest to psychologists and educators. We reported controlled experiments in which understanding of the concepts incorporated in a principle was found necessary but not sufficient for understanding the principle. In another experiment it was found that mastery of the multiple concepts of a taxonomy was associated with understanding of taxonomic relations among the concepts.

Analysis of the cross-sectional and longitudinal data showed that many students in the primary and intermediate grades mastered the concrete or identity level of the different concepts as their highest achievements but that they rarely mastered understanding principles, understanding taxonomic relations, or problem solving. The proportion of total instances of mastery of the uses to the number of students mastering either the concrete or the identity level was .08.

Substantial numbers of students at all grade levels mastered the classificatory level of one or more concepts as their highest achievement. The instances of uses mastered in relation to the numbers mastering the classificatory level increased across the grades. The proportion of total instances of mastery of the uses to the total number of students who mastered the classificatory level was .49.

Few students during the primary school years fully attained the formal level of any concept except *cutting tool,* and in Grade 6 only one had fully attained the formal level of *noun*. Unlike mastery of the other levels, mastery of the formal level was associated with far greater mastery of understanding taxonomic relations, understanding principles, and problem solving at all grade levels. The proportion of the instances of mastery of the uses to the number of students who mastered the formal level of one or more concepts was 2.03. The highest proportion possible was 3.0; each student could have mastered these uses.

INTERINDIVIDUAL AND INTRAINDIVIDUAL DIFFERENCES

By gathering information at three 12-month intervals on four longitudinal blocks of students, we were able to identify the many regularities noted in the previous pages in the sequence, rate, and pattern of developing the consecutively higher levels of the same concept and in understanding principles, understanding taxonomic relations, and solving problems. The same information was used in what we believe to be the first systematic attempt to identify and describe interindividual differences and intraindividual differences in these significant dimensions of cognitive growth. It is helpful for teachers and others to be able to identify interindividual and intraindividual differences on any dimension within any grade and also between grades.

The formal level and understanding principles in Grades 1, 3, 6, 9, and 12 were selected to illustrate the extent of interindividual differences in mastering the levels and uses of the concepts. Exceedingly large differences were found within each grade and across the grades in the number of students who did and who did not master the formal level of the various concepts and the understanding of principles. For example, 52% of the Grade 6 students had mastered the formal level of *equilateral triangle,* whereas 48% had not. The magnitude of the difference across grades was even more dramatic. For example, 3% of the Grade 3 children mastered the formal level of *equilateral triangle,* whereas 21% of the Grade 12 students did not. Of the Grade 6 students 38% mastered understanding of principles related to *equilateral triangle* but 27% of the twelfth-graders had not reached the mastery criterion.

The intraindividual variability in attaining the concept levels and uses was sharply differentiated from Grade 6 through Grade 12 and to a lesser extent in the earlier grades. In Grade 6 a separate factor was identified for each of the four concepts: *cutting tool, tree, equilateral triangle,* and *noun;* no other factors were identified. Moreover, in each grade from 6 through 12 only four or five factors were identified, and in all these grades, except Grade 7, the same four factors as in Grade 6, but with slightly different loadings, were found. A principle of highest significance may be inferred from the results of these and other factor analyses—namely, that individual cognitive development from about age 10 onward is sharply and clearly differentiated according to content fields. The differentiation starts to emerge in Grade 1. The individual's cognitive functioning is not unitary or global; it is not characterized by equally high or low performance across all concepts. Rather, individual students vary within themselves in their attainment of different concepts, their understanding of the related principles and taxonomic relations, and their development of problem solving skills. Other supporting evidence shows the intraindividual variability to be closely related to the subject fields of English, mathematics, science, and social studies.

RAPID AND SLOW COGNITIVE DEVELOPMENT

Uniformity in the rate at which individuals attain the levels and the uses of the four different concepts across the years is not expected in view of the finding regarding intraindividual variability. Rather, only a few exceptional individuals from each of the longitudinal blocks of students might be expected to have relatively high or low scores on the levels tests and uses tests of all four concepts. In actuality not a single individual of any longitudinal block had scores on the tests of all four concept batteries that fell entirely in either the top quartile or the bottom quartile during all 3 years. The four pairs of students whom we identified as representative examples of rapid and slow development had scores that fell in the top or bottom quartile of their respective longitudinal blocks on only part of the measures each year. Two scores were obtained for each student for this aspect of the study. One score was for the combined classificatory and formal level tests, the other for the combined uses tests.

The difference in the levels of performance between the rapid and slow developers on all these measures was quite large, as should be expected in terms of the selection method employed. Besides the difference in level of performance, the rate of growth of the rapid developers across the three annual measurements was more consistent than that of the slow developers; there were fewer plateaus and sharp dips in their developmental curves. The difference in the performance levels between the rapid and slow developers increased from Longitudinal Block B to C to D. The difference between the rapid and the slow developer when in Grade 12 was very large. It is possible that cognitive growth ceases or actually decreases for many slow developers from Grade 10 to Grade 12.

What may contribute to the very large interindividual differences that were identified? To answer this question, a different sample of rapidly and slowly developing Grade 6 and Grade 12 students was identified and studied intensively. The test protocols used in identifying the slow and rapid developers indicated large differences in the levels of performance on most of the tests of all four batteries, as was observed above. Intensive case studies indicated other large differences between the rapid and slow developers in three areas: self— abilities measured by the Primary Mental Abilities tests, self-esteem and perception of self, relations with others, attitude toward teachers and parents, and interests; school—attendance, courses taken, grades made, participation in school activities, and rapport with teachers; family—socioeconomic status, the parents' attitudes toward school and their expectations for the student, and the intellectual climate of the home.

In a subsequent study carried out with a group of younger elementary school students, many of the conditions associated with slow development were ameliorated through making changes in the home-and-family situation, the school curriculum and instruction of the child, and the relationships among teachers, parents, and the student. The intervention process, carried out for 7 weeks, involved more interactions between the teacher and parents and more parent participation in the child's educational and other activities in the home. The parents' attitudes toward the child, the teachers, and the school improved markedly. The children's self-esteem and motivation to learn improved and their attitudes toward learning, peers, and teacher authority and control changed from negative to positive. The children's attitudes toward reading became more positive and their reading achievement scores increased dramatically. The cooperative relationship established between the home and the school and the better relationships between the parents and the child were judged to ameliorate and possibly eliminate some of the conditions associated with a slow rate of cognitive development.

NURTURING COGNITIVE DEVELOPMENT THROUGH FORMAL EDUCATION

A large body of information concerning the development of concepts, principles, structures of knowledge, and problem solving has been summarized in
the preceding pages, and the crucial role of these products in cognitive
functioning has been indicated.

Interindividual and intraindividual differences derived from the longitudinal
study of cognitive development have also been described. This information
combined with principles derived from experimentation in school settings has
been incorporated into a design for preparing instructional materials and also
for guiding oral interactive instructional sequences. The strategy here has not
terminated with stating implications for improving instruction. Rather, the
information has been incorporated into materials and processes that have been
tested through controlled experiments in school settings.

Designing materials and oral interactive instructional sequences to nurture
cognitive development starts with outlining the taxonomy or other structure of
knowledge of which the concepts to be learned are a part. After this is done, the
defining attributes of the generic concepts and the critical attributes of the
coordinate concepts are identified. Outlining the structure of knowledge and
identifying the attributes enable the concept analyst to select rational sets of
examples and nonexamples of each concept to be used in teaching the concept, as well as other examples and nonexamples that can be used in later
testing to identify whether the student has attained the concept. As part of the
analysis, principles in which the concept is incorporated and problem-solving
exercises involving use of the concept are also identified. These principles and
problem-solving exercises are also used in the teaching sequence to assure that
transfer occurs.

Our experience in conducting concept analyses as a basis for preparing
printed lessons for use in experiments conducted in elementary schools and
high schools indicates that it is advantageous to carry out the analysis at the
formal level of concept attainment. Also, the complete analysis is expressed in
terminology appropriate for teaching senior high school students. The concept
analyzer needs at least this amount of information, even though subsequent
instruction may be carried out in the elementary school. What is eventually
included in a set of instructional materials or in oral interactive instructional
activities must be related to the level of cognitive functioning, reading
achievement, and other characteristics of the students who will receive the
instruction.

Our experience in the logical analysis of instruction and related experimentation has resulted in principles of instruction. The results of concept analyses
combined with the principles of instruction are used in preparing illustrated
printed lessons to teach single concepts or multiple concepts, including the
taxonomy of which the multiple concepts are a part. Two to four lessons

directed toward aiding elementary school children to progress from the classificatory level to the formal level have enabled a large percentage of the children to master the formal level. Through three lessons to teach multiple concepts, high school seniors were brought from functioning at a chance level to functioning at a high level with respect to mastering eight concepts at the formal level, understanding the supraordinate, coordinate, and subordinate relationships involved among the eight concepts, and placing the names of the concepts properly in the taxonomy. The effectiveness of the instructional materials for teaching single concepts and multiple concepts results from the precision with which the learning process is guided throughout the lessons.

Although printed lessons can be prepared to supplement oral interactive instruction, the lessons do not function equally well when students are instructed as age-graded, heterogeneous classroom groups. The age-graded elementary school in which one teacher instructs 20–40 children as a classroom group is no longer effective in nurturing the cognitive development of some of the students. The familiar age-graded high school in which each teacher instructs four to six classes of 20–40 students as classroom groups is also failing many students. The most powerful theories of development and learning are having very little effect, if any, on nurturing the cognitive development of children and youth in these familiar forms of schooling.

A model of instructional programming for the individual student was developed and tested in many schools of the nation as a means of improving education. Age-graded, self-contained and departmentalized schools were changed in many ways to make it possible for teachers to nurture the individual student's educational development more effectively. Three main features of this kind of instruction and schooling follow.

First, the individual student rather than the classroom group serves as the basic unit of instruction. Students may receive some of their instruction as part of class-size groups. However, this is done expressly to implement the instructional programs that have been designed for the individual students who are included in each instructional group. In Chapter 10 we reported that children learned the process concepts of science in groups of 18–24 in the science laboratory. The students were placed in these groups on the basis of their entry achievement levels and further individualization was carried out within the group through independent study, pairing of students, and small-group work. As we observed, this kind of instruction yielded a higher level of mastery of the process concepts of science than did instruction of heterogeneous classroom groups.

Second, instruction is personalized and interactive rather than impersonal and reactive on the part of the student. This is accomplished by forming smaller schools, or instructional units, of 75–200 students within the larger school of 500–4000 students. In the smaller school, or instructional unit, a group of students receives a considerable portion of their instruction and educational advising from teachers who are part of a cooperative instructional team. Each teacher serves as a personal educational adviser to a few of the students for a year or longer. The teacher–adviser also monitors the progress of these students. Parents are involved in planning the educational program of the students with the adviser, and the parents also interact freely and often with the teachers. In Chapter 8 we noted the positive effects of this kind of parent involvement.

Third, instructional decisions are made cooperatively at different levels in the educative process, and the individuals who share in making the decisions are accountable for implementing them. Individual teachers and students make decisions in the context of the larger unit of students and teachers. The cooperative instructional team with input from the students makes decisions affecting this larger group. Teachers who are team leaders share decision making regarding instruction and educational programs with school administrators and others of the school. Instructional programming for the individual student carried out in this kind of school environment includes formulating clearly stated educational objectives at the school level and instructional objectives at the student level. The objectives provide the basis for designing instructional programs for the students and also for accountability on the part of the students, teachers, and administrators.

The three preceding features of instruction and formal education designed to nurture each student's educational development are prominent aspects of Individually Guided Education. Individually Guided Education was developed and is practiced as an alternative to familiar age-graded, classroom group instruction and to the many varieties of unstructured open education.

COGNITIVE OPERATIONS, MEMORY, AND LANGUAGE

The previous account of the course of cognitive development was derived from the longitudinal study; the means of nurturing it through formal education may now be related to the earlier formulations regarding cognitive operations (Chapter 3), memory (Chapter 4), and the relationship between language and cognitive development (Chapter 5). The main purpose is to review how the invariant sequence in attainment of the successive levels is related to the successive emergence of new mental operations and how the gradual and continuous development of all the cognitive dimensions is related to the increasing competence of the individual in carrying out the operations on more content and more complex content in a greater variety of situational contexts.

Attending, discriminating, and remembering are the necessary operations for attaining the concrete level, and increasing competence in the use of these operations is necessary for attainment of the next three successive levels. Generalizing that an object or quality when experienced in a different context or modality is the same object or quality is the new operation necessary for attaining the identity level. Generalizing that two examples belong to the same class is the new operation necessary for attaining a concept at the classificatory level. One set of new operations is necessary for attaining the formal level when an inductive strategy is employed, another set when a meaningful reception strategy is followed. The inductive strategy involves formulating, remembering, and evaluating hypotheses regarding the attributes of the concept and then inferring either the concept definition or the concept itself. The reception operations include assimilating the information that is presented verbally and by other means. Having the name of the concept and the defining attributes may facilitate concept learning at the concrete, identity, and classificatory levels but it is not necessary for learning the concept at these levels. Having the names of the concept and the defining attributes is prerequisite for attaining the formal level.

Attending and discriminating are analogous to perception in the formulations of Gibson and Levin (1975). Gibson and Levin define perception as the process of extracting information from stimulation emanating from objects, places, and events. Three kinds of information are abstracted: distinctive features of all kinds of things, including people, objects, and symbols; invariants of events; and invariant relations among distinctive features or among the invariants of events. According to Gibson and Levin, as individuals gain experience and practice, they are able, with greater economy and flexibility, to discriminate the specific features of things, the invariants of events, and the invariants of relationships. As they become increasingly capable of these discriminations, they are also increasingly able to discriminate among things and events that are more similar. This kind of perceptual development is accounted for by the individual's learning to orient the sense organs selectively to the distinctive features and invariants while ignoring others, to abstract the distinctive features or invariants, and to filter the incoming sensations so as to retain the distinctive features or invariants but not the irrelevant.

Children's increasing competence in attending and discriminating identified in the longitudinal study appears to conform to the preceding principles of perceptual learning. The successive test items for measuring attainment of the concrete, identity, and classificatory levels were constructed in such manner that the student was required to attend to an increasing amount of information and also to make finer discriminations. The amount of information to attend to was controlled by increasing the number of nonexamples in the successive items. The discrimination requirement was controlled by making the nonexamples more like the examples in terms of both the variable attributes and the defining attributes shared by the examples and nonexamples. Older students at successively higher grade levels got more of the successive items correct; they had apparently learned to attend to the defining attributes and to ignore the variable ones, to discriminate the less obvious defining attributes, and to process the incoming information so as to retain the defining attributes but not the irrelevant contextual or other information.

The process of generalizing is necessary for attaining a concept at the identity, classificatory, and formal levels, and greater competence is necessary at the classificatory level than at the identity level. Attaining the identity level requires the individual to generalize that a single object or event is the same one experienced earlier despite a change in any aspect of the context or modality in which it is experienced. Generalizing at the initial classificatory level requires the preceding for at least two different examples of the same concept. Mastery of the classificatory level requires generalizing across many examples that are very different from one another in many attributes (e.g., animals). The items in the four batteries that were used in the longitudinal study to measure attainment at the classificatory level varied according to the nature of examples and nonexamples, but all the items were constructed to measure the student's ability to generalize from a given target example to one or more examples presented with three or more nonexamples. The successive items in the four batteries were constructed to require generalizing to a greater number of examples that shared values of the same variable attribute (e.g., size or color), while discriminating from nonexamples that were increasingly like the target example in both variable attributes and critical attributes. The rate of attaining the classificatory level varied among the concepts: Eighty-three percent or more of the Grade 1 children attained the classificatory levels of *cutting tool, equilateral triangle,* and *tree;* mastery of the classificatory level of *noun* was not reached until Grade 12. The form of this curve, which extended from Grade 1 through Grade 12, was natural log. There was a very rapid increase between Grades 1 and 2 and a continuing rapid but decelerating rate of increase thereafter into Grade 12. We may infer that competence in generalizing approximately paralleled attainment of the classificatory level.

The increasing competence in generalization appears to be interpretable in much the same manner as that regarding attending and discriminating. With increasing experience and practice, individuals attend selectively to the defining attributes of the class and increasingly ignore the variable attributes shared by members of the class. They carry out these operations across sensory modalities and also across situational contexts that are increasingly alike. The defining attributes of the members of the class are processed with increasing economy, and storage in secondary memory becomes more stable and permanent. Further, as we observed in the experiments dealing with the teaching of single concepts and multiple concepts, individuals learn strategies that aid them in identifying the defining attributes and ignoring the variable attributes and other irrelevant contextual information.

Remembering is essential for attaining all four levels of a concept, and greater memory requirements are experienced at each successive level. Knowledge concerning change in memory processes, structures, and capacities across the developmental years is very meager. However, Miller and Johnson-Laird (1976) have formulated a theory of perception and language in which they relate perceiving, intending, remembering, and knowing. Three particularly interesting aspects of their theory are related to the time dimension of memory, memory locations, and conceptual cores.

The time and capacity dimensions of memory are indicated by the terms *buffer memory, primary memory,* and *secondary memory.* In the buffer memory, stimulation from the perceptual field activates the receptors and the information received is transformed to neural information. Here the stimulus-induced transformed information persists in its entirety for a very short period of time, lasting only about a hundredth of a second. In primary memory, patterned information from the sensory register is stored briefly and processed further. It may be organized, rehearsed, or elaborated in primary memory and then translated and stored in secondary memory, or it may be translated into commands to the effectors. Incoming information is held in primary memory for about 1 second and may remain if undisturbed for as much as 10 seconds. Rehearsal, organization, and elaboration may extend the amount of time in working memory up to 30 seconds. Information from primary memory is translated into an appropriate neural form and stored in secondary memory. Secondary memory in adults is characterized by virtually unlimited capacity and high stability over long periods of time.

Persons gain increasing amounts of information and organize and store it in different locations in secondary memory. The memory locations are designated *semantic, episodic, action, geographic,* and *person.* Within each of these locations, sets of related concepts are organized and stored. The sets of concepts may be organized in taxonomies, other hierarchies, theories, part–whole relations, and other structures of knowledge. The important point is that the conceptual core of each set of concepts consists of the defining attributes and critical attributes that define the various individual concepts and the relationships among the concepts. According to Miller and Johnson-Laird, these conceptual cores originate initially as percepts consisting of the intrinsic and functional attributes of the objects, events, qualities, relations, and processes that are experienced. Miller and Johnson-Laird also explain how words expressing the concepts are organized into semantic fields. In their view the relationship between a percept and a concept is analogous to that between a conceptual core and a semantic field.

Following the Miller and Johnson-Laird theory, we have attempted to show how visual and other perceptual images may be initially stored in secondary memory and then retrieved in working memory to be used in testing whether an incoming image is the same as the one previously experienced. This partially accounts for memory at the concrete and identity levels of concept attainment. The memory trace of a concept attained at either the classificatory level or the formal level probably includes not only the intrinsic and functional properties but also the word that stands for the concept and contextual information. It may also include an image, particularly if the examples of the concept are concrete. Paivio (1974) has formulated a dual coding theory of information processing and memory that incorporates this view.

The effectiveness with which information is acquired and processed is dependent upon strategies of learning; the effectiveness with which it is stored and retrieved from memory is dependent upon strategies of remembering. With increased experience and practice persons develop more sophisticated strategies of learning and remembering. These more sophisticated strategies, as noted previously, contribute to the gradual and continuous increase in the ability to acquire concepts at the successively higher levels, to understand principles and taxonomic relations, and to solve problems.

The development of language itself is one of the most important areas of human cognitive development. The relationship between the acquisition of words, word meanings, and concepts is of particular interest in the study of conceptual development and the development of understanding of principles, taxonomic relations, and problem solving. We may examine the relationship between word meanings and the four levels of concept attainment, the relationship between conceptual cores and semantic fields, and the facilitative effects of language on concept attainment.

Let us assume that an individual acquires the name of a concept at about the same time as attaining the concrete level and then attains the three successively higher levels of the same concept. The meaning of the word parallels the attainment of the four levels; the individual's meaning of the word that expresses the concept is the same as the individual's mental construct at each level. At the formal level of attainment the individual has the name not only of the concept but also of the defining attributes. The word meaning at the formal level is the societally accepted meaning of the word. Miller and Johnson-Laird refer to this word meaning as a lexical concept. In their theory, having the meaning of a word enables the individual to ascertain what is and what is not an entity that can or cannot be labeled by the word. Having the word meaning also enables the individual to indicate the function or purpose of the entity that the word labels. Finally, having the meaning can help the individual retrieve from secondary memory everything that the individual knows about the particular entity.

A group of related lexical concepts forms a semantic field. Just as having a lexical concept requires knowing the defining attributes of the particular concept, so also a semantic field requires having formed a conceptual core. The conceptual core includes the defining attributes of the generic concept and the critical attributes of the coordinate concepts comprising the taxonomy or other structure of knowledge. In a taxonomy, the attributes of the generic class are common to all members of the taxonomy, but there are critical attributes that are unique to the members of each coordinate class. Knowledge of the critical attributes makes it possible to discriminate between members of the different coordinate subclasses, each of which is represented by a contrastive word.

This analysis of the relationship between concepts and the meaning of the words that express the concepts and between conceptual cores and semantic fields implies a need for the continuing study of these critical areas of human cognitive functioning. The descriptions of closely related dimensions of cognitive development in this book included attaining the successive levels of the concepts, acquiring the names of the concepts and of their defining attributes, acquiring concept definitions, and understanding taxonomic relations. They are regarded as a promising beginning point for further study of the relationship between cognitive development and semantic development.

The facilitative effects of language in concept attainment merit concluding remarks. Language is widely used in directing the attention of the young child to an object, person, process, quality, or relation. This directing of attention facilitates attainment of the concept at the concrete and identity levels. Language is also used to point to an attribute of a generic class or to the critical attribute of a coordinate class. This facilitates attending and discriminating at both the classificatory and formal levels. The facilitative effects of being taught the names of the concepts and the attributes have been interpreted as due to mediating between the environmental input and the individual's responding, enhancing the distinctiveness of the concept examples, and enhancing the individual's sensitivity to the defining attributes of the concept. Although theorists do not agree about the internal mechanisms that might explain the facilitative effects, it is clear that instruction that gives the name of the concept is helpful in increasing intraclass similarity and decreasing interclass similarity. This in turn enables individuals to classify members of coordinate concepts that have the same generic attributes and are much alike in variable attributes.

Increasing competence in language is also associated with more sophisticated strategies for acquiring and remembering information and for using the strategies under appropriate circumstances. Focusing strategies generally have been found to be more effective than scanning strategies in acquiring concepts. Rehearsal, elaborative, and organizing strategies are useful in processing and storing information. The increasing competence of the individual in learning and using the strategies contributes to the gradual and continuous development of concepts to successively higher levels, to more mature understanding of principles and taxonomies, and to more effective problem solving during the school years.

Appendix

TABLE A.1 Longitudinal Block and Grade at Which the Test for Each Level and Each Use of Each Concept Was and Was Not Administered

Longitudinal block and grade	Battery	Test[a]						
		CO	ID	CL	FO	PR	TAX	PS
A1	CT	A	A	A	A	A	A	A
	TR	A	A	A	A	*	A	A
	ET	A	A	A	A	*	A	*
	NN	A	A	A	*	*	*	*
A2	CT	A	A	A	A	A	A	A
	TR	A	A	A	A	A	A	A
	ET	A	A	A	A	*	A	*
	NN	A	A	A	A	*	*	*
A3	CT	A	A	A	A	A	A	A
	TR	A	A	A	A	A	A	A
	ET	A	A	A	A	A	A	A
	NN	A	A	A	A	A	A	A
B4	CT	A	A	A	A	A	A	A
	TR	A	A	A	A	A	A	A
	ET	A	A	A	A	A	A	A
	NN	A	A	A	A	A	A	A
B5	CT	A	A	A	A	A	A	A
	TR	A	A	A	A	A	A	A
	ET	A	A	A	A	A	A	A
	NN	A	A	A	A	A	A	A
B6	CT	A	A	A	A	A	A	A
	TR	A	A	A	A	A	A	A
	ET	A	A	A	A	A	A	A
	NN	A	A	A	A	A	A	A
C7	CT	**	**	A	A	A	A	A
	TR	**	**	A	A	A	A	A
	ET	**	**	A	A	A	A	A
	NN	A	A	A	A	A	A	A
C8	CT	**	**	A	A	A	A	A
	TR	**	**	A	A	A	A	A
	ET	**	**	A	A	A	A	A
	NN	**	**	A	A	A	A	A
C9	CT	**	**	A	A	A	A	A
	TR	**	**	A	A	A	A	A
	ET	**	**	A	A	A	A	A
	NN	**	**	A	A	A	A	A
D10	CT	**	**	A	A	A	A	A
	TR	**	**	A	A	A	A	A
	ET	**	**	A	A	A	A	A
	NN	**	**	A	A	A	A	A
D11	CT	**	**	A	A	A	A	A
	TR	**	**	A	A	A	A	A
	ET	**	**	A	A	A	A	A
	NN	**	**	A	A	A	A	A
D12	CT	**	**	A	A	A	A	A
	TR	**	**	A	A	A	A	A
	ET	**	**	A	A	A	A	A
	NN	**	**	A	A	A	A	A

[a] Single asterisk indicates test not administered because previous research showed that children at this grade responded at a chance level; double asterisk indicates test not administered because previous research showed 100% attainment at this grade.

TABLE A.2. Mean Score and Standard Deviation for Each Level and Each Use of Each Concept for Each Longitudinal Block, Grades 1-12

Longitudinal block and grade	Battery	Test[a]													
		CO		ID		CL		FO		PR		TAX		PS	
		Mean	SD	Mean	SD	Mean	SD	Mean	SD	Mean	SD	Mean	SD	Mean	SD
A1	CT	7.92	.27	7.89	.32	7.57	.80	13.71	3.02	5.32	1.52	5.87	1.57	3.13	1.06
	TR	7.79	.41	7.66	.54	6.34	2.01	14.94	4.20	*		1.79	1.06	1.65	1.24
	ET	7.86	.44	7.81	.51	2.50	.84	6.47	2.67	*		2.52	1.08	*	
	NN	6.94	1.08	4.86	1.87	.45	.95	*		*		*		*	
A2	CT	7.90	.39	7.89	.37	7.65	.85	13.13	2.51	3.81	1.64	5.65	1.65	2.44	1.00
	TR	7.47	.67	7.55	.74	7.36	1.16	19.84	3.76	1.11	1.07	2.65	1.10	2.92	1.91
	ET	7.92	.27	7.97	.25	2.84	.58	8.02	2.79	*		2.68	1.21	*	
	NN	7.84	.45	7.39	1.15	4.24	2.00	1.68	.84	*		*		*	
A3	CT	8.00	.00	8.00	.00	7.84	.58	14.47	2.13	5.27	1.63	5.71	2.02	3.31	.90
	TR	7.97	.25	7.87	.49	7.61	1.31	18.53	5.74	5.61	3.96	3.73	1.83	4.32	1.84
	ET	8.00	.00	8.00	.00	2.95	.28	9.94	2.81	4.85	2.07	3.63	1.94	3.27	1.45
	NN	7.77	.69	7.63	.91	5.79	2.01	8.06	2.92	2.73	1.81	2.92	1.53	1.19	.95
B4	CT	7.94	.29	7.92	.27	7.65	.98	14.16	2.73	5.34	2.33	6.79	1.30	3.61	1.22
	TR	7.86	.39	7.79	.41	7.35	1.37	22.05	5.09	8.26	3.41	4.30	1.33	3.01	1.61
	ET	7.82	.55	7.83	.41	2.70	.74	10.42	2.85	4.53	2.17	4.38	1.62	2.10	1.24
	NN	7.97	.16	7.88	.40	4.62	1.86	7.83	2.89	2.69	1.64	2.60	1.36	1.04	1.01
B5	CT	7.97	.16	7.97	.16	7.83	.41	15.01	2.08	5.55	2.50	6.61	1.23	3.81	1.12
	TR	7.78	.48	7.70	.61	7.60	.95	25.68	4.67	9.96	3.39	4.88	1.20	3.70	1.68
	ET	8.00	.00	8.00	.00	2.79	.52	12.05	2.90	5.68	2.35	4.60	1.51	2.23	1.30
	NN	7.99	.11	7.94	.25	6.05	1.72	11.25	3.20	3.73	1.77	3.92	1.00	1.58	1.20
B6	CT	8.00	.00	8.00	.00	7.99	.11	16.49	2.74	7.51	2.32	7.13	1.12	3.78	1.03
	TR	8.00	.00	8.00	.00	7.82	.81	23.55	7.29	9.29	5.08	5.69	1.76	5.33	2.21
	ET	8.00	.00	8.00	.00	2.96	.25	14.26	2.40	8.51	1.82	5.96	1.87	4.18	1.45
	NN	8.00	.00	8.00	.00	6.26	1.73	12.60	3.35	4.34	1.98	4.30	1.27	2.08	1.18

(continued)

TABLE A.2. (Continued)

Longitudinal block and grade	Battery	Test[a] CO Mean	CO SD	ID Mean	ID SD	CL Mean	CL SD	FO Mean	FO SD	PR Mean	PR SD	TAX Mean	TAX SD	PS Mean	PS SD
C7	CT	**		**		7.58	1.15	14.14	3.38	5.80	2.56	6.44	1.63	3.13	1.64
	TR	**		**		7.25	1.70	26.76	5.30	11.69	3.80	4.96	1.53	4.16	1.95
	ET	**		**		2.80	.56	12.95	3.18	7.23	2.53	4.48	1.68	3.10	1.38
	NN	7.99	.11	7.98	.15	6.55	1.70	12.43	4.65	4.91	2.10	4.09	1.55	2.28	1.23
C8	CT	**		**		7.23	.78	14.92	3.17	6.50	2.39	6.65	1.53	3.64	1.41
	TR	**		**		7.81	.73	27.06	4.89	12.29	3.67	5.71	1.39	4.70	2.20
	ET	**		**		2.88	.37	14.14	2.63	7.91	2.04	5.23	1.67	3.24	1.23
	NN	**		**		6.98	1.34	14.88	5.19	5.90	2.30	5.30	1.95	2.48	1.15
C9	CT	**		**		8.00	.00	16.55	2.44	7.90	2.16	7.35	1.15	3.75	.83
	TR	**		**		8.00	.00	30.39	4.72	14.94	3.88	7.15	1.34	7.95	1.66
	ET	**		**		3.00	.00	15.53	2.27	8.55	1.97	6.74	1.70	4.46	1.55
	NN	**		**		7.61	1.02	16.31	5.30	5.83	2.52	5.64	1.97	3.35	1.17
D10	CT	**		**		7.71	.59	16.36	1.89	7.73	2.59	7.32	.97	3.95	1.33
	TR	**		**		7.74	.75	30.71	2.56	15.90	3.66	6.11	1.48	5.73	2.20
	ET	**		**		2.88	.50	15.11	2.57	9.29	2.16	6.14	1.95	4.52	1.60
	NN	**		**		7.14	1.37	16.48	4.76	6.81	1.85	5.25	1.68	2.55	1.34
D11	CT	**		**		7.74	.71	16.33	2.06	7.93	2.45	7.38	.97	3.80	1.36
	TR	**		**		7.70	1.08	30.90	3.14	15.90	3.91	6.10	1.61	6.37	2.21
	ET	**		**		2.89	.51	15.29	2.88	9.14	2.56	6.60	1.72	4.42	1.61
	NN	**		**		7.07	1.53	18.27	4.36	7.04	1.95	6.10	1.54	3.00	1.05
D12	CT	**		**		7.75	.76	17.05	1.97	8.14	1.98	7.59	.85	3.96	1.21
	TR	**		**		8.00	.00	31.73	4.11	15.99	3.71	6.85	1.58	8.53	1.82
	ET	**		**		2.93	.30	15.84	2.71	9.38	2.45	6.33	2.11	4.79	1.36
	NN	**		**		7.84	.58	19.26	5.16	7.74	2.25	6.11	1.61	3.88	1.13

[a] Single asterisk indicates test not administered because previous research showed that children at this grade responded at a chance level; double asterisk indicates test not administered because previous research showed 100% attainment at this grade.

TABLE A.3. Percentage Correct for Each Level and Each Use of Each Concept for Each Longitudinal Block, Grades 1–12

Longitudinal block and grade	Battery	Test[a]						
		CO	ID	CL	FO	PR	TAX	PS
A1	CT	99	99	95	76	53	73	63
	TR	97	96	79	43	*	22	17
	ET	98	98	83	36	*	32	*
	NN	87	61	6	*	*	*	*
A2	CT	99	99	96	73	38	71	49
	TR	93	94	92	57	6	33	29
	ET	99	100	95	45	*	34	*
	NN	98	92	53	7	*	*	*
A3	CT	100	100	98	80	53	71	66
	TR	100	98	95	53	28	47	43
	ET	100	100	98	55	44	45	55
	NN	97	95	72	32	27	37	24
B4	CT	99	99	96	79	53	85	72
	TR	98	97	92	63	41	54	30
	ET	98	98	90	58	41	55	35
	NN	100	99	58	31	27	33	21
B5	CT	100	100	98	83	56	83	76
	TR	97	96	95	73	50	61	37
	ET	100	100	93	67	52	58	37
	NN	100	99	76	45	37	49	32
B6	CT	100	100	100	92	75	89	76
	TR	100	100	98	67	46	71	53
	ET	100	100	99	79	77	75	70
	NN	100	100	78	50	43	54	42
C7	CT	**	**	95	79	58	81	63
	TR	**	**	91	76	58	62	42
	ET	**	**	93	72	66	56	52
	NN	100	100	82	50	49	51	46
C8	CT	**	**	90	83	65	83	73
	TR	**	**	98	77	61	71	47
	ET	**	**	96	79	72	65	54
	NN	**	**	87	60	59	66	50
C9	CT	**	**	100	92	79	92	75
	TR	**	**	100	87	75	89	80
	ET	**	**	100	86	78	84	74
	NN	**	**	95	65	58	71	67
D10	CT	**	**	96	91	77	92	79
	TR	**	**	97	88	80	76	57
	ET	**	**	96	84	84	77	75
	NN	**	**	89	66	68	66	51

(continued)

TABLE A.3   (*Continued*)

Longitudinal block and grade	Battery	Test[a]						
		CO	ID	CL	FO	PR	TAX	PS
D11	CT	**	**	97	91	79	92	76
	TR	**	**	96	88	80	76	64
	ET	**	**	96	85	83	83	74
	NN	**	**	88	73	70	76	60
D12	CT	**	**	97	95	81	95	79
	TR	**	**	100	91	80	86	85
	ET	**	**	98	88	85	79	80
	NN	**	**	98	77	77	76	78

[a] Single asterisk indicates test not administered because previous research showed that children at this grade responded at a chance level; double asterisk indicates test not administered because previous research showed 100% attainment at this grade.

TABLE A.4.   Percentage of Students Who Mastered Each Level and Each Use of Each Concept for Each Longitudinal Block, Grades 1–12

Longitudinal block and grade	Battery	Test[a]						
		CO	ID	CL	FO	PR	TAX	PS
A1	CT	100	100	92	45	2	47	44
	TR	100	97	61	0	*	0	0
	ET	97	95	68	0	*	0	*
	NN	74	23	0	*	*	*	*
A2	CT	97	98	92	34	2	39	11
	TR	94	92	82	2	0	0	0
	ET	100	98	90	0	*	0	*
	NN	97	89	11	0	*	*	*
A3	CT	100	100	98	55	3	52	45
	TR	98	97	92	8	2	11	6
	ET	100	100	97	3	0	10	39
	NN	94	94	47	0	2	0	3
B4	CT	99	100	92	48	16	71	64
	TR	99	100	86	14	3	10	0
	ET	97	99	82	5	1	17	14
	NN	100	97	18	0	0	0	1
B5	CT	100	100	99	70	18	65	62
	TR	97	92	90	39	5	19	1
	ET	100	100	83	18	5	16	15
	NN	100	100	53	1	1	3	8

(*continued*)

TABLE A.4 (*Continued*)

Longitudinal block and grade	Battery	Test[a]						
		CO	ID	CL	FO	PR	TAX	PS
B6	CT	100	100	100	83	49	83	61
	TR	100	100	96	38	6	49	17
	ET	100	100	97	52	38	49	62
	NN	100	100	57	1	1	8	13
C7	CT	**	**	93	61	29	69	51
	TR	**	**	85	53	13	24	5
	ET	**	**	85	39	24	14	38
	NN	100	100	64	4	8	8	16
C8	CT	**	**	98	68	28	73	63
	TR	**	**	99	58	16	40	10
	ET	**	**	89	56	28	24	46
	NN	**	**	74	23	20	40	19
C9	CT	**	**	100	89	50	88	69
	TR	**	**	100	78	31	85	64
	ET	**	**	100	75	51	69	68
	NN	**	**	89	35	25	44	43
D10	CT	**	**	96	85	62	88	73
	TR	**	**	97	89	58	59	23
	ET	**	**	93	70	62	52	71
	NN	**	**	81	32	21	27	25
D11	CT	**	**	97	86	62	90	71
	TR	**	**	95	85	56	52	36
	ET	**	**	95	74	70	63	74
	NN	**	**	77	51	32	52	30
D12	CT	**	**	95	95	60	92	71
	TR	**	**	100	86	47	74	74
	ET	**	**	95	79	73	63	82
	NN	**	**	97	63	49	51	63

[a] Single asterisk indicates test not administered because previous research showed that children at this grade responded at a chance level; double asterisk indicates test not administered because previous research showed 100% attainment at this grade.

TABLE A.5.   Predicted Mean Percentage Score for Each Level and Each Use of Each Concept for Each Longitudinal Block, Grades 1–12

Longitudinal block and grade	Battery	Test[a]						
		CO	ID	CL	FO	PR	TAX	PS
A1	CT	99	99	96	72	45	72	56
	TR	96	95	84	39	*	19	21
	ET	99	98	88	36	*	24	*
	NN	90	67	21	*	*	*	*
A2	CT	99	99	96	77	48	74	62
	TR	97	96	88	53	9	37	26
	ET	99	99	91	45	*	40	*
	NN	94	83	43	10	*	*	*
A3	CT	99	99	96	80	52	76	66
	TR	97	97	91	61	25	48	31
	ET	99	99	92	53	40	49	41
	NN	97	94	55	25	25	31	21
B4	CT	100	99	96	82	55	79	68
	TR	98	97	93	66	37	55	36
	ET	99	99	93	61	50	56	46
	NN	98	100	65	35	31	40	27
B5	CT	100	100	96	84	59	81	70
	TR	99	98	94	71	46	61	41
	ET	100	100	94	67	57	61	50
	NN	100	100	72	43	37	47	33
B6	CT	100	100	96	85	62	83	72
	TR	99	99	95	74	54	66	46
	ET	100	100	95	72	64	65	54
	NN	100	100	77	50	43	53	38
C7	CT	**	**	96	87	66	85	73
	TR	**	**	96	78	60	70	51
	ET	**	**	96	77	69	68	58
	NN	100	100	82	55	49	58	44
C8	CT	**	**	96	88	69	87	74
	TR	**	**	97	80	66	73	56
	ET	**	**	96	81	73	71	63
	NN	**	**	87	60	55	63	50
C9	CT	**	**	97	88	73	90	75
	TR	**	**	98	83	71	76	61
	ET	**	**	97	84	78	74	67
	NN	**	**	90	64	60	66	55
D10	CT	**	**	97	89	76	92	76
	TR	**	**	98	85	75	79	66
	ET	**	**	97	86	81	76	71
	NN	**	**	94	68	66	70	61

(continued)

TABLE A.5   (Continued)

Longitudinal block and grade	Battery	Test[a]						
		CO	ID	CL	FO	PR	TAX	PS
D11	CT	**	**	97	90	80	94	77
	TR	**	**	99	87	79	81	71
	ET	**	**	98	87	84	79	76
	NN	**	**	97	72	72	73	67
D12	CT	**	**	97	91	83	96	78
	TR	**	**	99	88	83	84	76
	ET	**	**	98	87	87	80	80
	NN	**	**	99	75	78	76	72

[a] Single asterisk indicates test not administered because previous research showed that children at this grade responded at a chance level; double asterisk indicates test not administered because previous research showed 100% attainment at this grade.

TABLE A.6. Relationship between the Highest Level of Each Concept Attained and Mastery of Each Concept Use for Each Longitudinal Block, Grades 1–12[a]

Block/grade	Concrete												Identity											
	CT			TR			ET			NN			CT			TR			ET			NN		
	PR	TAX	PS	PR	TAX	PS	PR	TAX	PS	PR	TAX	PS	PR	TAX	PS	PR	TAX	PS	PR	TAX	PS	PR	TAX	PS
A1																								
N att. level	0			2			1			32			2			22			17			14		
Instances of uses mastery		0	0		0	0		0	*		*	*		1	1		0	0		0	*		*	*
A2																								
N att. level	0			1			1			5			4			9			5			48		
Instances of uses mastery		0	0		0	0		0	*		*	*		1	0		0	0		0	*		*	*
A3																								
N att. level	0			1			0			2			0			4			2			29		
Instances of uses mastery		0	0		0	0		0	0		0	0		1	0		0	0		0	0		0	0
B4																								
N att. level	0			0			1			2			5			10			12			61		
Instances of uses mastery		0	0		0	0		0	0		0	0		0	0		0	0		0	0		0	0
B5																								
N att. level	0			1			0			0			1			6			12			36		
Instances of uses mastery		0	0		0	0		0	0		0	0		0	0		0	0		2	2		0	0
B6																								
N att. level	0			0			0			0			0			3			2			33		
Instances of uses mastery		0	0		0	0		0	0		0	0		0	0		0	0		1	2		2	2

C7									
N att. level	*	*	*	*	0	5**	11**	9**	29
Instances of uses	*	*	*	0	0	2	0	1	2
mastery	*	*	*	0	0	1	2	2	5
C8									
N att. level	*	*	*	*	0	2**	1**	4**	20**
Instances of uses	*	*	*	0	1	0	1	0	3
mastery	*	*	*	0	1	0	0	0	1
C9									
N att. level	*	*	*	*	0	0	0	0	9**
Instances of uses	*	*	*	0	0	0	0	0	2
mastery	*	*	*	0	0	0	0	1	1
D10									
N att. level	*	*	*	*	2**	2**	1**	3**	14**
Instances of uses	*	*	*	1	1	0	0	0	2
mastery	*	*	*	1	2	0	0	0	1
D11									
N att. level	*	*	*	*	0	0	2**	2**	14**
Instances of uses	*	*	*	0	0	1	0	1	2
mastery	*	*	*	0	1	1	1	0	3
D12									
N att. level	*	*	*	*	0	0	0	0	1**
Instances of uses	*	*	*	0	0	0	0	0	0
mastery	*	*	*	0	0	0	0	1	0

(continued)

TABLE A.6 (Continued)

Block/grade	Classificatory												Formal											
	CT			TR			ET			NN			CT			TR			ET			NN		
	PR	TAX	PS	PR	TAX	PS	PR	TAX	PS	PR	TAX	PS	PR	TAX	PS	PR	TAX	PS	PR	TAX	PS	PR	TAX	PS
A1																								
N att. level		32			38			42			0			28			0			0			*	
Instances of uses mastery	2	15	10	*	0	0	*	0	*	*	*	*	0	13	16	*	0	0	*	0	*	*	*	*
A2																								
N att. level		37			50			56			7			21			1			0			0	
Instances of uses mastery	0	13	5	0	0	0	*	0	*	*	*	*	1	10	2	0	0	0	*	0	*	*	*	*
A3																								
N att. level		28			52			58			29			34			5			2			0	
Instances of uses mastery	0	7	11	1	6	4	0	5	23	1	0	2	2	25	17	0	1	0	0	1	1	0	0	0
B4																								
N att. level		35			56			60			14			37			11			4			0	
Instances of uses mastery	2	24	18	0	7	0	1	9	9	0	0	1	10	29	30	2	1	0	0	2	2	0	0	0
B5																								
N att. level		22			40			51			40			54			30			14			1	
Instances of uses mastery	0	13	6	1	5	0	1	6	7	1	1	6	14	37	42	3	9	1	3	4	2	0	0	0
B6																								
N att. level		13			45			35			43			64			29			40			1	
Instances of uses mastery	1	6	4	0	14	4	12	8	15	0	4	8	37	58	43	5	24	9	17	29	31	1	0	0

C7								
N att. level	26	27	40	48	49	42	31	3
Instances of uses	2	0	6	4	21	17	13	2
mastery	14	2	8	6	39	4	20	2
C8								
N att. level	24	33	31	42	54	46	45	18
Instances of uses	1	6	6	15	44	26	12	14
mastery	13	2	12	6	44	6	25	8
C9								
N att. level	9	18	20	43	71	62	60	28
Instances of uses	6	10	6	10	64	58	49	23
mastery	3	8	7	12	52	43	47	21
D10								
N att. level	9	7	19	36	62	65	51	23
Instances of uses	6	2	4	6	57	41	34	12
mastery	1	0	8	4	50	17	44	13
D11								
N att. level	10	9	17	22	63	62	54	37
Instances of uses	6	1	4	9	60	37	41	26
mastery	3	0	8	4	49	25	45	18
D12								
N att. level	4	10	15	26	69	63	58	46
Instances of uses	2	2	4	6	65	52	42	31
mastery	1	3	9	8	51	51	51	38

ᵃ Single asterisk indicates subtest not administered because previous research showed that children at this grade responded at a chance level; double asterisk indicates that although concrete and identity subtests were not administered, identity was assumed to be the highest level if classificatory and formal were not passed. Previous research showed 100% attainment at concrete and identity levels at this grade.

TABLE A.7. Correlation Matrix of Grade 6 Scores

Battery and test	CTCL	CTFO	CTPR	CTTAX	CTPS	TRCL	TRFO	TRPR	TRTAX	TRPS	ETCL	ETFO	ETPR	ETTAX	ETPS	NNCL	NNFO	NNPR	NNTAX
CTFO	-.02																		
CTPR	.13	.69																	
CTTAX	.12	.28	.43																
CTPS	-.14	.21	.35	.16															
TRCL	-.03	.01	.18	.13	.13														
TRFO	-.09	.36	.41	.23	.31	.30													
TRPR	-.11	.23	.25	.17	.31	.23	.61												
TRTAX	-.02	.30	.40	.21	.31	.42	.60	.42											
TRPS	.12	.28	.29	.13	.31	.09	.47	.50	.36										
ETCL	-.02	.05	.21	.02	-.13	-.04	.01	.04	.03	-.07									
ETFO	-.04	.10	.12	.16	.10	.06	.09	.30	.04	.17	.28								
ETPR	-.10	.01	.04	-.05	.12	.04	-.02	.18	-.03	.13	.16	.33							
ETTAX	-.13	.16	.10	.07	.15	.10	.07	.34	.23	.04	-.01	.50	.26						
ETPS	.17	-.11	.01	-.09	.06	.15	-.09	.11	.07	.16	-.05	.31	.28	.50					
NNCL	-.05	.13	.13	.22	.02	-.04	.29	.34	.26	.14	-.10	-.07	.08	.10	-.11				
NNFO	.06	.25	.36	.30	.31	-.01	.39	.39	.19	.31	.03	.31	.23	.23	-.03	.37			
NNPR	.02	.31	.48	.35	.23	.01	.41	.23	.20	.34	.08	.32	.07	.17	.02	.23	.55		
NNTAX	-.16	.04	.10	.10	.20	-.06	.16	.23	.21	.15	.04	.19	.18	.11	.05	.20	.15	.06	
NNPS	.01	.25	.28	.18	.23	-.10	.35	.17	.23	.30	.01	.19	.14	.12	-.05	.42	.43	.50	.12

TABLE A.8 Hoyt Reliability Coefficients and Standard Errors of Measurement for Grades 1, 4, 7, and 10 Combined in 1974

Test	Cutting tool (N=349)		Tree (N=354)		Equilateral triangle (N=351)		Noun (N=362)	
	Hoyt	SE_M	Hoyt	SE_M	Hoyt	SE_M	Hoyt	SE_M
Concrete	.51	.19	.16	.29	.46	.28	.63	.45
Identity	.53	.22	.15	.36	.26	.28	.85	.59
Classificatory	.63	.52	.84	.63	.71	.30	.91	.85
Formal	.77	1.39	.91	2.10	.83	1.64	.92	1.87
Combined levels	.78	1.62	.92	2.39	.83	1.88	.95	2.38
Principle	.73	1.26	.93	1.62	.91	1.12	.83	1.15
Taxonomic relations	.58	.91	.72	1.01	.69	1.10	.78	.99
Problem solving	.58	.80	.67	1.24	.79	.83	.67	.75
Combined uses	.82	1.87	.94	2.38	.93	1.91	.91	1.78

References

American Association for the Advancement of Science Commission on Science Education. *Science . . . A Process Approach.* Washington, D.C.: American Association for the Advancement of Science/Xerox, 1967.

Amster, H. Effect of instructional set and variety of instances on children's learning. *Journal of Educational Psychology,* 1966, *57,* 74–85.

Anderson, L. W. An empirical investigation of individual differences in time to learn. *Journal of Educational Psychology,* 1976, *68,* 226–233.

Anderson, R. C., & McGaw, B. On the representation of meaning of general terms. *Journal of Experimental Psychology,* 1973, *101,* 301–306.

Ausubel, D. P. *The psychology of meaningful verbal learning.* New York: Grune & Stratton, 1963.

Ausubel, D. P. Meaningful reception learning and the acquisition of concepts. In H. J. Klausmeier & C. W. Harris (Eds.), *Analyses of concept learning.* New York: Academic Press, 1966.

Ausubel, D. P. *Educational psychology: A cognitive view.* New York: Holt, Rinehart and Winston, 1968.

Ausubel, D. P. The facilitation of meaningful verbal learning in the classroom. *Educational Psychologist,* 1977, *12,* 162–178.

Ausubel, D. P., & Robinson, F. G. *School learning.* New York: Holt, Rinehart and Winston, 1969.

Baltes, P. B. Longitudinal and cross-sectional sequences in the study of age and generation effects. *Human Development,* 1968, *11,* 145–171.

Baltes, P. B., Cornelius, S. W., & Nesselroade, J. R. Cohort effects in behavioral development: Theoretical and methodological perspectives. In W. A. Collins (Ed.), *Minnesota Symposia on Child Psychology* (Vol. 11). Hillsdale, New Jersey: Lawrence Erlbaum Associates, in press.

Barnes, K. E. Preschool play norms: A replication. *Developmental Psychology,* 1971, *5,* 99–103.

Bayley, N. Some increasing parent-child similarities during the growth of children. *Journal of Educational Psychology,* 1954, *45,* 1–21.

Bayley, N. Behavioral correlates of mental growth: Birth to thirty-six years. *American Psychologist,* 1968, *23,* 1–17.

Bayley, N. Development of mental abilities. In P. H. Mussen (Ed.), *Carmichael's manual of child psychology* (Vol. 1, 3rd ed.). New York: Wiley, 1970. Pp. 1163–1209.

Bechtol, W. M., & Conte, A. E. *Individually guided social studies*. Reading, Mass.: Addison-Wesley, 1976.

Beilin, H. *Studies in the cognitive basis of language development*. New York: Academic Press, 1975.

Bernard, M. E. *Task analysis in instructional program development* (Theo. Paper No. 52). Madison: Wisconsin Research and Development Center for Cognitive Learning, 1975. (a)

Bernard, M. E. *The effect of advance organizers and within-text questions on the learning of a taxonomy of concepts* (Tech. Rep. No. 357). Madison: Wisconsin Research and Development Center for Cognitive Learning, 1975. (b)

Bijou, S. W., & Baer, D. M. Some methodological contributions from a functional analysis of child development. *Advances in Child Development and Behavior*, 1963, *1*, 197–231.

Bird, J. E., & Bennett, A. F. A developmental study of recognition of pictures and nouns. *Journal of Experimental Child Psychology*, 1974, *18*, 117–126.

Block, J. H. (Ed.). *Schools, society, and mastery learning*. New York: Holt, Rinehart and Winston, 1974.

Block, J. H., & Anderson, L. W. *Mastery learning in classroom instruction*. New York: Macmillan, 1975.

Block, J. H., & Burns, R. B. Mastery learning. In L. S. Shulman (Ed.), *Review of research in education 4*. Itasca, Ill.: F. E. Peacock, 1977.

Bloom, B. S. Learning for mastery. *UCLA Evaluation Comment*, 1968, *1*(2), 1–11.

Bloom, B. S. *Human characteristics and school learning*. New York: McGraw-Hill, 1976.

Bourne, L. E., Jr. Knowing and using concepts. *Psychological Review*, 1970, *77*(6), 546–556.

Bourne, L. E., Jr. Effects of rule, memory, and truth-table information on attribute identification. *Journal of Experimental Psychology*, 1973, *101*, 283–288.

Bourne, L. E., Jr., Ekstrand, B. R., & Dominowski, R. L. *The psychology of thinking*. Englewood Cliffs, N.J.: Prentice-Hall, 1971.

Bower, G., & Trabasso, T. Concept identification. In R. C. Atkinson (Ed.), *Studies in mathematical psychology*, Stanford, Calif.: Stanford University Press, 1964. Pp. 32–94.

Brainerd, C. J. *Piaget's theory of intelligence*. Englewood Cliffs, N.J.: Prentice-Hall, 1978.

Brainerd, C. J. The stage question in cognitive-developmental theory. *Behavioral and Brain Sciences*, 1978, *1*, No. 1, in press.

Brooks, L. R. Spatial and verbal components of the act of recall. *Canadian Journal of Psychology*, 1968, *22*, 349–368.

Brown, A. L. The development of memory: Knowing, knowing about knowing, and knowing how to know. In H. W. Reese (Ed.), *Advances in child development and behavior* (Vol. 10). New York: Academic Press, 1975.

Brown, R. *A first language: The early stages*. Cambridge, Mass.: Harvard University Press, 1973.

Bruner, J. S. *The process of education*. Cambridge: Harvard University Press, 1960.

Bruner, J. S. The course of cognitive growth. *American Psychologist*, 1964, *19*, 1–15.

Bruner, J. S. *Beyond the information given*. New York: W. W. Norton, 1973.

Bruner, J. S., Goodnow, J. J., & Austin, G. A. *A study of thinking*. New York: Wiley, 1956.

Bruner, J. S., Olver, R. R., & Greenfield, P. M. *Studies in cognitive growth*. New York: Wiley, 1966.

Buss, A., & Poley, W. *Individual differences: Traits and factors*. New York: Gardner Press, 1976.

Byrne, B. Item concreteness vs. spatial organization as predictors of visual imagery. *Memory & Cognition*, 1974, *2*, 53–59.

Cantor, J. H. Transfer of stimulus pretraining to motor paired-associate and discrimination learning tasks. In L. P. Lipsitt and C. C. Spiker (Eds.), *Advances in child development and behavior* (Vol. 2). New York: Academic Press, 1965. Pp. 19–58.

Carey, J. E., & Goss, A. E. The role of mediating verbal responses in the conceptual sorting behavior of children. *Journal of Genetic Psychology*, 1957, *90*, 69–74.

Carroll, J. B. A model of school learning. *Teachers College Record*, 1963, *64*, 723–733.

Carroll, J. B. Words, meanings, and concepts. *Harvard Educational Review*, 1964, *34*, 178–202. (a)

Carroll, J. B. *Language and thought*. Englewood Cliffs, N.J.: Prentice-Hall, 1964. (b)

Carroll, J. B. On learning from being told. *Educational Psychologist*, 1968, *5*, 2, 1, 5–10.

Carroll, J. B., & Freedle, R. O. (Eds.). *Language comprehension and the acquisition of knowledge*. Washington, D.C.: Winston & Sons, 1972.

Chase, F. S. IGE as a focus for educational reform and renewal. *Journal of Teacher Education*, 1976, *27*, 196–198.

Clark, D. C. Teaching concepts in the classroom: A set of prescriptions derived from experimental research. *Journal of Educational Psychology Monograph*, 1971, *62*, 253–278.

Clark, E. V. What's in a word? On the child's acquisition of semantics in his first language. In T. Moore (Ed.), *Cognitive development and the acquisition of language*. New York: Academic Press, 1973. Pp. 65–110.

Cole, M., & Scribner, S. *Culture and thought: A psychological introduction*. New York: Wiley, 1974.

Coltheart, M. Contemporary models of the cognitive processes, I. Iconic storage and visual masking. In V. Hamilton & M. D. Vernon (Eds.), *The development of cognitive processes*. London: Academic Press, 1976. Pp. 11–42.

Cooper, L. A., & Shepard, R. N. Chronometric studies of the rotation of mental images. In W. G. Chase (Ed.), *Visual information processing*. New York: Academic Press, 1973.

Coopersmith, S. *Antecedents of self-esteem*. San Francisco: Freeman, 1967.

Crandall, V. C., Katkovsky, W., & Crandall, V. J. Children's belief in their own control of reinforcements in intellectual academic achievement situations. *Child Development*, 1965, *36*, 91–109.

Cronbach, L. J., & Snow, R. E. *Aptitudes and instructional methods: A handbook for research on interactions*. New York: Halsted Press, 1977.

Crowder, R. G., & Morton, J. Precategorical acoustic storage (PAS). *Perception and Psychophysics*, 1969, *5*, 365–373.

Dale, P. S. *Language development: Structure and function* (2nd ed.). New York: Holt, Rinehart and Winston, 1976.

Datan, N., & Reese, H. W. (Eds.). *Life-span developmental psychology: Dialectical perspectives on experimental research*. New York: Academic Press, 1977.

Dewey, J. *How we think*. New York: Heath, 1933.

Dietze, D. A. The facilitating effect of words on discrimination and generalization. *Journal of Experimental Psychology*, 1955, *50*, 255–260.

DiLuzio, G. J., Katzenmeyer, C. G., & Klausmeier, H. J. *Technical manual for the conceptual learning and development assessment series I: Equilateral triangle* (Tech. Rep. No. 434). Madison: Wisconsin Research and Development Center for Cognitive Learning, 1975. (a)

DiLuzio, G. J., Katzenmeyer, C. G., & Klausmeier, H. J. *Technical manual for the conceptual learning and development assessment series III: Noun* (Tech. Rep. No. 436). Madison: Wisconsin Research and Development Center for Cognitive Learning, 1975. (b)

DiLuzio, G. J., Katzenmeyer, C. G., & Klausmeier, H. J. *Technical manual for the conceptual learning and development assessment series IV: Tree* (Tech. Rep. No. 437). Madison: Wisconsin Research and Development Center for Cognitive Learning, 1975. (c)

DiLuzio, G. J., Katzenmeyer, C. G., & Klausmeier, H. J. *Technical manual for the conceptual learning and development assessment series II: Cutting tool* (Tech. Rep. No. 435). Madison: Wisconsin Research and Development Center for Cognitive Learning, 1975. (d)

Di Vesta, F. J., Ingersoll, G., & Sunshine, P. A factor analysis of imagery tests. *Journal of Verbal Learning and Verbal Behavior*, 1971, *10*, 471–479.

Dodd, D. H., & Bourne, L. E., Jr. Test of some assumptions of a hypothesis-testing model of concept identification. *Journal of Experimental Psychology*, 1969, *80*, 69–72.

Erickson, J. R. Hypothesis sampling in concept identification. *Journal of Experimental Psychology*, 1968, *76*, 12–18.

Erickson, J. R., & Jones, M. R. Thinking. In M. R. Rosenzweig & L. W. Porter (Eds.), *Annual review of psychology* (Vol. 29). Palo Alto, Calif.: Annual Reviews Inc., 1978. Pp. 61–90.

Erickson, J. R., & Zajkowski, M. M. Learning several concept-identification problems concurrently:

A test of the sampling-with-replacement assumption. *Journal of Experimental Psychology,* 1967, *74,* 212–218.

Erickson, J. R., Zajkowski, M. M., & Ehrman, E. D. All-or-none assumptions in concept identification: Analysis of latency data. *Journal of Experimental Psychology,* 1966, *72,* 690–697.

Erikson, E. H. Identity and the life cycle: Selected papers. *Psychological Issues,* 1959, *1*(1, Whole No. 1).

Estes, W. K. (Ed.). *Handbook of learning and cognitive processes: Attention and memory* (Vol. 4). New York: John Wiley, 1976.

Farnham-Diggory, S. Development of logical operations and reasoning. In V. Hamilton & M. D. Vernon (Eds.), *The development of cognitive processes.* London: Academic Press, 1976. Pp. 359–412.

Feldman, C. F., & Toulmin, S. Logic and the theory of mind. In W. J. Arnold (Ed.), *Nebraska symposium on motivation 1975: Conceptual foundations of psychology.* Lincoln: University of Nebraska Press, 1975. Pp. 409–476.

Feldman, K. V. *The effects of number of positive and negative instances, concept definition, and emphasis of relevant attributes on the attainment of mathematical concepts* (Tech. Rep. No. 243). Madison: Wisconsin Research and Development Center for Cognitive Learning, 1972.

Feldman, K. V. *Instructional factors relating to children's principle learning* (Tech. Rep. No. 309). Madison: Wisconsin Research and Development Center for Cognitive Learning, 1974.

Feldman, K. V., & Klausmeier, H. J. Effects of two kinds of definition on the concept attainment of fourth and eighth graders. *Journal of Educational Research,* 1974, *67,* 219–223.

Fishman, J. A systematization of the Whorfian hypothesis. *Behavioral Science,* 1960, *5,* 323–339.

Flavell, J. H. Stage-related properties of cognitive development. *Cognitive Psychology,* 1971, *2,* 421–453.

Flavell, J. H. An analysis of cognitive–developmental sequences. *Genetic Psychology Monographs,* 1972, *86,* 279–350.

Flavell, J. H. *Cognitive development.* Englewood Cliffs, N.J.: Prentice-Hall, 1977.

Flavell, J. H., & Wohlwill, J. F. Formal and functional aspects of cognitive development. In D. Elkind & J. H. Flavell (Eds.), *Studies in cognitive development: Essays in honor of Jean Piaget.* London and New York: Oxford University Press, 1969. Pp. 67–120.

Frayer, D. A. *Effects of number of instances and emphasis of relevant attribute values on mastery of geometric concepts by fourth- and sixth-grade children* (Tech. Rep. No. 116). Madison: Wisconsin Research and Development Center for Cognitive Learning, 1970.

Frayer, D. A., & Klausmeier, H. J. *Variables in concept learning: Task variables* (Theo. Paper No. 28). Madison: Wisconsin Research and Development Center for Cognitive Learning, 1971.

Frayer, D. A., Klausmeier, H. J., & Nelson, G. K. *Pilot study of tasks to assess levels of mastery of the concepts equilateral triangle and cutting tool* (Working Paper No. 111). Madison: Wisconsin Research and Development Center for Cognitive Learning, 1973.

Fredrick, W. C., & Klausmeier, H. J. Instructions and labels in a concept attainment task. *Psychological Reports,* 1968, *23,* 1339–1342.

Fruth, M. J., Bowles, B. D., & Moser, R. H. Home–school–community relations in IGE. In H. J. Klausmeier, R. A. Rossmiller, & M. Saily (Eds.), *Individually guided elementary education: Concepts and practices.* New York: Academic Press, 1977. Pp. 260–290.

Gagné, R. M. The acquisition of knowledge. *Psychological Review,* 1962, *69,* 355–365. (a)

Gagné, R. M. (Ed.). *Psychological principles in system development.* New York: Holt, Rinehart and Winston, 1962. (b)

Gagné, R. M. Learning hierarchies. *Educational Psychologist,* 1968, *6,* 1–9.

Gagné, R. M. *The conditions of learning* (2nd ed.). New York: Holt, Rinehart and Winston, 1970.

Gagné, R. M. *Essentials of learning for instruction.* Hinsdale, Ill.: Dryden Press, 1974.

Gagné, R. M. *The conditions of learning* (3rd ed.). New York: Holt, Rinehart and Winston, 1977.

Gagné, R. M., & Briggs, L. J. *Principles of instructional design.* New York: Holt, Rinehart and Winston, 1974.

Gargiulo, R. M. *The effect of labels only and labels with instruction on the concept attainment of educable mentally retarded and normally developing boys of school age* (Tech. Rep. No. 301). Madison: Wisconsin Research and Development Center for Cognitive Learning, 1974.

Gazzaniga, M. S. *The bisected brain.* New York: Appleton-Century-Crofts, 1970.

Gelman, R. Cognitive development. In M. R. Rosenzweig & L. W. Porter (Eds.), *Annual review of psychology* (Vol. 29). Palo Alto, Calif.: Annual Reviews Inc., 1978. Pp. 297–332.

Gesell, A., & Ilg, F. L. *Infant and child in the culture of today.* New York: Harper, 1943.

Gesell, A., & Ilg, F. L. *The child from five to ten.* New York: Harper, 1946.

Gesell, A., Ilg, F. L., & Ames, L. B. *Youth: The years from ten to sixteen.* New York: Harper, 1956.

Ghatala, E. S., & Levin, J. R. Children's recognition memory processes. In J. R. Levin & V. L. Allen (Eds.), *Cognitive learning in children: Theories and strategies.* New York: Academic Press, 1977. Pp. 61–100.

Gibbons, M. *The new secondary education* (A Phi Delta Kappa Task Force Report). Bloomington, Ind.: Phi Delta Kappan, 1976.

Gibson, E. J. *Principles of perceptual learning and development.* New York: Appleton-Century-Crofts, 1969.

Gibson, E. J., Gibson, J. J., Pick, A. D., & Osser, H. A developmental study of the discrimination of letter-like forms. *Journal of Comparative and Physiological Psychology*, 1962, *55*, 897–906.

Gibson, E. J., & Levin, H. *The psychology of reading.* Cambridge, Mass.: The M.I.T. Press, 1975.

Ginsburg, H., & Koslowski, B. Cognitive development. In M. R. Rosenzweig & L. W. Porter (Eds.), *Annual review of psychology.* Palo Alto, Calif.: Annual Reviews, Inc., 1976.

Glaser, R. *Adaptive education: Individual diversity and learning.* New York: Holt, Rinehart, and Winston, 1977.

Goss, A. E., & Moylan, M. C. Conceptual block-sorting as a function of type and degree of mastery of discriminative verbal responses. *Journal of Genetic Psychology*, 1958, *93*, 191–198.

Guilford, J. P. *The nature of human intelligence.* New York: McGraw-Hill, 1967.

Haney, R. E., & Sorenson, J. S. *Individually guided science.* Reading, Mass.: Addison-Wesley, 1977.

Harris, C. W. Some Rao-Guttman relationships. *Psychometrika*, 1962, *27*, 247–263.

Harris, M. L., & Harris, C. W. *A structure of concept attainment abilities: Wisconsin monograph series.* Madison: Wisconsin Research and Development Center for Cognitive Learning, 1973.

Hebb, D. O. Concerning imagery. *Psychological Review*, 1968, *75*, 466–477.

Horn, J. L. Human abilities: A review of research and theory in the early 1970s. In M. R. Rosenzweig & L. W. Porter (Eds.), *Annual review of psychology* (Vol. 27). Palo Alto, Calif.: Annual Reviews Inc., 1976. Pp. 437–485.

Huttenlocher, J., & Presson, C. C. Mental rotation and the perspective problem. *Cognitive Psychology*, 1973, *4*, 277–299.

Instructional Objectives Exchange. *Attitude toward school, Grades K–12.* Los Angeles, Calif.: Instructional Objectives Exchange, 1972.

Johnson, D. M., & O'Reilly, C. A. Concept attainment in children: Classifying and defining. *Journal of Educational Psychology*, 1964, *55*, 71–74.

Johnson, E. S. Objective identification of strategy on a selection concept learning task. *Journal of Experimental Psychology Monograph*, 1971, *90*, 167–196.

Jöreskog, K. G. Some contributions to maximum likelihood factor analysis. *Psychometrika*, 1967, *32*, 443–482.

Kagan, J. A developmental approach to conceptual growth. In H. J. Klausmeier & C. W. Harris (Eds.), *Analyses of concept learning.* New York: Academic Press, 1966. Pp. 97–116.

Kail, R. V., & Hagen, J. W. (Eds.). *Memory in cognitive development.* Hillsdale, N.J.: Lawrence Erlbaum Associates, 1976.

Kail, R. V., & Hagen, J. W. *Perspectives on the development of memory and cognition.* New York: Halstead Press, 1977.

Kalish, P. W. *Concept attainment as a function of monetary incentives, competition, and instructions* (Tech. Rep. No. 8). Madison: Wisconsin Research and Development Center for Cognitive Learning, 1966.

Katz, Selena. *The effects of five instructional treatments on the learning of principles by children*

(Tech. Rep. No. 381). Madison: Wisconsin Research and Development Center for Cognitive Learning, 1976.

Kendler, H. H., Glasman, L. D., & Ward, J. W. Verbal-labeling and cue-training in reversal-shift behavior. *Journal of Experimental Child Psychology,* 1972, *13,* 195–209.

Kendler, T. S., & Kendler, H. H. Reversal and nonreversal shifts in kindergarten children. *Journal of Experimental Psychology,* 1959, *58,* 56–60.

Kessen, W. Research design in the study of developmental problems. In P. H. Mussen (Ed.), *Handbook of research methods in child development.* New York: Wiley, 1960. Pp. 36–70.

Kimura, D. The asymmetry of the human brain. *Scientific American,* 1973, *228,* 70–78.

Klausmeier, H. J. Cognitive operations in concept learning. *Educational Psychologist,* 1971, *9,* 1–8.

Klausmeier, H. J. "IGE": An alternative form of schooling. In H. Talmage (Ed.), *Systems of individualized education.* Berkeley, Calif.: McCutchan, 1975.

Klausmeier, H. J. Continuity in learning: Long-range effects. In K. H. Hansen (Ed.), *Learning: An overview & update* (A report of the Chief State School Officers 1976 Summer Institute, San Diego, Calif.). Washington, D.C.: U.S. Office of Education, 1976. Pp. 15–42. (a)

Klausmeier, H. J. Instructional design and the teaching of concepts. In J. R. Levin & V. L. Allen (Eds.), *Cognitive learning in children: Theories and strategies.* New York: Academic Press, 1976. Pp. 191–217. (b)

Klausmeier, H. J. Problem solving and complex learning. In B. B. Wolman (Ed.), *International encyclopedia of psychiatry, psychology, psychoanalysis, and neurology* (Vol. IX). New York: Van Nostrand Reinhold, 1977. Pp. 82–85. (a)

Klausmeier, H. J. *Principals' ratings of the desirability of the comprehensive and enabling objectives for individually guided education/secondary* (Working Paper No. 207). Madison: Wisconsin Research and Development Center for Cognitive Learning and Development, 1977. (b)

Klausmeier, H. J. Instructional programming for the individual student. In H. J. Klausmeier, R. A. Rossmiller, & M. Saily (Eds.), *Individually guided elementary education: Concepts and practices.* New York: Academic Press, 1977. Pp. 55–76. (c)

Klausmeier, H. J. Origin and overview of IGE. In H. J. Klausmeier, R. A. Rossmiller, & M. Saily (Eds.), *Individually guided elementary education: Concepts and practices.* New York: Academic Press, 1977. Pp. 1–24. (d)

Klausmeier, H. J., Allen, P. S., Sipple, T. S., & White, K. M. *Second cross-sectional study of attainment of the concepts equilateral triangle, cutting tool, noun, and tree by children age 6 to 16 of city B* (Tech. Rep. No. 347). Madison: Wisconsin Research and Development Center for Cognitive Learning, 1976. (a)

Klausmeier, H. J., Allen, P. S., Sipple, T. S., & White, K. M. *Third cross-sectional study of attainment of the concepts equilateral triangle, cutting tool, noun, and tree by children age 7 to 17* (Tech. Rep. No. 427). Madison: Wisconsin Research and Development Center for Cognitive Learning, 1976. (b)

Klausmeier, H. J., Bernard, M., Katzenmeyer, C., & Sipple, T. S. *Development of conceptual learning and development assessment series II: Cutting tool* (Tech. Rep. No. 431). Madison: Wisconsin Research and Development Center for Cognitive Learning, 1973.

Klausmeier, H. J., & Feldman, K. V. Effects of a definition and a varying number of examples and nonexamples on concept attainment. *Journal of Educational Psychology,* 1975, *67,* 174–178.

Klausmeier, H. J., Ghatala, E. S., & Frayer, D. A. *Conceptual learning and development: A cognitive view.* New York: Academic Press, 1974.

Klausmeier, H. J., & Goodwin, W. L. *Learning and human abilities: Educational psychology* (4th ed.). New York: Harper & Row, 1975.

Klausmeier, H. J., & Harris, C. W. (Eds.). *Analyses of concept learning.* New York: Academic Press, 1966.

Klausmeier, H. J., Harris, C. W., Davis, J. K., Schwenn, E., & Frayer, D. *Strategies and cognitive processes in concept learning* (Project No. 2850). Madison: University of Wisconsin Department of Educational Psychology, March 1968.

Klausmeier, H. J., Harris, C. W., & Wiersma, W. *Strategies of learning and efficiency of concept attainment by individuals and groups* (Cooperative Research Project Number 1442). Madison: University of Wisconsin Department of Educational Psychology, July 1964.

Klausmeier, H. J., & Associates. *Cognitive development from a Piagetian and an information-processing view: Results of a longitudinal study*. Madison: University of Wisconsin—Madison, in preparation.

Klausmeier, H. J., Ingison, L. J., Sipple, T. S., & Katzenmeyer, C. G. *Development of conceptual learning and development assessment series I: Equilateral triangle* (Tech. Rep. No. 430). Madison: Wisconsin Research and Development Center for Cognitive Learning, 1973. (a)

Klausmeier, H. J., Ingison, L. J., Sipple, T. S., & Katzenmeyer, C. G. *Development of conceptual learning and development assessment series III: Noun* (Tech Rep. No. 432). Madison: Wisconsin Research and Development Center for Cognitive Learning, 1973. (b)

Klausmeier, H. J., Jeter, J. T., Quilling, M. R., Frayer, D. A., & Allen, P. S. *Individually guided motivation*. Madison: Wisconsin Research and Development Center for Cognitive Learning, 1975.

Klausmeier, H. J., & Loughlin, L. J. Behaviors during problem solving among children of low, average, and high intelligence. *Journal of Educational Psychology*, 1961, *52*, 148–152.

Klausmeier, H. J., Marliave, R. S., Katzenmeyer, C. G., & Sipple, T. S. *Development of conceptual learning and development assessment series IV: Tree* (Tech. Rep. No. 433). Madison: Wisconsin Research and Development Center for Cognitive Learning, 1974.

Klausmeier, H. J., & Meinke, D. L. Concept attainment as a function of instructions concerning the stimulus material, a strategy, and a principle for securing information. *Journal of Educational Psychology*, 1968, *59*, 215–222.

Klausmeier, H. J., Morrow, R. G., & Walter, J. E. *Individually guided education in the multiunit elementary school: Guidelines for implementation*. Madison: Wisconsin Research & Development Center for Cognitive Learning, 1968.

Klausmeier, H. J., & Pellegrin, R. J. The multiunit school: A differentiated staffing approach. In D. S. Bushnell & D. Rappaport (Eds.), *Planned change in education*. New York: Harcourt Brace Jovanovich, 1971. Pp. 107–126.

Klausmeier, H. J., Quilling, M. R., Sorenson, J. S., Way, R. S., & Glasrud, G. R. *Individually guided education and the multiunit elementary school: Guidelines for implementation*. Madison: Wisconsin Research and Development Center for Cognitive Learning, 1971.

Klausmeier, H. J., Rossmiller, R. A., & Saily, M. (Eds.). *Individually guided elementary education: Concepts and practices*. New York: Academic Press, 1977.

Klausmeier, H. J., Schilling, J., & Feldman, K. V. *The effectiveness of experimental lessons in accelerating children's attainment of the concept tree* (Tech. Rep. No. 372). Madison: Wisconsin Research and Development Center for Cognitive Learning, 1976.

Klausmeier, H. J., Sipple, T. S., & Allen, P. S. *First cross-sectional study of attainment of the concepts equilateral triangle, cutting tool, and noun by children age 5 to 16 of city A* (Tech. Rep. No. 287). Madison: Wisconsin Research and Development Center for Cognitive Learning, 1974. (a)

Klausmeier, H. J., Sipple, T. S., & Allen, P. S. *First cross-sectional study of attainment of the concepts equilateral triangle and cutting tool by children age 5 to 16 of city B* (Tech. Rep. No. 288). Madison: Wisconsin Research and Development Center for Cognitive Learning, 1974. (b)

Klausmeier, H. J., Sipple, T. S., & Frayer, D. A. *An individually administered test to assess level of attainment and use of concept, equilateral triangle* (Tech. Rep. No. 257). Madison: Wisconsin Research and Development Center for Cognitive Learning, 1973.

Klausmeier, H. J., Sipple, T. S., Swanson, J. E., & Schilling, J. M. *Second-year intervention study to facilitate children's concept learning* (Working Paper No. 193). Madison: Wisconsin Research and Development Center for Cognitive Learning, 1976.

Klausmeier, H. J., Sorenson, J. S., & Quilling, M. R. Instructional programming for the individual pupil in the multiunit elementary school. *Elementary School Journal,* 1971, *72*(2), 88–101.

Klausmeier, H. J., Swanson, J. E., & Sipple, T. S. *The analysis of nine process-concepts in elementary science* (Tech. Rep. No. 428). Madison: Wisconsin Research and Development Center for Cognitive Learning, 1976.

Klee, H., & Eysenck, M. W. Comprehension of abstract and concrete sentences. *Journal of Verbal Learning and Verbal Behavior,* 1973, *12,* 522–529.

Kohlberg, L. State and sequence: The cognitive–developmental approach to socialization. In D. A. Goslin (Ed.), *Handbook of socialization theory and research.* Chicago: Rand McNally, 1969. Pp. 347–480.

Krechevsky, I. "Hypotheses" in rats. *Psychological Review,* 1932, *39,* 516–532.

Kurtines, W., & Greif, E. B. The development of moral thought: Review and evaluation of Kohlberg's approach. *Psychological Bulletin,* 1974, *81,* 453–470.

Landau, B. L., & Hagen, J. W. The effect of verbal cues on concept acquisition and retention in formal and educable mentally retarded children. *Child Development,* 1974, *45,* 643–650.

Lashley, K. S. The mechanism of vision: XV. Preliminary studies of the rat's capacity for detail vision. *Journal of Genetic Psychology,* 1938, *18,* 123–193.

Laughlin, P. R., Doherty, M. A., & Dunn, R. F. Intentional and incidental concept formation as a function of motivation, creativity, intelligence, and sex. *Journal of Personality and Social Psychology,* 1968, *8,* 401–409.

LeFurgy, W. G., Woloshin, G. W., & Sandler, R. J. High speed prompting effect: Children's attainment and generalization of an unverbalized concept. *Proceedings of the 77th Annual Convention of the American Psychological Association,* 1969, *4,* 277–278.

Levine, M. A model of hypothesis behavior in discrimination learning set. *Psychological Review,* 1959, *66,* 353–366.

Levine, M. Cue neutralization: The effects of random reinforcements upon discrimination learning. *Journal of Experimental Psychology,* 1962, *63,* 438–443.

Levine, M. Mediating processes in humans at the outset of discrimination learning. *Psychological Review,* 1963, *70,* 254–276.

Levine, M. Hypothesis behavior by humans during discrimination learning. *Journal of Experimental Psychology,* 1966, *71,* 331–336.

Levine, M., Leitenberg, H., & Richter, M. The blank trials law: The equivalence of positive reinforcement and nonreinforcement. *Psychological Review,* 1964, *71,* 94–103.

Lipham, J. M. *Abstracts of completed research on administration and organization for instruction in IGE schools.* Madison: Wisconsin Research and Development Center for Cognitive Learning, 1977.

Lipham, J. M., & Fruth, M. J. *The principal and individually guided education.* Reading, Mass.: Addison-Wesley, 1976.

Mackworth, J. F. Development of attention. In V. Hamilton & M. D. Vernon (Eds.), *The development of cognitive processes.* London: Academic Press, 1976. Pp. 111–152.

Macnamara, J. (Ed.). *Language learning and thought.* New York: Academic Press, 1977.

Mager, R. F. *Preparing instructional objectives.* Palo Alto, Calif.: Fearon, 1962.

Markle, S. M. They teach concepts, don't they? *Educational Researcher,* 1975, *4,* 3–9.

Markle, S. M. *The implications of semantic archaeology for semantic architecture, if any.* Paper presented at the American Psychological Association Convention, San Francisco, August 1977.

Markle, S. M., & Tiemann, P. W. *Really understanding concepts: Or in frumious pursuit of the jabberwock.* Champaign, Ill.: Stipes, 1969.

Marliave, R. S. *The effects on concept attainment of instructing children to hypothesize and evaluate* (Tech. Rep. No. 383). Madison: Wisconsin Research and Development Center for Cognitive Learning, 1976.

McCall, R. B. Challenges to a science of developmental psychology. *Child Development,* 1977, *48,* 333–344.

McMurray, N. E., Bernard, M. E., & Klausmeier, H. J. *An instructional design for accelerating children's attainment of the concept equilateral triangle* (Tech. Rep. No. 321). Madison: Wisconsin Research and Development Center for Cognitive Learning, 1975.

McNeill, D. The development of language. In P. H. Mussen (Ed.), *Carmichael's manual of child psychology* (3rd ed., Vol. 1). New York: Wiley, 1970. Pp. 1061–1161.

Meinke, D. L., George, C. S., & Wilkinson, J. M. Concrete and abstract thinkers at three grade levels and their performance with complex concepts. *Journal of Educational Psychology,* 1975, *67,* 154–158.

Melton, Arthur W., & Martin, E. *Coding processes in human memory.* New York: Halsted Press, 1972.

Merrifield, P. R., Guilford, J. P., Christensen, P. R., & Frick, J. W. A factor-analytic study of problem-solving abilities. *Report of Psychology Laboratory,* University of Southern California, 1960, No. 22.

Merrill, M. D., & Tennyson, R. D. *Attribute prompting errors as a function of relationships between positive and negative instances* (Working Paper No. 28). Provo, Utah: Instructional Research and Development, Brigham Young University, 1971.

Merrill, M. D., & Tennyson, R. D. *Teaching concepts: An instructional design guide.* Englewood Cliffs, N.J.: Educational Technology Publications, 1977.

Messick, S., & Associates. *Individuality in learning.* San Francisco: Jossey-Bass, 1976.

Miller, L. A. Hypothesis analysis of conjunctive concept-learning situations. *Psychological Review,* 1971, *78,* 262–271.

Miller, G. A., Galanter, E., & Pribram, K. H. *Plans and the structure of behavior.* New York: Holt, Rinehart and Winston, 1960.

Miller, G. A., & Johnson-Laird, P. N. *Language and perception.* Cambridge, Mass.: Harvard University Press, 1976.

Miller, N. E., & Dollard, J. *Social learning and imitation.* New Haven, Conn.: Yale University Press, 1941.

Milner, B., & Teuber, H. L. Alteration of perception and memory in man: Reflections on methods. In L. Weiskrantz (Ed.), *Analysis of behavioral change.* New York: Harper & Row, 1968.

Mize, G. K. *The influence of increased parental involvement in the educational process of their children* (Tech. Rep. No. 418). Madison: Wisconsin Research and Development Center for Cognitive Learning, 1977.

Mize, G. K., & Klausmeier, H. J. *Factors contributing to rapid and slow cognitive development among elementary and high school children* (Working Paper No. 201). Madison: Wisconsin Research and Development Center for Cognitive Learning, 1977.

Morrison, H. C. *The practice of teaching in the secondary school.* Chicago: University of Chicago Press, 1926.

Mueller, D. J. Mastery learning: Partly boon, partly boondoggle. *Teachers College Record,* 1976, *78*(1), 41–52.

Mussen, P. H. (Ed.). *Carmichael's manual of child psychology* (Vol. 1, 3rd ed.). New York: Wiley, 1970.

Mussen, P. H., Conger, J. J., & Kagan, J. *Child development and personality* (4th ed.). New York: Harper & Row, 1974.

Nahinsky, T. D., & Slaymaker, F. L. Sampling without replacement and information processing following correct responses in concept identification. *Journal of Experimental Psychology,* 1969, *80,* 475–482.

Neimark, E. D., & Santa, J. L. Thinking and concept attainment. In M. R. Rosenzweig & L. W. Porter (Eds.), *Annual review of psychology.* Palo Alto, Calif.: Annual Reviews, Inc., 1975. Pp. 173–205.

Nelson, G. K. Concomitant effects of visual, motor, and verbal experiences in young children's concept development. *Journal of Educational Psychology,* 1976, *68*(4), 466–473.

Nelson, G. K., & Klausmeier, H. J. Classificatory behaviors of low-socioeconomic-status children. *Journal of Educational Psychology,* 1974, *66,* 432–438.

Nelson, K. Concept, word, and sentence: Interrelations in acquisition and development. *Psychological Review,* 1974, *81,* 267–285.

Nelson, K. E., & Bonvillian, J. D. Concepts and words in the 18-month-old: Acquiring concept names under controlled conditions. *Cognition,* 1973, *2*(4), 435–450.

Nesselroade, J. R., & Reese, H. W. (Eds.). *Life-span developmental psychology: Methodological issues.* New York: Academic Press, 1973.

Newell, A., & Simon, H. A. *Human problem solving.* Englewood Cliffs, N.J.: Prentice-Hall, 1972.

Nodine, C. F., & Evans, J. D. Eye movements of prereaders containing letters of high and low confusability. *Perception and Psychophysics,* 1969, *6,* 39–41.

Nodine, C. F., & Lang, N. J. The development of visual scanning strategies for differentiating words. *Developmental Psychology,* 1971, *5,* 221–232.

Norcross, K. J. Effects on discrimination performance of similarity of previously acquired stimulus names. *Journal of Experimental Psychology,* 1958, *56,* 305–309.

Nunnally, J. C. Research strategies and measurement methods for investigating human development. In J. R. Nesselroade & H. W. Reese (Eds.), *Life-span developmental psychology: Methodological issues.* New York: Academic Press, 1973. Pp. 87–109.

Nussel, E. J., Inglis, J. D., & Wiersma, W. *The teacher and individually guided education.* Reading, Mass.: Addison-Wesley, 1976.

Olson, G. M. Developmental changes in memory and the acquisition of language. In T. Moore (Ed.), *Cognitive development and the acquisition of language.* New York: Academic Press, 1973. Pp. 145–158.

Osler, S. F., & Madden, J. The verbal label: Mediator or classifier? *Journal of Experimental Child Psychology,* 1973, *16,* 303–317.

Osler, S. F., & Weiss, S. R. Studies in concept attainment: III. Effect of instructions at two levels of intelligence. *Journal of Experimental Psychology,* 1962, *63,* 528–533.

Otto, W., & Chester, R. D. *Objective-based reading.* Reading, Mass.: Addison-Wesley, 1976.

Paivio, A. *Imagery and verbal processes.* New York: Holt, Rinehart and Winston, 1971.

Paivio, A. Language and knowledge of the world. *Educational Researcher,* 1974, *3*(9), 5–12.

Parten, M. B. Social participation among preschool children. *Journal of Abnormal and Social Psychology,* 1932, *27,* 243–269.

Peterson, L. R. Verbal learning and memory. In M. R. Rosenzweig & L. W. Porter (Eds.), *Annual review of psychology* (Vol. 28). Palo Alto, Calif.: Annual Reviews Inc., 1977. Pp. 393–415.

Peterson, P. L. A review of the research on mastery–learning strategies. Unpublished manuscript, International Association for the Evaluation of Educational Achievement, Stockholm, Sweden, 1972.

Piaget, J. *Play, dreams, and imitation in childhood.* New York: Norton, 1951.

Piaget, J. *The construction of reality in the child.* New York: Basic Books, 1954.

Piaget, J. *The origins of intelligence in children.* New York: Norton, 1963.

Piaget, J. Development and learning. In R. E. Ripple & V. N. Rockcastle (Eds.), *Piaget rediscovered.* Ithaca, N.Y.: Cornell University Press, 1964. Pp. 1–12.

Piaget, J. Piaget's theory. In P. H. Mussen (Ed.), *Carmichael's manual of child psychology* (Vol. 1, 3rd ed.). New York: Wiley, 1970. Pp. 703–732.

Poggio, J. P., Glasnapp, D. R., & Ory, J. C. The impact of test anxiety on formative and summative exam performance in the mastery learning model. Paper presented at the annual meeting of the National Council on Measurement in Education, Washington, D.C., 1975.

Postman, L. Methodology of human learning. In W. K. Estes (Ed.), *Handbook of learning and cognitive processes: Approaches to human learning and motivation* (Vol. 3). New York: John Wiley, 1976. Pp. 11–70.

Preyer, W. *Die seele des kindes.* Liepzig: Grieben, 1882.

Price-Williams, D. R. Cross-cultural differences in cognitive development. In V. Hamilton & M. D. Vernon (Eds.), *The development of cognitive processes.* London: Academic Press, 1976. Pp. 549–590.

Rampaul, W. E. *The relationship between conceptual learning and development, concept achievement, educational achievement, and selected cognitive abilities* (Tech. Rep. No. 382). Madison: Wisconsin Research and Development Center for Cognitive Learning, 1976.

Reese, H. W., & Lipsitt, L. P. *Experimental child psychology.* New York: Academic Press, 1970.

Resnick, L. B., Wang, M. C., & Kaplan, J. Task analysis in curriculum design: A hierarchically sequenced introductory mathematics curriculum. *Journal of Applied Behavior Analysis,* 1973, *6,* 697–710.

Restle, F. A theory of discrimination learning. *Psychological Review,* 1955, *62,* 11–19.

Restle, F. The selection of strategies in cue learning. *Psychological Review,* 1962, *69,* 329–343.

Restle, F., & Emmerich, D. Memory in concept attainment: Effect of giving several problems concurrently. *Journal of Experimental Psychology,* 1966, *71,* 794–799.

Roget's International Thesaurus (3rd ed.). New York: Crowell, 1962.

Rohwer, W. D., Jr. Cognitive development and education. In P. H. Mussen (Ed.), *Carmichael's manual of child psychology* (Vol. 1, 3rd ed.). New York: Wiley, 1970. Pp. 1379–1454.

Rohwer, W. D., Jr. Elaboration and learning in childhood and adolescence. In H. W. Reese (Ed.), *Advances in child development and behavior* (Vol. 8). New York: Academic Press, 1973.

Romberg, T. A. *Individually guided mathematics.* Reading, Mass.: Addison-Wesley Publishing Company, 1976.

Rosch, E. Universals and cultural specifics in human categorization. In W. S. Lonner and R. Breslin (Eds.), *Cross-cultural perspectives on learning.* London: Sage Publications, 1974.

Rossman, J. *The psychology of the inventor.* Washington D.C. Inventors, 1931.

Rourke, D., & Trabasso, T. Hypothesis sampling and prior experience. *Proceedings of the 76th convention of the American Psychological Association,* 1968, *3,* 47–78.

Rydberg, S., & Arnberg, P. W. Attending and processing broadened within children's concept learning. *Journal of Experimental Child Psychology,* 1976, *22,* 161–177.

Scandura, J. M. *Problem solving: A structural/process approach with instructional implications.* New York: Academic Press, 1977.

Schaie, K. W. A general model for the study of developmental problems. *Psychological Bulletin,* 1965, *64,* 92–107.

Seymour, P. H. K. Contemporary models of the cognitive processes, II. Retrieval and comparison operations in permanent memory. In V. Hamilton & M. D. Vernon (Eds.), *The development of cognitive processes.* London: Academic Press, 1976. Pp. 43–110.

Shaycoft, M. G. *The high school years: Growth in cognitive skills.* Pittsburgh: American Institutes of Research, 1967.

Shepard, R. N., & Metzler, J. Mental rotation of three-dimensional objects. *Science,* 1971, *171,* 701–703.

Smith, B. O. IGE and teacher education. *Journal of Teacher Education,* in press.

Sontag, L. W., Baker, C. T., & Nelson, V. L. Mental growth and personality development: A longitudinal study. *Monographs of the Society for Research in Child Development,* 1958, *23* (2, Serial No. 68).

Sorenson, J. S., Poole, M., & Joyal, L. H. *The unit leader and individually guided education.* Reading, Mass.: Addison-Wesley, 1976.

Sperling, G. A. The information available in brief visual presentation. *Psychological Monographs,* 1960, *74* (11, Whole No. 498).

Sperry, R. W. Lateralization of function in the surgically separated hemispheres. In F. J. McGuigan & R. Schoonover (Eds.), *The psychophysiology of thinking.* New York: Academic Press, 1973.

Spiker, C. C. The concept of development: Relevant and irrelevant issues. *Monographs of the Society for Research in Child Development,* 1966, *31,* 40–54.

Staats, A. *Child learning, intelligence and personality.* New York: Harper & Row, 1971.

Stein, K. K., & Erickson, J. R. Some characteristics of hypothesis sampling in concept identification.

Paper presented at the annual meeting of the Midwestern Psychological Association, May 1967.

Steinberg, B. M. Information processing in the third year: Coding, memory, transfer. *Child Development,* 1974, *45,* 503–507.

Swanson, J. E. *The effects of number of positive and negative instances, concept definition, and emphasis of relevant attributes on the attainment of three environmental concepts by sixth-grade children* (Tech. Rep. No. 244). Madison: Wisconsin Research and Development Center for Cognitive Learning, 1972.

Sweet, R. C. *Educational attainment and attitudes toward school as a function of feedback in the form of teachers' written comments* (Tech. Rep. No. 15). Madison: Wisconsin Research and Development Center for Cognitive Learning, 1966.

Tagatz, G. E. Effects of strategy, sex, and age of conceptual behavior of elementary school children. *Journal of Educational Psychology,* 1967, *58,* 103–109.

Tagatz, G. E., Walsh, M. R., & Layman, J. A. Learning set and strategy interaction in concept learning. *Journal of Educational Psychology,* 1969, *60,* 488–493.

Talmage, H. (Ed.). *Systems of individualized education.* Berkeley, Calif.: McCutchan, 1975.

Tennyson, R. D. Effect of negative instances in concept acquisition using a verbal-learning task. *Journal of Educational Psychology,* 1973, *64,* 247–260.

Tennyson, R. D., Woolley, F. R., & Merrill, M. D. Exemplar and nonexemplar variables which produce correct concept classification behavior and specified classification errors. *Journal of Educational Psychology,* 1972, *63,* 144–152.

Terman, L. M. *Genetic studies of genius. Vol. I. The mental and physical traits of a thousand gifted children.* Stanford, Calif.: Stanford University Press, 1925.

Thurstone, T. G. *Examiner's manual IBM 805 edition, PMA primary mental abilities for grades 6–9.* Chicago: Science Research Associates, 1963.

Tiemann, P. W., Kroeker, L. P., & Markle, S. M. *Teaching verbally-mediated concepts in an ongoing college course.* Paper presented at American Educational Research Association Convention, New York, April 5, 1977.

Tighe, T. J., & Tighe, L. S. Differentiation theory and concept-shift behavior. *Psychological Bulletin,* 1968, *70,* 756–761.

Tulving, E. Episodic and semantic memory. In E. Tulving & W. Donaldson (Eds.), *Organization of memory.* New York: Academic Press, 1972. Pp. 381–403.

Tyler, L. E. *Individual differences: Abilities and motivational directions.* Englewood Cliffs, N.J.: Prentice-Hall, 1974.

Van den Daele, L. D. Qualitative models in developmental analysis. *Developmental Psychology,* 1969, *1,* 303–310.

Vernon, M. D. *Perception through experience,* New York: Barnes & Noble, 1970.

Vurpillot, E. Development of identification of objects. In V. Hamilton & M. D. Vernon (Eds.), *The development of cognitive processes.* London: Academic Press, 1976. Pp. 191–236.

Vygotsky, L. S. *Thought and language.* Cambridge, Mass.: The M. I. T. Press, 1962.

Wagner, D. A. The effects of verbal labeling on short-term and incidental memory: A cross-cultural and developmental study. *Memory & Cognition,* 1975, *3*(6), 595–598.

Washburne, C. *Adjusting the school to the child.* New York: World Book Company, 1932.

Whorf, B. L. *Language, thought, and reality.* New York: Wiley; and Cambridge, Mass.: The M. I. T. Press, 1956.

Wickelgren, W. A. The long and the short of memory. *Psychological Bulletin,* 1973, *80*(6), 425–438.

Wittrock, M. C., & Lumsdaine, A. A. Instructional psychology. In M. R. Rosenzweig & L. W. Porter (Eds.), *Annual review of psychology* (Vol. 28). Palo Alto, Calif.: Annual Reviews Inc., 1977. Pp. 417–459.

Wiviott, S. P. *Bases of classification of geometric concepts used by children of varying characteris-*

tics (Tech. Rep. No. 143). Madison: Wisconsin Research and Development Center for Cognitive Learning, 1970.

Wirtz, W., et al. *On further examination: Report of the advisory panel on the scholastic aptitude test score decline.* New York: College Entrance Examination Board, 1977.

Wohlwill, J. F. *The study of behavioral development.* New York: Academic Press, 1973.

Woodruff, A. D. *Basic concepts of teaching* (Concise edition). San Francisco: Chandler Publishing, 1961.

Yonas, A. *The acquisition of information-processing strategies in a time-dependent task.* Unpublished doctoral dissertation. Department of Psychology, Cornell University, 1969.

Zaphorozhets, A. V. The development of perception in the preschool child. In P. H. Mussen (Ed.), *European research in cognitive development,* Monographs of the Society for Research in Child Development, 1965, *30* (2, Whole No. 100). Pp. 82–101.

Author Index

Subject Index

A

Ability(ies), verbal and nonverbal, independence of, 98
Achievement motivation, rate of cognitive development and, 202, 203
Adaptable Environments for Learning (AEL), 241
Age
  attainment of classificatory and formal level and, 175–177, 272
  developmental studies and, 31
    comparability of groups in, 32
Attending, 60
  at concrete level, 60, 61
  developmental trends in, 67–68
  directing, 283
  at formal level, 63
  at identity and classificatory levels, 62–63
  origination of, 85
  perceptual theory and, 64–66, 279
Attitude(s)
  toward family and home, rate of cognitive development and, 202, 203
  toward school, rate of cognitive development and, 202, 203
Attribute(s), 11–12
  common to examples, cognizing, 77–78
  critical, 12, 215

defining, 12, 24–26
  acquisition of, 132
  emphasizing, 226–227
  generalizing and, 71–72
  hypothesis testing and, 73–74
  specifying, 215–216
definition of, 11
discrimination of, developmental trends in, 68–69
variable, 12–13
  specifying, 216
Attribute prompting questions, 231
Axioms, 13

B

Baby biographies, 34
Behavior, nonverbal, language and, 108
Behavioral analysis, 208
  process of, 220–221

C

Cause-and-effect, 13
Classificatory level, 19
  age of attainment of, 175–177, 272, 273
  attending at, 62–63
  beginning, instructional analysis at, 222–223

developmental norms for, 167–169, 271, 272
Probability, 13
Problem solving, 14, 268
  age of mastery of, 273
  concept level mastery and, 177–181
  developmental norms for, 171–173, 272
  exercises in, 219–220
  lack of attention to, 15–16
  utilization of concepts in, 24

R

Reaction time
  dual-coding theory of memory and, 99
  memory for hypotheses and, 76
Reading, rate of cognitive development and, 202, 203
Reception operations, 21
Recognition, development of, 94
Rehearsal, language and, 129
Relational questions, 231
Reliability, of tests, 47–50
Retest effects, 53, 144, 268–269
Rotation, recognition and, 94

S

Sampling, in longitudinal approach, 34
Scanning, developmental trends in, 64
Schema, 113
  conceptual core and, 113–114
School(s)
  attitudes toward, rate of cognitive development and, 202, 203
  changing, 240–246, 277–278
School absenteeism, rate of cognitive development and, 202
School achievement
  factors affecting, 255
  mastery approach and, 256
  rate of cognitive development and, 202
Science . . . A Process Approach (SAPA), 258–265
Selective dropout, in longitudinal studies, 35
Selective survival, longitudinal studies and, 34–35
Self-esteem, rate of cognitive development and, 202, 203
Semantic field, 114, 282
  conceptual core and, 114
Sensory register, 84

Sentence meanings, word meanings and, 122–123
Sequencing, see Invariant sequencing
Social skills, rate of cognitive development and, 202
Socioeconomic status, rate of cognitive development and, 202
Stage theories, 136
Strategy(ies), 100
  for acquiring and remembering, language and, 129
  for differentiating examples and nonexamples, 227
  experimental investigations of, 100–103
  focusing, 101–102
  ideal, 101
  scanning, 101
Structure, of concepts, 8–10
Substitution sequences, 157
Systemwide Program Committee, 242, 244

T

Taxonomy(ies), 14–15, 171, 268
  age of mastery of, 273
  analysis of, 210, 212
  defining concepts in, 214–215
  formulation of, 213–214
  outlining, for concept analysis, 209–214
  understanding, 22–23
    concept level mastery and, 177–181
    developmental norms for, 169–170, 271–272
Test(s)
  construction and validation of, 42–44
    criteria for, 41–42
  reliability of, 47–50
Test-Operate–Test-Exit (TOTE) units, 77
Textbooks, taxonomic relations in, 170
Time, episodic memory and, 88
Trace, 91

U

Undergeneralization, 217
Usability, of concepts, 7

V

Validity
  of concepts, 7–8
  of longitudinal studies, 34

A
B
C 8
D 9
E 0
F 1
G 2
H 3
I 4
J 5